Graham
Audrey   Connor

D0305905

FRENCH-ENGLISH
ENGLISH-FRENCH
DICTIONARY

GEDDES &
GROSSET

FRENCH-ENGLISH
ENGLISH-FRENCH
DICTIONARY

**GEDDES &
GROSSET**

This edition published 2003 by Geddes & Grosset,
David Dale House, New Lanark, ML11 9DJ, Scotland

© 2001 Geddes & Grosset

First published 2001
Reprinted 2003, 2004

ISBN 1 84205 133 4

Printed and bound in Poland, OZGraf S.A.

	Abbreviations	**Abréviations**
abrev	abbreviation	abréviation
adj	adjective	adjectif
adv	adverb	adverbe
art	article	articule
auto	automobile	automobile
aux	auxiliary	auxiliaire
bot	botany	botanique
chem, chim	chemistry	chimie
col	colloquial term	expression familière
com	commerce	commerce
compd	compound	compound
comput	computers	informatique
conj	conjunction	conjonction
culin	culinary term	vocabulaire culinaire
excl	exclamation	exclamation
f	feminine noun	substantif fémenin
fam	colloquial term	expression familière
fig	figurative	figuré
geol	geology	géologie
gr	grammar	grammaire
imp	impersonal	impersonnel
inform	computers	informatique
interj	interjection	interjection
invar	invariable	invariable
irr	irregular	irrégulier
jur	law term	jurisprudence
law	law term	jurisprudence
ling	linguistics	linguistique
m	masculine noun	substantif masculin
mar	marine term	vocabulaire marin
mat, math	mathematics	matémathiques
med	medicine	médicine

mil	military term	vocabulaire militaire
mus	music	musique
n	noun	substantif
orn	ornithology	ornithologie
pej	pejorative	péjoratif
pl	plural	pluriel
pn	pronoun	pronom
poet	poetical term	vocabulaire poétique
pol	political term	vocabulaire politque
pp	past participle	participe passé
prep	preposition	préposition
rad	radio	radio
rail	railway	chemin de fer
sl	slang	argot
teat	theatre	théâtre
tec	technology	technologie
TV	television	télévision
vi	intransitive verb	verbe intransitif
vr	reflexive verb	verbe réfléchi
vt	transitive verb	verbe transitif
zool	zoology	zoologie

French-English Dictionary

A

à *prép* (in)to; at; on; by; per:—**aller ~ l'école** to go to school.

abaisser *vt* to lower.

abandon *m* abandonment, desertion.

abandonner *vt* to abandon, leave.

abattement *m* despondency; exhaustion.

abattoir *m* abattoir, slaughterhouse.

abattu *adj* despondent; exhausted.

abbaye *f* abbey.

abcès *m* abscess.

abdomen *m* abdomen.

abeille *f* bee.

aberration *f* aberration.

abîmer *vt* spoil, damage.

abolir *vt* to abolish.

abolition *f* abolition.

abondamment *adv* abundantly.

abondance *f* abundance.

abondant *adj* abundant, plentiful.

abonder *vi* to be abundant *ou* plentiful.

abonné *m*, **-ée** *f*:—*adj* subscriber.

abonnement *m* subscription.

abonner s'~ *vr* to subscribe, take out a subscription *(à* to).

abord *m*:—**d'~** first (of all).

aborder *vt* to approach.

aboutir *vi* to succeed.

aboutissement *m* outcome; success.

abréger *vt* to shorten; abridge.

abréviation *f* abbreviation.

abri *m* shelter.

abriter *vt* to shelter:—**s'~** *vr* to shelter.

abrupt *adj* abrupt:—**~ement** *adv* abruptly.

absence *f* absence.

absent *adj* absent.

absenter (s') *vr* to leave, go out.

absolu *adj* absolute:—**~ment** *adv* absolutely:—*m* absolute.

absorbant *adj* absorbent.

absorber *vt* to absorb.

absorption *f* absorption.

abstinence *f* abstinence.

abstrait *adj* abstract.

absurde *adj* absurd:—**~ment** *adv* absurdly.

absurdité *f* absurdity.

abus *m* abuse.

abuser *vt* ~ **de** to exploit; abuse.

académie *f* academy.

accélérateur *m* accelerator.

accélération *f* acceleration.

accélérer *vi* to speed up, accelerate.

accent *m* accent.

accentuer *vt* to accentuate.

acceptable *adj* acceptable.

accepter *vt* to accept.

accès *m* access.

accessible *adj* accessible.

accident *m* accident.

accidentel *adj* accidental:—**-lement** *adv* accidentally.

accommodant *adj* accommodating.

accommoder *vt* to prepare; adapt.

accompagner *vt* to accompany.

accomplir *vt* to do, accomplish.

accomplissement *m* accomplishment.

accord *m* agreement:—**d'~!** okay!, all right!:—**être d'~** to agree.

accorder *vt* to give:—**s'~** *vr* to agree.

accoucher *vi* to give birth.

accrocher *vt* to hang up (*à* on).

accroissement *m* increase.

accroître *vt* to increase.

accueil *m* welcome, reception.

accueillir *vt* to welcome.

accumuler *vt* to accumulate.

accusation *f* accusation.

accusé *m*, **-ée** *f* accused, defendant.

accuser *vt* to accuse.

achat *m* purchase.

acheter *vt* to buy.

acheteur *m* **-euse** *f* buyer.

achèvement *m* completion.

achever *vt* to finish; complete.

acide *adj* acidic:—*m* acid.

acier *m* steel.

acoustique *adj* acoustic:—*f* acoustics.

acquérir *vt* to buy, purchase.

acrobate *mf* acrobat.

acte *m* act; deed.

acteur *m* **actrice** *f* actor.

actif *adj* active.

action *f* act, action; share.

activement *adv* actively.

activer *vt* to speed up.

activité *f* activity.

actualité *f*:—**l'~** current events.

actuel *adj* current, present:— **~lement** *adv* currently.

adaptable *adj* adaptable.

adaptation *f* adaptation.

adapter *vt* to adapt (*à* to):—**s'~** *vr* to adapt (*à* to).

addition *f* addition; bill.

adéquat *adj* suitable, appropriate.

adhérer *vi* to adhere, stick.

adhésif *adj* adhesive.

adjectif *m* adjective.

admettre *vt* to admit; accept; assume.

administrer *vt* to run; administer.

admirable *adj* admirable:-**ment** *adv* admirably, brilliantly.

admiration *f* admiration.

admirer *vt* to admire.

adolescence *f* adolescence.

adolescent *m*, **-e** *f* adolescent.

adopter *vt* to adopt.

adorer *vt* to adore, worship.

adrénaline *f* adrenalin.

adresse *f* address; skill.

adresser *vt* to address; send.

adroit *adj* deft, skilful:—**~ement** *adv* deftly, skilfully.

adulte *mf* adult, grown-up:—*adj* adult, full-grown.

adversité *f* adversity.

aérodrome *m* aerodrome, airfield.

aéroport *m* airport.

affable *adj* affable.

affaiblir *vt* to weaken:—**s'~** *vr* to weaken, grow weaker.

affaire *f* matter.

affamé *adj* starving.

affamer *vt* to starve.

affection *f* affection.

affectueusement *adv* affectionately.

affectueux *adj* affectionate.

affermir *vt* to strengthen.

affiche *f* poster.

affiner *vt* to refine.

affirmatif *adj* affirmative.

affirmation *f* assertion.

affirmer *vt* to assert.

affluent *m* tributary.

affoler *vt* to throw into a panic:—**s'~** *vr* to get into a panic.

affréter *vt* to charter.

affreux *adj* horrible; awful.

afin *prép*:—~ **de** (in order) to:—~ **que** in order that.

africain *adj*, *mf* African.

Afrique *f* Africa.

âge *m* age:—**quel ~ as-tu?** how old are you?

âgé *adj* old:—~ **de 10 ans** 10 years old.

agence *f* agency; branch; offices.

agenda *m* diary.

agenouiller (s') *vr* to kneel (down).

agent *m* agent; policeman.

agglomération *f* town, urban area.

aggraver *vt* to make worse; increase.

agile *adj* agile, nimble:—~**ment** *adv* nimbly.

agilité *f* agility.

agir *vi* to act.

agitation *f* agitation.

agiter *vt* to shake; wave:—**s'~** *vr* to move about; fidget.

agneau *m* lamb.

agrandir *vt* to make bigger; to widen; to expand.

agrandissement *m* enlargement.

agréable *adj* agreeable, pleasant.

agressif *adj* aggressive.

agression *f* attack.

agriculteur *m* farmer.

agriculture *f* agriculture, farming.

ahuri *adj* stunned; stupefied.

aide *f* help; aid;

aider *vt* to help.

aigle *m* eagle.

aigre *adj* sour, bitter:—~**ment** *adv* sourly.

aigu *adj* (*f* **aiguë**) shrill; acute.

aiguille *f* needle.

ail *m* garlic.

ailleurs *adv* elsewhere:—**partout ~** everywhere else:—**nulle part ~** nowhere else:—**d'~** moreover; by the way.

aimable *adj* kind:—~**ment** *adv* kindly.

aimant *m* magnet.

aimer *vt* to love.

aîné *m*, **aînée** *f* eldest child:—*adj* elder; eldest.

ainsi *adv* so, thus.

air *m* air:—**avoir l'~ content** to look happy.

aire *f* area.

aisé *adj* easy; well-off:—~**ment** *adv* easily.

ajouter *vt* to add.

ajuster *vt* to adjust.

alarme *f* alarm.

alarmer *vt* to alarm:—**s'~** *vr* to get alarmed (*de* at, about).

album *m* album.

alcool *m* alcohol.

alentours *mpl* surroundings, neighbourhood.

alerte *adj* alert; agile:—**f** alarm, alert.

alerter *vt* to alert; notify; warn.

algue *f* seaweed.

aligner *vt* to align, line up.

aliment *m* food.

alimenter *vt* to feed:—**s'~** *vr* to eat.

alinéa *m* paragraph.

allée *f* avenue; path.

alléger *vt* to make lighter; alleviate.

aller *vi* to go:—**comment allez-vous?** how are you?:—**allons-y** let's go:—**s'en aller** to go away, leave:—*m* single ticket.

allergie *f* allergy.

alliance *f* alliance; marriage; wedding ring.

allô *excl* hello!

allocation *f* allocation; allowance.

allouer *vt* to allocate.

allumer *vt* to light; turn *ou* switch on.

allumette *f* match.

allure *f* speed; look.

alors *adv* then:—**~ que** while; whereas.

alphabet *m* alphabet.

alpiniste *mf* mountaineer.

altérer *vt* to change, alter.

alternatif *adj* alternate.

alternative *f* alternative.

altitude *f* altitude, height.

amabilité *f* kindness.

amaigrir *vt* to make thin.

amant *m* lover.

amas *m* pile, heap.

amasser *vt* to amass, pile up.

amateur *m* amateur; connaisseur.

ambassade *f* embassy.

ambassadeur *m*, **-drice** *f* ambassador.

ambiance *f* atmosphere.

ambigu *adj*, *f* **ambiguë** ambiguous.

ambitieux *adj* ambitious.

ambition *f* ambition.

ambulance *f* ambulance.

âme *f* soul.

amélioration *f* improvement.

améliorer *vt* to improve:—**s'~** *vr* to improve.

aménagement *m* fitting out; adjustment; development.

aménager *vt* to fit out; adjust; develop.

amener *vt* to bring.

amer *adj* bitter.

Américain *m*, **-e** *f* American.

américain *adj* American.

Amérique *f* America.

ameublement *m* furniture.

ami *m*, **-ie** *f* friend.

amical *adj* friendly:—**-ement** *adv* in a friendly manner.

amitié *f* friendship.

amnistie *f* amnesty.

amoindrir *vt* to weaken; reduce.

amorcer *vt* to bait; begin.

amortir *vt* to soften; deaden.

amour *m* love.

amoureux *adj* in love *(de* with*)*.

amovible *adj* detachable.

amphibie *adj* amphibious.

ample *adj* roomy; wide.

ampleur *f* fullness; range.

amplifier *vt* to increase; amplify.

amusant *adj* amusing.

amuser *vt* to amuse.

an *m* year:—**avoir vingt ~s** to be 20 (years old).

analogie *f* analogy.

analphabète *adj* illiterate.

analyse *f* analysis; test.

analyser *vt* to analyse.

analyste *mf* analyst; psychoanalyst.

ananas *m* pineapple.

anarchie *f* anarchy.

anatomie *f* anatomy.

ancestral *adj* ancestral.

ancêtre *m* ancestor.

ancien *adj* old; former:——**nement** *adv* formerly.

ancre *f* anchor.

âne *m* ass, donkey.

anecdote *f* anecdote.

anesthésie *f* anaesthetic; anaesthesia.

ange *m* angel.

Anglais *m*, **-e** *f* Englishman; Englishwoman.

anglais *adj* English:——*m (ling)* English.

angle *m* angle; corner.

Angleterre *f* England.

anglophone *adj* English-speaking:——*mf* English speaker.

angoisse *f* anguish.

animal *m* animal.

animation *f* animation.

animé *adj* busy; lively.

animosité *f* animosity.

anneau *m* ring.

année *f* year:——**les ~s soixante** the Sixties.

annexe *f* annexe:——*adj* subsidiary.

annexer *vt* to annex; append.

anniversaire *m* birthday:——**joyeux ~!** happy birthday!

annonce *f* advertisement; announcement.

annoncer *vt* to announce *(à to)*.

annuaire *m* telephone directory, phone book.

annuel *adj* annual:——**lement** *adv* annually.

annuler *vt* to cancel; nullify.

anomalie *f* anomaly.

anonyme *adj* anonymous; impersonal:——**ment** *adv* anonymously.

anorexique *adj*, *mf* anorexic.

anormal *adj* abnormal:——**ement** *adv* abnormally.

antagonisme *m* antagonism.

antenne *f (rad, tv)* aerial; *(zool)* feeler.

antérieur *adj* earlier, previous.

anthologie *f* anthology.

anticancéreux *adj* cancer.

anticipation *f* anticipation.

anticonceptionnel *adj* contraceptive.

anticyclone *m* anticyclone.

antidote *m* antidote.

antigel *m* antifreeze.

antipathie *f* antipathy.

antipathique *adj* unpleasant.

antique *adj* ancient.

antiquité *f* antiquity; antique.

antirouille *adj invar* rustproof.

antisocial *adj* antisocial.

antithèse *f* antithesis.

antonyme *m* antonym.

anxiété *f* anxiety.

anxieux *adj* anxious.

août *m* August.

apaisant *adj* soothing.

apaiser *vt* to calm (down); relieve.

apathie *f* apathy.

apathique *adj* apathetic.

apercevoir *vt* to see; catch a glimpse of.

apéritif *m* aperitif.

apeuré *adj* frightened.

aphone *adj* voiceless, hoarse.

aphrodisiaque *adj, m* aphrodisiac.

apitoyer *vt* to move to pity:—**s'~** *vr* to feel pity (*sur* for).

aplanir *vt* to level (out); smooth away.

aplati *adj* flat.

apolitique *adj* apolitical; non-political.

apologie *f* apology.

apostrophe *f* apostrophe.

apparaître *vi* to appear.

appareil *m* device; appliance; (tele)-phone;—**~-photo** camera.

apparence *f* appearance.

apparent *adj* apparent.

appartement *m* flat, apartment.

appartenir *vi*:—**~ à** to belong to.

appauvrir *vt* to impoverish:—**s'~** *vr* to grow poorer.

appel *m* call; appeal.

appeler *vt* to call:—**s'~** *vr* **je m'appelle Léon** my name is Leon.

appellation *f* appellation; name.

appétissant *adj* appetising.

appétit *m* appetite (*de* for).

applaudir *vt vi* to applaud.

application *f* application; use.

appliquer *vt* to apply:—**s'~** *vr* to apply oneself.

apporter *vt* to bring.

appréciation *f* estimation, assessment

apprécier *vt* to assess; appreciate.

appréhender *vt* to apprehend; to dread.

appréhension *f* apprehension.

apprendre *vt* to learn:—**~ à lire** to learn to read:—**~ à lire à un enfant** to teach a child to read.

apprenti *m*, **-ie** *f* apprentice.

apprentissage *m* apprenticeship.

approbation *f* approval.

approche *f* approach.

approcher *vt* to move near; approach:—**s'~** *vr* to approach.

approuver *vt* to approve of.

approvisionner *vt* to supply:—**s'~** *vr* to stock up (*de, en* with).

approximatif *adj* approximate.

appui *m* support.

appuyer *vt* to support *vi* to press:—*vr* **s'~ sur** to lean on.

âpre *adj* bitter:—**~ment** *adv* bitter-ly.

après *prép* after:—**après tout** after all:—**d'~ elle** according to her.

après-midi *m/f invar* afternoon.

apte *adj* capable (*à* of).

aptitude *f* aptitude:—ability.

aquatique *adj* aquatic.

araignée *f* spider.

arbitraire *adj* arbitrary:—**~ment** *adv* arbitrarily.

arbitre *m* arbiter; referee.

arbitrer *vt* to arbitrate; referee.

arbre *m* tree.

arc *m* bow; arc; arch.

arc-en-ciel *m*, *pl* **arcs-en-ciel** rainbow.

arche *f* arche.

archéologie *f* archaeology.

archipel *m* archipelago.

architecte *mf* architect.

architecture *f* architecture.

archiver *vt* to file, archive.

archives *fpl* archives, records.

ardu *adj* difficult.

argent *m* silver; money.

argument *m* argument.

argumenter *vi* to argue (*sur* about).

aride *adj* arid.

aristocrate *mf* aristocrat.

aristocratie *f* aristocracy.

arithmétique *f* arithmetic:—*adj* arithmetical.

arme *f* arm, weapon.

armée *f* army.

armer *vt* to arm:—**s'~** *vr* to arm oneself.

armoire *f* cupboard; wardrobe.

aromatique *adj* aromatic.

arôme *m* aroma; flavour.

arqué *adj* curved, arched.

arracher *vt* to pull (out); to tear off.

arrangement *m* arrangement.

arranger *vt* to arrange:—**s'~** *vr* to come to an arrangement.

arrêt *m* stopping; stop (button).

arrêter *vt* to stop:—**s'~** *vr* to stop.

arrière *m invar* back:—**en ~** back(wards):—**à l'~** at the back:—*adj invar* back, rear.

arrière-plan *m* background.

arrivant *m*, **-e** *f* newcomer.

arrivée *f* arrival, coming.

arriver *vi* to arrive, come.

arrogant *adj* arrogant.

arrondir *vt* to make round; to round off.

arrondissement *m* district.

arsenal *m* arsenal.

art *m* art.

artère *f* artery; road.

article *m* article.

articuler *vt* to articulate.

artificiel *adj* artificial:—**~lement** *adv* artificially.

artisan *m* artisan, craftsman.

artisanat *m* craft industry.

artiste *mf* artist.

artistique *adj* artistic:—**~ment** *adv* artistically.

ascenseur *m* lift, elevator.

ascension *f* ascent.

asiatique *adj* Asian.

asile *m* refuge; asylum.

aspect *m* appearance, look.

asphyxier *vt* to asphyxiate, suffocate.

aspirateur *m* vacuum cleaner.

aspirine *f* aspirin.

assaillant *m* assailant.

assaillir *vt* to assail.

assainir *vt* to clean up; to purify.

assaisonner *vt* to season.

assassin *m* murderer; assassin.

assassiner *vt* to assassinate.

assaut *m* assault, attack.

assemblage *m* assembly; assembling.

assemblée *f* meeting.

assembler *vt* to assemble:—**s'~** *vr* to assemble.

asseoir (s') *vr* to sit down.

assertion *f* assertion.

asservissement *m* enslavement; slavery.

assez *adv* enough; quite, rather:—**avoir ~ d'argent** to have enough money:—**~ bien** quite well.

assidu *adj* assiduous; regular.

assiette *f* plate.

assigner *vt* to assign.

assimiler vt to assimilate.

assis adj seated, sitting (down).

assistant(e) m(f) assistant.

assister vt to attend; to assist.

association f association.

associé(e) m(f) associate, partner.

assombrir vt to darken:—**s'~** to darken.

assommer vt to stun.

assortir vt to match:—**s'~** vr to go well together.

assoupir (s') vr to doze off.

assourdir vt to deafen; to muffle.

assourdissant adj deafening.

assouvir vt to satisfy.

assumer vt to assume.

assurance f (self-)assurance; assurance; insurance (policy).

assuré m, -e assured:—adj assured.

assurer vt to assure:—**s'~** vr to insure oneself.

asthme m asthma.

astre m star.

astreignant adj demanding.

astreindre vt to force, compel.

astrologie f astrology.

astrologue m astrologer.

astronaute m astronaut.

astronome m astronomer.

astronomie f astronomy.

astuce f shrewdness; (clever) trick; pun.

astucieux adj astute.

atelier m workshop; studio.

athée mf atheist:—adj atheistic.

athlète mf athlete.

athlétisme m athletics.

atlas m atlas.

atmosphère f atmosphere.

atome m atom.

atomique adj atomic.

atout m trump; advantage, asset.

atroce adj atrocious; dreadful.

atrocité f atrocity.

attaché m, -e attaché; assistant.

attacher vt to tie together; tie up; fasten; attach (à to).

attaque f attack.

attaquer vt to attack; tackle.

attarder (s') vr to linger.

atteindre vt to reach; affect; contact.

atteinte f attack (à on):—**hors d'~** beyond ou out of reach.

attendre vt to wait:—**s'~** vr :—**s'~ à qch** to expect something.

attendrir vt to fill with pity:—**s'~** vr to be moved (sur by).

attendrissant adj touching, moving.

attendu adj expected; long-awaited.

attentat m attack (contre on); murder attempt.

attente f wait; expectation.

attention f attention; care.

attentionné adj considerate, thoughtful (pour towards).

atténuer vt to alleviate; ease.

atterrir vi to land, touch down.

atterrissage m landing, touch down.

attester vt to testify to.

attirant adj attractive.

attirer vt to attract.

attitude f attitude; bearing.

attrait m attraction, appeal.

attraper vt to catch.

attribuer vt to attribute; award.

attribut m attribute.

attribution f attribution.

attrister vt to sadden.

au = à le.

aube f dawn, daybreak.

auberge f inn:—**de jeunesse** youth hostel.

aucun adj no; not any; any:—**~ement** adv in no way:—pron none; not any; any (one):—**~ d'entre eux** none of them.

audacieux adj audacious, bold; daring.

audience f audience; hearing.

auditeur m, **-trice** f listener; auditor.

auditoire m audience.

augmentation f increase, rise (de in); increasing(de of).

augmenter vt to increase, raise.

aujourd'hui adv today.

auparavant adv before, previously; before, first.

auprès prép ~ **de** next to; compared (with).

auquel = à lequel.

aurore f dawn, first light.

aussi adv too, also; so:—**nous ~** us too:—**une ~ belle journée** such a beautiful day.

aussitôt adv immediately:—**~ dit, ~ fait** no sooner said than done:—**~ que** as soon as.

autant adv as much; as many; so much; such; so many; such a lot of; the same:—**~ que je sache** as far as I know:—**~ que possible** as much as possible.

autel m altar.

auteur m author.

authentique adj authentic:—**~ment** adv authentically.

auto-école f driving school.

auto-stop m hitchhiking:—**faire de l'~** to hitchhike.

auto-stoppeur m, **-euse** f hitchhiker.

autobiographie f autobiography.

autocar m coach.

autodéfense f self-defence.

autodidacte mf self-taught.

automatique adj automatic:—**~ment** adv automatically.

automne m autumn.

automobile f motor car.

automobiliste mf motorist.

autonome adj autonomous.

autopsie f autopsy, post-mortem (examination).

autorisation f authorisation, permission; permit.

autoriser vt to authorise, give permission for.

autorité f authority.

autoroute f motorway.

autour prép ~ **de** (a)round:—adv (a)round.

autre adj other:—**~ chose** something else ou different:—**~ part** somewhere else:—**d'~ part** on the other hand:—pn another.

autrefois adv in the past, in days gone by.

autrement adv differently; otherwise:—**je n'ai pas pu faire ~** I couldn't do differently ou otherwise.

aux = à les.

auxiliaire adj auxiliary:—m auxiliary:—mf assistant.

avalanche f avalanche.

avaler vt to swallow.

avance f advance; lead:—**arriver en**

~ to arrive early:—**payer d'**~ to pay in advance.

avancer *vt* to move forward:—**s'**~ *vr* to advance, move forward:—*vi* move forward, advance; make progress.

avant *prép* before:—~ **peu** shortly:—~ **tout** above all:—*adv* before:—**en** ~ in front, ahead:—*m* front; bow; forward.

avant-bras *m invar* forearm.

avant-hier *adv* the day before yesterday.

avantage *m* advantage.

avantageux *adj* profitable, worthwhile; attractive; flattering.

avarie *f* damage.

avec *prép* with; to.

avenir *m* future.

aventure *f* adventure; venture; experience.

avenue *f* avenue.

avérer (s') *vr* to turn out, prove to be.

aversion *f* aversion.

avertir *vt* to warn; inform.

avertissement *m* warning.

aveugle *adj* blind:—*mf* blind person.

aveuglement *m* blindness.

aveugler *vt* to blind.

aviation *f* flying; aviation.

avide *adj* greedy; eager.

avion *m* (air)plane, aircraft.

avis *m* opinion.

avisé *adj* wise, sensible.

aviser *vt* to advise:—**s'**~ *vr* **s'aviser de** to realise suddenly.

avoir *vt* to have:—**il y a** there is/are **il y a deux mois** two months ago:—**qu'as-tu?** what's the matter?:—*m* resources; credit.

avortement *m* abortion.

avoué *m* solicitor.

avril *m* April.

axe *m* axis; axle; main road.

B

babiole *f* trinket, trifle.

bac *m* ferry.

badge *m* badge.

bagage *m* luggage.

bagarre *f* fight, brawl.

bagatelle *f* trinket; trifling sum.

bague *f* ring.

baguette *f* stick; loaf of French bread.

baie *f (geog)* bay.

baigner *vt vi* to bathe:—**se** ~ *vr* to have a bathe, swim.

baignoire *f* bathtub.

bâiller *vi* to yawn.

bain *m* bath; bathe, swim.

baiser *m* kiss:—*vt* to kiss.

baisse *f* fall, drop.

baisser *vi* to fall, drop *vt* to lower.

bal *m* dance.

balai *m* broom, brush.

balance *f* balance; scales.

balançoire *f* swing; seesaw.

balayer *vt* to sweep, brush.

balbutier *vt* to stammer, mumble.

balcon *m* balcony.

baleine *f* whale.

balle *f* bullet; ball.

ballon *m* ball; balloon.

balustrade *f* balustrade; handrail.

bambou *m* bamboo.

banal *adj* banal, trite:—**~ement** *adv* tritely.

banane *f* banana.

bancaire *adj* banking, bank.

bandage *m* bandage.

bande *f* band; tape.

bandeau *m* headband; blindfold.

bander *vt* to bandage; stretch.

bandit *m* bandit.

banlieue *f* suburbs.

bannière *f* banner.

bannir *vt* to banish.

banque *f* bank; banking.

banquette *f* seat, stool.

banquier *m* banker.

baptiser *vt* to baptise.

bar *m* bar.

barbare *adj* barbarian; barbaric.

barbe *f* beard.

barème *m* list, schedule.

baril *m* barrel, cask.

baromètre *m* barometer.

barque *f* small boat.

barre *f* bar, rod.

barrer *vt* to bar, block.

barricader *vt* to barricade:—**se ~** *vr* to barricade o.s.

barrière *f* barrier; fence.

bas *adj* low, base:—*n* stocking; sock.

bascule *f* weighing machine, scales.

base *f* base; basis.

baser *vt* to base:—**se baser sur** *vr* to depend on, rely on.

basse *f (mus)* bass; shoal, reef.

bassesse *f* meanness; vulgarity.

bassin *m* pond, pool; dock.

bataille *f* battle.

batailler *vi* to battle.

bateau *m* boat, ship.

bâtiment *m* building.

bâtir *vt* to build.

bâton *m* stick, staff.

batte *f* bat; beating.

batterie *f* battery.

battre *vt* to beat, defeat.

baume *m* balm, balsam.

bavard *m*, **-e** *f* chatterbox:—*adj* talkative, loquacious.

bavardage *m* chatting, gossiping.

bavarder *vi* to chat, gossip.

bazar *m* bazaar; general store.

béat *adj* blessed; complacent.

béatitude *f* beatitude; bliss.

beau, *f* **belle** *adj* beautiful, lovely.

beaucoup *adv* a lot, a great deal:—**~ de monde** a lot of people.

beauté *f* beauty, loveliness.

beaux-arts *m pl* fine art.

bébé *m* baby.

bec *m* beak, bill.

bégayer *vi* to stammer, stutter.

beige *adj* beige:—*m* beige.

bêler *vi* to bleat.

Belge *mf* Belgian.

belge *adj* Belgian.

Belgique *f* Belgium.

belligérant *m*, **-ante** *f* belligerent:—*adj* belligerent.

bénédiction *f* benediction, blessing.

bénéfice *m* profit; benefit.

bénéficier *vi* to benefit; enjoy.

bénin, *f* **bénigne** *adj* benign; harmless.

bénir *vt* to bless.

bénit *adj* consecrated, holy.

béquille *f* crutch; prop.

berceau *m* cradle.

bercer *vt* to rock, cradle.
béret *m* beret.
berge *f* riverbank; barge.
berger *m* shepherd:-**ère** *f* shepherdess.
besogne *f* work; job.
besoin *m* need; want:—**avoir ~ de** to need.
bête *adj* stupid, silly:—**~ment** *adv* stupidly, foolishly:—*f* animal.
bêtise *f* stupidity, foolishness.
béton *m* concrete.
beurre *m* butter.
biberon *m* baby's bottle.
bible *f* bible.
bibliographie *f* bibliography.
bibliothécaire *mf* librarian.
bibliothèque *f* library; bookcase.
bicyclette *f* bicycle.
bidon *m* tin, can; flask.
bien *adv* well; properly; very:—*n* property, estate.
bien-être *m* well-being.
bienfaiteur *m* benefactor, **-trice** *f* benefactress.
bienheureux *adj* blessed; lucky; happy.
bientôt *adv* soon.
bienvenu *adj* welcome.
bière *f* beer; coffin.
bifteck *m* steak.
bigot *adj* bigoted.
bijou *m* jewel.
bijouterie *f* jewellery.
bilan *m* balance sheet; assessment.
bilingue *adj* bilingual.
billet *m* ticket; note.
billetterie *f* cash dispenser.
billion *m* billion.

binaire *adj* binary.
biodégradable *adj* biodegradable.
biographie *f* biography.
biologie *f* biology.
biologiste *mf* biologist.
bipède *m* biped.
biscuit *m* cake; biscuit.
bisexuel *adj* bisexual.
bissextile *adj* bissextile, leap (year).
bitumer *vt* to asphalt, tarmac.
bizarre *adj* bizarre, strange:—**~ment** *adv* strangely, oddly.
blague *f* joke, trick.
blaguer *vi* to joke.
blagueur *m*, **-euse** *f* joker, wag:—*adj* jokey, teasing.
blaireau *m* badger.
blâme *m* blame, rebuke.
blâmer *vt* to blame, rebuke.
blanc *adj*, *f* **blanche** white:—*m* white; blank:—*mf* white person:—*f* minim.
blancheur *f* whiteness.
blanchir *vi* to turn white:—*vt* to whiten.
blanchisserie *f* laundry.
blasphème *m* blasphemy.
blé *m* wheat.
blêmir *vi* to turn pale.
blessé *adj* injured, wounded.
blesser *vt* to injure, wound.
bleu *adj* blue:—*n* blue; bruise.
bleuir *vi* to turn blue:—*vt* to make blue.
bloc *m* block, group, unit.
blond *adj* blond, fair.
blondir *vi* to turn blond, turn golden:—*vt* to bleach.
bloquer *vt* to block, blockade.

blouse f blouse; overall.

bœuf m ox, bullock.

boire vt to drink:—vi to drink, tipple.

bois m wood.

boisson f drink.

boîte f box.

boiter vi to limp.

boiteux adj lame.

bol m bowl.

bombarder vt to bombard, bomb.

bombe f bomb.

bon adj, f **bonne** good:—m slip, coupon, bond.

bonbon m sweet, candy.

bond m leap; bounce.

bondir vi to jump, leap; to bounce.

bonheur m happiness; luck.

bonhomme m, pl **bonshommes** chap, fellow.

bonifier vt to improve:—**se ~** vr to improve.

bonjour m hello, good morning.

bonsoir m good evening.

bonté f goodness, kindness.

bord m side, edge.

border vt to edge, border.

borner vt to restrict, limit.

botanique f botany:—adj botanical.

botaniste f botanist.

botte f boot.

bouche f mouth.

bouché adj cloudy, overcast.

bouche-à-bouche m kiss of life.

bouchée f mouthful.

boucher vt to butcher:—m, **-ère** f butcher.

boucherie f butcher's; butchery.

bouchon m cork.

boudeur adj sullen, sulky.

boudin m pudding.

boue f mud.

bouée f buoy.

bouger vi to move:—vt to move, shift.

bougie f candle.

bouillir vi to boil.

bouilloire f kettle.

boulanger m, **-ère** f baker.

boulangerie f bakery.

boule f ball, bowl.

boulevard m boulevard.

bouleversement m confusion, disruption.

bouleverser vt to confuse, disrupt.

boulon m bolt.

bourdon m bumblebee.

bourdonner vi to buzz, hum.

bourg m market-town.

bourgeois m, **-e** f bourgeois, middle-class person:—adj bourgeois, middle-class.

bourse f purse; stock exchange.

boursier m, **-ière** f broker; speculator.

bousculer vt to jostle, hustle.

bout m end; piece, scrap.

bouteille f bottle.

boutique f shop, store.

bouton m button.

boutonner vt to button.

boxe f boxing.

boxer vi to box.

boycotter vt to boycott.

bracelet m bracelet.

braguette f fly (trousers).

brancher vt to connect, link.

bras m arm.

brasse f breaststroke.

brasser vt to brew; to mix.

brasserie *f* bar; brewery.
brave *adj* brave, courageous.
braver *vt* to brave, defy.
brèche *f* breach, gap.
bredouiller *vi* to stammer, mumble.
bref *adj*, *f* **brève** brief, concise:—**en ~** *adv* in short.
brevet *m* licence, patent.
bric-à-brac *m* bric-a-brac.
bricolage *m* DIY, odd jobs.
bricoler *vi* to do odd jobs.
bride *f* bridle.
brider *vt* to restrain, restrict.
brièveté *f* brevity.
brillant *adj* brilliant, shining.
briller *vi* to shine.
brique *f* brick, slab.
brise *f* breeze.
briser *vt* to smash, shatter.
broche *f* brooch.
brochure *f* brochure, pamphlet.
bronze *m* bronze.
bronzer *vi* to get a tan.
brosse *f* brush.
brosser *vt* to brush.
brouette *f* wheelbarrow.
brouillard *m* fog, mist.
brouter *vt vi* to graze.
bruine *f* drizzle.

bruit *m* noise, sound.
bruitage *m* sound-effects.
brûler *vt vi* to burn.
brûlure *f* burn.
brume *f* haze, mist.
brun *m* dark-haired man, **brune** *f* brunette:—*adj* brown.
brusque *adj* brusque, abrupt.
brut *adj* crude, raw.
brutal *adj* brutal, rough.
brutalité *f* brutality.
brute *f* brute; animal.
bruyant *adj* noisy.
bûche *f* log.
bûcheron(ne) *m(f)* woodcutter, lumberjack.
budget *m* budget.
buée *f* condensation; steam.
buffet *m* sideboard, buffet.
bulbe *m* bulb.
bulletin *m* bulletin.
bureau *m* office; desk.
bureaucrate *mf* bureaucrat.
bus *m* bus.
buste *m* bust, chest.
but *m* objective, goal.
buvable *adj* drinkable.
buvette *f* refreshment-room.
buveur *m*, **-euse** *f* drinker.

C

ça *pron* that; it:—**~ va?** How goes it?:—**~ alors!** you don't say!
cabaret *m* cabaret; tavern.
cabine *f* cabin, cab; cockpit.
cabinet *m* surgery; office, study.
câble *m* cable.
cacahouète *f* peanut.

cacao *m* cocoa.
caché *adj* hidden, secluded.
cacher *vt* to hide, conceal.
cadavre *m* corpse.
cadeau *m* present.
cadenasser *vt* to padlock.
cadet *m*, **-ette** *f* youngest child.

cadre *m* frame; context; scope.
caduc *adj f* **caduque** null and void; obsolete.
café *m* coffee.
cafétéria *f* cafeteria.
cafetière *f* coffeepot.
cage *f* cage.
cahier *m* notebook.
caillou *m* stone; pebble.
caisse *f* box; till; fund.
caissier *m*, **-ière** *f* cashier.
calcul *m* sum, calculation.
calculatrice, calculette *f* calculator.
calculer *vt* to calculate, reckon:—*vi* to budget carefully.
caleçon *m* shorts, pants.
calendrier *m* calendar.
calibre *m* calibre, bore.
calmant *m* tranquilliser, sedative:— *adj* tranquillising.
calme *m* calm, stillness:—*adj* calm, still.
calmer *vt* calm, soothe, pacify.
calorie *f* calorie.
camarade *mf* companion, friend.
camaraderie *f* camaraderie, friendship.
cambrioler *vt* to burgle.
caméra *f* camera.
camion *m* lorry.
camionneur *m* lorry driver, trucker.
camouflage *m* camouflage.
camp *m* camp.
campagnard *m* countryman, **-e** *f* countrywoman:—*adj* country, rustic.
campagne *f* country, countryside.
camper *vi* to camp.
canal *m* canal, channel.
canapé *m* sofa, settee.

cancer *m* cancer.
cancéreux *adj* cancerous.
candidat *m*, **-e** *f* candidate.
candide *adj* frank, ingenuous.
canne *f* cane, rod.
canoë *m* canoe.
canon *m* cannon, gun.
cantatrice *f* singer.
cantine *f* canteen.
caoutchouc *m* rubber.
cap *f* cape; course.
capable *adj* capable, competent.
capacité *f* capacity.
capitaine *m* captain.
capital *adj* capital, cardinal, major:—*m* capital, stock.
capitale *f* capital (letter, city).
capitaliste *mf* capitalist.
capituler *vt* to capitulate.
capoter *vt* to capsize, overturn.
caprice *m* caprice, whim.
capricieux *adj* capricious.
capsule *f* capsule.
captif *m*:—**ve** *f* captive:—*adj* captive.
captiver *vt* to captivate, enthrall.
captivité *f* captivity.
capture *f* capture.
capturer *vt* to capture.
car *conj* for; because:—*m* bus; van.
caractère *m* character, disposition.
caractériser *vt* to characterise.
caractérisque *f* characteristic, feature:—*adj* characteristic.
carat *m* carat.
caravane *f* caravan.
carbone *m* carbon.
carburant *m* motor-fuel.
cardiaque *adj* cardiac.

carence *f* deficiency; insolvency.
caressant *adj* affectionate.
caresse *f* caress.
caresser *vt* to caress, fondle.
cargaison *f* cargo, freight.
caricature *f* caricature.
caricaturer *vt* to caricature.
caritatif *adj* charitable.
carnaval *m* carnival.
carnet *m* notebook; logbook.
carnivore *mf* carnivore:—*adj* carnivorous.
carotte *f* carrot.
carreau *m* tile; pane.
carrefour *m* crossroads.
carrière *f* career.
carrosserie *f* bodywork, coachwork.
carte *f* card; map.
cartilage *m* cartilage.
carton *m* cardboard.
cartonner *vt* to bind (book).
cas *m* case; circumstance.
cascade *f* waterfall.
case *f* square; box.
casier *m* compartment; filing cabinet.
casino *m* casino.
casque *m* helmet.
cassant *adj* brittle.
casse-croûte *m invar* snack.
casser *vt* to break:—**se ~** *vr* to break.
casserole *f* saucepan.
cassette *f* cassette; cash-box.
catalogue *m* catalogue.
cataloguer *vt* to catalogue.
catastrophe *f* catastrophe.
catastrophique *adj* catastrophic.
catégorie *f* category.
catégorique *adj* categorical.
cathédrale *f* cathedral.

catholique *adj* Catholic.
cauchemar *m* nightmare.
cause *f* cause, reason.
causer *vt* to cause; to chat:—*vi* to talk, chat.
cavalerie *f* cavalry.
cavalier *m*, **-ière** *f* rider.
cave *f* cellar.
caverne *f* cave, cavern.
cavité *f* cavity.
ce *adj* **cet** (*bef.* vowel and mute h), *f* **cette**, *pl* **ces** this, these:—**cet homme-là** that man:—*pron:*—**c'est le facteur** it's the postman:—**~ sont mes lunettes** these are my glasses.
ceci *pron* this.
céder *vi* to give in:—*vt* to give up, transfer.
ceinture *f* belt, girdle.
cela *pron* that:—*emphasis* **qui ~?** who? (do you mean)?:—**comment ~?** how? (do you mean?).
célèbre *adj* famous.
célébrer *vt* to celebrate.
célébrité *f* fame, celebrity.
célibataire *mf* single person:—*adj* single, unmarried.
cellule *f* cell, unit.
celluloïde *m* celluloid.
celui *pron*, *f* **celle** this one, *pl* **ceux** these ones.
cendre *f* ash.
censure *f* censorship.
cent *adj* a hundred:—**tu as ~ fois raison** you are absolutely right:—*m* a hundred:—**~ pour ~** per cent.
centenaire *m* centenarian:—*adj* a hundred years old.

centigrade *m* centigrade.
centigramme *m* centigram.
centime *m* centime.
centimètre *m* centimetre.
central *adj* central.
centre *m* centre.
cependant *conj* however.
cercle *m* circle, ring.
céréale *f* cereal.
cérébral *adj* cerebral.
cérémonie *f* ceremony.
certain *adj* certain, sure:—**~s** *pn*
  some, certain.
certificat *m* certificate.
certifier *vt* to certify; to guarantee.
certitude *f* certainty, certitude.
cervelle *f* brain.
cesser *f* to cease, stop.
cessez-le-feu *m* cease-fire.
cet *adj f* **cette** *see* **ce**.
ceux *see* **ce**.
chacun *pron* each one:—**~e d'entre
  elles** each of them.
chagrin *m* sorrow, chagrin.
chaîne *f* chain.
chair *f* flesh.
chaise *f* chair.
châlet *m* chalet.
chaleur *f* heat.
chaleureux *adj* warm, cordial.
chambre *f* room.
chameau *m* camel.
champ *m* field.
champignon *m* mushroom.
champion *m*, **-onne** *f* champion.
championnat *m* championship.
chance *f* luck.
chanceler *vi* to stagger, totter.
chanceux *adj* lucky, fortunate.

changement *m* change, changing.
changer *vi* to change:—*vt* to change.
chanson *f* song.
chantage *m* blackmail.
chanter *vi, vt* to sing.
chanteur *m*, **-euse** *f* singer.
chantier *m* building site.
chaos *m* chaos.
chapeau *m* hat.
chapelle *f* chapel.
chapitre *m* chapter.
chaque *adj* each.
charbon *m* coal.
charge *f* load; responsibility.
charger *vt* to load:—**se ~ de** to take
  responsibility for, attend to.
charisme *m* charisma.
charitable *adj* charitable, kind.
charité *f* charity.
charme *m* charm.
charmer *vt* to charm, beguile.
charpente *f* structure, framework.
charpentier *m* carpenter.
charrue *f* plough.
chasse-neige *m invar* snowplough.
chasser *vt* to hunt, chase.
châssis *m* chassis.
chat *m*, **chatte** *f* cat.
château *m* castle, château.
châtiment *m* chastisement, punishment.
chaud *adj* warm, hot.
chaudière *f* boiler.
chauffage *m* heating.
chauffer *vi* to heat:—*vt* to heat up.
chauffeur *m* driver.
chaumière *f* cottage.
chaussée *f* road, street.
chaussette *f* sock.

chaussure f shoe.

chauve-souris f bat.

chef m head, boss; chef.

chef-d'œuvre m masterpiece.

chemin m way, road:—**~ de fer** railway.

cheminée f chimney.

chemise f shirt.

chêne m oak.

chèque m cheque.

chéquier m chequebook.

cher adj f **chère** dear, expensive.

chercher vt to look for.

chéri m, **-ie** f darling:—adj cherished.

cheval m horse.

cheveu m hair.

cheville f ankle.

chèvre f goat.

chez prép at home:—**je rentre ~ moi** I'm going home.

chic m style, stylishness.

chien m, **chienne** f dog.

chiffre m figure.

chimie f chemistry.

chimiste mf chemist.

chimpanzé m chimpanzee.

chirurgie f surgery.

chirurgien m surgeon.

choc m shock, crash.

chocolat m chocolate.

choir vi to fall.

choisir vt to choose.

choix m choice.

chômage m unemployment.

chômeur m, **-euse** f unemployed person.

choquer vt to shock.

chose f thing, matter, object.

chou m cabbage.

chouette f owl.

chrétien m, **-ienne** f Christian, adj christian.

christianisme m Christianity.

chronologie f chronology.

chuchoter vi to whisper.

chuinter vi to hiss.

chute f fall, drop.

chuter vi to fall.

ci adv:—**ces fleurs-ci** these flowers:—**ci-joint** enclosed.

cible f target.

cicatrice f scar.

cidre m cider.

ciel m, pl **cieux, ciels** sky.

cierge m candle.

cigare m cigar.

cigarette f cigarette.

cil m eyelash.

ciment m cement.

cimetière m cemetery.

cinéma m cinema.

cingler vt to lash, sting.

cinq m five.

cinquante m fifty.

cinquième mf fifth, adj fifth.

cirage m polish.

circonférence f circumference.

circonspect adj circumspect.

circonstance f circumstance.

circuit m circuit, tour.

circulaire adj circular.

circulation f circulation; traffic.

circuler vi to circulate, move.

cirer vt to polish.

cirque m circus.

ciseau m chisel; scissor(s).

citadelle f citadel.

citadin(e) *m(f)* city dweller:—*adj* town, urban.

citation *f* citation, summons.

cité *f* city.

citer *vt* to quote, cite.

citoyen *m*, **-enne** *f* citizen.

citron *m* lemon.

civil *adj* civil:—**~ement** *adv* civilly.

civilisation *f* civilisation.

civiliser *vt* to civilise.

clair *adj* clear, bright:—**~ement** *adv* clearly.

clameur *f* clamour.

clandestin *adj* clandestine.

claque *f* slap, smack.

claquer *vi* to bang, slam.

clarifier *vt* to clarify:—**se ~** *vr* to become clear.

clarté *f* light, brightness.

classe *f* class, standing.

classer *vt* to file, classify.

classification *f* classification.

classique *adj* classical, standard.

clause *f* clause.

claustrophobie *f* claustrophobia.

clavier *m* keyboard.

clé, clef *f* key.

cliché *m* cliché; negative.

client *m*, **-e** *f* client.

cligner *vi* to blink.

clignoter *vi* to blink, flicker.

climat *m* climate.

climatisation *f* air conditioning.

clinique *f* clinic.

clochard *m*, **-e** *f* down-and-out.

cloche *f* bell.

cloison *f* partition.

clore *vt* to close, conclude.

clou *m* nail.

clouer *vt* to nail.

coalition *f* coalition.

cochon *m*, **-onne** *f* pig.

code *m* code.

cœur *m* heart.

coffre *m* chest:—**~-fort** safe.

cohabitation *f* cohabitation.

cohérent *adj* coherent.

cohésion *f* cohesion.

coiffer *vt* to arrange so's hair:—**se ~** *vr* to do one's hair.

coiffeur *m*, **-euse** *f* hairdresser.

coin *m* corner.

coïncidence *f* coincidence.

col *m* neck.

colère *f* anger.

colis *m* parcel.

collaborateur *m*, **-trice** *f* collaborator, colleague.

collaborer *vi* to collaborate.

collection *f* collection.

collectionner *vt* to collect.

collège *m* college, school.

collègue *mf* colleague.

coller *vt* to stick, glue:—*vi* to stick, be sticky.

colline *f* hill.

collision *f* collision.

colonie *f* colony.

coloniser *vt* to colonise.

coloration *f* colouring, staining.

colorier *vt* to colour in.

coma *m* coma.

comateux *adj* comatose.

combat *m* combat, fight.

combattre *vt* to fight, combat:—*vi* to fight.

combien *adv* how much, how many:—**~ de temps** how much time.

combiner *vt* to combine.

combustible *m* fuel.

combustion *f* combustion.

comédie *f* comedy.

comédien *m*:-**ienne** *f* actor.

comète *f* comet.

comique *adj* comic:——**ment** *adv* comically.

comité *m* committee.

commande *f* command, order.

commander *vt vi* to order, command.

comme *conj* as, like:—— **ci ~ ça** so-so:—*adv* how.

commémorer *vt* to commemorate.

commencer *vt* to begin:-*vi* to begin, start.

comment *adv* how:—— **dire?** how shall we say?

commentaire *m* comment; commentary.

commenter *vt* to comment.

commerçant *m*, -**e** *f* merchant, trader.

commerce *m* business, commerce.

commercial *adj* commercial:——**ement** *adv* commercially.

commercialiser *vt* to market.

commettre *vt* to commit.

commission *f* commission, committee.

commodité *f* convenience.

commun *adj* common, joint.

communal *adj* common, communal.

commune *f* town, district.

communication *f* communication.

communiquer *vt* to communicate, transmit:—*vi* to communicate.

communiste *mf* communist.

compact *adj* compact, dense.

compagne *f* companion.

compagnon *m* companion.

comparable *adj* comparable.

comparaison *f* comparison.

comparer *vt* to compare.

compartiment *m* compartment.

compas *m* compass.

compassion *f* compassion.

compatible *adj* compatible.

compatriote *mf* compatriot.

compensation *f* compensation.

compenser *vt* to compensate; offset.

compétence *f* competence.

compétitif *adj* competitive.

compétitivité *f* competitiveness.

complaisant *adj* kind; complacent.

complément *m* complement; extension.

complet *adj* complete, full.

compléter *vt* to complete.

complexe *adj* complex, complicated.

complication *f* complication.

complice *mf* accomplice.

compliment *m* compliment.

compliquer *vt* to complicate.

comportement *m* behaviour; performance.

comporter *vt* to consist of:——**se ~** *vr* to behave.

composer *vt* to compose, make up:—**se ~** *vr*:—**se ~ de** to be made up of.

compréhensible *adj* comprehensible.

compréhensif *adj* comprehensive, understanding.

comprendre *vt* to understand; consist of.

compression *f* compression; reduction.

comprimer *vt* to compress; to restrain.

compromettre *vt* to compromise.

comptable *mf* accountant.

compter *vt vi* to count.

comptoir *m* counter, bar.

concentration *f* concentration.

concept *m* concept.

conception *f* conception, design.

concerner *vt* to concern, regard.

concert *m* concert.

concession *f* concession; privilege.

concevoir *vt* to imagine, conceive.

concierge *mf* caretaker, concierge.

conciliation *f* conciliation; reconciliation.

concilier *vt* to reconcile; to attract.

concision *f* conciseness, brevity.

conclure *vt* to conclude; to decide.

conclusion *f* conclusion.

concours *m* competition; conjuncture.

concret *adj* concrete, solid.

concubin *m*, **-e** *f* concubine; cohabitant.

concurrence *f* competition.

condamnation *f* condemnation; sentencing.

condamner *vt* to condemn; to sentence.

condensation *f* condensation.

condenser *vt* to condense, compress.

condition *f* condition, term.

conditionner *vt* to condition; to package.

conducteur *m*, **-trice** *f* driver; operator.

conduire *vt vi* to lead; to drive.

conduite *f* conduct; driving; running.

cône *m* cone.

conférence *f* conference.

confession *f* confession.

confiance *f* confidence, trust.

confidence *f* confidence; disclosure.

confidentiel *adj* confidential.

confier *vt* to confide, entrust:—**se ~** *vr* to confide in.

confiner *vt* to confine:—**se ~** to be confined.

confirmer *vt* to confirm:—**se ~** *vr* to be confirmed.

confiserie *f* confectionery.

confiture *f* jam.

conflit *m* conflict, contention.

confondre *vt* to confuse, mingle.

conforme *adj* consistent; true.

conformer *vt* to model:—**se ~** *vr* to conform.

confort *m* comfort.

confortable *adj* comfortable, cosy.

confronter *vt* to confront.

confus *adj* confused, indistinct.

confusion *f* confusion, disorder.

congédier *vt* to dismiss.

congeler *vt* to freeze.

congratuler *vt* to congratulate.

congrégation *f* congregation.

congrès *m* congress, conference.

conjurer *vt* to conspire; to implore.

connaissance *f* knowledge; consciousness.

connaisseur *m*, **-euse** *f* connoisseur; expert.

connaître *vt* to know, be acquainted with.

connecter *vt* to connect.

connexion *f* connection, link.

connu *adj* known; famous.

conquérir *vt* to conquer.

conquête *f* conquest.

conscience *f* consciousness; conscience.

consciencieux *adv* conscientious.

conscient *adj* conscious, aware.

consécutif *adj* consecutive.

conseil *m* advice, counsel.

conseiller *vt* to advise, counsel.

consentir *vi* to consent, acquiesce.

conséquence *f* consequence, result.

conséquent *adj* consequent, logical.

conservateur *m*, **-trice** *f* conservative; curator.

conservation *f* conservation.

conserver *vt* to keep, preserve:—**se ~** *vr* to keep.

considérable *adj* considerable; notable.

considération *f* consideration, respect.

considérer *vt* to consider, regard.

consistance *f* consistency; strength.

consister *vi*:—~ **en** to consist of.

consolation *f* consolation, solace.

consoler *vt* to console, comfort.

consolider *vt* to consolidate, reinforce.

consommateur *m*, **-trice** *f* consumer.

consommation *f* consumption; accomplishment.

consommer *vt* to consume, use.

conspirer *vi* to conspire, plot.

constant *adj* constant, continuous.

constat *m* report; acknowledgement.

constater *vt* to record; to verify.

constellation *f* constellation, galaxy.

consterner *vt* to dismay.

constipation *f* constipation.

constituer *vt* to constitute, form.

constitution *f* constitution, formation.

constructeur *m*, **-trice** *f* builder, maker.

construction *f* building, construction.

construire *vt* to construct, build.

consulat *m* consulate.

consultant *m*, **-e** *f* consultant.

consulter *vt* to consult, take advice from.

consumer *vt* to consume, spend.

contact *m* contact, touch.

contagieux *adj* contagious, infectious.

contaminer *vt* to contaminate, pollute.

conte *m* story, tale.

contempler *vt* to contemplate, meditate.

contemporain *adj* contemporary.

contenir *vt* to contain.

contentement *m* contentment, satisfaction.

contenter *vt* to please, satisfy.

contenu *m* contents, enclosure.

contester *vt* to contest, dispute.

contexte *m* context.

continent *m* continent.

continental *adj* continental.

continuation *f* continuation.

continuel *adj* continual, continuous.

continuer *vt* to continue, proceed with:—*vi* to continue, go on.

contour *m* contour, outline.

contraceptif *adj* contraceptive.

contracter *vt* to contract, acquire:—**se ~** *vr* to contract, shrink.

contradiction f contradiction, discrepancy.

contraindre vt to constrain, compel.

contraire m opposite, contrary:—adj opposite, contrary.

contrarier vt to annoy; to oppose.

contraste m contrast.

contrat m contract, agreement.

contre prép against:—**par ~** on the other hand.

contre-attaquer vi to counter-attack.

contrebande f contraband, smuggling.

contrecœur:—à ~ reluctantly.

contredire vt to contradict, refute.

contrefaire vt to counterfeit, forge.

contrepartie f compensation; consideration.

contresens m nonsense; misunderstanding; mistranslation.

contribuer vt vi to contribute.

contribution f contribution; tax.

contrôler vt to control, check.

contrôleur m, **-euse** f inspector; auditor.

controverse f controversy.

convaincre vt to convince, persuade.

convalescence f convalescence.

convenable adj fitting, suitable:— **~ment** adv suitably, fitly.

convenir vi to agree, accord.

convention f convention, agreement.

conventionnel adj conventional; contractual.

conversation f conversation, talk.

conversion f conversion.

convertir vt to convert:—**se ~** vr to be converted.

conviction f conviction.

convoi m convoy; train.

convoquer vt to convoke, convene.

coopération f cooperation.

coopérative f cooperative.

coopérer vi to cooperate, collaborate.

coordination f coordination; committee.

copain m friend, pal.

copie f copy, reproduction.

copier vt to copy, reproduce.

copilote m co-pilot.

coq m cock, rooster.

coquet adj stylish, smart.

coquin m, **-e** f naughty, mischievous.

corail m coral.

coran m Koran.

corbeille f basket.

corde f rope; string.

cordial adj cordial, warm.

cordialité f cordiality, warmth.

cordon m cord, string; cordon.

corne f horn, antler.

corneille f crow.

cornet m cornet, cone.

corporatif adj corporative, corporate.

corporation f corporation, guild.

corps m body, corpse.

corpulent adj corpulent.

correct adj correct, accurate.

correcteur m, **-trice** f examiner; proofreader.

correction f correction; proofreading.

correspondance f correspondence, communication.

correspondre vi to correspond, communicate.

corridor m corridor, passage.

corriger *vt* to correct.

corroder *vt* to corrode.

corrompre *vt* to corrupt, debase.

corrosion *f* corrosion.

corruption *f* corruption, debasement.

corset *m* corset.

cortège *m* cortège, procession.

cosmétique *m* cosmetic.

cosmique *adj* cosmic.

cosmopolite *adj* cosmopolitan.

cosmos *m* cosmos.

costume *m* costume, dress.

côte *f* coast; rib; slope.

côté *m* side; point.

coteau *m* hill.

coter *vt* to quote; to classify.

coton *m* cotton.

cou *m* neck.

couche *f* layer, coat.

coucher *vt* to put to bed:—**se ~** *vr* to go to bed.

coucou *m* cuckoo.

coude *m* elbow.

coudre *vt vi* to sew.

couler *vi* to flow, run.

couleur *f* colour, shade.

coulisser *vi* to slide, run.

couloir *m* corridor, passage.

coup *m* blow; shot:—**tout à ~** suddenly:—**après ~** afterwards, after the event:—**~ de feu** shot:—**jeter un ~ d'œil** to glance.

coupable *mf* culprit:—*adj* guilty.

coupe *f* cut; cutting.

couper *vt* to cut, slice.

couple *m* couple, pair.

coupon *m* coupon, voucher, ticket.

cour *f* court, yard, courtyard.

courage *m* courage, daring.

courageux *adj* courageous.

courant *adj* current; present:—*m* stream, current.

courbe *f* curve; contour.

courber *vt* to curve, bend.

coureur *m*, **-euse** *f* runner.

courir *vi* to run, race.

couronne *f* crown, wreath.

courrier *m* mail, post.

cours *m* course; flow; path.

course *f* running; race; flight; journey.

coursier *m*, **-ière** *f* courier, messenger.

court *adj* short, brief.

court-circuiter *vt* to short-circuit.

courtier *m*, **-ière** *f* broker, agent.

courtois *adj* courteous.

cousin *m*, **-e** *f* cousin.

coussin *m* cushion, pillow.

coût *m* cost, charge.

couteau *m* knife.

coûter *vi*, *vt* to cost.

coûteux *adj* costly, expensive.

coutume *f* custom, habit.

couvent *m* convent.

couvercle *m* lid, cap.

couvert *m* shelter; cover; pretext:—*adj* covered; secret.

couverture *f* blanket; cover; roofing.

couvrir *vt* to cover.

crabe *m* crab.

cracher *vt* to spit.

craie *f* chalk.

craindre *vt* to fear.

crampe *f* cramp.

crâne *m* cranium, skull.

crapaud *m* toad.

craquement *m* crack, creaking, snap.

craquer *vi* to creak, squeak, crack.

cratère *m* crater.

cravate *f* tie.

créateur *m*, **-trice** *f* creator, author.

création *f* creation.

créature *f* creature.

crèche *f* creche; crib.

crédible *adj* credible.

crédit *m* credit, trust.

crédule *adj* credulous, gullible.

créer *vt* to create, produce.

crème *f* cream.

crémerie *f* dairy.

crêpe *f* pancake:—*m* crepe.

crépiter *vi* to crackle; to rattle.

crépuscule *m* twilight, dusk.

crête *f* crest, comb.

crétin *m*, **-e** *f* cretin, idiot.

creuser *vi* to dig, burrow:—*vt* to dig, hollow.

crevaison *f* puncture, flat.

crever *vt* to burst; to gouge:—*vi* to burst; to split.

cri *m* cry, howl, yell.

crible *m* riddle, sieve.

crier *vi* to cry, shout.

crime *m* crime, offence.

criminel *m*, **elle** *f* criminal:—*adj* criminal.

crise *f* crisis, attack.

cristal *m* crystal, glassware.

cristalliser *vt* to crystallise.

critère *m* criterion, standard.

critique *adj* critical, censorious:—*f* criticism; critique.

critiquer *vt* to criticise, censure.

crochet *m* hook, clip.

crocodile *m* crocodile.

croire *vt* to believe, think.

croiser *vt* to cross; to fold:—**se ~** *vr* to cross, intersect.

croisière *f* cruise.

croissance *f* growth, increase.

croître *vi* to grow, rise.

croix *f* cross.

croquer *vt* to crunch, munch.

croquette *f* croquette.

croquis *m* sketch, outline.

croustiller *vi* to be crusty, crispy.

croûte *f* crust.

croyance *f* belief.

croyant *adj* believing.

cru *adj* raw, uncooked:—*m* vineyard; wine.

cruauté *f* cruelty, inhumanity.

crucial *adj* crucial, decisive.

crucifix *m* crucifix.

crudité *f* crudity, coarseness.

cruel *adj* cruel.

crypter *vt* to encode, scramble.

cube *m* cube, block.

cueillir *vt* to pick, gather.

cuiller, cuillère *f* spoon, spoonful.

cuir *m* leather, hide.

cuire *vi* to cook.

cuisine *f* kitchen; cookery.

cuisiner *vt vi* to cook.

cuisinier *m*, **-ière** *f* cook.

cuisse *f* thigh.

cuisson *f* cooking, baking.

cuit *adj* cooked.

cul-de-sac *m* blind alley, cul-de-sac.

culminer *vi* to culminate, tower.

culotte *f* knickers; underpants; shorts.

culpabiliser *vt* to make someone feel guilty.

culte *m* cult, veneration.

cultivateur m, **-trice** f farmer.
cultiver vt to cultivate:—**se ~** vr to improve oneself
culture f culture; cultivation.
culturel adj cultural.
cumuler vt to accumulate.
cupide adj greedy.
cure f cure; treatment.
curé m parish priest, parson.
curieux adj curious, inquisitive.
cuvette f basin, bowl.

cycle m cycle; stage.
cyclique adj cyclical.
cyclisme m cycling.
cycliste mf cyclist.
cyclone m cyclone.
cygne m swan.
cylindre m cylinder.
cynique adj cynical:—**~ment** adv cynically.
cynisme m cynicism.

D

dactylographe mf typist.
dactylographier vt to type.
dame f lady.
damier m draughtboard.
danger m danger, risk.
dangereux adj dangerous, risky.
dans prép in; into.
danse f dance; dancing.
danser vi to dance.
danseur m **-euse** f dancer.
dard m dart; sting.
date f date.
dater vt to date.
dauphin m dolphin.
davantage adv more.
de prép of; from:—**deux ~ plus** two more:—**art** some, any.
dé m die; thimble.
débâcle f disaster; collapse.
débarquer vt to land, unship:—vi to disembark, land.
débarrasser vt to clear, rid.
débat m debate; dispute, contest.
débattre vi to debate, discuss.
débile adj weak, feeble.
débilitant adj debilitating, weakening.

débiteur m, **-trice** f debtor.
débloquer vt to release, unlock.
déboiser vt to deforest.
débordant adj exuberant, overflowing.
déborder vi to overflow; to outflank.
debout adv upright, standing:—**être ~** to stand.
débris m debris, waste.
début m beginning, outset.
débuter vi to start, begin:—vt to lead, start.
décadence f decadence, decline.
décadent adj decadent.
décaféiné adj decaffeinated.
décaler vt to stagger; to shift.
décathlon m decathlon.
décéder vi to die.
déceler vt to detect; to disclose.
décembre m December.
décence f decency.
décennie f decade.
décent adj decent, proper.
décentraliser vt to decentralise.
déception f disappointment; deceit.
décès m death, decease.

décevoir vt to disappoint; to deceive.
déchaîner vt to unleash.
décharge f discharge; receipt.
décharger vt to unload, discharge.
déchet m loss, waste.
déchiffrer vt to decipher, decode.
déchirer vt to tear, rip.
décibel m decibel.
décidé adj decided; determined.
décimal adj decimal.
décision f decision.
déclarer vt to declare, announce.
déclencher vt to release, set off.
décliner vi to decline, refuse.
décollage m take-off, lift-off.
décoller vi to unpaste.
décolleté adj low-cut.
décomposer vt to decompose; to break up.
décompte m discount; deduction.
décongeler vt to thaw, defrost.
déconnecter vt to disconnect.
décontenancé adj embarrassed; disconcerted.
décor m scenery; setting.
décorateur m, **-trice** f decorator; set designer.
décoration f decoration, embellishment.
décorer vt to decorate, adorn.
découper vt to carve, cut up.
décourageant adj discouraging, disheartening.
décourager vt discourage, dishearten.
découvert adj uncovered; open.
découverte f discovery.
découvrir vt to discover.
décréter vt to decree, enact.

décrire vt to describe.
décroître vi to decrease, diminish.
déçu adj disappointed.
dédaigner vt to disdain, scorn.
dédaigneux adj disdainful, scornful.
dedans adv inside, indoors:—m inside:—**au ~ inside**.
dédier vt to consecrate, dedicate to.
dédommager vt to compensate, indemnify.
déduction f deduction.
déduire vt to deduct; to deduce.
défaire vt to undo, dismantle.
défaite m defeat, overthrow.
défaut m defect, fault.
défavorable adj unfavourable.
défection f defection.
défectueux adj defective, faulty.
défendeur m, **-deresse** f defendant.
défendre vt to defend, protect; to prohibit.
défense f defence; prohibition.
défi m defiance; challenge.
déficience f deficiency.
déficit m deficit, shortfall.
défier vt to challenge, defy.
défiler vi to parade, march.
définir vt to define, specify.
définitif adj definitive, final.
définition f definition.
déformation f deformation, distortion.
déformer vt to deform.
défouler vt to unwind, relax.
défunt m, **-e** f deceased:—adj late, deceased.
dégagement m freeing, clearance.
dégager vt to free, clear:—**se ~** vr to free oneself.

dégât m havoc, damage.

dégel m thaw.

dégénérer vi to degenerate, decline.

dégoût m disgust, distaste.

dégradation f degradation, debasement.

dégrader vt to degrade, debase.

degré m degree; grade.

déguiser vt to disguise:—**se ~** vr to disguise oneself.

dégustation f tasting, sampling.

dehors adv outside, outdoors:—**en ~ de** outside; apart from:—m outside, exterior.

déjà adv already.

déjeuner vi to lunch:—m lunch.

delà adv:—**au ~ de** beyond:—**par ~** beyond.

délai m delay; respite; time limit.

délaisser vt to abandon, quit.

délasser vt to refresh, relax:—**se ~** vr to rest, relax.

délayer vt to thin; to drag out.

délectation f delectation, delight.

délégation f delegation.

délégué m, **-e** f delegate:—adj delegated.

déléguer vt to delegate.

délibéré adj deliberate; resolute.

délicat adj delicate, dainty.

délicieux adj delicious, delightful.

délimiter vt to delimit, demarcate.

délinquant m, **-e** f delinquent, offender:—adj delinquent.

délire m delirium, frenzy.

délirer vi to be delirious.

délit m offence, misdemeanour.

délivrer vt to deliver; to release.

déloyal adj disloyal, unfaithful.

delta m delta.

demain adv tomorrow.

demande f request, petition; question.

demander vt to ask, request:—**se ~** vr to wonder.

démaquiller vt to remove make-up.

démarche f bearing; gait, walk.

déménager vi to move house.

dément adj mad, insane, crazy.

démentir vt to deny, refute.

demeure f residence, dwelling place.

demeurer vi to live at, reside, stay.

demi adj half:—**à ~** halfway:—m half.

demi-cercle m semicircle.

demi-douzaine f half-dozen.

demi-heure f half hour.

demi-lune f half-moon.

démilitariser vt to demilitarise.

démission f resignation.

démissionner vi to resign.

démocrate mf democrat.

démocratie f democracy.

démocratique adj democratic.

démodé adj old-fashioned, out-of-date.

demoiselle f young lady.

démolir vt to demolish, knock down.

démolition f demolition.

démonstration f demonstration, proof.

démonter vt to dismantle, take down, dismount.

démontrer vt demonstrate; to prove.

démoraliser vt to demoralise.

déni m denial, refusal.

dénier vt to deny, disclaim.

dénigrer vt to denigrate, disparage.

dénombrer *vt* to number, enumerate.

dénomination *f* denomination, designation.

dénoncer *vt* to denounce; to inform against.

dénonciation *f* denunciation.

dénoyauter *vt* to stone (fruit).

dense *adj* dense, thick.

densité *f* density, denseness.

dent *f* tooth.

dentelle *f* lace.

dentifrice *m* toothpaste.

dentiste *mf* dentist.

dénuder *vt* to bare, denude.

dépanner *vt* to repair, fix.

dépanneur *m*, **-euse** *f* breakdown mechanic.

départ *m* departure; start.

département *m* department.

dépasser *vt* to exceed; to go past.

dépêcher *vt* to dispatch, send:—**se ~** *vr* to hurry, rush.

dépendant *adj* dependent.

dépendre *vi* to depend on, be dependent on.

dépenser *vt* to expend, spend:—**se ~** *vr* to exert oneself.

dépérir *vi* to decline, waste away.

dépit *m* spite; grudge:—**en ~ de** in spite of.

déplacement *m* displacement; removal.

déplacer *vt* to displace; to move:—**se ~** *vr* to change residence.

déplaire *vi* to displease; to offend.

déplaisant *adj* disagreeable, unpleasant.

déplorable *adj* deplorable, disgraceful.

déployer *vt* to deploy; to display.

déportation *f* deportation, transportation.

déporter *vt* to deport, transport.

déposer *vt* to lodge, deposit.

dépôt *m* deposit; warehouse.

dépouillement *m* scrutiny, perusal; despoiling.

dépréciation *f* depreciation.

déprécier *vt* to depreciate.

dépression *f* depression, slump; dejection.

déprimant *adj* depressing.

déprimer *vt* to depress; to discourage.

depuis *prép* since, from; after.

déraillement *m* derailment.

dérangement *m* derangement; inconvenience.

déranger *vt* to upset, unsettle.

déraper *vi* to skid, slip.

dérision *f* derision, mockery.

dérisoire *adj* derisory; pathetic.

dériver *vi* to drift.

dernier *adj* last; latest; back:—*m*, **-ière** *f* last one; latter.

dernièrement *adv* recently; lately.

dérober *vt* to steal; to hide:—**se ~** *vr* to steal away, escape.

déroger *vi* to derogate; to detract.

déroulement *m* unfolding; progress, development.

dérouler *vt* to unwind, uncoil:—**se ~** *vr* to develop; to unfold.

dérouter *vt* to rout, overthrow.

derrière *prép* behind:—*adv*:—**par ~** by the back:—*m* bottom; back:—**de ~** back, rear.

des *art* = de les:—*see* **un, une.**

dès *prép* from, since:—~ **que** when; as soon as.

désaccord *m* disagreement, discord.

désaffecté *adj* disused.

désagréable *adj* disagreeable, unpleasant.

désagréger *vt* to separate:—**se ~** *vr* to become separated.

désagrément *m* displeasure, annoyance.

désapprobation *f* disapproval.

désapprouver *vt* to disapprove, object.

désarmement *m* disarmament.

désarroi *m* disarray, confusion.

désastre *m* disaster.

désavantage *m* disadvantage; prejudice.

désavantager *vt* to disadvantage, handicap.

descendant *m*, **-e** *f* descendant.

descendre *vi* to descend, go down:—*vt* to take down.

descente *f* descent, way down.

descriptif *adj* descriptive, explanatory.

description *f* description.

désenchantement *m* disenchantment; disillusion.

déséquilibré *adj* unbalanced, unhinged.

désert *m* desert, wilderness:—*adj* deserted.

déserter *vt* to desert.

désespéré *adj* desperate, hopeless.

désespérer *vi* to despair, give up hope.

désespoir *m* despair, despondency.

déshabiller *vt* to undress:—**se ~** *vr* to undress.

déshériter *vt* to disinherit.

désignation *f* designation, nomination; name.

désigner *vt* to designate, indicate.

désillusionner *vt* to disillusion; to disappoint.

désinfectant *m* disinfectant:—*adj* disinfectant.

désintégration *f* disintegration.

désintégrer *vt* to split, break up:—**se ~** *vr* to disintegrate.

désintéressé *adj* disinterested, unselfish.

désir *m* desire, wish, longing.

désirable *adj* desirable.

désirer *vt* to desire, wish, long.

désobéir *vi* to disobey.

désolation *f* desolation; ruin; grief.

désolé *adj* desolate; disconsolate; grieved.

désordonné *adj* untidy; inordinate; reckless.

désordre *m* disorder, confusion, disturbance.

désorienté *adj* disorientated.

désormais *adv* from now on, henceforth.

dessécher *vt* to dry, parch:—**se ~** *vr* to dry out.

dessein *m* design, plan, scheme:—**à ~** intentionally.

desserrer *vt* to unscrew:—**se ~** *vr* to work loose.

dessert *m* dessert, sweet.

dessin *m* drawing, sketch; draft.

dessiner *vt* to draw, sketch; to design.

dessous *adv* under, beneath:—*m* underside, bottom.

dessus *adv* over, above:—*m* ~ top.

destin *m* destiny, fate, doom.

destinataire *mf* addressee, consignee.

destination *f* destination; purpose.

destiner *vt* to determine; to intend, destine, aim.

destruction *f* destruction.

détachable *adj* detachable.

détachement *m* detachment, indifference.

détacher *vt* to detach, unfasten.

détail *m* detail, particular.

détaillant *m*, **-e** *f* retailer.

détailler *vt* to detail; to sell retail.

détecter *vt* to detect.

détecteur *m* detector.

détection *f* detection.

détective *m* detective.

détendre *vt* to release, loosen.

détenir *vt* to detain; to hold.

détente *f* relaxation, easing.

détérioration *f* deterioration.

détériorer *vt* to damage, impair:—**se ~** *vr* to deteriorate, worsen.

détermination *f* determination; resolution.

déterminer *vt* to determine, decide.

détestable *adj* detestable, odious.

détester *vt* to detest, hate.

détonation *f* detonation, explosion.

détour *m* detour; curve; evasion.

détournement *m* diversion, rerouting.

détourner *vt* to divert, reroute.

détresse *f* distress, trouble.

detruire *vt* to destroy, demolish.

dette *f* debt.

deuil *m* mourning, bereavement, grief.

deux *adj* two:—*m* two:—**en moins de** ~ in a jiffy.

deuxième *adj* second:—*mf* second.

dévaliser *vt* to burgle; to rifle.

dévaloriser *vt* to depreciate, reduce the value of.

dévaluation *f* devaluation.

devancer *vt* to outstrip, outrun; to precede.

devant *prép* in front of, before:—*adv* in front:—*m* front.

devanture *f* display; shop-front.

développement *m* development; growth; progress.

développer *vt* to develop, expand:—**se ~** *vr* to develop, grow.

devenir *vi* to become, grow.

dévêtir *vt* to undress:—**se ~** *vr* to get undressed.

déviation *f* deviation; diversion.

deviner *vt* to guess; to solve; to foretell.

devise *f* currency.

dévisser *vt* to unscrew, undo.

devoir *m* duty; homework:—*vt* to owe; to have to.

dévorer *vt* to devour, consume.

dévotion *f* devotion, piety.

dextérité *f* dexterity, adroitness.

diabétique *adj* diabetic.

diable *m* devil.

diagnostic *m* diagnosis.

diagnostiquer *vt* to diagnose.

diagonale *f* diagonal.

diagramme *m* diagram; graph.

dialecte *m* dialect.

dialogue *m* dialogue, conversation.

diamant *m* diamond.

diamètre *m* diameter.

dictateur *m*, **-trice** *f* dictator.

dictée *f* dictating; dictation.

dictionnaire *m* dictionary.

diesel *m* diesel.

diète *f* diet.

diététicien *m*, **-ienne** *f* dietician.

dieu *m* god.

diffamer *vt* to defame, slander.

différence *f* difference.

différencier *vt* to differentiate.

différent *adj* different; various.

différer *vt* to differ; to vary.

difficile *adj* difficult; awkward, tricky.

difficulté *f* difficulty; problem.

diffuser *vt* to diffuse, circulate, broadcast.

digérer *vt* to digest.

digestion *f* digestion.

digne *adj* worthy; dignified.

dignité *f* dignity.

dilapider *vt* to squander; to embezzle.

dilemme *m* dilemma.

diluer *vt* to dilute.

dimanche *m* Sunday.

dimension *f* dimension, size.

diminuer *vt* to diminish, reduce:—*vi* to diminish, lessen.

diminutif *m* diminutive.

diminution *f* reduction, lessening.

dîner *vi* to dine:—*m* dinner.

diocèse *m* diocese.

diplomate *m* diplomat.

diplomatie *f* diplomacy.

diplomatique *adj* diplomatic.

diplôme *m* diploma, certificate.

dire *vt* to say; to tell:—**se ~** to say to oneself; to call oneself:—*vr* **se ~ que** to be said that.

direct *adj* direct:—*m* express.

directeur *m*, **-trice** *f* director.

direction *f* direction, management.

diriger *vt* to run, direct:—**se ~** *vr*:— **se ~ vers** to head for, make for.

discerner *vt* to discern, distinguish.

disciple *m* disciple.

discipline *f* discipline.

discorde *f* discord, dissension.

discothèque *f* discotheque.

discours *m* speech, talking.

discréditer *vt* to discredit.

discret *adj* discreet.

discrétion *f* discretion, prudence.

discrimination *f* discrimination.

discriminer *vt* to distinguish; to discriminate.

disculper *vt* to excuse, exonerate.

discussion *f* discussion, debate.

discuter *vi*, *vt* to discuss, debate.

disgrâce *f* disgrace.

disparaître *vi* to disappear, vanish.

disparité *f* disparity, incongruity.

disparition *f* disappearance; death; extinction.

dispenser *vt* to dispense, exempt.

dispersion *f* dispersal, scattering.

disponible *adj* available; transferable.

disposer *vt* to arrange, dispose.

dispositif *m* device, mechanism.

disposition *f* arrangement, layout.

dispute *f* dispute, argument.

disque *m* disk; record.

disquette *f* diskette.

dissertation *f* dissertation.

dissidence *f* dissidence, dissent.

dissident *adj* dissident.

dissimuler *vt* to dissemble, conceal.

dissipation *f* dissipation, waste.

dissiper *vt* to dispel; to dissipate.

dissolution *f* dissolution.

dissoudre *vt* to dissolve.

dissuader *vt* to dissuade.

distance *f* distance, interval.

distant *adj* distant.

distiller *vt* to distil.

distillerie *f* distillery.

distinct *adj* distinct, different.

distinction *f* distinction.

distingué *adj* distinguished.

distinguer *vt* to distinguish; to discern.

distraire *vt* to distract; to amuse:—**se ~** *vr* to enjoy oneself.

distrait *adj* inattentive, absentminded.

distribuer *vt* to distribute.

distribution *f* distribution.

district *m* district.

divaguer *vi* to ramble, rave.

divergence *f* divergence.

diverger *vi* to diverge, differ.

divers *adj* diverse, varied.

diversification *f* diversification.

diversifier *vt* to vary, diversify:—**se ~** *vr* to diversify.

diversité *f* diversity, variety.

divertir *vt* to amuse, entertain:—**se ~** *vr* to amuse oneself.

divertissant *adj* amusing, entertaining.

divin *adj* divine, exquisite.

divinité *f* divinity.

diviser *vt* to divide, split.

division *f* division.

divorce *m* divorce.

divorcer *vi* to get divorced.

dix *adj, m* ten.

dix-huit *adj, m* eighteen.

dix-huitième *adj, mf* eighteenth.

dix-neuf *adj, m* nineteen.

dix-neuvième *adj, mf* nineteenth.

dix-sept *adj, m* seventeen.

dix-septième *adj, mf* seventeenth.

dixième *adj, mf* tenth.

docile *adj* docile, submissive.

docteur *m* doctor.

doctrine *f* doctrine.

document *m* document.

documentaire *adj* documentary.

documentation *f* documentation; information.

documenter *vt* to document.

dogmatique *adj* dogmatic.

doigt *m* finger.

doigté *m* touch; fingering technique.

domaine *m* domain, estate; sphere.

domestique *adj* domestic, household.

domestiquer *vt* to domesticate, tame.

domicile *m* domicile, address.

dominant *adj* dominant, prevailing.

domination *f* domination; to dominion.

dominer *vt* to dominate; to prevail:—**se ~** to control oneself.

dommage *m* damage; harm:—**c'est ~** it's a pity.

dompter *vt* to tame, train.

don *m* gift; talent.

donation *f* donation.

donc *conj* so, therefore, thus:—**pourquoi ~?** why was that?.

donné *adj* given; fixed:—**étant ~** seeing that, in view of.

donnée *f* datum.

donner *vt* to give:—*vi* to knock, beat.

donneur *m*, **-euse** *f* giver, donor; dealer.

dont *pron* whose, of which.

dormir *vi* to sleep, be asleep; to be still.

dortoir *m* dormitory.

dos *m* back; top; ridge.

dose *f* dose; amount; quantity.

dossier *m* dossier, file; case.

douane *f* customs.

douanier *adj* custom(s).

double *adj* double, duplicate, dual:—*m* copy, double.

doubler *vt vi* to double, duplicate.

douceur *f* softness, gentleness.

douche *f* shower.

doucher (se) *vr* to take a shower.

doué *adj* gifted, endowed with.

douleur *f* pain, ache; anguish.

douloureux *adj* painful, grievous.

doute *m* doubt, misgiving:—**sans ~** without doubt.

douter *vi* to doubt, question:—**se ~ que** to suspect that, expect that.

douteux *adj* doubtful, dubious.

doux *adj* (*f* **douce**) soft; sweet; mild.

douzaine *f* dozen.

douze *adj m* twelve.

douzième *adj* twelfth:—*mf* twelfth.

dragon *m* dragon.

dramatique *adj* dramatic.

dramaturge *mf* playwright.

drame *m* drama.

drap *m* sheet.

drapeau *m* flag.

drogue *f* drug.

drogué(e) *m(f)* drug addict:—*adj* drugged.

droguer *vt* to drug, administer drugs.

droit *adj* right; straight; sound; honest:—*adv* straight, straight ahead:—*m* right; law; tax.

droite *f* right side; right (wing); straight line.

droitier *adj* right-handed.

drôle *adj* funny, amusing; peculiar.

du *art* of the.

dû *adj* owed; due:—**~ment** *adv* duly.

dubitatif *adj* doubtful, dubious.

duc *m* duke, **duchesse** *f* duchess.

dune *f* dune.

duo *m* duo; duet.

duper *vt* to dupe, take in.

dupliquer *vt* to duplicate.

dur *adj* hard, tough; difficult.

durable *adj* durable, lasting.

durant *prép* during, for.

durcir *vt vi* to harden:—**se ~** *vr* to become hardened.

durée *f* duration, length.

durer *vi* to last.

duvet *m* down.

dynamique *f* dynamic; dynamics:—*adj* dynamic.

dynamite *f* dynamite.

dynamo *f* dynamo.

dynastie *f* dynasty.

dyslexie *f* dyslexia.

dyslexique *adj* dyslexic.

E

eau *f* water; rain.

eau-de-vie *f* brandy.

éblouir *vt* to dazzle; to fascinate.

ébriété *f* intoxication.

écart *m* distance; interval; discrepancy.

écarter *vt* to separate; to avert; to dismiss.

ecclésiastique *adj* ecclesiastical:— *m* ecclesiastic, clergyman.

échange *m* exchange, barter, trade.

échanger *vt* to exchange.

échantillon *m* sample.

échappement *m* exhaust; release.

échapper *vi* to escape, avoid, elude.

écharpe *f* scarf; arm-sling.

échauffer *vt* to heat, overheat; to excite.

échec *m* failure, defeat.

échelle *f* ladder; scale.

échelonner *vt* to grade; to stagger, set at intervals.

échine *f* backbone, spine.

écho *m* echo; rumour.

échoir *vi* to fall due; to befall.

éclair *m* flash; lightning flash; spark.

éclairage *m* lighting, light.

éclaircir *vt* to lighten, brighten up.

éclairer *vt* to light; clarify, explain.

éclat *m* brightness; splendour.

éclatement *m* explosion, bursting, rupture.

éclipse *f* eclipse.

éclipser *vt* to eclipse, overshadow.

écœurer *vt* to nauseate, disgust.

école *f* school, schooling; sect, doctrine.

écolier *m* schoolgirl, **-ière** *f* schoolgirl.

écologie *f* ecology.

écologiste *mf* ecologist.

économe *adj* thrifty.

économie *f* economy, thrift; economics.

économique *adj* economic.

économiser *vt* to economise, save.

Écossais *m* Scotsman, **-e** *f* Scotswoman.

écossais *adj* Scottish.

Écosse *f* Scotland.

écoulement *m* flow, discharge, outlet.

écouler *vt* to flow, discharge; to sell.

écouter *vt* to listen to, hear.

écran *m* screen.

écraser *vt* to crush; to run over:—**s'~** *vr* to crash.

écrire *vt* to write; to spell.

écriture *f* writing; handwriting; script.

écrivain *m* writer.

écrouler (s') *vr* to collapse, crumble.

écume *f* foam, froth; scum.

écureuil *m* squirrel.

édifice *m* edifice, building.

édifier *vt* to build, construct; to edify.

éditer *vt* to publish, produce; to edit.

éditeur *m* **-trice** *f* publisher; editor.

éducation *f* education; upbringing.

éduquer *vt* to educate; to bring up, raise.

effacer *vt* to efface, erase, wipe off.

effaroucher *vt* to frighten; to shock.

effectif *m* staff; size, complement:— *adj* effective, positive.

effectuer *vt* to effect, execute, carry out.

effet *m* effect; bill, note.

efficace *adj* effective; efficient.

efficacité *f* effectiveness, efficiency.

efforcer (s') *vr* to endeavour, do one's best.

effort *m* effort, exertion; stress, strain.

effrayer *vt* to frighten, scare.

effroi *m* terror, dismay.

effronté *adj* shameless, impudent, cheeky.

effroyable *adj* horrifying, appalling.

égal *adj* equal; even, level; equable.

égaler *vt* to equal, match.

égaliser *vt* to equalise; to level out.

égalité *f* equality; equableness; evenness.

égard *m* consideration, respect:—**à l'~ de** concerning, regarding.

égarer *vt* to mislead, lead astray:—**s'~** *vr* to get lost.

église *f* church.

égoïsme *m* selfishness, egoism.

égoïste *mf* egotist:—*adj* egotistic.

éjecter *vt* to eject, throw out.

élaborer *vt* to elaborate, develop.

élan *m* surge, momentum, speed; spirit, elan.

élargir *vt* to widen, stretch:—**s'~** *vr* to get wider.

élastique *adj* elastic; flexible:—*m* elastic, elastic band.

élection *f* election; choice.

électorat *m* electorate; constituency; franchise.

électricité *f* electricity.

électrique *adj* electric.

électroménager *m* household appliance.

élégance *f* elegance, stylishness.

élégant *adj* elegant, stylish.

élémentaire *adj* elementary; basic.

éléphant *m* elephant.

élève *mf* pupil, student.

élever *vt* to bring up, raise:—**s'~** *vr* to rise, go up.

éligible *adj* eligible.

élimination *f* elimination.

éliminer *vt* to eliminate, discard.

élire *vt* to elect.

élite *f* elite.

elle *pron* she; it; her:—**~-même** herself.

élocution *f* elocution, diction.

éloigné *adj* distant, remote.

éloigner *vt* to move away:—**s'~** *vr* to go away.

éloquent *adj* eloquent.

émancipation *f* emancipation, liberation.

émanciper *vt* to emancipate:—**s'~** *vr* to become emancipated.

emballer *vt* to pack up, wrap up.

embarcation *f* boat, craft.

embargo *m* embargo.

embarquer *vt* to embark:—*vi* to embark.

embarras *m* embarrassment, confusion; trouble.

embarrasser *vt* to embarrass; to hamper.

embaucher *vt* to take on, hire.

embellir *vt* to beautify, make more attractive.

emblème *m* symbol, emblem.

embouteillage *m* traffic jam; bottling.

embrasser *vt* to kiss, embrace.

embrayage *m* clutch.

embryon *m* embryo.

embuscade *f* ambush.

émerger *vi* to emerge; to stand out.

émerveiller *vt* to astonish, amaze:—**s'~** *vr* to marvel at.

émettre *vt* to send out, emit, transmit.

émeute *f* riot.

émigration *f* emigration.

émigrer *vi* to emigrate.

éminent *adj* eminent, distinguished.

émission *f* sending out; transmission; broadcast; emission.

emménager *vi* to move in.

emmener *vt* to take away; to lead.

émoi *m* agitation, emotion.

émotion *f* emotion; commotion.

émouvoir *vt* to move, upset:—**s'~** *vr* to be moved.

empaqueter *vt* to parcel up, pack.

emparer (s') *vr* to seize, grab; to take possession of.

empêcher *vt* to prevent, stop.

empereur *m* emperor.

empiler *vt* to pile up, stack.

empire *m* empire; influence, ascendancy.

empirer *vi* to get worse, deteriorate.

emplacement *m* site, location.

emploi *m* use; job, employment.

employé *m*, **-e** *f* employee.

employer *vt* to use, spend; to employ.

employeur *m*, **euse** *f* employer.

empoisonner *vt* to poison.

emporter *vt* to take; to carry off.

emprisonner *vt* to imprison, trap.

emprunter *vt* to borrow; to assume; to derive.

ému *adj* moved, touched, excited.

en *prép* in; to; by; on:—**~ tant que** as:—*pn* from there; of it, of them:—**je n'~ veux plus** I don't want any more.

encadrer *vt* to frame; to train; to surround.

encaisser *vt* to collect, receive; to cash.

enceinte *f* pregnant.

encercler *vt* to encircle, surround.

enchaînement *m* linking; link; sequence.

enchaîner *vt* to chain.

enchanté *adj* enchanted, delighted.

enchanter *vt* to enchant, delight.

enclave *f* enclave.

encombrer *vt* to clutter, obstruct.

encore *adv* still; only; again; more:—**~ que** even though.

encouragement *m* encouragement.

encourager *vt* to encourage; to incite.

encre *f* ink.

encyclopédie *f* encyclopaedia.

endetter (s') *vr* to get into debt.

endommager *vt* to damage.

endormir *vt* to put to sleep:—**s'~** *vr* to fall asleep.

endosser *vt* to put on; to shoulder; to endorse.

endroit *m* place.

enduit *m* coating.

endurance *f* endurance, stamina.

endurcir *vt* to harden:—**s'~** *vr* to become hardened.

endurer *vt* to endure, bear.

énergie *f* energy; spirit, vigour.

énergique *adj* energetic, vigorous.

énerver *vt* to irritate, annoy:—**s'~** *vr* to get worked up.

enfance *f* childhood; infancy.

enfant *mf* child; native.

enfer *m* hell.

enfermer *vt* to lock up; to confine.

enfin *adv* at last; in short; after all.

enflammer *vt* to set on fire:—**s'~** *vr* to ignite.

enfler *vi* to swell up, inflate.

enfuir (s') *vr* to run away, flee.

engagement *m* agreement, commitment.

engager *vt* to bind; to involve:—**s'~** *vr* to undertake to.

engin *m* machine; instrument; contraption.

engouffrer *vt* to engulf.

engourdi *adj* numb; dull.

engraisser *vi* to get fatter.

énigme *f* enigma, riddle.

enivrer *vt* to intoxicate, make drunk:—**s'~** *vr* to get drunk.

enlever *vt* to remove; to abduct.

enneigé *adj* snowy, snowbound.

ennemi(e) *m(f)* enemy.

ennui *m* boredom, tedium, weariness.

ennuyer *vt* to bore, bother:—**s'~** *vr* to get bored.

énorme *adj* enormous, huge.

enquête *f* inquiry, investigation; survey.

enquêter *vi* to hold an inquiry; to investigate.

enraciner *vt* to implant, root.

enregistrer *vt* to record; to register.

enrichir *vt* to enrich, expand:—**s'~** *vr* to get rich.

enrober *vt* to wrap, cover, coat.

enrôler *vt* to enlist, enrol.

enrouler *vt* to roll up, wind up.

enseignant(e) *m(f)* teacher.

enseignement *m* education, training, instruction.

enseigner *vt* to teach.

ensemble *adv* together, at the same time:—*m* unity; whole.

ensoleillé *adj* sunny.

ensuite *adv* then, next, afterwards.

entasser *vt* to pile up, heap up.

entendement *m* understanding, comprehension.

entendre *vt* to hear; to intend, mean; to understand:—**s'~** *vr* to agree; to know how to.

entendu *adj* agreed:—**bien ~** of course.

enterrer *vt* to bury, inter.

entêté *adj* stubborn, obstinate.

enthousiasme *m* enthusiasm.

enthousiaste *adj* enthusiastic:—*mf* enthusiast.

entier *adj* entire, whole; intact.

entité *f* entity.

entourer *vt* to surround, frame, encircle:—*vr*:—**s'~ de** to surround oneself with.

entraider (s') *vr* to help one another.

entrain *m* spirit, liveliness.

entraîner *vt* to drag; to lead; to train:—**s'~** *vr* to train oneself.

entraîneur *m* trainer, coach.

entre *prép* between, among, into.

entrée *f* entry, entrance; insertion:—**d'~ de jeu** from the outset.

entremêler *vt* to intermingle, intermix.

entrepôt *m* warehouse, bonded warehouse.

entreprendre *vt* to embark upon, undertake.

entrepreneur *m* **-euse** *f* contractor; entrepreneur.

entreprise *f* company; venture, business.

entrer *vi* to enter, go in.

entretemps *adv* meanwhile.

entretenir *vt* to maintain, look after; to speak with.

entretien *m* upkeep, maintenance; conversation.

entrevue *f* meeting, interview.

énumérer *vt* to enumerate, list.

envahir *vt* to invade, overrun.

enveloppe *f* envelope; covering; exterior.

envelopper *vt* to envelop; to wrap up; to veil.

envers *prép* towards, to:—*m*:—**à l'~** inside out, upside down.

envie *f* desire, longing, inclination; envy.

envier *vt* to envy.

environ *adv* about, around:—**~s** *mpl* vicinity, neighbourhood.

environnement *m* environment.

environnemental *adj* environmental.

environner *vt* to surround, encircle.

envisager *vt* to view, envisage.

envoi *m* dispatch, remittance; kick-off.

envoyer *vt* to send, dispatch; hurl, fire.

épais *adj* thick; deep.

épaissir *vi* to thicken:—*vt*; **s'~** *vr* to get thicker.

épanouir *vt* to brighten; to open out:—**s'~** *vr* to bloom.

épargner *vt* to save; to spare.

épaule *f* shoulder.

épeler *vt* to spell.

éperdu *adj* distraught, overcome.

épice *m* spice.

épicier *m*, **-ière** *f* grocer.

épidémie *f* epidemic.

épier *vt* to spy on.

épine *f* spine; thorn; quill.

épingle *f* pin.

épiscopal *adj* episcopal.

épisode *m* episode.

épitaphe *f* epitaph.

éponge *f* sponge.

éponger *vt* to sponge, mop.

époque *f* time, epoch, age, period.

épouser *vt* to marry, wed; espouse.

épouvanter *vt* to terrify, appall.

époux *m*, **épouse** *f* spouse.

éprendre(s') *vr* to fall in love with.

épreuve *f* test; ordeal, trial; proof.

éprouver *vt* to feel, experience.

épuisement *m* exhaustion.

épuiser *vt* to exhaust, wear out.

épurer *vt* to purify, refine.

équateur *m* equator.

équation *f* equation.

équilibre *m* balance, equilibrium; harmony.

équilibrer *vt* to balance.

équipe *f* team, crew, gang, staff.

équipement *m* equipment; fitting out, fittings.

équiper *vt* to equip, fit out.

équitable *adj* equitable, fair.

équivalence f equivalence.

équivalent adj equivalent, same:—m equivalent.

équivoque adj equivocal, questionable.

ère f era.

érection f erection; establishment.

ergot m spur; lug.

ermite m hermit.

éroder vt to erode.

érotique adj erotic.

errer vi to wander, roam.

erreur f error, mistake, fault.

érudition f erudition, learning.

éruption f eruption.

escalade f climbing; escalation.

escalader vt to climb, scale.

escalier m stairs, steps.

escargot m snail.

esclavage m slavery, bondage.

esclave mf slave.

escompte m discount.

escompter vt to discount.

escorte f escort; retinue.

escorter vt to escort.

espace m space, interval.

espacer vt to space out.

espèce f sort, kind; species.

espérance f hope, expectation.

espérer vt to hope.

espion m, **-onne** f spy.

espionner vt to spy.

espoir m hope.

esprit m mind, intellect; spirit; wit.

esquisse f sketch, outline.

esquisser vt to sketch, outline.

esquiver vt to dodge; to shirk.

essai m test, trial; attempt; essay.

essayer vt to test, try, try on.

essence f petrol; essential oil.

essentiel adj essential, basic.

essieu m axle.

essuyer vt to wipe, mop:—**s'~** vr to wipe oneself.

est m east.

esthéticien(ne) m(f) beautician.

estimation f valuation; estimation, reckoning.

estimer vt to value, assess, estimate.

estival adj summer.

estivant m, **-e** f holidaymaker, summer visitor.

estomac m stomach.

et conj and.

établi adj established:—m workbench.

établir vt to establish **s'~** vr to become established.

établissement m establishing, building; establishment.

étage m floor, storey; stage, level.

étanche adj waterproof.

étang m pond.

étape f stage, leg; staging point.

état m state, condition; statement.

étayer vt to prop up, support.

été m summer.

éteindre vt to put out, extinguish.

étendre vt to spread, extend:—**s'~** vr to spread; to stretch out.

étendue f expanse, area; duration.

éternel adj eternal, everlasting.

éternité f eternity; ages.

éternuer vi to sneeze.

éthnique adj ethnic.

ethnologie f ethnology.

étinceler vi to sparkle, gleam.

étincelle f spark; gleam, glimmer.

étiquette f label, ticket; etiquette.

étoffe f material, fabric; stuff.

étoile f star.

étonnement m surprise, astonishment.

étonner vt to astonish, surprise:—**s'~** vr to be astonished.

étouffer vt to suffocate:—**s'~** vr to be suffocated, to swelter.

étourdi adj absentminded.

étourdir vt to stun, daze; to deafen.

étourdissement m blackout, dizzy spell.

étrange adj strange, funny.

étranger m, **-ère** f foreigner, stranger, alien:—adj foreign, strange, unknown.

étrangeté f strangeness, oddness.

étrangler vt to strangle, stifle:—**s'~** vr to strangle oneself, choke.

être vi to be:—**c'est-à-dire** namely, that is to say:—m being, person, soul.

étreindre vt to embrace, hug; to seize.

étroit adj narrow; strict.

étude f study; survey; office.

étudier vt to study, examine.

étymologie f etymology.

eu = p.p. **avoir** had.

eucalyptus m eucharist.

eucharistie f euphoria.

européen m, **-enne** f European:—adj European.

euthanasie f euthanasia.

eux pron they, them:—**c'est à ~** it's up to them; it's theirs:—**~-mêmes** themselves.

évacuer vt to evacuate, clear.

évader (s') vr to escape.

évaluation f evaluation, appraisal.

évaluer vt to evaluate, appraise.

évanouir (s') vr to faint, pass out.

évanouissement m faint, blackout.

évaporation f evaporation.

évaporer (s') vr to evaporate.

évasion f escape; escapism.

éveiller vt to waken, arouse:—**s'~** vr to wake up.

événement m event, incident.

éventualité f eventuality, possibility.

éventuel adj possible.

évêque m bishop.

évidence f evidence, proof.

évident adj obvious, evident.

évier m sink.

éviter vt to avoid; to spare.

évoluer vi to evolve, develop.

évolution f evolution, development.

évoquer vt to evoke, recall.

exacerber vt to exacerbate, aggravate.

exact adj exact, accurate.

exagération f exaggeration.

exagéré adj exaggerated, excessive.

exagérer vt to exaggerate.

examen m examination, survey, investigation.

examiner vt to examine, survey.

exaspérer vt to exasperate.

excellent adj excellent.

exceller vi to excel.

excentrique adj eccentric.

excepté adj apart, aside:—prép except, but for.

exception f exception, derogation.

exceptionnel adj exceptional.

excès m excess, surplus.

excitant *m* stimulant:—*adj* exciting, stimulating.

exciter *vt* to excite, stimulate:—**s'~** *vr* to get excited.

exclamation *f* exclamation.

exclamer (s') *vr* to exclaim.

exclure *vt* to exclude, oust, expel.

exclusif *adj* exclusive.

exclusion *f* exclusion, suspension.

excursion *f* excursion, trip.

excuse *f* excuse, pretext.

excuser *vt* to excuse, forgive:—**s'~** *vr* to apologise for.

exécuter *vt* to execute, carry out, perform; to produce.

exécution *f* execution, carrying out, performance.

exemple *m* example, model, instance.

exercer *vt* to exercise, perform, fulfil:—**s'~** *vr* to practise.

exercice *m* exercise, practice, use; financial year.

exhaustif *adj* exhaustive.

exhiber *vt* to exhibit, show.

exhibition *f* exhibition, show; display.

exhorter *vt* to exhort, urge.

exiger *vt* to demand, require.

exiler *vt* to exile, banish:—**s'~** *vr* to go into exile.

existence *f* existence, life.

exister *vi* to exist; to be.

exonérer *vt* to exempt.

exotique *adj* exotic.

expansion *f* expansion, development.

expectative *f* expectation, hope.

expédier *vt* to send, dispatch; to dispose of.

expédition *f* dispatch; consignment.

expérience *f* experience; experiment.

expérimental *adj* experimental.

expérimentation *f* experimentation.

expérimenter *vt* to test; to experiment with.

expert *adj* expert, skilled in:—*m* expert; connoisseur; assessor.

expertise *f* expertise; expert appraisal.

explicatif *adj* explanatory.

explication *f* explanation, analysis.

explicite *adj* explicit.

expliquer *vt* to explain, account for; to analyse.

exploitation *f* working; exploitation; concern.

exploiter *vt* to work, exploit; run, operate.

explorer *vt* to explore.

exploser *vi* to explode.

explosion *f* explosion.

exportation *f* export, exportation.

exporter *vt* to export.

exposer *vt* to display; to expose.

exposition *f* display; exposition; exposure.

express *adj* fast:—*m* fast train.

expression *f* expression.

exprimer *vt* to express, voice:—**s'~** *vr* to express oneself.

expropriation *f* expropriation.

expulser *vt* to expel; to evict.

exquis *adj* exquisite.

extase *f* ecstasy; rapture.

extension *f* extension; stretching; expansion.

exténuer *vt* to exhaust:—**s'~** *vr* to exhaust oneself.

extérieur *m* exterior, outside:—*adj* outer, external, exterior.

exterminer *vt* exterminate.

externe *adj* external, outer.

extinction *f* extinction, extinguishing.

extradition *f* extradition.

extraire *vt* to extract; to mine.

expertise (*expertise* expert appraisal

fable *f* fable, story, tale.

fabricant *m*, **-ante** *f* manufacturer, maker.

fabrique *f* factory.

fabriquer *vt* to manufacture; to forge; to fabricate.

façade *f* façade, front.

face *f* face, side, surface, aspect:—**en ~** opposite:—**~ à** facing.

fâcher *vt* to anger; to grieve:—**se ~** *vr* to get angry.

fâcheux *adj* deplorable, regrettable.

facile *adj* easy; facile.

facilité *f* easiness, ease; ability; facility.

faciliter *vt* to make easier, facilitate.

façon *f* way, fashion; make; imitation:—**de toute ~** at any rate.

façonner *vt* to shape, fashion.

facteur *m* postman.

facture *f* bill, invoice; construction, technique.

facturer *vt* to invoice, charge for.

faculté *f* faculty; power; ability; right.

fade *adj* insipid, bland, dull.

faible *adj* weak, feeble; slight, poor.

faiblesse *f* weakness, feebleness, faintness.

extraordinaire *adj* extraordinary.

extravagant *adj* extravagant, wild.

extraverti *m*, **-e** *f* extrovert:—*adj* extrovert.

extrême *adj* extreme.

extrémiste *mf*, *adj* extremist.

exubérance *f* exuberance.

exubérant *adj* exuberant.

F

faillir *vi* to come close to; to fail:— **j'ai failli tomber** I almost fell.

faim *f* hunger; appetite; famine.

faire *vt* to do; to make:—**rien à ~!** nothing doing!:—**s'en ~** to worry.

faisable *adj* feasible.

fait *m* event; fact; act.

falaise *f* cliff.

falloir *vi* to be necessary:—**il faut que tu partes** you must leave.

falsifier *vt* to falsify, alter.

familial *adj* family, domestic.

familiariser *vt* to familiarise:—**se ~** *vr* to familiarise oneself.

familiarité *f* familiarity.

familier *adj* familiar; colloquial; informal.

famille *f* family.

famine *f* famine.

fanatique *adj* fanatic:—*mf* fanatic.

faner *vt* to fade:—**se ~** *vr* to wither, fade.

fantaisie *f* whim, extravagance; imagination.

fantastique *adj* fantastic.

fantôme *m* ghost, phantom.

farce *f* joke, prank; farce.

farcir *vt* to stuff, cram.

fardeau *m* load, burden.

farine f flour.

farouche adj shy, timid; unsociable.

fascination f fascination.

fasciner vt to fascinate, bewitch.

fasciste mf, adj fascist.

fastidieux adj tedious, boring.

fatal adj fatal, deadly; fateful.

fatalité f fatality; inevitability.

fatigue f fatigue, tiredness.

fatiguer vt to tire; to overwork, strain:—**se** ~ vr to get tired.

faubourg m suburb.

faune f wildlife, fauna.

faussaire mf forger.

fausser vt to distort, alter; to warp.

faute f mistake, foul, fault:—~ **de mieux** for lack of anything better.

fauteuil m armchair.

fautif m, **-ive** f culprit:—adj at fault.

faux adj false, forged, fake; wrong; bogus.

faux-semblant m sham, pretence.

faveur f favour.

favorable adj favourable, sympathetic.

favori m, **-ite** f favourite:—adj favourite.

favoriser vt to favour, further.

fécond adj fertile; prolific, fruitful; creative.

féconder vt to impregnate; to fertilise, pollinate.

fédéral adj federal.

fédération f federation.

feindre vt to feign, pretend.

fêlé adj cracked, hare-brained.

félicitation f congratulation.

féliciter vt to congratulate.

femelle f female.

féminin adj feminine, female.

féministe mf adj feminist.

féminité f femininity.

femme f woman; wife.

fendre vt to split, cleave, crack:—**se** ~ vr to crack.

fenêtre f window.

fente f crack, fissure; slot.

fer m iron, point, blade:—~ **à cheval** horseshoe.

férié adj holiday.

ferme adj firm, steady; definite:—f farm.

ferment m ferment, leaven.

fermentation f fermentation, fermenting.

fermer vt to close; block; turn off:—**se** ~ vr to close, shut up; to close one's mind to.

fermeté f firmness, steadiness.

fermier m, **-ière** f farmer.

féroce adj ferocious, savage.

férocité f ferocity, fierceness.

ferroviaire adj railway.

fertile adj fertile, productive.

fertilité f fertility.

fervent adj fervent, ardent.

festin m feast.

festival m festival.

fête f feast, holiday.

fêter vt to celebrate, fête.

feu m fire; light; hearth:—**en** ~ on fire.

feuille f leaf.

feuilleter vt to leaf through.

fiable adj reliable; dependable.

fiancer (se) vr to become engaged.

fiasco m fiasco.

fibre f fibre.

ficelle *f* string; stick (bread).

fiche *f* card; sheet; certificate.

ficher *vt* to file, put on file.

fictif *adj* fictitious; imaginary.

fiction *f* imagination, fiction.

fidèle *adj* faithful, loyal.

fidélité *f* fidelity, loyalty.

fier *adj* proud, haughty; noble.

fier (se) *vr* to trust, rely on.

fierté *f* pride; arrogance.

fièvre *f* fever, temperature; excitement.

figuratif *adj* figurative, representational.

figure *f* face; figure; illustration, diagram.

figurer *vt* to represent:—*vi* to appear, feature:—**se ~** *vr* to imagine.

fil *m* thread; wire; cord:—**~ de fer** wire.

file *f* line, queue:—**à la ~** in line, in succession.

filer *vt* to spin.

filière *f* path; procedures; network.

fille *f* daughter, girl.

fillette *f* (small) girl.

film *m* film, picture.

filmer *vt* to film.

fils *m* son.

filtre *m* filter.

fin *f* end, finish:—*adj* thin, fine; delicate.

final *adj* final.

finance *f* finance.

financer *vt* to finance.

financier *m*, **-ière** *f* financier.

finesse *f* fineness; neatness.

fini *adj* finished, over, complete.

finir *vt* to finish, complete:—*vi* to finish, end; to die.

fissure *f* crack, fissure.

fixe *adj* fixed, permanent, set:—**~ment** *adv* fixedly, steadily.

fixer *vt* to fix; to arrange.

flacon *m* bottle, flask.

flagrant *adj* flagrant, blatant.

flair *m* sense of smell, nose; intuition.

flambeau *m* torch; candlestick.

flamme *f* flame; fervour; ardour.

flanc *m* flank, side.

flâner *vi* to stroll; to lounge about.

flatter *vt* to flatter, gratify.

flatterie *f* flattery.

flèche *f* arrow.

fléchir *vi* to bend, yield, weaken:—*vt* to bend, sway.

fleur *f* flower.

fleurir *vi* to blossom, flower:—*vt* to decorate with flowers.

fleuve *m* river.

flexibilité *f* flexibility.

flexible *adj* flexible, pliant.

flocon *m* fleck, flake.

flore *f* flora.

flot *m* stream, flood; floodtide; wave.

flotte *f* fleet; rain.

flotter *vi* to float; to drift; to wander; to waver.

fluctuation *f* fluctuation.

fluide *adj* fluid, flowing.

flux *m* flood; flow; flux.

foi *f* faith, trust.

foie *m* liver.

foin *m* hay.

foire *f* fair, trade fair.

fois *f* time, occasion.

folie *f* madness, insanity; extravagance.

foncé *adj* dark, deep (colours).

fonction f post, duty; function.

fonctionnaire mf civil servant.

fonctionner vi to work, function, operate.

fond m bottom, back:—**au ~** basically, in fact:—**à ~** thoroughly, in depth.

fondamental adj fundamental, basic.

fondamentaliste mf:—adj fundamentalist.

fondateur m, **-trice** f founder.

fondation f foundation.

fonder vt to found; to base.

fondre vi to melt:—vt to melt; to cast.

fonds m business; fund; money; stock.

fontaine f fountain, spring.

football m football, soccer.

force f strength, force, violence, energy.

forcé adj forced; emergency:—**~ment** adv inevitably.

forcer vt to force:—vi to overdo:—**se ~** vr to force oneself to.

forêt f forest.

forger vt to forge, form, mould.

formalité f formality.

formation f formation; training.

forme f form, shape; mould, fitness.

formel adj definite; positive; formal.

former vt to form; to train:—**se ~** vr to form; to train oneself

formidable adj tremendous:—**~ment** adv tremendously.

formulaire m form.

formule f formula; phrase; system.

formuler vt to formulate; express.

fort adj strong; high; loud; pro-

nounced:—adv loudly; greatly; most:—m fort; strong point, forte.

fortifier vt to fortify, strengthen:—**se ~** vr to grow stronger.

fortuit adj fortuitous, chance.

fortune f fortune, luck.

fosse f pit; grave.

fou adj, f **folle** mad, wild; tremendous; erratic.

foudre f lightning, thunderbolt.

foudroyer vt to strike (lightning).

fouiller vt to search, scour.

foulard m scarf.

foule f crowd; masses, heaps.

four m oven; furnace; fiasco.

fourgon m coach, wagon, van.

fourmi f ant.

fourmiller vi to swarm, teem.

fournir vt to supply, provide.

fournisseur m, **-euse** f purveyor, supplier.

fourrer vt to stuff; to line.

fourrure f coat, fur.

foyer m home; fireplace; focus.

fracas m crash; roar, din.

fraction f fraction, part.

fracture f fracture.

fragile adj fragile, delicate.

fragment m fragment.

fragmenter vt to break up:—**se ~** vr to fragment.

fraîcheur f freshness, coolness.

frais mpl expenses:—adj, f **fraîche** fresh, cool.

franc adj, f **franche** frank, open.

Français m Frenchman, **-e** f Frenchwoman.

français adj French:—m French.

France f France.

franchir *vt* to clear, get over, cross.

francophone *mf* French-speaker, *adj* French-speaking.

frange *f* fringe; threshold.

frapper *vt* to hit; to strike down:—*vi* to strike, knock.

fraternel *adj* fraternal.

fraternité *f* fraternity.

fraude *f* fraud, cheating.

frein *m* brake; check.

freiner *vi* to brake, slow down:—*vt* to slow down; to curb, check.

frémir *vi* to quiver, tremble.

frénétique *adj* frenetic.

fréquence *f* frequency.

fréquent *adj* frequent.

frère *m* brother.

friand *adj* partial to, fond of.

frigidaire *m* refrigerator.

frire *vt* to fry.

frisé *adj* curly, curly-haired.

frisson *m* shiver, shudder.

frissonner *vi* to shudder, tremble, shiver.

frite *f* chip.

frivole *adj* frivolous, shallow.

frivolité *f* frivolity.

froid *adj* cold, cool:—*m* cold; coolness; refrigeration.

froideur *f* coldness, chilliness.

fromage *m* cheese.

front *m* forehead; face; front.

frontière *f* border, frontier.

frotter *vt* to rub, scrape.

fructueux *adj* fruitful, profitable.

frugal *adj* frugal.

frugalité *f* frugality.

fruit *m* fruit, result.

frustration *f* frustration.

frustrer *vt* to frustrate, deprive.

fugitif *m*, **-ive** *f* fugitive:—*adj* fugitive, runaway.

fuir *vi* to avoid; to flee; to leak.

fuite *f* flight, escape; leak.

fumé *adj* smoked.

fumée *f* smoke; vapour.

fumer *vi* to smoke, steam, give off smoke:—*vt* to smoke.

fumeur *m*, **-euse** *f* smoker.

funérailles *fpl* funeral.

funéraire *adj* funeral, funerary.

fureur *f* fury; violence.

furieux *adj* furious, violent.

furtif *adj* furtive; stealthy.

fusée *f* rocket, missile.

fusil *m* rifle, gun.

fusiller *vt* to shoot.

fusion *f* fusion; melting; merger; blending.

fusionner *vt* to merge, combine.

futile *adj* futile.

futilité *f* futility.

futur *adj* future:—*m* intended, fiancé; future.

fuyard *m*, **-e** *f*:—*adj* runaway.

G

gâcher *vt* to mix; to waste.

gachette *f* trigger.

gadget *m* gadget; gimmick.

gage *m* security; pledge; proof.

gagnant *m*, **-e** *f* winner:—*adj* winning.

gagner *vt* to earn, to win:—*vi* to win.

gai *adj* cheerful, happy, gay.

gain *m* earnings; gain, profit, benefit; saving.

gala *m* official reception; gala.

galant *adj* gallant, courteous.

galaxie *f* galaxy.

galerie *f* gallery; tunnel.

galet *m* pebble.

Gallois *m* Welshman, **-e** *f* Welshwoman.

gallois *adj* Welsh:—*m* Welsh.

galop *m* gallop; canter.

galoper *vi* to gallop; to run wild.

gamin *m*, **-e** *f* kid, street urchin.

gamme *f* range; scale.

gant *m* glove.

gap *m* gap; difference, discrepancy.

garage *m* garage.

garagiste *mf* garage owner.

garantie *f* guarantee, surety.

garantir *vt* to guarantee, secure.

garçon *m* boy; assistant; waiter.

garde *f* custody; guard; surveillance:
—*m* guard, warder.

garde-boue *m* mudguard.

garder *vt* to look after; to stay in; to keep on.

garde-robe *f* wardrobe.

gardien *m*, **-ienne** *f* guard, guardian, warden; protector.

gare *f* rail station; basin; depot.

gargouiller *vi* to gurgle; to rumble.

garnir *vt* to fit with; to trim, decorate.

garnison *f* (*mil*) garrison.

gaspiller *vt* to waste, squander.

gastronomie *f* gastronomy.

gâté *adj* ruined; spoiled.

gâteau *m* cake.

gâter *vt* to ruin; to spoil:—**se ~** *vr* to go bad, go off.

gauche *adj* left; awkward, clumsy:—*f* left; left wing.

gaucher *adj* left-handed.

gaz *m invar* gas; fizz; wind.

gazeux *adj* gaseous; fizzy.

gazon *m* lawn; turf.

géant *m* giant, **-e** *f* giantess.

gel *m* frost; gel.

geler *vi* to freeze, be frozen:—*vt* to freeze.

gémir *vi* to groan, moan.

gendarme *m* policeman; gendarme.

gendarmerie *f* police force, constabulary.

gêne *f* discomfort; trouble:—**être sans ~** to be inconsiderate.

généalogie *f* genealogy.

gêner *vt* to bother; to hinder; to make uneasy.

général *adj* general, broad; common:—*m* general.

généralisation *f* generalisation.

généraliser *vt* to generalise:—**se ~** *vr* to become widespread.

générateur *m* generator.

génération *f* generation.

générer *vt* to generate

généreux *adj* generous; noble; magnanimous.

générosité *f* generosity; nobility; magnanimity.

génétique *adj* genetic.

génie *m* genius; spirit; genie.

genou *m* knee.

genre *m* kind, type; gender; genre.

gens *mpl* people, folk.

gentil adj, f **gentille** kind; good; pleasant.

géographie f geography.

géographique adj geographic.

géologie f geology.

géométrie f geometry.

géométrique adj geometric.

gérant m, **-e** f manager.

gérer vt to manage, administer.

germe m germ; seed.

geste m gesture; act, deed.

gesticuler vi to gesticulate.

gestion f management, administration.

ghetto m ghetto.

gicler vi to spurt, squirt.

gifler vt to slap, smack.

gilet m waistcoat.

girafe f giraffe.

gisement m deposit; mine; pool.

gîte m shelter; home; self-catering holiday cottage.

givre m frost, rime.

glace f ice; ice cream; mirror.

glacer vt to freeze; to chill; to glaze.

glaçon m icicle; ice cube.

glande f gland.

glaner vt to glean.

glissement m sliding; gliding; downturn, downswing.

glisser vi to slide, slip, skid.

global adj global, overall:—**ement** adv globally.

globe m globe, sphere; earth.

gloire f glory; distinction; celebrity.

glorieux adj glorious.

glorifier vt to glory, honour:—**se ~** vr to glory in; to boast.

glossaire m glossary.

gluant adj sticky, gummy.

gobelet m beaker, tumbler.

golf m golf.

golfeur m, **-euse** f golfer.

gomme f gum; rubber, eraser.

gommer vt to rub out; to gum.

gonflable adj inflatable.

gonfler vt to pump up, inflate:—**se ~** vr to swell; to be puffed up.

gorge f throat.

gothique m, adj Gothic.

goudronner vt to tar.

goulu adj greedy, gluttonous.

goupille f pin.

gourde f gourd; flask.

gourmand adj greedy.

gourmet m gourmet.

goût m taste; liking; style.

goûter vt to taste; to appreciate:— vi to have a snack; to taste good:—m snack.

goutte f drop; gout.

gouvernail m rudder; helm.

gouvernement m government.

gouverner vt to govern, rule; to control; to steer.

grâce f grace; favour; mercy; pardon:—**~ à** thanks to.

gracieux adj gracious.

grade m rank; grade; degree.

graduel adj gradual; progressive.

graduer vt to step up; to graduate.

grain m grain, seed; bead.

graisse f grease, fat.

grammaire f grammar.

grammatical adj grammatical.

gramme m gram.

grand adj big; tall; great; leading:— **pas ~-chose** not up to much.

grand-mère *f* grandmother.

grand-parents *mpl* grandparents

grand-père *m* grandfather.

grandeur *f* size; greatness; magnitude.

grandir *vi* to grow bigger, increase:—*vt* to magnify; to exaggerate.

graphique *m* graph:—*adj* graphic.

gras *adj f* **grasse** fatty; fat; greasy; crude.

gratification *f* gratuity; bonus.

gratis *adv* free, gratis.

gratitude *f* gratitude, gratefulness.

gratuit *adj* free, gratuitous.

grave *adj* grave, solemn.

graver *vt* to engrave, imprint.

gravitation *f* gravitation.

gravité *f* gravity.

gravure *f* engraving, carving.

gré *m* liking, taste:—**au ~ de** depending on, at the mercy of:— **savoir ~** to be grateful.

greffer *vt* to transplant, graft.

grêle *f* hail.

grelotter *vi* to shiver.

grenier *m* attic, garret.

grenouille *f* frog.

grève *f* strike; shore.

griffe *f* claw.

griffer *vt* to scratch.

griffonner *vt* to scribble, jot down.

grillade *f* grill.

grille *f* railings; gate; grill.

grille-pain *m invar* toaster.

griller *vt* to toast, scorch; to put bars on:—*vi* to toast, grill.

grimace *f* grimace.

grimper *vi* to climb up.

grippe *f* flu, influenza.

gris *adj* grey.

griser *vt* to intoxicate:—**se ~** *vr* to get drunk.

grogner *vi* to grumble, moan.

grommeler *vi* to mutter; to grumble:—*vt* to mutter.

gronder *vt* to scold:—*vi* to rumble, growl.

gros *adj*, *f* **grosse** big; fat; serious; coarse:—**en ~** in bulk:—*m* bulk; wholesale; fat man.

grossesse *f* pregnancy.

grosseur *f* thickness; weight; fatness.

grossir *vi* to get fatter; to swell, grow:—*vt* to magnify; to exaggerate.

grossiste *mf* wholesaler.

grotesque *adj* grotesque, ludicrous.

groupe *m* group; party; cluster.

grouper *vt* to group together; to bulk:—**se ~** *vr* to gather.

grue *f* crane.

guépard *m* cheetah.

guêpe *f* wasp.

guère *adv* hardly, scarcely.

guérir *vi* to get better; to heal:—*vt* to cure, heal:—**se ~** *vr* to get better; to recover from.

guérison *f* recovery; curing.

guerre *f* war; warfare.

guerrier *m*, **-ière** *f* warrior.

guetter *vt* to watch; to lie in wait for.

gueule *f* mouth; face; muzzle.

guichet *m* counter; ticket office, booking office.

guichtier m, **-ière** f counter clerk.
guide m guide.
guider vt to guide:—**se ~** vr to be guided by.
guidon m handlebars.
guillotine f guillotine.
guise f manner, way:—**en ~ de** by way of:—**à ta ~** as you please.
guitare f guitar.
guitariste mf guitarist.
gymnastique f gymnastics.
gynécologue, gynécologiste mf gynaecologist.

H

habile adj skilful, skilled.
habiliter vt to qualify; to authorise.
habiller vt to dress, clothe:—**s'~** vr to get dressed.
habitant(e) m(f) inhabitant; occupant; dweller.
habitation f dwelling; residence; house.
habiter vi to live:—vt to live in; to occupy.
habitude f habit, custom, routine.
habituel adj usual, customary.
habituer vt to accustom; to teach:—**s'~** vr to get used to.
hache f axe, hatchet.
haie f hedge.
haine f hatred.
haïr vt to hate, detest.
hâle m tan, sunburn.
haleine f breath, breathing.
haleter vi to pant, gasp for breath.
hall m hall, foyer.
halle f covered market; hall.
hallucination f hallucination.
halte f stop, break; stopping place.
hameçon m fish-hook.
hanche f hip; haunch.
handicap m handicap.
hanter vt to haunt.
harceler vt to harass; to pester; to plague.

hardi adj bold, daring; brazen.
hargne f spite.
haricot m bean.
harmonie f harmony; wind section.
harmoniser vt to harmonise:—**s'~** vr to be in harmony.
harpe f harp.
hasard m chance; accident; hazard; risk.
hasardeux adj hazardous, risky.
hâte f haste; impatience.
hâter vt to hasten; to quicken:—**se ~** vr to hurry.
hâtif adj precocious; early; hasty.
hausse f rise, increase.
hausser vt to raise; to heighten.
haut adj high, tall; upper; superior.
haut-parleur m loudspeaker.
hauteur f height; elevation; haughtiness; bearing.
hebdomadaire adj:—m weekly.
hélice f propeller; helix.
hélicoptère m helicopter.
hémisphère m hemisphere.
hémophile adj haemophiliac.
herbe f grass:—**en ~** under grass.
herboriste mf herbalist.
héréditaire adj hereditary.

hérédité f heredity; heritage; right of inheritance.

hérisser vt to bristle; to spike.

hérisson m hedgehog.

héritage m inheritance; heritage, legacy.

hériter vi to inherit.

héritier m heir, **-ière** f heiress.

hermétique adj hermetic.

hernie f hernia, rupture.

héroïne f heroine; heroin.

héroïque adj heroic.

héroïsme m heroism.

héros m hero.

hésitation f hesitation.

hésiter vi to hesitate.

hétérosexuel adj heterosexual.

heure f hour; time of day:—**de bonne ~** early.

heureux adv lucky; happy.

heurter vt to strike, hit; to jostle.

hibernation f hibernation.

hibou m owl.

hier adv yesterday.

hilarité f hilarity, laughter.

hippopotame m hippopotamus.

hirondelle f swallow.

hisser vt to hoist, haul up.

histoire f history; story; business:—**~ de dire** just to say.

historien m, **-ienne** f historian.

historique adj historic; historical.

hiver m winter.

hivernal adj winter; wintry.

hocher vt to nod; to shake one's head.

homard m lobster.

homicide m homicide.

homme m man.

homogène adj homogeneous.

homologuer vt to ratify; to approve.

homosexuel(le) m(f) homosexual.

honnête adj honest; decent; honourable.

honnêteté f honesty, decency.

honneur m honour; integrity; credit:—**en l'~ de** in honour of.

honorable adj honourable; reputable.

honorer vt to honour; to esteem.

honte f shame, disgrace.

honteux adj shameful; disgraceful.

hôpital m hospital.

horaire m timetable:—adj hourly.

horizon m horizon.

horizontal adj horizontal.

horloge f clock.

hormone f hormone.

horreur f horror.

horrible adj horrible; dreadful.

horrifier vt to horrify.

hors prép outside; beyond; save; except.

hors-d'œuvre m invar hors d'œuvre, starter.

hospice m home, asylum; hospice.

hospitalier adj hospital; hospitable.

hospitaliser vt to hospitalise.

hospitalité f hospitality.

hostile adj hostile.

hostilité f hostility.

hôte m, **hôtesse** f host; landlord.

hôtel m hotel.

hôtelier m, **-ière** f hotelier:—adj hotel.

houle f swell.

huer *vt* to boo.

huile *f* oil; petroleum.

huit *adj, m* eight.

huitième *adj* eighth:—*mf* eighth.

huître *f* oyster.

humain *adj* human; humane:—*m* human.

humanitaire *adj* humanitarian.

humanité *f* humanity.

humble *adj* humble; modest.

humeur *f* mood, humour; temper.

humide *adj* humid.

humidité *f* humidity.

humilier *vt* to humiliate.

humilité *f* humility.

humour *m* humour.

hurler *vi*:—*vt* to roar, yell.

hutte *f* hut.

hybride *adj m* hybrid.

hydraulique *adj* hydraulic.

hygiène *f* hygienics; hygiene.

hygiénique *adj* hygienic.

hymne *m* hymn.

hypermarché *m* hypermarket.

hypnose *f* hypnosis

hypnotiser *vt* to hypnotise.

hypocondriaque *mf adj* hypochondriac.

hypocrisie *f* hypocrisy.

hypocrite *mf* hypocrite:—*adj* hypocritical.

hypothèque *f* mortgage.

hypothéquer *vt* to mortgage.

hypothèse *f* hypothesis; assumption.

hypothétique *adj* hypothetical.

hystérie *f* hysteria.

hystérique *mf* hysterical:—*adj* hysteric.

I

iceberg *m* iceberg.

idéal *adj*:—*m* ideal.

idée *f* idea.

identifier *vt* to identify:—**s'~** *vr* to identify with.

identique *adj* identical.

identité *f* identity; similarity.

idiot *m*, **-e** *f* idiot, fool:—*adj* idiotic, stupid.

ignorance *f* ignorance.

ignorant *adj* ignorant; unacquainted; uninformed.

ignorer *vt* to be ignorant of; to be unaware of; to ignore.

il *pron* he, it.

île *f* island, isle.

illégal *adj* illegal; unlawful.

illégitime *adj* illegitimate; unwarranted.

illicite *adj* illicit.

illogique *adj* illogical.

illusion *f* illusion

illustration *f* illustration.

illustrer *vt* to illustrate.

image *f* image, picture; reflection.

imagination *f* imagination.

imaginer *vt* to imagine; to suppose.

imbécile *mf* idiot, imbecile:—*adj* stupid, idiotic.

imitation *f* imitation; mimicry; forgery.

imiter *vt* to imitate.

immatriculation *f* registration.

immédiat *adj* immediate; instant.

immense *adj* immense, boundless.

immeuble *m* building; block of flats; real estate.

immigrant *m*, **-e** *f* immigrant.

immigration *f* immigration.

imminent *adj* imminent, impending.

immobilier *adj* property:—*m* property business.

immobiliser *vt* to immobilise; to bring to a standstill/

immoral *adj* immoral.

immortel *adj* immortal.

immunité *f* immunity.

impair *adj* odd, uneven.

imparfait *adj* imperfect.

impartial *adj* impartial.

impartialité *f* impartiality.

impassible *adj* impassive.

impatience *f* impatience.

impatient *adj* impatient.

imperceptible *adj* imperceptible.

impersonnel *adj* impersonal.

impertinence *f* impertinence.

impertinent *adj* impertinent.

imperturbable *adj* unshakeable; imperturbable.

impétueux *adj* impetuous.

impitoyable *adj* merciless, pitiless.

implacable *adj* implacable.

implantation *f* implantation; establishment; introduction.

implanter *vt* to introduce; to establish; to implant.

implication *f* implication; involvement.

implicite *adj* implicit.

impliquer *vt* to imply; to necessitate; to implicate.

impoli *adj* impolite, rude.

impolitesse *f* impoliteness, rudeness.

importance *f* importance, significance; size.

important *adj* important, significant; sizeable.

importation *f* import, importation.

importer *vt* to import:—*vi* to matter:—**n'importe qui** anybody:—**n'importe quoi** anything.

imposer *vt* to impose, lay down.

impossibilité *f* impossibility.

impossible *adj* impossible.

impôt *m* tax, duty.

imprégner *vt* impregnate; to permeate; to imbue.

impression *f* feeling, impression.

impressioniste *mf:*—*adj* impressionist.

impressionner *vt* to impress; to upset.

imprévisible *adj* unforeseeable; unpredictable.

imprévu *adj* unforeseen, unexpected.

imprimer *vt* to print.

imprimeur *m* printer.

improbable *adj* improbable, unlikely.

improviser *vt* to improvise.

imprudent *adj* careless, imprudent.

impudence *f* impudence; shamelessness.

impuissant *adj* powerless, helpless.

impulsif *adj* impulsive.

inacceptable *adj* unacceptable.

inaccessible *adj* inaccessible.

inactif *adj* inactive, idle.

inactivité *f* inactivity.

inadmissible *adj* inadmissible.

inanimé *adj* inanimate; unconscious.

inaperçu *adj* unnoticed.

inattendu *adj* unexpected, unforeseen.

incapable *adj* incapable; incompetent.

incapacité *f* incompetence; disability.

incarcérer *vt* to incarcerate.

incendie *m* fire, blaze.

incertain *adj* uncertain, unsure.

incessant *adj* incessant, ceaseless.

incident *m* incident, point of law.

inciter *vt* to incite, urge.

inclure *vt* to include; to insert.

incommoder *vt* to disturb, bother.

incomparable *adj* incomparable.

incompatible *adj* incompatible.

incompréhensible *adj* incomprehensible.

inconfortable *adj* uncomfortable; awkward.

incongru *adj* unseemly; incongruous.

inconnu *m*, **-e** *f* stranger, unknown person:—*m* unknown:—*adj* unknown.

inconscience *f* unconsciousness; thoughtlessness.

inconscient *adj* unconscious; thoughtless, reckless:—*m* subconscious, unconscious.

inconsidéré *adj* inconsiderate; thoughtless.

incontestable *adj* incontestable, unquestionable.

inconvénient *m* drawback, inconvenience.

incorporer *vt* to incorporate, integrate.

incorrect *adj* faulty, incorrect.

incroyable *adj* incredible; unbelievable.

indécis *adj* indecisive; unsettled; undefined.

indéfini *adj* undefined; indefinite:—**~ment** *adv* indefinitely.

indemne *adj* unharmed, unhurt.

indemnité *f* compensation; indemnity.

indéniable *adj* undeniable, indisputable.

indépendant *adj* independent.

indéterminé *adj* undetermined; unspecified.

index *m* index; index finger.

indication *f* indication; piece of information; instruction.

indice *m* indication; clue; sign.

indifférent *adj* indifferent; immaterial.

indigène *mf* native; local:—*adj* indigenous, native.

indigestion *f* indigestion.

indigne *adj* unworthy; undeserving.

indiquer *vt* to indicate, point out; to tell.

indirect *adj* indirect; circumstantial; collateral.

indiscret *adj* indiscreet; inquisitive.

indispensable *adj* indispensable; essential.

indisponible *adj* unavailable.

individu *m* individual.

individuel *adj* individual.

indulgent *adj* indulgent; lenient.

industrie *f* industry; dexterity, ingenuity.

industriel *m*, **-elle** *f* industrialist, manufacturer:—*adj* industrial.

inédit *adj* unpublished; original.

inefficace *adj* ineffective; inefficient.

inégal *adj* unequal; uneven; irregular.

inépuisable *adj* inexhaustible.

inertie *f* inertia, apathy.

inévitable *adj* inevitable, unavoidable.

inexact *adj* inexact, inaccurate.

inexplicable *adj* inexplicable.

infaillible *adj* infallible.

infantile *adj* infantile, childish.

infecter *vt* to infect; to contaminate:—**s'~** *vr* to become infected.

infection *f* infection.

inférieur *adj* inferior; lower.

infériorité *f* inferiority.

infester *vt* to infest; overrun.

infidèle *adj* unfaithful, disloyal.

infini *adj* infinite; interminable.

infirme *adj* feeble; crippled, disabled.

infirmier *m*, **-ière** *f* nurse.

infirmité *f* disability; infirmity.

inflation *f* inflation.

inflexible *adj* inflexible, rigid.

influence *f* influence.

influencer *vt* to influence, sway.

information *f* piece of information; information; inquiry.

informatique *f* computing; data processing:—*adj* computer.

informer *vt* to inform, tell.

ingénieur *m* engineer.

ingénieux *adj* ingenious, clever.

ingénu *adj* ingenuous, naive.

ingrédient *m* ingredient; component.

initial *adj* initial.

initiative *f* initiative; enterprise.

initier *vt* to initiate.

injecter *vt* to inject.

injure *f* injury; insult.

injuste *adj* unjust, unfair.

injustice *f* injustice.

inné *adj* innate, inborn.

innocence *f* innocence.

innocent *m*, **-e** *f* innocent person; simpleton:—*adj* innocent.

innovation *f* innovation.

inondation *f* inundation.

inouï *adj* unprecedented, unheard of.

inquiet *adj* worried, anxious, uneasy.

inscription *f* inscription; registration; matriculation.

inscrire *vt* to inscribe; to register:—**s'~** *vr* to join.

insecte *m* insect.

insensible *adj* insensible, insensitive.

insérer *vt* to insert.

insinuer *vt* to insinuate, imply.

insipide *adj* insipid, tasteless.

insister *vi* to insist, be insistent; to stress.

insolent *adj* insolent; brazen.

insomnie *f* insomnia.

insoutenable *adj* unbearable; untenable.

inspecter *vt* to inspect, examine.

inspection *f* inspection.

inspiration *f* inspiration; suggestion.

inspirer *vt* to inspire; to breathe in.

instable *adj* unstable; unsettled.

installation *f* installation; installing.

installer *vt* to install; to fit out.

instant *m* moment, instant.

instinct *m* instinct.

instinctif *adj* instinctive.

institut *m* institute; school.

institution *f* institution; establishment.

instruction *f* instruction; education; inquiry.

instruire *vt* to instruct; to teach; to conduct an inquiry.

instrument *m* instrument, implement.

insuffisant *adj* insufficient, inadequate.

insulte *f* insult.

insulter *vt* to insult, affront.

insupportable *adj* unbearable, intolerable.

intact *adj* intact.

intégral *adj* integral, complete.

intégrer *vt* to integrate:—**s'~** *vr* to become integrated; to fit in.

intégrité *f* integrity.

intellectuel *m*, **-uelle** *f* intellectual:—*adj* intellectual, mental.

intelligence *f* intelligence; understanding.

intelligent *adj* intelligent.

intelligible *adj* intelligible.

intense *adj* intense; severe.

intensifier *vt* to intensify:—**s'~** *vr* to intensify.

intensité *f* intensity; severity.

intention *f* intention; purpose, intent.

intercepter *vt* to intercept.

interdire *vt* to forbid, ban, prohibit.

intéressant *adj* interesting; attractive, worthwhile.

intéresser *vt* to interest; to affect:—**s'~** *vr*:—**s'~ à** to be interested in.

intérêt *m* interest; significance, importance.

interférence *f* interference; conjunction.

intérieur *adj* interior, internal, inland.

interlocuteur *m*, **-trice** *f* interlocutor, speaker.

intermittent *adj* intermittent, sporadic.

international *adj* international.

interne *adj* internal:—*mf* boarder; house doctor.

interprète *mf* interpreter.

interpréter *vt* to interpret; to perform.

interrogation *f* interrogation, questioning; question.

interroger *vt* to question; to interrogate:—**s'~** *vr* to wonder.

interrompre *vt* to interrupt, break.

interruption *f* interruption, break.

intervalle *m* interval; space, distance.

intervenir *vi* to intervene; to take part in.

intervention f intervention; operation.

intime adj intimate; private:—mf close friend.

intimider vt to intimidate.

intimité f intimacy; privacy.

intolérance f intolerance.

intolérant adj intolerant.

intrépide adj intrepid, fearless.

introduction f introduction; launching; institution.

introduire vt to introduce, insert; to present.

introverti m, **-e** f introvert:—adj introverted.

intuitif adj intuitive.

intuition f intuition.

inutile adj useless; unavailing; pointless.

invalide adj disabled; invalid.

invariable adj invariable; unvarying.

invasion f invasion.

inventer vt to invent; to devise; to make up.

invention f invention; inventiveness.

inverse adj opposite:—m opposite, reverse.

inversion f inversion; reversal.

investissement m investment; investing.

invincible adj invincible, indomitable.

invisible adj invisible; unseen.

invitation f invitation.

inviter vt to invite, ask.

involontaire adj involuntary; unintentional.

invoquer vt to invoke; to call up; to plead.

invraisemblable adj unlikely, improbable.

invulnérable adj invulnerable.

Irlandais m Irishman, **-e** f Irishwoman.

irlandais adj Irish.

Irlande f Ireland.

ironique adj ironic:—~ment adv ironically.

irrationnel adj irrational.

irréel adj unreal.

irrégularité f irregularity; variation; unevenness.

irrégulier adj irregular; varying; uneven.

irremplaçable adj irreplaceable.

irrésistible adj irresistible:— ~ment adv irresistibly.

irresponsable adj irresponsible

irrigation f irrigation.

irriter vt to irritate; to provoke.

isoler vt to isolate; to insulate.

issue f outlet; solution; outcome.

ivre adj drunk, inebriated.

ivrogne mf drunkard.

J

jadis adv formerly, long ago.

jalousie f jealousy, envy.

jaloux adj jealous, envious.

jamais adv never:—**à ~** for ever.

jambe f leg.

jambon m ham.

janvier m January.

jardin m garden.

jardinier *m*, **-ière** *f* gardener.

jargon *m* jargon, slang; gibberish.

jaune *adj* yellow:—*m* yellow.

jaunir *vi* to yellow, turn yellow:—*vt* to make yellow.

jazz *m* jazz.

je, j' *pron* I.

jetable *adj* disposable.

jetée *f* pier.

jeter *vt* to throw.

jeton *m* token; counter.

jeu *m* play; game; gambling:**—— de mots** pun.

jeudi *m* Thursday.

jeune *adj* young:—*m* youth, young man:—*f* young girl.

jeûne *m* fast.

jeunesse *f* youth, youthfulness.

joaillerie *f* jewelling; jewellery.

joie *f* joy, happiness; pleasure.

joindre *vt* to join, link.

jointure *f* joint *(anat)*.

joli *adj* pretty; good, handsome.

jonction *f* junction.

joue *f* cheek.

jouer *vi* to play; to gamble; to act.

jouet *m* toy.

joueur *m*, **-euse** *f* player; gambler.

jouir *vi* to enjoy; to delight in.

jouissance *f* enjoyment; use.

jour *m* day; daylight:—**tous les ~s** every day:—**à ~** up to date:—**—— férié** public holiday:—**mise à ~** updating; update.

journal *m* newspaper; bulletin:—**—— télévisé** television news.

journaliste *mf* journalist.

journée *f* day; day's work.

jovial *adj* jovial, jolly.

joyau *m* jewel, gem.

joyeux *adj* joyful.

judaïsme *m* Judaism.

judiciaire *adj* judicial, legal.

judicieux *adj* judicious.

juge *m* judge.

jugement *m* judgment.

juger *vt* to judge; to decide; to consider.

juif *m* Jew; Jewish:—**juive** *f* Jewess; Jewish.

juillet *m* July.

juin *m* June.

jumeau *m*, **-elle** *f* twin:—*adj* twin; double.

jumelle(s) *f(pl)* binoculars.

jungle *f* jungle.

jupe *f* skirt.

jurer *vt* to swear, pledge.

juridiction *f* jurisdiction; court of law.

juridique *adj* legal, juridical.

jury *m* jury; board of examiners.

jus *m* juice.

jusque, jusqu' *prép* to, as far as; until.

juste *adj* just, fair; exact; sound.

justesse *f* accuracy; aptness; soundness.

justice *f* justice, fairness.

justification *f* justification; proof.

justifier *vt* to justify, prove.

juteux *adj* juicy; lucrative.

juvénile *adj* young, youthful.

K

kaléidoscope *m* kaleidoscope.
kangourou *m* kangaroo.
karaté *m* karate.
képi *m* kepi.
kermesse *f* fair; bazaar.
kidnapper *vt* to kidnap, abduct.
kidnappeur *m*, **-euse** *f* kidnapper.

kilogramme *m* kilogramme.
kilomètre *m* kilometre.
kiosque *m* kiosk, stall.
klaxon *m* horn.
klaxonner *vi* to sound one's horn.
koala *m* koala.

L

la *art pn see* **le**.
là *adv* there; over there; then:—**par ~** that way;**~-dedans** inside, in there:—**~-dessous**, under there:—**~-dessus** on that; thereupon:—**~-haut** up there:—**celui-~** that one.
label *m* label; seal.
labeur *m* labour, toil.
laborantin(e) *m(f)* laboratory assistant.
laboratoire *m* laboratory.
lac *m* lake.
lacer *vt* to lace up; to tie up.
lâche *adj* slack; lax; cowardly.
lâcher *vt* to loosen; to release.
laid *adj* ugly, unsightly.
laideur *f* ugliness, unsightliness.
laine *f* wool.
laisser *vt* to leave; to let:—**~ tomber** to drop.
laisser-passer *m invar* pass, permit.
lait *m* milk
laitue *f* lettuce.
lame *f* blade; strip; metal plate.
lamentable *adj* lamentable, distressing.
lamenter (se) *vr* to lament, bewail.

lampe *f* lamp, light; bulb.
lance *f* lance, spear.
lancement *m* launching; starting up; throwing.
lancer *vt* to throw; to launch.
langage *m* language, speech.
langoureux *adj* languid, languorous.
langouste *f* spiny lobster.
langue *f* tongue; language.
langueur *f* languor.
lanterne *f* lantern; lamp.
lapin *m*, **-e** *f* rabbit.
large *adj* wide; generous; lax; great.
largeur *f* width, breadth.
larme *f* tear.
las *adj*, *f* **lasse** weary, tired.
lasser *vt* to tire:—**se ~** *vr* to grow tired of.
latéral *adj* lateral, side.
latin *adj* Latin:—*m* Latin.
latitude *f* latitude; margin.
lavabo *m* washbasin.
lavage *m* washing; bathing.
laver *vt* to wash; to cleanse:—**se ~** *vr* to wash oneself.
laxatif *adj* laxative:—*m* laxative.

68

le *art*, *f* **la**, *devant voyelle* **l'**, *pl* **les** the:—*pron* him, her, them.

leçon *f* lesson; reading; class.

lecteur *m*, **-trice** *f* reader.

lecture *f* reading; perusal.

légal *adj* legal, lawful.

légalité *f* legality, lawfulness.

légendaire *adj* legendary.

légende *f* legend; inscription.

léger *adj* light; inconsiderate.

légèreté *f* lightness; thoughtlessness.

législatif *adj* legislative:—*m* legislature.

législation *f* legislation, laws.

légitime *adj* legitimate, lawful.

légitimité *f* legitimacy.

légume *m* vegetable.

lendemain *m* next day, day after.

lent *adj* slow; tardy; sluggish.

lenteur *f* slowness.

lequel *pron*, *f* **laquelle**, *pl* **lesquels**, **lesquelles** who, whom, which.

leste *adj* nimble, agile:—**~ment** *adv* nimbly.

léthargie *f* lethargy.

léthargique *adj* lethargic.

lettre *f* letter, note; literature:— **suivre à la ~** to carry out to the letter.

leur *pron* them:—**le ~**, **la ~**, **les ~s** theirs.

lever *vt* to lift, raise; to levy:—**se ~** *vr* to get up.

levier *m* lever.

lèvre *f* lip.

lexique *m* vocabulary, lexis.

lézard *m* lizard.

liaison *f* connection; liaison, link.

libéral *adj* liberal:—*m* liberal.

libération *f* release, liberation.

libérer *vt* to release; to liberate.

liberté *f* liberty, freedom.

libraire *mf* bookseller.

librairie *f* bookshop; bookselling.

libre *adj* free; independent.

licence *f* degree; permit; licentiousness.

licenciement *m* redundancy; dismissal.

licencier *vt* to make redundant; to dismiss.

lien *m* bond; link, connection; tie.

lier *vt* to bind; to link:—**se ~** *vr:*— **se ~ avec** to make friends.

lieu *m* place; occasion:—**avoir ~** to take place:—**au ~ de** instead of.

lièvre *m* hare.

ligne *f* line; row; range.

lignée *f* lineage; offspring.

ligue *f* league.

lime *f* file.

limitation *f* limitation, restriction.

limite *f* boundary, limit:—**à la ~** ultimately.

limiter *vt* to limit, restrict.

limonade *f* lemonade.

limpide *adj* limpid, clear.

linéaire *adj* linear.

linge *m* linen; washing.

lingerie *f* linen room; underwear, lingerie.

linguiste *mf* linguist.

lion *m* lion, **lionne** *f* lioness

liquéfier *vt* to liquefy:—**se ~** *vr* to liquefy.

liqueur *f* liqueur; liquid.

liquide *m* liquid.

liquider *vt* to wind up; to eliminate
lire *vt* to read.
lisible *adj* legible; readable.
lisse *adj* smooth, glossy.
lisser *vt* to smooth, gloss.
liste *f* list; schedule.
lit *m* bed; layer.
litige *m* lawsuit; dispute.
litre *m* litre.
littéral *adj* literal.
littérature *f* literature; writing.
littoral *m* coast:—*adj* coastal.
livraison *f* delivery; number, issue.
livre *m* book:—*f* pound (weight, currency).
livrer *vt* to deliver, hand over; to give away.
livreur *m* delivery man, **-euse** *f* delivery woman.
local *adj* local.
localité *f* locality; town.
locataire *mf* tenant; lodger.
location *f* renting; lease, leasing.
loge *f* lodge; dressing room; box.
logement *m* housing; accommodation.
loger *vt* to accommodate; to billet:—*vi* to live in.
logiciel *m* software.
logique *f* logic:—*adj* logical.
logo *m* logo.
loi *f* law;act, statute; rule.
loin *adv* far, a long way:—*m* distance; background:—**au ~** in the distance:—**de ~** from a distance.
lointain *adj* distant, remote:—*m* distance; background
loisir *m* leisure, spare time.
long *adj*, *f* **longue** long, lengthy.

longévité *f* longevity.
longitude *f* longitude.
longtemps *adv* for a long time.
longueur *f* length.
loquace *adj* loquacious, talkative.
lors *adv* then **~ de** at the time of:—**dès ~** from that time.
lorsque *conj* when.
lot *m* prize; lot; portion.
loterie *f* lottery; raffle.
lotion *f* lotion.
louange *f* praise, commendation.
louer *vt* to rent, lease; to book.
loup *m* wolf.
lourd *adj* heavy; sultry.
lourdeur *f* heaviness.
loyal *adj* loyal, faithful.
loyauté *f* loyalty
loyer *m* rent.
lucide *adj* lucid, clear.
lucidité *f* lucidity, clearness.
lueur *f* glimmer, gleam; glimpse.
lugubre *adj* lugubrious, gloomy.
lui *pron* him, her, it:—**c'est à ~** it is his:—**~-même** himself, herself, itself.
luire *vt* to shine, gleam.
lumière *f* light; daylight; lamp; insight.
lumineux *adj* luminous; illuminated.
lunaire *adj* lunar, moon.
lundi *m* Monday.
lune *f* moon.
lunette *f* telescope; sight:—**~s** glasses.
lutte *f* struggle; contest; strife.
lutter *vi* to struggle, fight.
luxe *m* luxury, excess.

luxueux *adj* luxurious.
lycée *m* secondary school.
lyncher *vt* to lynch.

lyre *f* lyre.
lyrique *adj* lyric.
lyrisme *m* lyricism.

M

mâcher *vt* to chew.
machinal *adj* mechanical, automatic.
machine *f* machine; engine; apparatus.
machinerie *f* machinery, plant.
mâchoire *f* jaw.
maçon *m* builder, mason.
madame *f* Madam; Mrs; lady.
mademoiselle *f* Miss; young lady.
magasin *m* shop, store; warehouse.
magazine *m* magazine.
magicien(ne) *m(f)* magician.
magie *f* magic
magistrat *m* magistrate.
magnanime *adj* magnanimous.
magnétique *adj* magnetic.
magnétophone *m* tape recorder.
magnifique *adj* magnificent; sumptuous.
mai *m* May.
maigre *adj* thin; meagre, scarce.
maigrir *vi* to get thinner; to waste away.
maillot *m* jersey; leotard.
main *f* hand:—**avoir la ~** to have the lead.
main-d'œuvre *f* workforce.
maintenance *f* maintenance, servicing.
maintenant *adv* now:—**à partir de ~** from now on.
maintenir *vt* to keep.
maintien *m* maintenance; preservation; keeping up.

maire *m* mayor, **-esse** *f* mayoress.
mais *conj* but.
maison *f* house; home; building; premises.
maître *m* **-esse** *f* master; ruler; lord; proprietor.
maîtresse *f* mistress; teacher
maîtrise *f* mastery; control; expertise.
majoritaire *adj* majority.
majorité *f* majority.
mal *adv* wrong, badly:—*m* evil, wrong; harm; pain.
malade *adj* sick, ill; diseased:—*mf* invalid, sick person.
maladie *f* illness; malady, complaint; disorder.
maladroit *adj* clumsy, awkward.
malchanceux *adj* unlucky, unfortunate.
mâle *m* male:—*adj* male; manly, virile.
malentendu *m* misunderstanding.
malgré *prép* in spite of; despite.
malheur *m* misfortune; calamity.
malheureux *adj* unfortunate; unlucky; unhappy.
malhonnête *adj* dishonest, crooked; uncivil.
malicieux *adj* malicious, spiteful; mischievous.
malnutrition *f* malnutrition.
malsain *adj* unhealthy, unwholesome; immoral.

maltraiter vt to abuse; to handle roughly.

malveillant adj malevolent, spiteful.

maman f mother, mummy, mum.

mammifère m mammal.

manche f sleeve; game, round:—m handle, shaft.

mangeable adj edible.

manger vt to eat; to consume, squander

maniable adj handy, workable.

manier vt to handle; to manipulate.

manière f manner, way, style.

manifeste adj manifest, evident, obvious:—m manifesto.

manifester vt to display, make known; to demonstrate.

manipulation f handling; manipulation.

manipuler vt to handle; to manipulate

manœuvre f manoeuvre, operation; scheme:—m labourer.

manœuvrer vt to manoeuvre:—vi to manoeuvre, move.

manque m lack, shortage; shortcoming, deficiency.

manquer vt to miss; to fail; to be absent.

manteau m coat; mantle, blanket; cloak.

manuel m manual, handbook:—adj manual.

manufacture f factory; manufacture.

manufacturier m -ière f factory owner; manufacturer:—adj manufacturing.

manuscrit m manuscript; typescript:—adj handwritten.

maquillage m make-up.

marathon m marathon.

marbre m marble; marble statue.

marchand(e) m(f) merchant:—adj market, trade.

marchandise f merchandise, commodity; goods.

marche f walk; journey; progress; movement:—**mettre en ~** to start up; to turn on.

marché m market; transaction, contract.

marcher vi to walk, march; to progress; to work.

mardi m Tuesday.

marée f tide.

marge f margin; latitude, freedom; mark-up.

marginal adj marginal.

mari m husband.

mariage m marriage.

marié m bridegroom:—adj married.

marier vt to marry; blend, harmonise:—**se ~** vr to get married.

marin m sailor.

marine f navy; seascape; marine.

maritime adj maritime; seaboard.

marque f mark, sign; brand; make.

marquer vt to mark; to note down; to score.

mars m March.

marteau m hammer; knocker.

masculin adj masculine.

masque m mask; facade, front.

massage m massage.

masse f mass, heap; bulk; mob.

masser *vt* to mass, assemble; to massage.

masseur *m* masseur, **euse** *f* masseuse.

massif *adj* massive, solid, heavy:— *m* massif; clump.

match *m* match; game.

matelas *m* mattress.

matérialiser (se) ~ *vr* to materialise.

matériaux *mpl* material, materials.

matériel *adj* material, physical; practical.

maternel *adj* maternal, motherly.

maternité *f* motherhood; pregnancy; maternity hospital.

mathématicien(ne) *m(f)* mathematician.

mathématique *adj* mathematical:— *f* mathematics.

matière *f* material, matter; subject:—~ **première** raw material.

matin *m* morning; dawn.

matrice *f* womb; mould; matrix.

maturité *f* maturity; prime.

maussade *adj* sulky, sullen.

mauvais *adj* bad; wicked; faulty; hurtful; poor.

maximum *m* maximum.

me, m' *pn* me; myself.

mécanicien(ne) *m(f)* mechanic; engineer.

mécanique *f* mechanics:—*adj* mechanical.

méchant *adj* spiteful; wicked; mischievous.

méconnu *adj* unrecognised; misunderstood.

mécontentement *m* discontent; displeasure.

médecin *m* doctor, physician.

médecine *f* medicine

médical *adj* medical.

médiocre *adj* mediocre; indifferent.

méditation *f* meditation.

méditer *vi* to meditate:—*vt* to contemplate, have in mind.

méfier (se) *vr* to mistrust, distrust; to be suspicious.

meilleur *adj* better, preferable:—**le** ~, **la** ~**e** the best.

mélancolique *adj* melancholy; melancholic.

mélange *m* mixture.

mélanger *vt* to mix, blend; to muddle.

mêler *vt* to mix; to combine:—**se** ~ *vr* to mix, mingle

mélodie *f* melody, tune.

membre *m* member; limb.

même *adv* even:—**tout de** ~ nevertheless, all the same:—*adj* same, identical:—*pn*:—**le/la** ~, **les** ~**s** the same one(s).

mémoire *f* memory:—*m* memorandum, report.

mémorable *adj* memorable.

menace *f* threat; intimidation; danger.

menacer *vt* to threaten, menace; to impend.

ménage *m* housework, housekeeping; household.

ménager *vt* to treat with caution; to manage; to arrange:—*adj* household, domestic.

ménagère *f* housewife.

mendiant(e) *m(f)* beggar, mendicant.

mener *vt* to lead, guide; to steer; to manage.

ménopause *f* menopause.

mensonge *m* lie, falsehood; error, illusion.

menstruation *f* menstruation.

mental *adj* mental.

menteur *m* **-euse** *f* liar:—*adj* lying, deceitful.

mention *f* mention; comment; grade.

mentionner *vt* to mention.

mentir *vi* to lie, tell lies; to be deceptive.

menton *m* chin.

menu *m* menu; meal:—*adj* slender, thin; petty, minor.

mépriser *vt* to scorn, despise.

mer *f* sea; tide.

merci *m* thank you:—*f* mercy:— **sans ~** merciless.

mercredi *m* Wednesday.

mère *f* mother.

méridien *m* meridian; midday.

mériter *vt* to deserve, merit.

merveilleux *adj* marvellous, wonderful.

message *m* message.

messager *m* **-ère** *f* messenger.

messe *f* mass

mesure *f* measure; gauge; measurement:—**au fur et à ~** as; one by one:—**dans la mesure où** insofar as:—**en ~** in time.

mesurer *vt* to measure; to assess; to limit:—**se ~** *vr* to try one's strength.

métal *m* metal.

métaphore *f* metaphor.

météore *m* meteor.

météoroloque, météorologiste *mf* meteorologist.

méthode *f* method, way.

méthodique *adj* methodical.

métier *m* job; occupation:—**à tisser** weaving loom.

mètre *m* metre.

métro *m* underground, metro.

métropole *f* metropolis.

mettre *vt* to put, place; to put on:—**en marche** to start up:—**se ~ à** to begin to:—**se ~ en route** to start off.

meuble *m* piece of furniture.

meurtrier *m* murderer, **-ière** *f* murderess.

mi- *adj* half:—**à ~chemin** halfway:— **~clos** half-closed:—**à ~jambe** up to the knees:—**à ~voix** in a low voice.

miauler *vi* to mew.

micro-onde *f* microwave:—*m* **micro-ondes** microwave oven.

micro-ordinateur *m* microcomputer.

microbe *m* germ, microbe.

microfilm *m* microfilm.

microphone *m* microphone.

microscope *m* microscope.

midi *m* midday, noon.

miel *m* honey.

mien *pron*, *f* **mienne:—le ~, la mienne, les ~s, les miennes** mine, my own.

mieux *m* improvement:—**le ~** the best:—**de ~ en ~** better and better.

migraine *f* headache; migraine.

migrateur *m* migrant.

migration *f* migration.

milieu *m* middle, centre; medium; environment.

militaire *m* serviceman:—*adj* military, army.

militant(e) *m(f) adj* militant.

militer *vi* to militate; to be a militant.

mille *m adj* one thousand.

milliard *m* thousand million; milliard.

millième *m adj* thousandth.

millier *m* thousand.

million *m* million.

millionnaire *adj* millionaire; worth millions:—*mf* millionaire.

mime *m* mime:—*mf* mimic.

mimer *vt* to mime; to mimic, imitate.

mince *adj* thin, slender; meagre, trivial.

mincir *vi* to get slimmer, get thinner.

mine *f* expression; appearance; mine:—**avoir bonne ~** to look good.

minéral *adj* mineral; inorganic:—*m* mineral.

mineur(e) *m(f)* minor:—*adj* minor:—*m* miner.

mini-jupe *f* miniskirt.

miniature *f* miniature.

minimal *adj* minimal, minimum.

minimum *m* minimum.

ministère *m* ministry; agency.

ministre *m* minister; clergyman.

minorité *f* minority.

minuit *m* midnight.

minute *f* minute, moment.

minutieux *adj* meticulous; minute.

miracle *m* miracle, wonder.

miraculeux *adj* miraculous.

mirage *m* mirage.

miroir *m* mirror, reflection.

mise *f* putting, placing; stake; deposit; investment:—**~ en scène** production, staging:—**~ en liberté** release: **—~ en ordre** ordering, arrangement:—**~ en œuvre** implementation.

misérable *adj* miserable; destitute; pitiable.

misère *f* misery; poverty; destitution.

mission *f* mission, assignment.

missionnaire *m* missionary.

mitigé *adj* mitigated; lukewarm.

mitoyen *adj* common; semi-detached.

mixer *vt* to mix; to blend.

mixte *adj* mixed; joint; combined.

mobile *adj* moving; movable:—*m* motive; moving body.

mobilier *m* furniture.

mobilité *f* mobility.

mode *f* fashion; custom:—*m* form, mode; way.

modèle *m* model; pattern; design; example.

modeler *vt* to model; to shape.

modem *m* modem.

modération *f* moderation; diminution.

modéré *adj* moderate

modérer *vt* to moderate.

moderne *adj* modern, up-to-date.

moderniser *vt* to modernise.

modeste *adj* modest, simple; unassuming.

modestie *f* modesty.

modification *f* modification, alteration.

modifier *vt* to modify, alter.

moelle *f* marrow; core.

mœurs *fpl* morals; customs.

moi *pn* me, I:—**c'est à ~** it is mine, it is my turn:—**~-même** myself.

mois *m* month.

moisson *f* harvest.

moissonner *vt* to reap, mow.

moite *adj* moist, damp.

moitié *f* half.

molécule *f* molecule.

moment *m* moment, instant, while; time; opportunity.

momentané *adj* momentary; brief.

mon *pron, f* **ma**, *pl* **mes** my.

monastère *m* monastery.

mondain *adj* worldly, mundane; society, fashionable.

monde *m* world, earth; society, company.

mondial *adj* world, worldwide.

moniteur *m* **-trice** *f* instructor, coach; supervisor.

monnaie *f* currency; coin; change.

monopole *m* monopoly.

monopoliser *vt* to monopolise.

monotone *adj* monotonous.

monsieur *m* sir, gentleman, Mr, *pl* **messieurs** gentlemen, Messrs.

monstre *m* monster.

mont *m* mountain; mount.

montage *m* assembly; setting up; editing.

montagne *f* mountain.

montagneux *adj* mountainous.

montée *f* climb, climbing; ascent; rise.

monter *vi* to go up, ascend; get into (vehicle):—*vt* to go up; to carry/ bring up.

montre *f* watch.

montrer *vt* to show, point to; prove.

monument *m* monument, memorial.

moquer (se) *vr* to make fun, jeer, laugh at.

moqueur *m* **-euse** *f* mocker, scoffer:—*adj* mocking.

moral *adj* moral, ethical; intellectual.

moralité *f* morals, morality.

morceau *m* piece, morsel, fragment; extract.

mordre *vt* to bite, gnaw; to grip.

morose *adj* sullen, morose.

mort *m* dead man, **-e** *f* dead woman:—*adj* dead:—*f* death.

mortalité *f* mortality; death rate.

mortel *adj* mortal; fatal.

mortuaire *adj* mortuary; funeral.

mosquée *f* mosque

mot *m* word; saying:—**~s croisés** crossword.

moteur *m* engine, motor:—*adj* motor, driving.

motif *m* motive, grounds; motif, design.

motivation *f* motivation.

motiver *vt* to justify; to motivate.

moto *f* motorbike.

mou *adj* (*f* **molle**) soft; gentle; muffled.

mouche *f* fly.

moucher (se) *vr* to blow one's nose.

mouchoir *m* handkerchief.

moudre *vt* to mill, grind.

mouiller *vt* to wet; to water down:— **se ~** *vr* to get wet.

moule *m* mould:—*f* mussel.
mouler *vt* to mould; to model.
moulin *m* mill.
mourir *vi* to die.
mousser *vi* to froth, foam
mousseux *adj* sparkling; frothy:—
m sparkling wine.
moustache *f* moustache; whiskers.
moustique *m* mosquito.
mouton *m* sheep; mutton.
mouvement *m* movement, motion;
animation.
mouvoir *vt* to drive, power:—**se ~**
vr to move.
moyen *m* means; way:—*adj* average, medium, moderate:—**âge**
Middle Ages.
moyenne *f* average.
muet(te) *m*(*f*) mute:—*adj* dumb; silent, mute.
multicolore *adj* multicoloured.
multiple *adj* numerous, multiple:—
m multiple.
multiplication *f* multiplication.
multiplier (se) *vr* to multiply, increase.
municipal *adj* municipal; local.

municipalité *f* town, municipality.
munir *vt* to provide, equip with:—
se ~ *vr* to equip oneself.
mur *m* wall.
mûr *adj* ripe, mature; worn out.
mûrir *vi* to ripen, mature.
murmure *m* murmur; muttering;
grumbling.
murmurer *vi* to murmur.
muscle *m* muscle.
musculaire *adj* muscular.
musée *m* art gallery, museum.
musicien(ne) *m*(*f*) musician:—*adj*
musical.
musique *f* music.
musulman(e) *m*(*f*) *adj* Moslem.
muter *vt* to transfer, move.
myope *mf* short-sighted person:—
adj short-sighted.
myopie *f* short-sightedness, myopia.
mystère *m* mystery.
mystérieux *adj* mysterious.
mystifier *vt* to mystify; to hoax.
mystique *adj* mystical:—*mf* mystic.
mythe *m* myth.
mythique *adj* mythical.
mythologie *f* mythology.

N

nager *vi* to swim.
nageur *m*, **-euse** *f* swimmer; rower.
naissance *f* birth, extraction; dawn,
beginning.
naître *vi* to be born; to arise, spring
up.
naïveté *f* naïvety, artlessness, gullibility.
narcotique *m* drug, narcotic:—*adj*
narcotic.

narrateur *m*, **-trice** *f* narrator.
nasal *adj* nasal.
natalité *f* birth rate.
nation *f* nation.
national *adj* national; domestic.
nationaliste *mf* nationalist:—*adj*
nationalist.
nationalité *f* nationality.
nature *f* nature; kind, sort; temperament.

naturel *adj* natural; bodily; native; unsophisticated:—**~lement** *adv* naturally; of course.

nautique *adj* nautical.

navigation *f* sailing, navigation.

navire *m* ship, vessel.

ne *adv* no, not.

né *adj* born

néanmoins *adv* nevertheless.

nécessaire *adj* necessary; requisite; indispensable.

nécessité *f* necessity; need; inevitability.

nécessiter *vt* to require, necessitate.

négatif *adj* negative.

négligent *adj* negligent, careless; nonchalant.

négliger *vt* to neglect; to be negligent about.

négociation *f* negotiation.

négocier *vi* to negotiate; to trade:—*vt* to negotiate.

neige *f* snow.

neiger *vi* to snow, be snowing.

nerf *m* nerve.

nerveux *adj* nervous; vigorous; excitable.

net *adj*, *f* **nette** clean; clear; plain; sharp; net.

nettoyage *m* cleaning; clearing up.

nettoyer *vt* to clean; to ruin, clean out.

neuf *adj* nine:—*m* nine.

neutre *adj* neutral; neuter.

neuvième *adj* ninth:—*mf* ninth.

neveu *m* nephew.

nez *m* nose; flair:—**avoir du ~** to have flair.

niais *adj* silly, simple, inane.

nid *m* nest; den; berth.

nièce *f* niece.

nier *vt* to deny; to repudiate.

niveau *m* level; standard; par; gauge.

noble *adj* noble, dignified.

noce *f* wedding, wedding feast; marriage ceremony.

nocif *adj* noxious, harmful.

nocturne *adj* nocturnal, night.

Noël *m* Christmas.

nœud *m* knot, bow; crux.

noir *adj* black; dark:—*m* black; darkness; black man

noircir *vt* to blacken; to dirty:—**se ~** *vr* to darken, grow black.

noix *f* walnut

nom *m* name; fame; noun.

nombre *m* number, quantity.

nombreux *adj* numerous, frequent.

nommer *vt* to appoint; nominate.

non *adv* no; not.

non-sens *m* nonsense.

nonchalant *adj* nonchalant.

nord *m* north, northerly (wind)

normal *adj* normal, usual; standard-sized.

norme *f* norm; standard.

nostalgique *adj* nostalgic.

notable *adj* notable; noteworthy.

note *f* note; minute; mark; bill.

noter *vt* to note down; to notice; to mark.

notice *f* note; directions; instructions.

notion *f* notion, idea.

notoire *adj* notorious; well-known, acknowledged.

notre *adj* (*pl* **nos**) ours, our own.

nôtre *poss pn:*—**le ~, la ~, les ~s** ours, our own.

nouer *vt* to tie, knot.

nourrir *vt* to feed, provide for; to stoke:—**se ~** *vr* to feed o.s.

nourriture *f* food; sustenance.

nous *pron* we; us:—**c'est à ~** it's ours; it's our turn:—**~-mêmes** ourselves.

nouveau *adj* new; recent; additional.

nouvelle *f* piece of news; short story.

novembre *m* November.

novice *mf* novice, beginner.

noyer *vt* to drown; to flood:—**se ~** *vr* to drown.

nu *adj* naked, nude; plain, unadorned.

nuage *m* cloud.

nucléaire *adj* nuclear:—*m* nuclear energy.

nudité *f* nakedness, nudity.

nuire *vi* to harm, injure; to prejudice.

nuisible *adj* harmful; noxious.

nuit *f* night, darkness.

nul *adj* no; nil; null and void:—**~lement** *adv* not at all.

numérique *adj* numerical; digital.

numéro *m* number; issue.

numéroter *vt* to number.

nylon *m* nylon.

O

obéir *vt* to obey, be obedient; to comply.

obéissant *adj* obedient.

obèse *adj* obese.

objecter *vt* to object.

objectif *adj* objective, unbiased:—*m* objective, target.

objection *f* objection.

objet *m* object, thing; purpose; matter.

obligation *f* obligation, duty; bond.

obligatoire *adj* obligatory, compulsory.

obliger *vt* to oblige, require; to bind.

oblitérer *vt* to obliterate; to cancel (stamp)

obscène *adj* obscene.

obscur *adj* obscure, dark, gloomy.

obscurcir *vt* to darken; to obscure:—**s'~** *vr* to get dark.

obscurité *f* obscurity; darkness.

observation *f* observation; remark.

observatoire *m* observatory.

observer *vt* to observe.

obsession *f* obsession.

obstacle *m* obstacle, hindrance.

obstination *f* obstinacy, stubbornness.

obstiné *adj* obstinate, stubborn.

obstiner (s') *vr* to insist, persist.

obtenir *vt* to obtain.

occasion *f* occasion, opportunity; bargain.

occidental *adj* western.

occupant *m*, **-e** *f* occupant, occupier.

occupation *f* occupation; occupancy.

occuper *vt* to occupy:—**s'~** *vr* to keep busy.

océan *m* ocean.

octobre *m* October.

odeur *f* smell, odour.

odieux *adj* hateful, obnoxious.

odorat *m* smell (sense).

œil *m* (*pl* **yeux**) eye; look; bud.

œuf *m* egg.

œuvre *f* work; action, deed; production.

offense *f* offence; injury.

offenser *vt* to offend:—**s'~** *vr* to take offence.

offensif *adj* offensive.

office *m* office; duty; function.

officiel *adj* official.

officier *m* officer.

officieux *adj* officious; unofficial.

offre *f* offer, tender, bid.

offrir *vt* to offer.

oie *f* goose.

oignon *m* onion; bulb.

oiseau *m* bird.

oisif *adj* idle.

oisiveté *f* idleness.

olive *f* olive.

olivier *m* olive tree.

olympique *adj* Olympic.

ombre *f* shade, shadow.

omelette *f* omelette.

omettre *vt* to omit.

omission *f* omission.

omniprésent *adj* omnipresent.

on *pn* one; someone, anyone.

once *f* ounce.

oncle *m* uncle.

onde *f* wave.

onduler *vi* to undulate; to ripple.

onéreux *adj* onerous; costly.

ongle *m* nail; claw, talon; hoof.

onze *adj* eleven:—*m* eleven.

onzième *adj* eleventh:—*mf* eleventh.

opaque *adj* opaque; impenetrable.

opéra *m* opera.

opération *f* operation, performance.

opérationnel *adj* operational.

opérer *vt* to operate.

opiniâtre *adj* stubborn; persistent.

opinion *f* opinion, view.

opportun *adj* timely, opportune.

opposant *m*, **-e** *f* opponent:—*adj* opposing.

opposé *adj* opposite:—*m* opposite:—**à l'~** contrary to.

opposer *vt* to oppose.

opposition *f* opposition; conflict.

oppresser *vt* to oppress, weigh down.

oppressif *adj* oppressive.

optimiste *mf* optimist:—*adj* optimistic.

option *f* option, choice.

optionnel *adj* optional.

opulent *adj* opulent, wealthy.

or *m* gold:—*conj* now.

orage *m* storm.

orageux *adj* stormy.

oral *adj* oral, verbal.

orange *f* orange:—*adj* orange.

orateur *m*, **-trice** *f* orator.

orbite *f* orbit; socket; sphere.

orchestre *m* orchestra.

ordinaire *adj* ordinary:—*m* usual routine:—**d'~**, **à l'~** ordinarily, usually.

ordinateur *m* computer.

ordonner *vt* to order.

ordre *m* order, command; class.

ordure *f* filth; rubbish.

oreille *f* ear; hearing.

oreiller *m* pillow.

organe *m* organ; instrument; medium.

organique *adj* organic.

organisateur *m*, **-trice** *f* organiser.

organisation *f* organisation.

organiser *vt* to organise, arrange.

orgueil *m* pride, arrogance.

orgueilleux *adj* proud, arrogant.

orient *m* orient, east.

oriental *adj* eastern, oriental.

orienter *vt* to orientate.

original *adj* original, novel:—*m* original.

originalité *f* originality.

origine *f* origin:—**à l'~** originally.

originel *adj* original, primitive.

orner *vt* to adorn, decorate.

orphelin *m*, **-e** *f* orphan.

orteil *m* toe.

orthodoxe *adj* orthodox:—*mf* orthodox.

os *m* bone

oser *vt* to dare.

ossature *f* skeleton; framework.

ostensible *adj* open, conspicuous.

otage *m* hostage.

ôter *vt* to take away.

ou *conj* or

où *adv* where, in which; *pron* where.

oubli *m* forgetfulness; oblivion.

oublier *vt* to forget.

ouest *m* west; *adj* west.

oui *adv* yes.

ouïe *f* hearing.

ouragan *m* hurricane, whirlwind.

ours *m*, **-e** *f* bear.

outil *m* tool, implement.

outillage *m* (set of) tools; equipment.

outiller *vt* to equip; to provide with tools.

outrage *m* outrage, insult, wrong.

outre *prép* as well as, besides:—**en ~** moreover.

ouvert *adj* open; exposed; frank.

ouverture *f* opening.

ouvrable *adj* working, business.

ouvrage *m* work; piece of work.

ouvrier *m*, **-ière** *f* worker:—*adj* labour.

ouvrir *vt* to open; to unlock; to broach.

oxygène *m* oxygen.

ozone *f* ozone.

P

pacifier *vt* to pacify.

pacifique *adj* peaceful.

pacte *m* pact, treaty.

page *f* page; passage.

paiement *m* payment

païen(ne) *m(f)* pagan:—*adj* pagan.

paille *f* straw.

pain *m* bread; loaf; bar.

pair *adj* even:—*m* peer; par.

paire *f* pair

paisible *adj* peaceful; calm.

paix *f* peace; stillness.

palais *m* palace.

pâle *adj* pale, pallid.

pâleur *f* paleness, pallor.

pâlir *vi* to turn pale; to dim; to fade.

pallier *vt* to palliate; to offset.

palme *f* palm leaf; palm.

palmier *m* palm tree.
palpable *adj* palpable.
palper *vt* to feel, touch; to palpate.
palpiter *vi* to palpitate; to beat; to race.
panache *m* panache; gallantry
pancarte *f* sign, notice; placard.
panda *m* panda.
panique *f* panic.
paniquer *vi* to panic.
panne *f* breakdown; fault.
panneau *m* panel; sign, notice.
pansement *m* dressing, bandage.
panser *vt* to dress, bandage.
pantalon *m* trousers.
pantomime *f* pantomime; mime.
pantoufle *f* slipper.
papa *m* dad; daddy.
pape *m* pope.
papeterie *f* stationery.
papier *m* paper.
papillon *m* butterfly.
Pâques *fpl* Easter.
paquet *m* packet, pack.
par *prép* by, with, through; from; along:—**~-ci, ~-là** here and there.
parachever *vt* to perfect; to complete.
parachute *m* parachute.
parade *f* parade, show; parry.
paradis *m* paradise; gallery.
paradoxal *adj* paradoxical.
paradoxe *m* paradox.
paragraphe *m* paragraph.
paraître *vi* to appear; to seem.
parallèle *adj* parallel.
paralyser *vt* to paralyse.
paralysie *f* paralysis.
paranoïaque *adj* paranoid.

parapluie *m* umbrella.
parasite *m* parasite, sponger.
parasol *m* parasol; sunshade.
parc *m* park; grounds; depot.
parce que *conj* because
parcelle *f* particle; parcel.
parcourir *vt* to travel through.
pardon *m* pardon, forgiveness.
pardonner *vt* to pardon.
pare-brise *m invar* windscreen.
pare-chocs *m invar* bumper.
pareil(le) *m(f)* equal; match:—*adj* like, similar; identical.
parent(e) *m(f)* relative, relation; (*pl*) parents.
parental *adj* parental.
parenté *f* relationship, kinship.
paresse *f* laziness.
paresseux *adj* lazy.
parfaire *vt* to perfect.
parfait *adj* perfect, flawless.
parfois *adv* sometimes.
parfumer *vt* to perfume.
pari *m* bet, wager.
parier *vt* to bet, wager.
parking *m* car park; parking.
parlement *m* Parliament.
parlementaire *adj* parliamentary:— *mf* MP.
parler *vi* to talk, speak:—*vt* to speak.
parmi *prép* among.
paroi *f* wall; surface.
parole *f* word; speech; voice; lyrics.
parquer *vt* to park.
parrain *m* godfather; patron.
parrainer *vt* to sponsor, propose.
part *f* part; share; portion:—**prendre ~ à** to participate in:—**autre ~** elsewhere:—**nulle ~** nowhere.

partage *m* sharing, distribution.
partager *vt* to divide up.
partenaire *mf* partner.
parti *m* party; match.
partial *adj* partial, biased.
participant(e) *m(f)* participant, member.
participation *f* participation.
participer *vi* to participate.
particulier *adj* particular, specific:—*m* person, private individual.
partie *f* part; subject; party.
partiel *adj* part, partial.
partir *vi* to leave.
partisan(e) *m(f)* partisan.
partout *adv* everywhere.
parvenir *vi:—~ à* to reach.
pas *m* step; pace:—*adv* no, not.
passable *adj* passable, tolerable.
passage *m* passage; transit.
passager *m* **-ère** *f* passenger:—*adj* passing, transitory.
passant(e) *m(f)* passer-by.
passe *f* pass; permit; channel.
passé *m* past.
passe-temps *m invar* pastime
passeport *m* passport.
passer *vi* to pass:—**se ~** *vr* to take place.
passion *f* passion.
passionné *adj* passionate.
passionner (se) *vr* to be fascinated by, have a passion for.
passivité *f* passivity.
paternel *adj* paternal, fatherly.
paternité *f* paternity; fatherhood.
pathétique *adj* pathetic.
patience *f* patience.

patient *adj* patient.
patin *m* skate.
patiner *vi* to skate; to slip; to spin.
patineur *m* **-euse** *f* skater.
pâtisserie *f* cake shop, confectioner's.
pâtissier *m* **-ière** *f* pastry cook, confectioner.
patrie *f* homeland, country.
patriotisme *m* patriotism.
patron(ne) *m(f)* owner, boss.
patronner *vt* to patronise.
patte *f* leg, paw, foot.
paume *f* palm.
paupière *f* eyelid.
pause *f* pause; half-time.
pauvre *adj* poor; indigent:—*mf* pauper.
paye *f* pay, wages.
payer *vt* to pay.
pays *m* country; region.
paysage *m* landscape; scenery.
paysan *m* countryman **-anne** *f* countrywoman.
péage *m* toll; tollgate.
peau *f* skin; hide, pelt.
pêche *f* peach; fishing.
pécher *vi* to sin.
pêcher *vt* to fish; to catch.
pécheur *m* **-eresse** *f* sinner.
pêcheur *m* fisherman.
pédale *f* pedal; treadle.
pédaler *vi* to pedal.
pédestre *adj* pedestrian.
peigne *m* comb.
peigner (se) *vr* to comb one's hair.
peindre *vt* to paint.
peine *f* effort; pain; punishment.
peiner *vi* to toil; to struggle.

peintre *m* painter.

peinture *f* painting; paintwork.

peler *vi* to peel.

pèlerinage *m* pilgrimage.

peloton *m* pack; platoon.

pelouse *f* lawn.

pénaliser *vt* to penalise.

pencher *vi* to lean:—**se ~** *vr* to bend down.

pendant *prép* during; for:—**~ que** while.

pendre *vi* to hang.

pendule *f* clock:—*m* pendulum.

pénétrer *vi* to enter, penetrate:—*vt* to penetrate.

pénible *adj* hard, tiresome.

péninsule *f* peninsula.

pénis *m* penis.

pénitencier *m* prison, penitentiary.

pensée *f* thought.

penser *vt* to think, suppose, believe: —*vi* to think.

pension *f* pension; boarding house.

pensionnaire *mf* boarder; lodger.

pente *f* slope; gradient.

Pentecôte *f* Pentecost.

pépère *m* granddad, grandpa.

percée *f* opening, breach.

perception *f* perception.

percer *vt* to pierce.

percevoir *vt* to perceive; to collect.

percussion *f* percussion.

percuter *vt* to strike.

perdant(e) *m(f)* loser.

perdre *vt* to lose.

père *m* father; sire.

perfection *f* perfection.

perfectionnement *m* perfection.

perfectionner *vt* to perfect.

perfectionniste *mf* perfectionist:— *adj* perfectionist.

performance *f* performance.

performant *adj* high-performance

péril *m* peril, danger.

périmètre *m* perimeter.

période *f* period; epoch, era.

périodique *adj* periodic.

péripétie *f* event, episode.

périphérie *f* periphery.

périphérique *adj* peripheral

périple *m* voyage; journey.

périr *vi* to perish, die.

permanence *f* permanence.

permanent *adj* permanent.

perméable *adj* permeable.

permettre *vt* to allow, permit.

permis *adj* permitted:—*m* permit, licence.

permission *f* permission; leave.

permuter *vt* to permutate.

perpendiculaire *adj* perpendicular.

perpétuel *adj* perpetual.

perpétuité *f* perpetuity.

perplexe *adj* perplexed, confused.

perplexité *f* perplexity, confusion.

perquisition *f* search.

perroquet *m* parrot.

persécuter *vt* to persecute.

persécution *f* persecution.

persévérance *f* perseverance.

persévérer *vi* to persevere; to persist in.

persil *m* parsley.

persistance *f* persistence.

persister *vi* to persist, keep up.

personnage *m* character, individual.

personnalité *f* personality.

personne f person; self; appearance:—**en ~** in person:—*pron* anyone, anybody; nobody.

personnel *adj* personal.

perspective f perspective; view; angle.

perspicace *adj* perspicacious.

persuader *vt* to persuade; to convince.

persuasion f persuasion; conviction.

perte f loss, losing; ruin.

pertinent *adj* pertinent.

perturber *vt* to disrupt, disturb.

pervers *adj* perverse; perverted.

perversité f perversity.

pesanteur f gravity; heaviness.

peser *vt* to weigh.

pessimisme *m* pessimism.

pessismiste *mf* pessimist:—*adj* pessimistic.

peste f pest, nuisance; plague.

petit *adj* small, tiny; slim; young.

petit-fils *m* grandson.

petite-fille f granddaughter.

petitesse f smallness; meanness.

pétition f petition.

petits-enfants *mpl* grandchildren.

pétrifié *adj* petrified.

pétrole *m* oil, petroleum.

peu *adv* little, not much, few:—**un petit ~** a little bit:—**quelque ~** a little:—**pour ~ que** however little:—**~ de** little, few.

peuple *m* people, nation; crowd.

peupler *vt* to populate, stock; to plant.

peur f fear, terror, apprehension:—**avoir ~** to be afraid.

peut-être *adv* perhaps.

phare *m* lighthouse; headlight.

pharmaceutique *adj* pharmaceutical.

pharmacie f pharmacy; pharmacology.

pharmacien(ne) *m(f)* pharmacist.

phase f phase, stage.

phénoménal *adj* phenomenal.

phénomène *m* phenomenon.

philosophe *mf* philosopher.

philosophie f philosophy.

philosophique *adj* philosophical.

phobie f phobia.

phonétique f phonetics:—*adj* phonetic.

photo f photo.

photocopie f photocopy.

photogénique *adj* photogenic.

photographe *mf* photograph.

photographie f photography.

photographier *vt* to photograph.

phrase f sentence; phrase.

physicien(ne) *m(f)* physicist.

physiologique *adj* physiological.

physionomie f countenance, physiognomy.

physiothérapie f physiotherapy.

physique f physics:—*adj* physical.

pianiste *mf* pianist.

piano *m* piano.

pic *m* peak.

pictural *adj* pictorial.

pièce f piece; room; document.

pied *m* foot; **à ~** on foot.

piège *m* trap; pit; snare.

piéger *vt* to trap, set a trap.

pierre f stone.

piété f piety.

piéton *m* pedestrian.

pieu *m* post, stake, pile.

pieux *adj* pious, devout.

pigment *m* pigment.

pile *f* pile; battery.

piler *vt* to crush, pound.

pilier *m* pillar.

pilote *m* pilot; driver.

piloter *vt* to pilot, fly; to drive.

pilule *f* pill.

piment *m* pepper.

pin *m* pine.

pinceau *m* brush, paintbrush.

pincer *vt* to pinch.

pingouin *m* penguin.

pinte *f* pint.

piolet *m* ice axe.

pionnier *m* pioneer.

pipe *f* pipe.

pique-nique *m* picnic.

pique-niquer *vi* to picnic.

piquer *vt* to sting.

piqûre *f* prick; sting; bite.

pirate *m* pirate.

pire *adj* worse:—**le ~** the worst.

pis-aller *m invar* last resort, stop-gap.

piscine *f* swimming pool.

piste *f* track; clue.

pistolet *m* pistol, gun.

piteux *adj* pitiful, pathetic.

pitié *f* pity, mercy.

pittoresque *adj* picturesque.

pivoter *vi* to revolve, pivot.

placard *m* poster, notice.

place *f* place; square; seat:—**à la ~ de** instead of.

placer *vt* to place; to invest.

placide *adj* placid, calm.

plafond *m* ceiling; roof.

plage *f* beach.

plaider *vt* to plead.

plaie *f* wound, cut.

plaignant(e) *m(f)* plaintiff.

plaindre *vt* to pity:—**se ~** *vr* to complain.

plaine *f* plain.

plainte *f* complaint.

plaire *vi* to please:—**se ~** *vr* to enjoy.

plaisant *adj* pleasant, agreeable.

plaisanter *vi* to joke, jest.

plaisir *m* pleasure.

plan *m* plan; plane, level.

planche *f* plank, board.

plancher *m* floor.

planer *vi* to glide, soar.

planète *f* planet.

planeur *m* glider.

planifier *vt* to plan.

plante *f* plant.

planter *vt* to plant.

plaque *f* sheet, plate; plaque.

plastique *m* plastic:—*adj* plastic.

plat *adj* flat; straight; dull:—*m* plate; course.

plateau *m* tray; turntable; plateau.

plâtre *m* plaster.

plâtrer *vt* to plaster.

plébiscite *m* plebiscite.

plein *adj* full; entire.

pleur *m* tear, sob:—**en ~s** in tears.

pleurer *vi* to cry, weep.

pleuvoir *vi* to rain.

pli *m* fold; crease; envelope.

pliant *adj* collapsible, folding.

plier *vt* to fold; to bend.

plissement *m* creasing, folding.

plisser *vt* to pleat, fold.

plomb *m* lead; sinker; fuse.

plomber *vt* to weight; to fill.

plomberie *f* plumbing.

plongée *f* diving, dive.

plongeon *m* dive.

plonger *vi* to dive; to plunge.

plongeur *m* **-euse** *f* diver.

pluie *f* rain; shower.

plume *f* feather.

plupart *f* most; majority.

pluriel *m* plural:—*adj* plural.

plus *adv* more, most:—~ **grand que** bigger than:—**de ~ en ~** more and more:—**de ~** moreover:—**non ~** neither, not either.

plusieurs *adj* several.

plutôt *adv* rather, quite, fairly.

pluvieux *adj* rainy, wet.

pneu *m* tyre.

pneumonie *f* pneumonia.

poche *f* pocket; pouch; bag.

poêle *m* stove:—*f* frying pan.

poème *m* poem.

poète *m* poet.

poids *m* weight, influence.

poignée *f* handful:—~ **de mains** handshake.

poil *m* hair; bristle.

poinçon *m* hallmark.

poinçonner *vt* to hallmark.

poing *m* fist:—**coup de** ~ punch.

point *m* point; full stop:—**mettre au** ~ to finalise; to perfect:—**être sur le** ~ **de** to be about to:—**à~** medium, just right:—~ **de vue** point of view.

pointe *f* point, head; spike:—**sur la** ~ **des pieds** on tiptoe.

pointu *adj* pointed, sharp.

poire *f* pear.

poireau *m* leek.

pois *m* pea.

poison *m* poison.

poisson *m* fish.

poitrine *f* chest, breast; bosom.

poivre *m* pepper.

poivrer *vt* to pepper.

polaire *adj* polar.

pôle *m* pole; centre.

polémique *f* controversy:—*adj* controversial.

poli *adj* polite; polished, smooth.

police *f* police.

policier *m* policeman, **-ière** *f* policewoman.

polir *vt* to polish; to refine.

politesse *f* politeness, courtesy.

politicien(ne) *m(f)* politician.

politique *f* politics; policy:—*adj* political.

politiser *vt* to politicise.

polluer *vt* to pollute.

pollution *f* pollution.

polyglotte *adj* polyglot:—*mf* polyglot.

pomme de terre *f* potato.

pomme *f* apple.

pompe *f* pump.

pomper *vt* to pump.

pompeux *adj* pompous; pretentious.

pompier *m* fireman.

poncer *vt* to sand down, rub down.

ponctualité *f* punctuality.

ponctuel *adj* punctual.

ponctuer *vt* to punctuate.

pondre *vt* to lay; to produce.

pont *m* bridge; deck; axle.

ponton *m* pontoon; landing stage.
populaire *adj* popular.
popularité *f* popularity.
population *f* population.
porc *m* pig; pork.
porche *m* porch.
pore *m* pore.
poreux *adj* porous.
port *m* port; pass; wearing.
portatif *adj* portable.
porte *f* door; gate; threshold.
porte-avions *m invar* aircraft carrier.
porte-clefs, porte-clés *m invar* key ring.
porte-parole *m invar* spokesperson.
portée *f* reach, range; significance:—**à la ~ de** within reach:—**hors de ~** out of reach.
portefeuille *m* wallet; portfolio.
porter *vt* to carry; to take; to wear.
porteur *m* **-euse** *f* porter; carrier:—*adj* booster; strong, buoyant.
portière *f* door.
portion *f* portion, share.
portrait *m* portrait.
pose *f* pose, posture; setting.
poser *vt* to put; to install:—**se ~** *vr* to land, settle.
positif *adj* positive, definite.
position *f* position; situation; state; stance.
positionner *vt* to position, locate.
posséder *vt* to possess.
possesseur *m* possessor, owner.
possession *f* possession.
possibilité *f* possibility; potential.
possible *adj* possible; potential:—*m* **faire son ~** to do one's best.

postal *adj* postal, mail.
poste *f* post office, post:—*m* position; job.
poster *vt* to post, mail; to position.
postérieur *adj* subsequent.
postérité *f* posterity; descendants.
postier *m* **-ière** *f* post office worker.
postuler *vt* to apply for; to postulate.
posture *f* posture, position.
pot *m* jar; pot; can.
pot-de-vin *m* bribe.
potable *adj* drinkable; passable.
potage *m* soup.
poteau *m* post, stake.
potentiel *adj* potential:—*m* potential
poterie *f* pottery.
potier *m* potter.
poubelle *f* dustbin.
pouce *m* thumb; big toe; inch.
poudre *f* powder, dust.
poudrer *vt* to powder.
poule *f* hen, fowl.
poulet *m* chicken.
pouls *m* pulse.
poumon *m* lung.
poupon *m* baby.
pouponnière *f* creche.
pour *prép* for; to; in favour of; in order:—**~ que** in order that.
pourboire *m* tip.
pourcentage *m* percentage.
pourparlers *mpl* talks, negotiations.
pourquoi *adv* why:—**~ pas?** why not?:—*m* reason, question.
pourri *adj* rotten.
pourrir *vi* to rot.
pourriture *f* rot, rottenness.

poursuite f pursuit; prosecution.

poursuivre vt to pursue; to prosecute.

pourtant adv however, yet, nevertheless.

pourvoir vt to provide, equip.

pourvu conj:—~ que provided that.

poussée f pressure; thrust.

pousser vt to push:—vi to push; to grow.

poussière f dust.

poussiéreux adj dusty.

pouvoir vi can, be able; may:—m power; authority.

pragmatique adj pragmatic.

prairie f meadow, prairie.

praticable adj practicable; passable.

pratique f practice; exercise; observance:—adj practical.

pratiquer vt to practise, exercise; to carry out.

pré m meadow.

préalable adj preliminary.

préavis m notice, advance warning.

précaire adj precarious.

précaution f precaution; care.

précédent adj previous:—m precedent.

précéder vt to precede.

prêcher vt to preach.

précieux adj precious.

précipice m precipice.

précipitation f haste, violent hurry.

précipiter vt to hasten, precipitate.

précis adj precise, exact.

préciser vt to specify:—se ~ vr to become clear.

précision f precision.

précoce adj precocious.

précurseur m precursor.

prédateur m predator.

prédécesseur m predecessor.

prédiction f prediction.

prédire vt to predict, foretell.

prédominance f predominance.

prédominer vi to predominate.

préfabriqué adj prefabricated.

préférable adj preferable.

préféré(e) m(f) favourite.

préférence f preference.

préférer vt to prefer.

préjudice m loss; damage.

préjudiciable adj prejudicial.

préjudicier vt to be prejudicial.

préjugé m prejudice.

préliminaire m preliminary:—adj preliminary.

prématuré adj premature.

préméditation f premeditation.

premier m first:—adj first; primary

prémonition f premonition.

prénatal adj prenatal.

prendre vt to take:—se ~ vr to consider oneself.

prénom m first name, forename.

préoccuper vt to preoccupy:—se ~ vr to concern oneself.

préparation f preparation.

préparer vt to prepare.

prérogative f prerogative.

près adv near; almost:—de ~ closely:—à peu ~ just about.

prescrire vt to prescribe.

présence f presence.

présent m present:—adj present:— m present:—à ~ just now.

présentation *f* presentation; introduction.

présenter *vt* to introduce; to present.

préservatif *m* condom.

préserver *vt* to preserve.

présidence *f* presidency.

président(e) *m(f)* president.

présider *vt* to preside, chair.

présomption *f* presumption.

présomptueux *adj* presumptuous.

presque *adv* almost.

presse *f* press.

pressentiment *m* presentiment.

pressentir *vt* to have a presentiment of.

presser *vt* to press; to hurry up:— **se ~** *vr* to hurry.

pression *f* pressure.

pressoir *m* press (wine, cider)

prestation *f* benefit; payment.

prestige *m* prestige.

présumer *vt* to presume.

prêt *adj* ready; prepared:—*m* loan.

prêt-à-porter *m* ready-to-wear.

prétendant(e) *m(f)* candidate.

prétendre *vt* to claim; to want; to intend.

prétendu *adj* so-called, supposed.

prétentieux *adj* pretentious.

prétention *f* pretension, claim.

prêter *vt* to lend; to attribute.

prétexte *m* pretext, excuse.

prêtre *m* priest.

preuve *f* proof, evidence.

prévaloir *vi* to prevail.

prévenant *adj* considerate.

prévenir *vt* to prevent; to warn.

prévention *f* prevention.

prévisible *adj* foreseeable.

prévision *f* prediction; forecast.

prévoir *vt* to anticipate; to plan.

prévoyance *f* foresight.

prévoyant *adj* provident.

prévu *adj* provided for.

prier *vi* to pray.

prière *f* prayer; entreaty.

primaire *adj* primary.

primate *m* primate.

prime *f* premium, subsidy.

primer *vi* to dominate:—*vt* to outdo.

primitif *adj* primitive.

primordial *adj* primordial.

prince *m* prince.

princesse *f* princess.

principal *m* principal:—*adj* main, principal.

principe *m* principle; origin.

printanier *adj* spring.

printemps *m* spring.

prioritaire *adj* priority.

priorité *f* priority.

prise *f* hold, grip; catch; plug; dose —**~ de sang** blood sample:—**~ de courant** plug, power point:—**~ de conscience** awareness, realisation.

prison *f* prison; jail.

prisonnier *m* **-ière** *f* prisoner:—*adj* captive.

privation *f* deprivation.

privatiser *vt* to privatise.

privé *adj* private; unofficial.

priver *vt* to deprive.

privilège *m* privilege.

privilégié *adj* privileged, favoured.

privilégier *vt* to favour.

prix *m* price, cost; prize.
probabilité *f* probability.
probable *adj* probable, likely.
problématique *adj* problematical.
problème *m* problem, issue.
procédé *m* process; behaviour.
procéder *vi* to proceed.
procédure *f* procedure; proceedings.
procès *m* proceedings; lawsuit.
procès-verbal *m* minutes; report.
procession *f* procession.
prochain *adj* next; imminent:—*m* neighbour.
proche *adj* nearby; close.
proclamation *f* proclamation.
proclamer *vt* to proclaim, declare.
procurer *vt* to procure.
procureur *m* prosecutor.
prodigieux *adj* prodigious.
producteur *m* **-trice** *f* producer.
productif *adj* productive.
production *f* production.
productivité *f* productivity.
produire *vt* to produce.
produit *m* product; yield.
profane *adj* secular, profane.
professeur *m* teacher, professor.
profession *f* profession; occupation.
professionnel(le) *m(f)* professional; skilled worker:—*adj* professional.
profil *m* profile, outline.
profiler *vt* to profile.
profit *m* profit; advantage.
profitable *adj* profitable.
profiter *vi* to profit.
profond *adj* deep, profound.

profondeur *f* depth; profundity.
profusion *f* profusion.
programme *m* programme.
programmer *vt* to programme; to schedule.
progrès *m* progress; improvement; advance.
progresser *vi* to progress; to advance.
progression *f* progress
prohiber *vt* to prohibit, ban.
proie *f* prey, victim.
projection *f* projection, casting.
projet *m* plan; draft.
projeter *vt* to plan; to cast, project.
prolétaire *mf* proletarian.
prolifération *f* proliferation.
proliférer *vi* to proliferate.
prolongement *m* continuation, extension.
prolonger *vt* to prolong.
promenade *f* walk, stroll.
promener (se) *vr* to go for a walk.
promeneur *m* **-euse** *f* walker.
promesse *f* promise.
promettre *vt* to promise.
promotion *f* promotion.
promouvoir *vt* to promote.
prompt *adj* prompt.
prononcer *vt* to pronounce.
prononciation *f* pronunciation.
pronostic *m* forecast; prognosis.
pronostiquer *vt* to forecast, prognosticate.
propagande *f* propaganda.
propagation *f* propagation.
propager *vt* to propagate.
prophète *m* prophet.
prophétique *adj* prophetic.

prophétiser *vt* to prophesy.

propice *adj* propitious.

proportion *f* proportion, ratio.

proportionnel *adj* proportional.

propos *m* talk, remarks; intention:—**à ~ de** about, on the subject of.

proposer *vt* to propose.

proposition *f* proposition.

propre *adj* clean; own; suitable.

propreté *f* cleanliness; tidiness.

propriétaire *mf* owner; landlord.

propriété *f* ownership; suitability.

propulser *vt* to propel, power.

propulsion *f* propulsion.

prorogation *f* prorogation.

proroger *vt* to prorogue.

proscrire *vt* to proscribe.

prose *f* prose.

prospecter *vt* to prospect.

prospecteur *m* **-trice** *f* prospector.

prospectus *m* leaflet; prospectus.

prospère *adj* prosperous.

prospérer *vi* to prosper, flourish.

prospérité *f* prosperity.

prostituée *f* prostitute.

prostitution *f* prostitution.

protagoniste *m* protagonist

protection *f* protection.

protéger *vt* to protect.

protestant(e) *m(f)* Protestant:—*adj* Protestant.

protestation *f* protest.

protester *vi* to protest; to affirm.

prototype *m* prototype.

prouesse *f* prowess.

prouver *vt* to prove; to demonstrate.

provenir *vi* to come from.

proverbe *m* proverb.

province *f* province.

provincial *adj* provincial

provision *f* provision; supply.

provisoire *adj* provisional, temporary.

provocation *f* provocation.

provoquer *vt* to provoke; to cause.

proximité *f* proximity.

prudence *f* prudence, care.

prudent *adj* prudent, careful.

pseudonyme *m* pseudonym.

psychanalyser *vt* to psychoanalyse

psychanalyste *mf* psychoanalyst.

psychiatre *mf* psychiatrist

psychiatrie *f* psychiatry.

psychique *adj* psychic.

psychisme *m* psyche, mind.

psychologie *f* psychology.

psychologique *adj* psychological.

psychologue *mf* psychologist:— *adj* psychological.

psychosomatique *adj* psychosomatic.

puberté *f* puberty.

public *adj*, *f* **publique** public:—*m* public, audience.

publicité *f* publicity.

publier *vt* to publish.

puce *f* flea.

pudique *adj* modest; chaste.

puer *vi* to stink:—*vt* to stink.

puéril *adj* puerile, childish.

puérilité *f* puerility, childishness.

puis *adv* then, next.

puisque *conj* since; as.

puissance *f* power, strength.

puissant *adj* powerful.

puits *m* well; shaft.

pulmonaire *adj* pulmonary, lung.

pulsation *f* pulsation.

pulvériser *vt* to pulverise; to powder.

punir *vt* to punish.

punition *f* punishment.

pupille *f* pupil; ward.

pupitre *m* desk; console.

pur *adj* pure; neat.

pureté *f* purity, pureness.

purifier *vt* to purify, cleanse.

puritain(e) *m(f) adj* puritan.

pur-sang *m invar* thoroughbred.

putréfier *vt* to putrefy, rot.

pyjama *m* pyjamas.

pylône *m* pylon.

pyramide *f* pyramid.

Q

quai *m* quay, wharf; platform.

qualificatif *adj* qualifying.

qualification *f* qualification.

qualifier *vt* to describe; to qualify.

qualitatif *adj* qualitative.

qualité *f* quality; skill; position.

quand *conj* when, while.

quant *prép*:—~ **à lui** as for him/it.

quantifier *vt* to quantify.

quantitatif *adj* quantitative.

quantité *f* quantity, amount.

quarante *adj, m inv* forty.

quarantième *adj, mf* fortieth.

quart *m* quarter; watch.

quartier *m* district; quarter.

quasi *adv* almost, nearly.

quatorze *adj m* fourteen.

quatorzième *adj mf* fourteenth.

quatre *adj m* four.

quatre-vingt(s) *adj m* eighty.

quatre-vingt-dix *adj m* ninety.

quatre-vingtième *adj mf* eightieth.

quatrième *adj mf* fourth.

que *conj* that; than:—*pron* that; whom; what; which.

quel, *f* **quelle** *adj* who, what, which.

quelconque *adj* some, any; least, indifferent.

quelqu'un, *f* **-une** someone *pl* **quelques-uns, -unes** *pron* some.

quelque *adj* some:—~ **part** somewhere.

quelque chose *pron* something.

quelquefois *adv* sometimes.

querelle *f* quarrel; row; debate.

quereller (se) *vr* to quarrel.

question *f* question; issue.

questionnaire *m* questionnaire.

questionner *vt* to question.

quête *m* quest, search.

queue *f* tail; stalk; queue.

qui *pn* who, whom; which.

quiconque *pn* whoever, whosoever.

quiétude *f* quiet; peace.

quincaillerie *f* hardware, ironmongery.

quintuple *adj* quintuple:—*m* quintuple.

quintupler *vi* to quintuple.

quinzaine *f* about fifteen; fortnight.

quinze *adj, m* fifteen.

quinzième *adj, mf* fifteenth.

quitter *vt* to leave.

quoi *pn* what:—~ **que** whatever.
quoique *conj* although, though.

R

rabais *m* reduction, discount.
rabaisser *vt* to humble.
rabattre *vt* to close; to reduce.
rabbin *m* rabbi.
raccommoder *vt* to mend, repair.
raccord *m* join; link; pointing.
raccorder *vt* to link up.
raccourci *m* shortcut.
raccourcir *vt* to shorten.
raccrocher *vt* to ring off, hang up.
race *f* race; stock; breed.
rachat *m* repurchase, purchase.
racheter *vt* to repurchase.
racial *adj* racial.
racine *f* root:—~ **carrée** square
  root.
raciste *mf* racist:—*adj* racist.
raconter *vt* to tell, recount.
radar *m* radar.
rade *f* harbour, roads.
radiateur *m* radiator; heater.
radiation *f* radiation.
radical *adj* radical.
radieux *adj* radiant, dazzling.
radio *f* radio; X-ray.
radio-taxi *m* radio taxi.
radioactif *adj* radioactive.
radiodiffuser *vt* to broadcast (radio).
radiographie *f* radiography; X-ray
  photography.
radiologue *mf* radiologist.
radis *m* radish.
radoucir *vt* to soften.
rafale *f* gust, blast; flurry.

raffermir *vt* to harden.
raffinage *m* refining.
raffiné *adj* refined, sophisticated.
raffiner *vt* to refine.
raffoler *vi*:—~ **de** to be crazy about.
rafraîchir *vt* to cool, freshen.
rafraîchissant *adj* refreshing, cool-
  ing.
rage *f* rage, fury; mania; rabies.
raid *m* raid; trek.
raide *adj* stiff; steep; broke.
raideur *f* stiffness; steepness.
raidir *vt* to stiffen.
raie *f* line; furrow; scratch.
rail *m* rail; railway.
railler *vt* to scoff at, mock.
raillerie *f* mockery, scoffing.
raisin *m* grape.
raison *f* reason; motive; ratio:—
  avoir ~ to be right:—**en** ~ **de** because of.
raisonnable *adj* reasonable, sensible.
raisonnement *m* reasoning.
raisonner *vi* to reason; to argue.
rajeunir *vt* to rejuvenate.
rajuster *vt* to readjust.
ralenti *adj* slow:—*m* slow motion:—**au** ~ ticking over, idling.
ralentir *vi* to slow down.
ralentissement *m* slowing down.
râler *vi* to groan, moan.
rallier *vt* to rally; to win over.
rallumer *vt* to relight.
ramadan *m* Ramadan.

ramassage m gathering.

ramasser vt to collect, gather.

rame f oar; underground train.

rameau m branch.

ramener vt to bring back, restore.

ramer vi to row.

rameur m, **euse** f rower.

ramollir (se) vr to soften.

ramoner vt to sweep.

rampe f ramp, slope; gradient.

ramper vi to crawl, slither.

rance adj rancid, rank.

rançon f ransom.

rancune f grudge, rancour.

randonnée f drive; ride; ramble.

randonneur m, **-euse** f hiker, rambler.

rang m row, line; rank; class.

rangée f row, range, tier.

ranger vt to arrange.

ranimer vt to reanimate.

rapatriement m repatriation.

rapatrier vt to repatriate.

rapide adj rapid, quick.

rapidité f rapidity, quickness.

rapiécer vt to patch up.

rappel m recall; reminder.

rappeler vt to recall; to remind:—**se ~** vr to remember.

rapport m report; relation; reference.

rapporter vt to report; to bring back.

rapporteur m, **-euse** f reporter.

rapprochement m reconciliation.

rapprocher (se) vr to approach; to be reconciled.

raquette f racket.

rare adj rare; odd.

raréfier (se) vr to rarefy.

rareté f rarity; scarcity.

ras adj close-shaven, shorn.

raser vt to shave off; to raze:—**se ~** vr to shave.

rasoir m razor.

rassemblement m assembling; crowd.

rassembler vt to rally:—**se ~** vr to gather, assemble.

rasseoir (se) vr to sit down again.

rassurant adj reassuring, comforting.

rassurer vt to reassure.

rat m rat.

raté m **-e** f failure:—m misfire.

rater vt to miss; to fail:—vi to misfire.

ratification f ratification.

ratifier vt to ratify, confirm.

ration f ration, allowance.

rationnel adj rational.

rationner vt to ration.

rattacher vt to refasten; to attach; to link.

rattraper vt to catch again; to recover.

rature f deletion, erasure.

raturer vt to delete, erase.

rauque adj hoarse, raucous.

ravage m havoc; devestation.

ravager vt to ravage; devastate.

ravin m ravine, gully.

ravir vt to delight.

raviser (se) vr to change one's mind.

ravissant adj ravishing, delightful.

ravitaillement m revictualling.

ravitailler vt to revictual.

raviver vt to revive.

rayer vt to scratch; to cross out.

rayon m ray, beam; spoke; shelf.

rayonnement m radiance.

rayonner vi to radiate, shine.

rayure f stripe; streak; groove.

réaccoutumer (se) vr to become reaccustomed.

réacteur m reactor; jet-engine.

réaction f reaction.

réactionnaire adj reactionary:—mf reactionary.

réagir vi to react.

réalisateur m, **-trice** f director, film-maker.

réalisation f realisation.

réaliser vt to realise:—**se ~** vr to be realised, come true.

réalisme m realism.

réalité f reality.

réanimation f resuscitation.

réanimer vt to reanimate.

réapparaître vi to reappear.

rebelle mf rebel:—adj rebel, rebellious.

rebeller (se) vr to rebel.

rébellion f rebellion.

reboiser vt to reafforest.

rebondir vi to rebound.

rebondissement m rebound.

rebut m scrap; repulse, rebuff.

receler vt to harbour.

récent adj recent; new.

réceptif adj receptive.

réception f reception, welcome.

réceptionniste mf receptionist.

récession f recession.

recette f recipe; formula; receipt.

receveur m, **-euse** f recipient; collector.

recevoir vt to receive.

rechange m spare.

recharge f reloading.

rechargeable adj reloadable.

recharger vt to reload.

réchauffer vt to reheat.

rêche adj rough, harsh.

recherche f search; research.

rechercher vt to seek; to investigate.

rechute f relapse; lapse.

récidiver vi to reoffend; to recur.

récif m reef.

récipient m container, receptacle.

réciproque adj reciprocal, mutual.

récit m account, story.

récitation f recitation.

réciter vt to recite.

réclamation f complaint; claim.

réclamer vt to claim.

réclusion f reclusion.

récolte f harvest; collection.

récolter vt to harvest; to collect.

recommandation f recommendation.

recommander vt to recommend; to register (letter).

recommencement m renewal.

recommencer vi to begin again.

récompense f reward; award.

réconciliation f reconciliation.

réconcilier vt to reconcile.

réconfort m comfort.

réconfortant adj comforting; tonic.

réconforter vt to comfort.

reconnaissance f recognition.

reconnaissant adj grateful.

reconnaître vt to recognise; to acknowledge; to be grateful.

reconsidérer vt to reconsider.

reconstituer vt to reconstitute.

reconstitution f reconstitution.

reconstruire vt to rebuild.

record *m* record.

recourbé *adj* curved, hooked.

recourir *vi* to run again.

recours *m* recourse; appeal.

récréatif *adj* recreative.

récréation *f* recreation.

récrimination *f* recrimination.

récriminer *vi* to recriminate.

recrue *f* recruit.

recrutement *m* recruitment.

recruter *vt* to recruit.

rectangle *m* rectangle.

rectangulaire *adj* rectangular.

rectification *f* rectification.

rectifier *vt* to rectify.

rectiligne *adj* rectilinear.

reçu *pp* **recevoir** accepted, successful: —*m* receipt.

recueil *m* collection, miscellany.

recueillir *vt* to gather:—**se ~** *vr* to collect one's thoughts.

reculer *vi* to fall back.

récupération *f* recovery.

récupérer *vt* to recover.

recycler *vt* to recycle.

rédacteur *m*, **-trice** *f* editor.

rédaction *f* drafting, drawing up.

rédemption *f* redemption.

redevance *f* rent; tax; fees.

rédiger *vt* to compile; to draft.

redire *vt* to repeat.

redoutable *adj* redoubtable, formidable.

redouter *vt* to dread, fear.

redresser *vt* to rectify; to true.

réduction *f* reduction.

réduire *vt* to reduce.

réduit *adj* reduced:—*m* retreat; recess.

rééducation *f* re-education.

rééduquer *vt* to re-educate.

réel *adj* real, genuine.

réélire *vt* to re-elect.

refaire *vt* to redo; to remake.

réfectoire *m* refectory.

référence *f* reference.

référendum *m* referendum.

réfléchir *vi* to think, reflect.

reflet *m* reflection.

refléter *vt* to reflect, mirror.

réflexe *m* reflex.

réflexion *f* thought, reflection:—~ **faite** all things considered.

réforme *f* reform.

réformer *vt* to reform.

réfraction *f* refraction.

réfréner *vt* to curb.

réfrigérateur *m* refrigerator.

réfrigérer *vt* to refrigerate.

refroidir *vt* to cool:—*vi* to get cold.

refuge *m* refuge.

réfugié(e) *m(f)* refugee:—*adj* refugee.

réfugier (se) *vr* to take refuge.

refus *m* refusal.

refuser *vt* to refuse.

réfuter *vt* to refute.

regagner *vt* to regain.

régaler *vt* to regale.

regard *m* look; glance.

regarder *vt* to look at.

régénération *f* regeneration.

régénérer *vt* to regenerate, revive.

régie *f* administration.

régime *m* system, régime.

région *f* region, area.

régional *adj* regional.

régir *vt* to govern, rule.

registre *m* register, record.

règle *f* rule; order.

règlement *m* regulation, rules.

réglementation *f* regulations; control.

réglementer *vt* to regulate.

régler *vt* to pay; to regulate.

règne *m* reign.

régner *vi* to reign.

régresser *vi* to regress.

régression *f* regression.

regret *m* regret.

regretter *vt* to regret, be sorry; to miss.

regroupement *m* reassembly

regrouper *vt* to reassemble:—**se ~** *vr* to assemble.

régulariser *vt* to regularise.

régularité *f* regularity.

régulier *adj* regular; consistent.

réhabilitation *f* rehabilitation.

réhabiliter *vt* to rehabilitate.

réhabituer (se) *vr* to reaccustom oneself.

rein *m* kidney.

réincarnation *f* reincarnation.

reine *f* queen.

réinsertion *f* reinsertion.

réintégrer *vt* to reinstate.

réitérer *vt* to reiterate.

rejet *m* rejection.

rejeter *vt* to reject.

rejoindre *vt* to rejoin.

rejouer *vt* to replay.

réjouir *vt* to delight:—**se ~** *vr* to rejoice.

réjouissance *f* rejoicing.

relâche *f* intermission, respite.

relâchement *m* relaxation.

relâcher (se) *vr* to relax; to become lax.

relais *m* relay.

relatif *adj* relative.

relation *f* relation; reference.

relaxation *f* relaxation.

relaxer (se) *vr* to relax.

relayer *vt* to relieve; to relay.

relecture *f* rereading.

reléguer *vt* to relegate.

relève *f* relief.

relevé *m* statement; bill.

relever *vt* to raise again; to rebuild.

relief *m* relief; contours; depth.

relier *vt* to link up; to bind.

religieux *m* monk, **-euse** *f* nun:—*adj* religious.

religion *f* religion.

relire *vt* to reread.

reluire *vi* to gleam, shine.

remaniement *m* recasting; revision.

remanier *vt* to recast; to amend.

remarquable *adj* remarkable.

remarque *f* remark, comment.

remarquer *vt* to remark; to notice.

remboursement *m* reimbursement.

rembourser *vt* to reimburse.

remède *m* remedy, cure.

remédier *vi* ~ **à** to remedy, cure.

remerciement *m* thanks; thanking.

remercier *vt* to thank.

remettre *vt* to replace:—**se ~** *vr* to recover.

réminiscence *f* reminiscence.

remise *f* delivery; remittance:—**~ en état** repairing:—**~ à neuf** restoration:—**~ en question** calling into question:—**~ en cause** calling into question.

remmener *vt* to take back.

remonter *vi* to go up again:—*vt* to take up.

remorque *f* trailer; towrope.

remorquer *vt* to tow.

remorqueur *m* tug.

rempart *m* rampart; defence.

remplaçant *m*, **-e** *f* replacement.

remplacer *vt* to replace.

remplir *vt* to fill.

remporter *vt* to take away.

remue-ménage *m invar* commotion; hullabaloo.

remuer *vi* to move; to fidget.

rémunération *f* remuneration.

rémunérer *vt* to remunerate, pay.

renaissance *f* rebirth, Renaissance.

renaître *vi* to be reborn.

renard *m* fox.

rencontre *f* meeting, encounter.

rencontrer *vt* to meet; to find.

rendement *m* yield; output.

rendez-vous *m* appointment; date; meeting place.

rendormir (se) *vr* to go back to sleep.

rendre *vt* to render; to give back:— **se ~** *vr* to surrender.

renfermer *vt* to contain, hold.

renflouer *vt* to refloat.

renforcer *vt* to strengthen.

renfort *m* reinforcement.

renifler *vt* to sniff.

renom *m* renown, fame.

renommée *f* renowned.

renoncement *m* renouncement.

renoncer *vi* to renounce.

renonciation *f* renunciation.

renouer *vt* to tie again.

renouveau *m* spring.

renouveler *vt* to renew.

renouvellement *m* renewal.

rénovation *f* renovation.

rénover *vt* to renovate.

renseignement *m* information.

renseigner *vt* to inform.

rentable *adj* profitable.

rente *f* rent; profit.

rentrer *vi* to re-enter; to return home.

renversement *m* reversal.

renverser *vt* to reverse; to overturn.

renvoi *m* sending back; dismissal.

renvoyer *vt* to send back;to dismiss.

réorganisation *f* reorganisation.

réorganiser *vt* to reorganise.

répandre *vt* to pour out.

répandu *adj* widespread.

réparation *f* repairing; restoration.

réparer *vt* to repair; to restore.

repartir *vi* to set off again.

répartir *vt* to share out.

répartition *f* sharing out.

repas *m* meal.

repeindre *vt* to repaint.

repentir (se) *vr* to repent, rue.

répercussion *f* repercussion.

répercuter (se) *vr* to reverberate; to echo.

repère *m* line, mark.

repérer *vt* to spot, pick out.

répertorier *vt* to itemise; to index.

répéter *vt* to repeat.

répétitif *adj* repetitive.

répétition *f* repetition; rehearsal.

répit *m* respite, rest.

repli *m* fold, coil, meander.

replier *vt* to fold up.

réplique *f* reply, retort.

répliquer *vt* to reply.

répondeur *m* answering machine.

répondre *vt* to answer, reply.

réponse *f* response, reply.

report *m* postponement, deferment.

reporter *vt* to take back:—*m* reporter.

repos *m* rest; landing.

reposer *vt* to put back:—**se ~** *vr* to rest oneself.

repoussant *adj* repulsive; repellent.

repousser *vt* to repel.

reprendre *vt* to retake, recapture.

représentant *m* representative.

représentation *f* representation; performance.

représenter *vt* to represent.

répressif *adj* repressive.

répression *f* repression.

réprimander *vt* to reprimand.

réprimer *vt* to repress.

reprise *f* resumption:—**à plusieurs ~s** several times.

reproche *m* reproach.

reprocher *vt* to reproach, blame.

reproduction *f* reproduction.

reproduire *vt* to reproduce.

reptile *m* reptile.

républicain *m*, **-e** *f* republican:—*adj* republican.

république *f* republic.

répudier *vt* to repudiate.

répugnance *f* repugnance.

répugnant *adj* repugnant.

réputation *f* reputation; character; fame.

réputé *adj* reputable, renowned.

requérir *vt* to request.

requête *f* request.

réquisition *f* requisition.

réseau *m* network, net.

réservation *f* reservation.

réserve *f* reserve; reservation.

réservé *f* reserved.

réserver *vt* to reserve.

réservoir *m* tank; reservoir.

résidence *f* residence.

résidentiel *adj* residential

résider *vi* to reside.

résignation *f* resignation.

résistance *f* resistance.

résistant *adj* resistant.

résister *vi* to resist, withstand.

résolu *adj* resolved, determined.

résolution *f* resolution; solution.

résonner *vi* to resonate.

résoudre *vt* to solve; to resolve.

respect *m* respect, regard.

respectable *adj* respectable.

respecter *vt* to respect.

respectif *adj* respective.

respectueux *adj* respectful.

respiration *f* respiration.

respiratoire *adj* respiratory.

respirer *vi* to breathe, respire.

responsabilité *f* responsibility.

responsable *adj* responsible; liable:—*mf* official, manager.

ressemblance *f* resemblance.

ressembler *vi* to resemble.

ressentiment *m* resentment.

ressentir *vt* to feel, experience.

resserrement *m* contraction.

resserrer *vt* to tighten.

ressort *m* spring.

ressortissant *m*, **-e** *f* national.

ressource *f* resource; resort.

ressusciter *vi* to reawaken.

restant *m* rest, remainder.

restaurant *m* restaurant.

restauration *f* restoration; catering.

restaurer *vt* to restore:—**se ~** *vr* to take refreshment.

reste *m* rest, remainder:—**du ~** besides.

rester *vi* to stay; to be left.

restituer *vt* to return; to refund.

restitution *f* restitution.

restreindre *vt* to restrict.

restrictif *adj* restrictive.

restriction *f* restriction, limitation.

résultat *m* result; profit.

résulter *vi*:—~ **de** to result from.

résumé *m* summary.

résumer *vt* to sum up.

résurrection *f* resurrection.

rétablir *vt* to re-establish, restore.

rétablissement *m* re-establishment, restoring.

retard *m* lateness; delay.

retardé *adj* backward, slow.

retarder *vt* to delay.

retenir *vt* to hold back, retain.

réticence *f* reticence.

réticent *adj* reticent.

retirer (se) *vr* to retire, withdraw.

rétorquer *vt* to retort.

retour *m* return; recurrence.

retourner *vi* to return, go back.

rétracter *vt* to retract.

retrait *m* retreat; withdrawal.

retraite *f* retreat; retirement.

retraité(e) *m(f)* pensioner:—*adj* retired.

rétrécissement *m* narrowing; shrinking.

rétribuer *vt* to remunerate.

rétribution *f* retribution.

rétroactif *adj* retroactive.

rétroaction *f* retroaction.

rétrograde *adj* reactionary.

rétrograder *vi* to go backward.

rétrospectif *adj* retrospective.

retrouver *vt* to find again; to recover:—**se ~** *vr* to meet up.

réunifier *vt* to reunify.

réunir (se) *vr* to meet; to assemble.

réussir *vi* to succeed.

réussite *f* success.

revanche *f* revenge:—**en ~** on the other hand.

rêve *m* dream, dreaming; illusion.

réveil *m* awaking; alarm clock.

réveiller *vt* to wake:—**se ~** *vr* to awaken.

révélation *f* revelation.

révéler *vt* to reveal.

revendeur *m*, **-euse** *f* retailer.

revendiquer *vt* to claim; to demand.

revendre *vt* to resell

revenir *vi* to come back, reappear.

revenu *m* income, revenue.

rêver *vi* to dream; to muse.

réverbère *m* street lamp.

révérer *vt* to revere.

rêverie *f* reverie, musing.

revers *m* back, reverse.

réversible *adj* reversible.

rêveur *m*, **-euse** *f* dreamer:—*adj* dreamy

revigorer *vt* to invigorate.

revirement *m* reversal; turnaround.

réviser *vt* to review; to revise.

révision *f* revision.

revivre *vt* to relive.

révocation *f* removal; revocation.

revoir *vt* to see again.

révolte *f* revolt, rebellion.

révolter (se) *vr* to rebel, revolt.
révolu *adj* past, bygone.
révolution *f* revolution.
révolutionnaire *mf* revolutionary:— *adj* revolutionary.
révoquer *vt* to revoke.
revue *f* review.
rez-de-chaussée *m invar* ground floor.
rhabiller (se) *vr* to dress again.
rhétorique *f* rhetoric:—*adj* rhetorical.
rhinocéros *m* rhinoceros.
rhum *m* rum.
rhume *m* cold.
riant *adj* smiling; cheerful.
riche *adj* rich, wealthy.
richesse *f* richness; wealth.
ride *f* wrinkle; ripple; ridge.
rideau *m* curtain.
ridicule *adj* ridiculous.
ridiculiser *vt* to ridicule.
rien *pron* nothing:—**de ~** don't mention it:—*m* nothingness; mere nothing.
rieur *adj* cheerful; laughing.
rigide *adj* rigid.
rigidité *f* rigidity.
rigoureux *adj* rigorous, harsh.
rigueur *f* rigour; harshness.
rime *f* rhyme.
rimer *vi* to rhyme (with)
rincer *vt* to rinse out; to rinse.
riposter *vi* to answer back, retaliate.
rire *vi* to laugh; to smile:—*m* laughter, laugh.
risée *f* laugh; ridicule.
risible *adj* laughable.
risque *m* risk, hazard.

risquer *vt* to risk; to venture.
rivage *m* shore.
rival *m*, **-e** *f* rival:—*adj* rival.
rivaliser *vi* to rival.
rivalité *f* rivalry.
rive *f* shore, bank.
riverain *adj* riverside, lakeside.
rivière *f* river.
riz *m* rice.
robe *f* dress; gown:—**~ de chambre** dressing gown.
robinet *m* tap.
robot *m* robot.
robuste *adj* robust.
roc *m* rock.
rocher *m* rock, boulder.
roder *vt* to grind.
rôder *vi* to roam; to prowl.
rôdeur *m*, **-euse** *f* prowler.
rognon *m* kidney.
roi *m* king
rôle *m* role, character; roll, catalogue.
roman *m* novel; romance.
romancier *m*, **-ière** *f* novelist.
romantique *adj* romantic.
rompre *vt* to break:—*vi* to break; to burst.
rond *m* circle, ring; round:—*adj* round; chubby.
rond-point *m* roundabout.
ronde *f* patrol; round; beat.
ronflement *m* snore, snoring.
ronfler *vi* to snore.
ronronner *vi* to purr; to hum.
rose *f* rose:—*adj* pink:—*m* pink.
rosée *f* dew.
rossignol *m* nightingale.
rotation *f* rotation; turnover.
rôti *m* joint, roast.

rôtir *vt* to roast.

rôtisserie *f* rotisserie, steakhouse.

roue *f* wheel.

rouge *adj* red:—*m* red.

rouge-gorge *m* robin.

rougeur *f* redness, blushing.

rougir *vi* to blush, go red:—*vt* to redden.

rouille *f* rust.

rouiller *vi* to rust.

roulement *m* rotation; movement.

rouler *vt* to wheel:—*vi* to drive.

roulotte *f* caravan.

route *f* road; way; direction.

routier *adj* road:—*m* lorry driver; transport cafe.

routine *f* routine.

routinier *adj* humdrum, routine.

roux *m*, **rousse** *f* redhead:—*adj* red, auburn.

royal *adj* royal, regal.

royaume *m* kingdom.

ruban *m* ribbon; tape.

rubis *m* ruby.

rubrique *f* column; rubric.

rude *adj* rough; hard; unrefined.

rudesse *f* roughness; harshness.

rudiment *m* rudiment; principle.

rudimentaire *adj* rudimentary.

rue *f* street.

ruelle *f* alley.

rugir *vi* to roar.

rugissement *m* roar, roaring.

ruine *f* ruin; wreck.

ruiner *vt* to ruin.

ruineux *adj* ruinous; extravagant.

ruisseau *m* stream, brook.

ruisseler *vi* to stream, flow.

rumeur *f* rumour; murmur.

rupture *f* break, rupture.

rural *adj* rural, country.

ruse *f* cunning, slyness.

rusé *adj* cunning, crafty.

rustique *adj* rustic.

rythme *m* rhythm; rate, speed.

rythmique *adj* rhythmic.

S

sable *m* sand.

sablé *adj* sandy, sanded.

sabotage *m* sabotage.

saboter *vt* to sabotage.

saboteur *m* **-euse** *f* saboteur.

sac *m* bag:—~ **à main** handbag.

saccade *f* jerk, jolt.

saccharine *f* saccharin.

sachet *m* bag; sachet; packet.

sacré *adj* sacred.

sacrifice *m* sacrifice.

sacrifier *vt* to sacrifice.

sacrilège *m* sacrilege.

sadique *adj* sadistic:—*mf* sadist.

safran *m* saffron.

saga *f* saga.

sagace *adj* sagacious, shrewd.

sage *adj* wise; well-behaved:—*m* sage, wise man.

sage-femme *f* midwife.

sagesse *f* wisdom, sense; good behaviour.

saignant *adj* bleeding.

saigner *vi* to bleed.

saillant *adj* protruding.

saillir *vi* to gush out; to project.

sain *adj* healthy; sound; sane.

saint(e) *m(f)* saint:—*adj* holy, saintly.

sainteté *f* saintliness; holiness.

saisie *f* seizure.

saisir *vt* to seize.

saison *f* season.

saisonnier *adj* seasonal.

salade *f* salad.

salaire *m* salary, pay; reward.

salarié(e) *m(f)* salaried employee:— *adj* salaried.

sale *adj* dirty, filthy; obscene.

salé *adj* salty, salted.

saler *vt* to salt, add salt.

saleté *f* dirt; rubbish; obscenity.

salière *f* saltcellar.

salir *vt* to make dirty:—**se ~** *vr* to get dirty.

salive *f* saliva.

salle *f* room; hall:—**~ de séjour** living room:—**~ à manger** dining room:—**~ de bain** bathroom.

salon *m* lounge; exhibition.

salubre *adj* healthy, salubrious.

saluer *vt* to greet; to salute.

salut *m* safety; welfare; salute.

salutation *f* salutation, greeting.

samedi *m* Saturday.

sanctifier *vt* to sanctify, bless.

sanction *f* sanction; approval.

sanctionner *vt* to punish; to sanction.

sanctuaire *m* sanctuary.

sandale *f* sandal.

sang *m* blood; race; kindred

sanglant *adj* bloody, gory.

sanglot *m* sob.

sangloter *vi* to sob.

sanguinaire *adj* sanguinary, blood-thirsty.

sanitaire *adj* health, sanitary.

sans-abris *mf invar* homeless person.

santé *f* health, healthiness.

saper *vt* to undermine, sap.

sapeur-pompier *m* fireman.

sapin *m* fir tree, fir.

sarcasme *m* sarcasm.

sarcastique *adj* sarcastic.

sardine *f* sardine.

sardonique *adj* sardonic

satellite *m* satellite.

satiété *f* satiety:—**à ~** ad nauseam.

satin *m* satin.

satire *f* satire, lampoon.

satirique *adj* satirical.

satisfaction *f* satisfaction.

satisfaire *vt* to satisfy.

satisfaisant *adj* satisfying.

saturation *f* saturation.

saturé *adj* saturated.

saturer *vt* to saturate.

sauce *f* sauce, dressing.

saucisse *f* sausage.

sauf *prép* save, except; unless:—*adj* safe, unhurt.

saumon *m* salmon.

saut *m* jump, bound; waterfall.

sauter *vi* to jump; to blow up.

sauvage *adj* savage; unsociable.

sauvegarde *f* safeguard; backup.

sauvegarder *vt* to safeguard.

sauver *vt* to save.

sauvetage *m* rescue; salvage.

sauveteur *m* rescuer.

savant *adj* learned; expert:—*m* scientist, scholar.

saveur *f* flavour; savour.

savoir *vt* to know; to be able:—*m* learning, knowledge.

savoir-faire *m* know-how.
savon *m* soap.
savonner *vt* to soap, lather.
savoureux *adj* tasty, savoury.
scandale *m* scandal.
scandaleux *adj* scandalous.
scandaliser *vt* to scandalise.
scaphandre *m* diving suit.
sceau *m* seal.
sceller *vt* to seal.
scénario *m* scenario; screenplay.
scénariste *mf* scriptwriter.
scène *f* stage; scenery, scene.
scepticisme *m* scepticism.
sceptique *adj* sceptical:—*mf* sceptic.
schéma *m* diagram, sketch; outline.
schizophrène *mf* schizophrenic:—*adj* schizophrenic.
schizophrénie *f* schizophrenia.
scie *f* saw; bore.
sciemment *adv* knowingly, on purpose.
science *f* science; skill; knowledge.
science-fiction *f* science fiction.
scientifique *adj* scientific.
scintillant *adj* sparkling, glistening.
scintiller *vi* to sparkle, glisten.
scolaire *adj* school; academic.
scolarité *f* schooling.
scooter *m* scooter.
score *m* score.
scout *m* scout, boy scout.
script *m* printing; script.
scrupule *m* scruple, doubt.
scrupuleux *adj* scrupulous.
sculpter *vt* to sculpt; to carve.
sculpteur *m* sculptor.
sculpture *f* sculpture.

se *pron* oneself, himself, herself, itself, themselves.
séance *f* meeting, session; seat.
seau *m* bucket, pail.
sec *adj*, *f* **sèche** dry, arid.
séchage *m* drying; seasoning.
sèche-cheveux *m* *invar* hairdrier.
sécher *vi* to dry.
sécheresse *f* drought.
second *adj* second.
secondaire *adj* secondary.
seconde *f* second.
secouer *vt* to shake, toss.
secourir *vt* to help, assist.
secouriste *mf* first-aid worker.
secours *m* help, assistance; relief; rescue.
secousse *f* jolt, bump.
secret *m* secret:—*adj* secret; discreet.
secrétaire *mf* secretary:—*m* writing desk.
sécrétion *f* secretion.
secte *f* sect.
secteur *m* sector, section.
section *f* section, division; branch.
séculaire *adj* secular.
sécuritaire *adj* security.
sécurité *f* security; safety.
sédatif *m* sedative:—*adj* sedative.
sédiment *m* sediment.
séduction *f* seduction; captivation
séduire *vt* to seduce; to charm, captivate.
segment *m* segment.
segmenter *vt* to segment.
ségrégation *f* segregation.
seigneur *m* lord, nobleman.

sein *m* breast, bosom; womb:—**au ~ de** within.

séisme *m* earthquake, seism.

seize *adj, m* sixteen.

seizième *adj, mf* sixteenth.

séjour *m* stay, sojourn.

séjourner *vi* to stay, sojourn.

sel *m* salt; wit.

sélectif *adj* selective.

sélection *f* choosing, selection.

sélectionner *vt* to select, pick.

selle *f* saddle.

selon *prép* according to.

semaine *f* week.

semblable *adj* like, similar.

semblant *m* appearance, look.

sembler *vi* to seem, appear.

semence *f* seed.

semer *vt* to sow.

semestre *m* half-year; semester.

semestriel *adj* half-yearly; semestral.

séminaire *m* seminary; seminar.

sénat *m* senate.

sénateur *m* senator.

sénile *adj* senile.

sénilité *f* senility.

sens *m* sense; judgement; meaning; direction.

sensation *f* sensation, feeling.

sensationnel *adj* sensational.

sensé *adj* sensible.

sensibiliser *vt* to make sensitive to.

sensibilité *f* sensitivity.

sensible *adj* sensitive; perceptive.

sensualité *f* sensuality.

sensuel *adj* sensual.

sentence *f* sentence.

sentier *m* path, track.

sentiment *m* sentiment; feeling.

sentimental *adj* sentimental.

sentir *vt* to feel; to perceive.

séparation *f* separation.

séparatiste *mf* separatist.

séparer *vt* to separate:—**se ~** *vr* to separate.

sept *adj, m* seven.

septembre *m* September

septième *adj, mf* seventh.

sépulture *f* sepulture, burial.

séquence *f* sequence.

serein *adj* serene, calm.

sérénité *f* serenity, calmness.

sergent *m* sergeant.

série *f* series.

sérieux *adj* serious.

seringue *f* syringe.

serment *m* oath.

séropositif *adj* HIV positive, seropositive.

serpent *m* serpent, snake.

serpenter *vi* to meander, wind.

serre *f* greenhouse; claw.

serrer *vt* to tighten.

serrure *f* lock.

sérum *m* serum.

servante *f* servant.

serveur *m* waiter, **-euse** *f* waitress.

service *m* service; function.

serviette *f* towel; serviette.

servile *adj* servile, slavish.

servilité *f* servility.

servir *vi* to be of use:—*vt* to serve:—**se ~ de** to make use of.

servitude *f* servitude.

session *f* session, sitting.

seuil *m* threshold.

seul *adj* alone; single.

sévère *adj* severe, austere.

sévérité *f* severity; strictness

sexe *m* sex.

sexiste *mf* sexist:—*adj* sexist.

sexualité *f* sexuality.

sexuel *adj* sexual.

sexy *adj* sexy.

short *m* shorts.

si *adv* so, so much; yes:—*conj* if; whether.

SIDA *m* AIDS.

sidérurgiste *mf* steel worker.

siècle *m* century.

siège *m* seat; head office.

siéger *vi* to sit; to be located.

sien *pron, f* **sienne:—le ~ his**, its, his own, its own, **la sienne** her, its, her own, its own, **les ~s, les siennes** their, their own.

siffler *vi* to whistle; to hiss.

sigle *m* abbreviation; acronym.

signal *m* signal, sign.

signaler *vt* to signal, indicate.

signature *f* signature; signing.

signe *m* sign; mark.

signer *vt* to sign.

signet *m* bookmark.

significatif *adj* significant.

signification *f* significance.

signifier *vt* to mean, signify.

silence *m* silence.

silencieux *adj* silent; still.

silhouette *f* silhouette.

similaire *adj* similar.

similarité *f* similarity.

simple *adj* simple; mere; single.

simplicité *f* simplicity.

simplification *f* simplification.

simplifier *vt* to simplify.

simulation *f* simulation.

simuler *vt* to simulate.

simultané *adj* simultaneous.

sincère *adj* sincere, honest.

sincérité *f* sincerity, honesty.

singe *m* monkey.

singularité *f* singularity.

singulier *adj* singular, peculiar.

sinistre *m* disaster; accident:—*adj* sinister.

sinistré(e) *m(f)* disaster victim.

sinon *conj* otherwise, if not; except.

sinueux *adj* sinuous, winding.

site *m* setting, beauty spot.

sitôt *adv* as soon:—**~ que** as soon as.

situation *f* situation, position.

situer *vt* to site, situate.

six *adj, m* six.

sixième *adj, mf* sixth.

ski *m* ski, skiing.

skier *vi* to ski.

skieur *m* **-euse** *f* skier.

slip *m* briefs; panties.

snob *adj* snobbish.

snobisme *m* snobbishness.

sobre *adj* sober, temperate.

sobriété *f* sobriety, temperance.

sociable *adj* sociable; social.

social *adj* social.

socialiste *mf* socialist:—*adj* socialist.

société *f* society; company.

sociologique *adj* sociological.

sociologue *mf* sociologist.

sœur *f* sister; nun.

sofa *m* sofa.

soi *pn* one(self); self:—**~-même** oneself, himself, herself, itself.

soie *f* silk.

soif *f* thirst.

soigner *vt* to look after.

soigneux *adj* neat; careful.

soin *m* care.

soir *m* evening; night.

soit *conj* either; or; whether:—*adv* granted; that is to say.

soixante *adj, m* sixty.

soixantième *adj, mf* sixtieth.

sol *m* ground; floor; soil.

soldat *m* soldier

solde *f* pay:—*m* balance.

solder *vt* to pay; to settle.

soleil *m* sun, sunshine; sunflower.

solennel *adj* solemn.

solidarité *f* solidarity.

solide *adj* solid; sound.

solidifier *vt* to solidify.

solitaire *mf* recluse:—*adj* solitary, lone.

solitude *f* solitude; loneliness.

solution *f* solution.

solvable *adj* solvent.

sombre *f* dark; gloomy.

sommaire *m* summary:—*adj* basic, summary.

sommeil *m* sleep; sleepiness.

sommeiller *vi* to slumber.

sommet *m* summit; crest.

somnambule *mf* sleepwalker:—*adj* sleepwalking.

somnifère *m* sleeping pill.

somnoler *vi* to doze.

somptueux *adj* sumptuous, lavish.

son *m* sound:—*adj, f* **sa**; *pl* **ses** his, her, its.

songe *m* dream.

songer *vt* to dream.

sonner *vi* to ring.

sonore *adj* resonant, deep-toned.

sophistiqué *adj* sophisticated.

sordide *adj* sordid, squalid.

sort *m* fate, destiny, lot.

sorte *f* sort, kind.

sortie *f* exit, way out; trip; sortie.

sortir *vi* to go out.

sot *adj* (*f* **sotte**) silly, foolish.

sottise *f* stupidity; stupid remark.

souci *m* worry; concern.

soucier *vr*:—**se ~ de** to care about.

soucieux *adj* concerned, worried.

soudain *adj* sudden, unexpected.

souder *vt* to solder; to weld.

souffle *m* blow, puff; breath.

souffler *vi* to blow; to breathe.

souffrance *f* suffering; pain

souffrir *vi* to suffer.

souhait *m* wish.

souhaiter *vt* to wish for, desire.

soulagement *m* relief.

soulager *vt* to relieve, soothe.

soulever *vt* to lift:—**se ~** *vr* to rise; to revolt.

soulier *m* shoe.

souligner *vt* to underline.

soumettre *vt* to subdue.

soumission *f* submission.

soupape *f* valve.

soupçon *m* suspicion.

soupçonner *vt* to suspect.

soupçonneux *adj* suspicious.

soupe *f* soup.

soupir *m* sigh; gasp.

soupirer *vi* to sigh; to gasp.

souple *adj* supple; pliable.

souplesse *f* suppleness.

source *f* source.

sourcil *m* eyebrow.

sourd(e) *m(f)* deaf person:—*adj* deaf; muted.

sourd(e)-muet(te) *m(f)* deaf-mute:—*adj* deaf and dumb.

souriant *adj* smiling, cheerful.

sourire *m* smile, grin.

souris *f* mouse.

sournois *adj* deceitful.

sous *prép* under, beneath, below.

sous-alimenté *adj* undernourished.

sous-développé *adj* underdeveloped.

sous-entendre *vt* to imply.

sous-estimer *vt* to underestimate.

sous-marin *m* submarine:—*adj* underwater.

sous-titre *m* subtitle.

sous-titrer *vt* to subtitle.

sous-traitant *m* subcontractor.

sous-traiter *vt* to subcontract.

souscrire *vi* to subscribe.

soustraction *f* subtraction.

soustraire *vt* to subtract.

soute *f* hold; baggage hold.

soutenir *vt* to sustain.

souterrain *adj* underground.

soutien *m* support.

soutien-gorge *m* bra.

souvenir *m* memory; recollection.

souvenir (se) *vr* to remember

souvent *adv* often, frequently.

souverain(e) *m(f)* sovereign:—*adj* sovereign.

spacieux *adj* spacious, roomy.

spaghettis *mpl* spaghetti.

spasme *m* spasm.

spécial *adj* special.

spécialiser *vt* to specialise.

spécieux *adj* specious.

spécification *f* specification.

spécifier *vt* to specify.

spécifique *adj* specific.

spécimen *m* specimen.

spectacle *m* spectacle, scene.

spectaculaire *adj* spectacular.

spectateur *m* **-trice** *f* spectator.

spectre *m* ghost.

spéculateur *m* **-trice** *f* speculator.

spéculer *vi* to speculate.

sphère *f* sphere.

spiritualité *f* spirituality.

spirituel *adj* witty; spiritual.

splendeur *f* splendour, brilliance.

splendide *adj* splendid.

spontané *adj* spontaneous.

sport *m* sport.

sportif *m* sportsman, **-ive** *f* sportswoman:—*adj* sports.

square *m* square.

squelette *m* skeleton.

stabiliser *vt* to stabilise.

stabilité *f* stability.

stable *adj* stable.

stade *m* stadium; stage.

stage *m* training course.

stagiaire *mf* trainee.

standard *adj* standard.

star *f* star.

starter *m* choke.

station *f* station; stage.

stationnaire *adj* stationary.

stationnement *m* parking.

stationner *vi* to park.

station-service *f* service station.

statique *adj* static.

statistique *f* statistics:—*adj* statistical.

statue *f* statue.

statuer *vt* to rule.

statut *m* statute.

statutaire *adj* statutory.

stencil *m* stencil.

sténodactylo *mf* shorthand typist.

sténographie *f* shorthand.

stéréotype *m* stereotype.

stérile *adj* sterile, infertile.

stériliser *vt* to sterilise.

stérilité *f* sterility.

stimulant *adj* stimulating:—*m* stimulant.

stimulation *f* stimulation.

stimuler *vt* to stimulate.

stipuler *vt* to stipulate.

stock *m* stock, supply.

stocker *vt* to stock, stockpile.

stoïque *adj* stoical.

stop *m* stop; stop sign.

stopper *vt* to stop.

store *m* blind, shade.

stratégie *f* strategy.

stratégique *adj* strategic.

stress *m* stress.

stressant *adj* stessful.

strict *adj* strict, severe.

strident *adj* strident, shrill.

structural *adj* structural.

structure *f* structure.

studieux *adj* studious.

studio *m* studio; film theatre.

stupéfier *vt* to stupefy; to astound.

stupeur *f* amazement; stupor.

stupide *adj* stupid, foolish.

stupidité *f* stupidity.

style *m* style; stylus.

styliste *mf* designer; stylist.

stylo *m* pen.

suave *adj* suave, smooth.

subconscient *m* subconscious:—*adj* subconscious.

subir *vt* to sustain; to undergo.

subit *adj* sudden.

subjectif *adj* subjective.

subjectivité *f* subjectivity.

subjuguer *vt* to subjugate.

sublime *adj* sublime.

submerger *vt* to submerge.

subséquent *adj* subsequent.

subside *m* grant.

subsistance *f* subsistence.

subsister *vi* to subsist.

substance *f* substance.

substantiel *adj* substantial.

substantif *m* noun, substantive.

substituer *vt* to substitute.

substitut *m* substitute.

substitution *f* substitution.

subtil *adj* subtle.

subtilité *f* subtlety.

subvention *f* grant, subsidy.

subventionner *vt* to subsidise.

subversif *adj* subversive.

succéder *vi*:—~ **à** to succeed, follow.

succès *m* success; hit.

successeur *m* successor.

succession *f* succession.

succinct *adj* succinct.

succomber *vi* to succumb.

succulent *adj* succulent, delicious.

sucursale *f* branch.

sucer *vt* to suck.

sucre *m* sugar.

sud *m* south.

suer *vi* to sweat, perspire.

sueur *f* sweat.

suffire *vi* to suffice.

suffisant *adj* sufficient, adequate.
suffoquer *vi* to choke, suffocate.
suffrage *m* suffrage; vote.
suggérer *vt* to suggest.
suggestion *f* suggestion.
suicide *m* suicide.
suicider (se) *vr* to commit suicide.
suite *f* continuation; series:—**tout de ~** at once:—**et ainsi de ~** and so on.
suivant *adj* following, next:—*prép* according to.
suivi *m* follow-up.
suivre *vt* to follow:—**~ son cours** to take its course:—**à suivre** to be continued.
sujet *m* subject, topic:—*adj* subject.
super *adj* ultra, super.
superbe *adj* superb.
superficie *f* area, surface.
superficiel *adj* superficial.
superflu *adj* superfluous.
supérieur *adj* upper; superior.
supériorité *f* superiority.
superlatif *m* superlative:—*adj* superlative.
superstitieux *adj* superstitious.
superstition *f* superstition.
superviser *vt* to supervise.
supplanter *vt* to supplant.
supplément *m* supplement.
supplémentaire *adj* supplementary.
support *m* support, prop; stand.
supporter *vt* to support; to endure.
supposer *vt* to suppose.
suppression *f* suppression.
supprimer *vt* to suppress.
suprématie *f* supremacy.
suprême *adj* supreme.

sur *prép* on; over, above; into; out of, from.
sûr *adj* sure, certain; secure:—**~ de soi** self-assured:—**bien ~** of course.
surabondance *f* overabundance.
suranné *adj* outmoded, outdated.
surcharge *f* surcharge.
surcroît *m* surplus:—**de ~** in addition.
surdité *f* deafness.
surélever *vt* to raise, heighten.
surestimer *vt* to overestimate.
sûreté *f* safety; guarantee.
surface *f* surface.
surgeler *vt* to deep-freeze.
surgir *vi* to appear; to arise.
surlendemain *m* day after tomorrow.
surmonter *vt* to surmount.
surnaturel *adj* supernatural.
surnom *m* nickname.
surnommer *vt* to nickname.
surpasser *vt* to surpass, outdo.
surplomber *vt* to overhang.
surplus *m* surplus.
surpopulation *f* overpopulation.
surprenant *adj* surprising.
surprendre *vt* to surprise.
surprise *f* surprise.
sursaut *m* start, jump.
sursauter *vi* to start, jump.
surtaxe *f* surcharge.
surtout *adv* especially; above all.
surveillance *f* surveillance.
surveiller *vt* to watch; to supervise.
survenir *vi* to take place, occur.
survie *f* survival.
survivant(e) *m(f)* survivor:—*adj* surviving.

survivre *vi* to survive.
survoler *vt* to fly over.
susceptible *adj* susceptible:—**être ~ de** to be likely to.
susciter *vt* to arouse, incite.
suspect(e) *m(f)* suspect.
suspecter *vt* to suspect.
suspendre *vt* to hang up; to suspend.
suspension *f* suspension.
suspicieux *adj* suspicious.
suspicion *f* suspicion.
susurrer *vt* to whisper.
svelte *adj* svelte, slim.
syllabe *f* syllable.
symbole *m* symbol
symbolique *adj* symbolic; token.
symboliser *vt* to symbolise.
symétrie *f* symmetry.

symétrique *adj* symmetrical.
sympathie *f* liking; sympathy.
sympathique *adj* likeable, nice; friendly.
symphonie *f* symphony.
symptôme *m* symptom.
synagogue *f* synagogue.
synchroniser *vt* to synchronise.
syndical *adj* trade-union.
syndicaliste *mf* trade unionist:—*adj* trade union.
syndicat *m* trade union; association.
synonyme *m* synonym:—*adj* synonymous.
synthèse *f* synthesis.
synthétique *adj* synthetic.
systématique *adj* systematic.
système *m* system.

T

tabac *m* tobacco.
table *f* table:—**~ ronde** round-table conference.
tableau *m* table; chart.
tablette *f* bar; tablet.
tablier *m* apron; overall.
tabouret *m* stool.
tache *f* mark; stain; spot.
tâche *f* task, assignment; work.
tacite *adj* tacit.
taciturne *adj* taciturn, silent.
tact *m* tact.
tactile *adj* tactile.
tactique *f* tactics:—*adj* tactical.
taille *f* height, stature, size.
tailler *vt* to cut; to carve.
taire(se) *vr* to be quiet.
talent *m* talent, ability.
talentueux *adj* talented.

talon *m* heel; crust; spur.
tambour *m* drum; barrel.
tamis *m* sieve; riddle.
tamiser *vt* to sieve; to sift.
tampon *m* stopper, plug; tampon.
tandem *m* tandem; duo.
tandis *conj*:—**~ que** while; whereas.
tangible *adj* tangible.
tank *m* tank.
tanner *vt* to tan, weather.
tant *adv* so much:—**~ que** as long as:—**~ mieux** that's a good job:—**~ pis** too bad.
tante *f* aunt.
tantôt *adv* sometimes; this afternoon; shortly.
tapage *m* din, uproar, racket.
tape *f* slap.

taper *vt* to beat; to slap; to type.

tapis *m* carpet; rug; cloth.

tapisser *vt* to wallpaper; to cover.

tapisserie *f* tapestry.

taquin *adj* teasing.

taquiner *vt* to tease; to plague.

tard *adv* late.

tarder *vi* to delay, put off; to dally.

tardif *adj* late; tardy.

tarif *m* tariff; price-list.

tarir (se) *vr* to dry up.

tarte *f* tart, flan.

tartre *m* tartar; fur, scale.

tas *m* heap, pile; lot, set.

tasse *f* cup; coffee cup.

tassement *m* settling, sinking.

tasser *vt* to heap up:—**se ~** *vr* to sink; subside.

tâter *vt* to feel, try.

tatonner *vi* to feel one's way.

tatouer *vt* to tattoo.

taudis *m* hovel, slum.

taureau *m* bull.

taux *m* rate; ratio:—**~ de change** exchange rate.

taverne *f* tavern.

taxation *f* taxation, taxing.

taxe *f* tax; duty; rate.

taxer *vt* to tax.

taxi *m* taxi.

te *pn* you, yourself.

technicien(ne) *m(f)* technician.

technique *f* technique:—*adj* technical.

technologie *f* technology.

technologique *adj* technological.

teindre *vt* to dye.

teint *m* complexion, colouring.

teinter *vt* to tint; to stain.

teinture *f* dye; dyeing.

tel *adj* such; like, similar:—**~ quel** such as it is:—**en tant que ~** as such.

télé *f* TV, telly.

télécommande *f* remote control.

télécopie *f* facsimile transmission; fax.

télégramme *m* telegram; cable.

télégraphier *vt* to telegraph, cable.

télépathie *f* telepathy.

téléphérique *m* cableway; cable-car.

téléphone *m* telephone.

téléphoner *vi* to telephone.

télescope *m* telescope.

télescopique *adj* telescopic.

téléviseur *m* television set.

télévision *f* television.

télex *m* telex.

tellement *adj* so, so much:—**~ de** so many, so much.

téméraire *adj* rash, reckless.

témoignage *m* testimony.

témoigner *vi* to testify.

témoin *m* witness.

témpérament *m* temperament.

température *f* temperature

tempête *f* tempest.

temple *m* temple.

temporaire *adj* temporary.

temps *m* time; while; tense; beat; weather:—**de ~ en ~** from time to time.

tenace *adj* tenacious, stubborn.

ténacité *f* tenacity; stubbornness.

tenaille *f* pincers; tongs.

tendance *f* tendency; trend.

tendancieux *adj* tendentious.

tendon *m* tendon, sinew.

tendre *adj* tender, soft; delicate.

tendresse *f* tenderness; fondness.

tendu *adj* tight; stretched; delicate.

ténébreux *adj* dark, gloomy.

teneur *f* terms; content; grade.

tenir *vt* to hold, keep:—**~ à** to value, care about.

tennis *m* tennis:—**~ de table** table tennis.

tentation *f* temptation.

tentative *f* attempt, bid.

tente *f* tent.

tenter *vt* to tempt.

tenue *f* holding; deportment; dress, appearance.

terme *m* term; termination; end; word.

terminaison *f* ending.

terminal *adj* terminal:—*m* terminal.

terminer *vt* to finish off:—**se ~** *vr* to terminate.

terminologie *f* terminology.

terne *adj* colourless; drab.

terrain *m* ground, earth; site; field.

terrasse *f* terrace.

terre *f* earth; ground, land:—**mettre pied à ~** to land, alight.

terrestre *adj* land; terrestrial.

terreur *f* terror, dread.

terrible *adj* terrible, dreadful; terrific, great.

terrier *m* burrow; earth; terrier.

terrifiant *adj* terrifying, fearsome.

terrifier *vt* to terrify.

territoire *m* territory, area.

territorial *adj* land, territorial.

terroir *m* soil.

terroriser *vt* to terrorise.

terroriste *mf* terrorist:—*adj* terrorist.

test *m* test.

testament *m* will, testament.

tester *vt* to test; to make out one's will.

tête à tête *m* private conversation.

tête *f* head; top; sense:—**tenir ~** to cope:—**être en ~** to head.

tétine *f* teat; udder; dummy.

téton *m* breast.

têtu *adj* headstrong, stubborn.

texte *m* text; theme; passage.

textile *adj* textile.

textuel *adj* textual, literal.

texture *f* texture.

thé *m* tea.

théâtral *adj* theatrical, dramatic.

théâtre *m* theatre; drama.

thème *m* theme.

théologie *f* theology.

théorie *f* theory.

théorique *adj* theoretical.

thérapeute *mf* therapist.

thérapie *f* therapy.

thermique *adj* thermal; thermic.

thermomètre *m* thermometer.

thermos *f/m* thermos.

thèse *f* thesis.

thym *m* thyme.

ticket *m* ticket.

tiède *adj* lukewarm, tepid.

tien *poss pn*:—**le ~, la ~ne, les ~(ne)s** yours.

tiers *adj* third:—**~-monde** Third World:—*m* third; third party.

tigre *m* tiger.

timbre *m* stamp; postmark; bell.

timbrer *vt* to stamp; to postmark.

timide *adj* timid, shy.

timidité *f* timidity, shyness.

tintement *m* ringing toll.

tinter *vi* to ring, toll; to chime.

tir *m* shooting; shot:—~ **à l'arc** archery.

tirailler *vt* to tug; to pester.

tire-bouchon *m* corkscrew.

tirelire *f* moneybox.

tirer *vt* to pull; to draw.

tiret *m* dash; hyphen.

tireur *m* **-euse** *f* gunner; drawer (cheque).

tiroir *m* drawer.

tisser *vt* to weave.

tissu *m* texture, fabric; tissue.

titre *m* title; heading; right; deed:— **à ~ de** by right of.

tituber *vi* to stagger.

titulaire *mf* incumbent, holder:—*adj* titular.

toi *pn* you:—~**-même** yourself:— **c'est à ~** it's your's; it's your turn.

toile *f* cloth; canvas; sheet.

toilette *f* cleaning, grooming:—**faire sa ~** to wash oneself.

toit *m* roof; home.

tolérable *adj* tolerable, bearable.

tolérant *adj* tolerant.

tolérer *vt* to tolerate.

tomate *f* tomato.

tombe *f* tomb; grave.

tomber *vi* to fall:—**laisser ~** to drop.

tome *m* book; volume.

ton *adj*, *f* **ta**, *pl* **tes** your:—*m* tone; pitch; shade.

tondre *vt* to shear; mow.

tonifiant *m* tonic.

tonifier *vt* to tone up.

tonique *adj* tonic; fortifying:—*m* tonic.

tonne *f* ton, tonne.

tonneau *m* barrel, cask.

tonnerre *m* thunder.

topographie *f* topography.

toquade *f* infatuation; fad, craze.

toquer *vi* to tap, rap.

torche *f* torch.

torcher *vt* to wipe, mop up.

torchon *m* cloth; duster.

tordre *vt* to twist, contort.

tordu *adj* twisted, crooked.

torpeur *f* torpor.

torrent *m* torrent.

torrentiel *adj* torrential.

torride *adj* torrid; scorching.

torse *m* chest; torso.

torsion *f* twisting; torsion.

tort *m* fault; wrong; prejudice:— **avoir ~** to be wrong:—**faire du ~** to harm.

tortiller *vt* to twist:—**se ~** *vr* to wriggle.

tortionnaire *mf* torturer.

tortue *f* tortoise.

tortueux *adj* tortuous, winding.

torture *f* torture.

torturer *vt* to torture.

tôt *adv* early; soon:—**au plus ~** as soon as possible:—**plus ~** sooner.

total *adj* total.

totalitaire *adj* totalitarian.

totalité *f* totality.

touche *f* touch.

toucher *vt* to touch.

touffe *f* tuft, clump.

toujours *adv* always; still.

tour *f* tower:—*m* turn, round; circuit; tour; trick:—~ **à ~** by turns.

tourbillon *m* whirlwind.
tourbillonner *vi* to whirl, eddy.
tourisme *m* tourism.
touriste *mf* tourist.
touristique *adj* tourist.
tourment *m* torment, agony.
tourmenter *vt* to torment.
tournant *m* bend; turning point:—
  adj revolving.
tournée *f* tour; round.
tourner *vi* to turn:—**se ~** *vr* to turn
  round.
tournesol *m* sunflower.
tournevis *m* screwdriver.
tournoi *m* tournament.
tournure *f* turn; turn of phrase.
tousser *vi* to cough.
tout *adj* (*pl* **tous, toutes**) all; whole;
  every:—**le monde** everybody:—
  pn everything; all:—*m* whole:—
  adv entirely, quite.
toutefois *adv* however.
toux *f* cough.
toxicomane *mf* drug addict.
toxique *adj* toxic.
trac *m* nerves, stage fright.
tracasser *vt* to worry; to harass.
trace *f* track; outline, trace.
tracer *vt* to trace.
tract *m* leaflet, tract.
tractation *f* transaction.
tracteur *m* tractor.
tradition *f* tradition.
traditionnel *adj* traditional; usual.
traducteur *m* **-trice** *f* translator.
traduction *f* translation.
traduire *vt* to translate.
trafic *m* traffic; trading.
trafiquer *vi* to traffic, trade.

tragédie *f* tragedy.
tragique *adj* tragic.
trahir *vt* to betray.
trahison *f* betrayal, treason.
train *m* train; pace, rate.
traîneau *m* sleigh, sledge.
traînée *f* trail, track; drag.
traîner *vi* to drag on, lag.
traire *vt* to milk.
trait *m* trait, feature; relation.
traite *f* trade; draft, bill; milking.
traité *m* treaty; treatise, tract.
traitement *m* treatment; salary.
traiter *vt* to treat; to process.
traiteur *m* caterer.
traître *m* traitor.
traîtrise *f* treachery.
trajet *m* distance; course.
tramer *vt* to plot; to weave.
trampoline *m* trampoline.
tranche *f* slice; edge; section.
trancher *vt* to cut, sever.
tranquille *adj* quiet, tranquil.
tranquilliser *vt* to reassure.
tranquillité *f* tranquillity.
transaction *f* transaction.
transatlantique *adj* transatlantic.
transcription *f* transcription.
transcrire *vt* to transcribe.
transe *f* trance.
tranférer *vt* to transfer.
transfert *m* transfer.
transformateur *m* transformer.
transformation *f* transformation.
transformer *vt* to transform.
transfusion *f* transfusion.
transgresser *vt* to transgress.
transgression *f* transgression.
transistor *m* transistor.

transiter *vi* to pass in transit.
transition *f* transition.
transitoire *adj* transitory.
transmettre *vt* to transmit.
transmissible *adj* transmissible.
transmission *f* transmission.
transparence *f* transparency.
transparent *adj* transparent.
transpercer *vt* to pierce.
transplanter *vt* to transplant.
transport *m* carrying; transport.
transporter *vt* to transport
transporteur *m* haulier; carrier.
transposer *vt* to transpose.
transversal *adj* transverse.
trapèze *m* trapeze.
trapéziste *mf* trapeze artist.
trappe *f* trap door.
trappeur *m* trapper.
traquer *vt* to track; to hunt down.
traumatiser *vt* to traumatise.
travail *m pl* **travaux** work, labour.
travailler *vi* to work.
travailleur *m*, **-euse** *f* worker:—*adj* diligent; hard-working.
travers *m* breadth:—**à ~** through, across.
traversée *f* crossing; traverse.
traverser *vt* to cross, traverse.
trébucher *vi* to stumble.
trèfle *m* clover.
treillis *m* trellis; wire mesh.
treize *adj*, m thirteen.
treizième *adj*, *mf* thirteenth.
tremblement *m* trembling **~ de terre** earthquake.
trembler *vi* to tremble, shake.
trémousser (se) *vr* to wriggle.
tremper *vt* to soak.

tremplin *m* springboard.
trentaine *f* about thirty.
trente *adj*, *m* thirty.
trentième *adj mf* thirtieth.
trépidant *adj* pulsating, quivering.
trépigner *vi* to stamp one's feet.
très *adv* very; most; very much.
trésor *m* treasure.
trésorier *m* **-ière** *f* treasurer.
tressaillir *vi* to thrill; to shudder.
tresse *f* plait, braid.
tresser *vt* to plait, braid.
trêve *f* truce; respite.
tri *m* sorting out; grading.
triangle *m* triangle.
triangulaire *adj* triangular.
tribal *adj* tribal.
tribu *f* tribe.
tribunal *m* court, tribunal.
tribune *f* gallery; rostrum.
tribut *m* tribute.
tricher *vi* to cheat.
tricheur *m*, **-euse** *f* cheater.
tricolore *adj* three-coloured, tricolour.
tricoter *vt* to knit.
tridimensionnel *adj* three-dimensional.
trier *vt* to sort out.
trilingue *adj* trilingual.
trimestre *m* quarter; term.
trimestriel *adj* quarterly; three-monthly.
trinquer *vi* to toast; to booze.
trio *m* trio.
triomphal *adj* triumphal.
triomphe *m* triumph, victory.
triompher *vi* to triumph.
triple *adj* triple, treble.

tripler *vi* to triple.

triste *adj* sad, melancholy.

tristesse *f* sadness.

trivial *adj* trivial; crude.

trivialité *f* triviality; crudeness.

troc *m* exchange; barter.

trois *adj, m* three.

troisième *adj, mf* third.

trombe *f:*—~ **d'eau** cloudburst.

trompe *f* trumpet; trunk.

tromper *vt* to deceive, trick:—**se ~**
vr to be mistaken.

tromperie *f* deception, deceit.

trompette *f* trumpet.

trompeur *adj* deceitful; deceptive.

tronc *m* trunk, shaft.

trône *m* throne.

tronquer *vt* to truncate, curtail.

trop *adv* too; too much:—*m* ~ excess.

trophée *m* trophy.

tropical *adj* tropical.

tropique *m* tropic.

troquer *vt* to barter, swap.

trotter *vi* to trot; to toddle.

trottinette *f* scooter.

trottoir *m* pavement.

trou *m* hole; gap; cavity.

troublant *adj* disturbing.

trouble *adj* unclear, murky:—*m* trouble, disturbance.

troubler *vt* to trouble, disturb.

trouer *vt* to make a hole in.

troupe *f* troupe; troop.

troupeau *m* herd, drove.

trousse *f* case, kit; wallet.

trouver *vt* to find.

truc *m* (*fam*) trick; gadget.

truite *f* trout.

truquage *m* rigging, fiddling.

truquer *vt* to rig, fiddle.

tu *pn* you.

tube *m* tube, pipe; duct.

tuer *vt* to kill.

tuerie *f* slaughter.

tueur *m* -**euse** *f* killer.

tuile *f* tile.

tulipe *f* tulip.

tumeur *f* tumour.

tumulte *m* tumult, commotion.

tumultueux *adj* tumultuous.

tunnel *m* tunnel.

turbine *f* turbine.

turbulence *f* turbulence.

turbulent *adj* turbulent.

tutelle *f* guardianship.

tuteur *m* **tutrice** *f* guardian:—*m*
stake, prop.

tutoyer *vt* to address s.o. as *tu*.

tuyau *m* pipe.

type *m* type; model; bloke, chap.

typhon *m* typhoon.

typique *adj* typical.

tyran *m* tyrant.

tyrannique *adj* tyrannical.

U

ulcère *m* ulcer.

ultérieur *adj* subsequent:—~**ement**
adv later.

ultimatum *m* ultimatum.

ultime *adj* ultimate, final.

un, une *art* a, an; one—**l'~ l'autre,
les ~s les autres** one another.

unanime *adj* unanimous.

unification f unification.
unifier vt to unify.
uniforme adj uniform.
uniformité f uniformity; regularity.
unilatéral adj unilateral.
union f union.
unique adj only, single; unique:—
~**ment** adv only, solely, exclusively.
unir vt to unite.
unisson m unison.
unité f unity; unit.
univers m universe; world.
universel adj universal.
universitaire adj university:—mf academic.
université f university.
urbain adj urban, city.
urbanisme m town planning.

urgence f urgency.
urgent adj urgent.
urne f ballot box; urn.
usage m use; custom.
usager m ère f user.
usé adj worn; banal, trite.
user vt to use.
usine f factory.
ustensile m implement; utensil.
usuel adj ordinary; everyday:—
~**lement** adv ordinarily.
usurper vt to usurp.
utérus m womb, uterus.
utile adj useful.
utilisateur m, -**trice** f user.
utiliser vt to use, utilise.
utilité f usefulness; use; profit.
utopie f utopia.
utopique adj utopian.

V

vacance f vacancy:—~**s** holiday, vacation.
vacancier m, -**ière** f holidaymaker.
vacant adj vacant.
vacarme m racket, row.
vaccin m vaccine.
vache f cow.
vagabond m, -**e** f tramp, vagabond.
vagin f vagina.
vague adj vague:—m vagueness:—f wave.
vaguer vi to wander, roam.
vaillant adj brave, courageous.
vain adj vain; shallow.
vaincre vt to defeat, overcome.
vainqueur m conqueror, victor.
vaisseau m vessel; ship.
vaisselle f crockery; dishes.

valable adj valid; worthwhile.
valeur f value, worth; security.
valider vt to validate.
valise f suitcase.
vallée f valley.
valoir vt to be worth.
valser vi to waltz.
vandale mf vandal.
vanité f vanity, conceit.
vaniteux adj vain, conceited.
vantard adj boastful, bragging.
vanter vt to praise, vaunt:—**se** ~ vr to boast.
vapeur f haze, vapour.
vaporiser vt to spray.
variable adj variable, changeable.
variation f variation, change.
varié adj varied; variegated.

varier *vi* to vary.

variété *f* variety, diversity.

vaste *adj* vast, huge.

vaurien(ne) *m(f)* good-for-nothing.

vautrer (se) *vr* to wallow in.

veau *m* calf; veal.

vedette *f* star; leading light.

végétal *adj* vegetable.

végétarien(ne) *m(f)* vegetarian:— *adj* vegetarian.

végétatif *adj* vegetative.

véhémence *f* vehemence.

véhément *adj* vehement.

véhicule *m* vehicle.

veille *f* wakefulness; watch; eve.

veiller *vi* to stay up, sit up.

veine *f* vein; inspiration; luck.

vélo *m* cycle.

vélodrome *m* velodrome.

velours *m* velvet.

vendange *f* wine harvest; vintage.

vendangeur *m* **-euse** *f* grape-picker.

vendeur *m* **-euse** *f* seller, salesperson.

vendre *vt* to sell.

vendredi *m* Friday.

vénéneux *adj* poisonous.

vénérable *adj* venerable.

vénérer *vt* to venerate.

vengeance *f* vengeance.

venger *vt* to avenge.

venin *m* venom.

venir *vi* to come.

vent *m* wind; breath; vanity.

vente *f* sale; selling.

ventre *m* stomach, belly; womb.

ventriloque *mf* ventriloquist.

venue *f* coming.

ver *m* worm; grub.

véracité *f* veracity; truthfulness.

verbal *adj* verbal.

verbe *m* verb; word.

verdict *m* verdict.

verdure *f* greenery, verdure.

verge *f* stick, cane.

verger *m* orchard.

vérification *f* check; verification.

vérifier *vt* to verify; to audit.

véritable *adj* real, genuine.

vérité *f* truth; truthfulness.

vermine *f* vermin.

verni *adj* varnished.

vernis *m* varnish; glaze.

verre *m* glass; lens; drink.

verrou *m* bolt.

verrouiller *vt* to bolt; to lock.

vers *prép* towards; around:—*m* line, verse.

versatile *adj* versatile.

verser *vt* to pour.

version *f* version.

vert *m* green:—*adj* green.

vertèbre *f* vertebra.

vertical *adj* vertical.

vertu *f* virtue.

vertueux *adj* virtuous.

verve *f* verve, vigour.

veste *f* jacket.

vestiaire *m* cloakroom.

vestibule *m* hall, vestibule.

veston *m* jacket.

vêtement *m* garment.

vêtir (se) *vr* to dress oneself.

veto *m* veto.

veuf *m* widower:—*adj* widowed.

veuve *f* widow:—*adj* widowed.

vexer *vt* to annoy; to hurt.

viable *adj* viable.

viande *f* meat.

vice *m* vice; fault, defect.

victime *f* victim, casualty.

victoire *f* victory.

victorieux *adj* victorious.

vide *adj* empty, vacant:—*m* vacuum.

vidéo *f* video:—*adj invar* video.

vidéocassette *f* videocassette.

vider *vt* to empty.

vie *f* life:—**être en ~** to be alive.

vieillard *m* old man.

vieillesse *f* old age.

vieillir *vi* to get old.

vierge *f* virgin:—*adj* virgin; blank; unexposed.

vieux *adj*, *f* **vieille** old; obsolete.

vif *adj* lively; quick; eager.

vigilant *adj* vigilant.

vigne *f* vine; vineyard.

vigneron *m*, **-onne** *f* wine grower.

vignoble *m* vineyard.

vigoureux *adj* vigorous.

vigueur *f* vigour, strength.

vil *adj* vile; lowly.

villa *f* villa, detached house.

village *m* village.

villageois *m*, **-e** *f* village, rustic.

ville *f* town, city.

vin *m* wine.

vinaigre *m* vinegar.

vindicatif *adj* vindictive.

vingt *adj*, *m* twenty.

vingtaine *f* about twenty.

vingtième *adj*, *mf* twentieth.

vinicole *adj* wine, wine-growing.

viol *m* rape.

violation *f* violation.

violence *f* violence; force.

violent *adj* violent.

violer *vt* to violate; to rape.

violet *adj* violet:—*m* violet.

violeur *m* rapist.

violon *m* violin.

violoniste *mf* violinist.

vipère *f* viper, adder.

virage *m* turn, bend.

virer *vt* to transfer:—*vi* to turn.

virginité *f* virginity; purity.

viril *adj* virile; male, masculine.

virilité *f* virility; masculinity.

virtuel *adj* virtual.

virulence *f* virulence.

virulent *adj* virulent.

virus *m* virus.

vis *f* screw.

visa *m* stamp, visa.

visage *m* face; expression.

vis-à-vis *prép* opposite:—*m* encounter:—**en ~** opposite each other.

viser *vt* to aim, target; to visa.

viseur *m* sights; viewfinder.

visibilité *f* visibility.

visible *adj* visible; evident.

vision *f* eyesight; vision.

visionnaire *mf* visionary:—*adj* visionary.

visite *f* visit; inspection; visitor.

visiter *vt* to visit.

visiteur *m*, **-euse** *f* visitor.

visqueux *adj* viscous, thick.

visser *vt* to screw on.

visuel *adj* visual.

vital *adj* vital.

vitalité *f* energy, vitality.

vitamine *f* vitamin.

vite *adv* quickly, fast.

vitesse f speed, swiftness; gear.

viticulteur m wine grower.

vitrail m stained-glass window.

vitre f pane, window.

vitreux adj glassy, vitreous.

vitrier m glazier.

vitrine f shop window.

vitupérer vi to vituperate.

vivace adj hardy, perennial.

vivacité f vivacity, liveliness.

vivant adj alive, living; lively.

vivement adv quickly; keenly.

vivifiant adj refreshing.

vivifier vt to enliven.

vivre vi to live.

vivres mpl victuals, supplies.

vocabulaire m vocabulary.

vocal adj vocal.

vocation f vocation, calling.

vœu m vow; wish.

vogue f fashion:—**en ~** in fashion.

voici prép here is, here are; ago, past.

voie f way, road; means:—**~ ferrée** railway.

voilà prép there is, there are; ago.

voile f sail:—m veil.

voiler vt to veil.

voir vt to see:—**avoir à ~ avec** to have to do with.

voisin m, **-e** f neighbour:—adj neighbouring.

voisinage m neighbourhood.

voiture f car; carriage; cart.

voix f voice; vote.

vol m flight:—**à ~ d'oiseau** as the crow flies.

volant m steering wheel:—adj flying.

volatile adj volatile.

volcan m volcano.

volcanique adj volcanic.

volée f flight; volley.

voler vi to fly:—vt to steal; to rob.

volet m shutter; flap, paddle.

voleur m, **-euse** f thief.

volontaire adj voluntary.

volonté f will; willpower.

volontiers adv willingly.

volubile adj voluble.

volume m volume.

volumineux adj voluminous.

volupté f voluptuousness.

voluptueux adj voluptuous.

vomir vi to vomit.

vorace adj voracious.

voracité f voracity.

vos = pl **votre**.

votant m, **-e** f voter.

vote m vote; voting.

voter vi to vote.

votre adj, pl **vos** your, your own.

vôtre poss pn:—**le/la ~, les ~s** yours.

vouer vt to vow.

vouloir vt to want, wish.

voulu adj required; deliberate.

vous pn you, yourself.

voûte f vault.

vouvoyer vt to address someone as vous.

voyage m journey, trip; travelling.

voyager vi to travel, journey.

voyageur m **-euse** f traveller, passenger.

voyelle f vowel.

vrac adv:—**en ~** in bulk.

vrai adj true, genuine.

vraisemblable adj likely, probable.

vrille f tendril; spiral.
vu adj seen:—prép in view of.
vue f sight, eyesight.

WXYZ

wagon m wagon, truck.
wagon-restaurant m restaurant car.
W.-C. (water-closet) mpl lavatory.
week-end m weekend.
whisky m whisky.
xénophobe mf xenophobe:—adj xenophobic.
xénophobie f xenophobia.
xylophone m xylophone.
yacht m yacht.
yaourt m yoghurt.
yeux = pl œil.
yoga m yoga
yoghurt m = yaourt.
yogi m yogi.

vulgaire adj vulgar.
vulgarité f vulgarity, coarseness.
vulnérable adj vulnerable.

yucca m yucca.
zèle m zeal.
zélé adj zealous.
zénith m zenith.
zéro m zero, nought, nothing.
zézayer vi to lisp.
zigzag m zigzag.
zigzaguer vi to zigzag.
zodiaque m zodiac.
zone f zone, area.
zoo m zoo.
zoologie f zoology.
zoologiste mf zoologist.
zut interj damn!, rubbish!

English-French Dictionary

A

a *art* un, une.

abacus *n* abaque, boulier *m*.

abandon *vt* abandonner, laisser.

abash *vt* couvrir de honte.

abate *vt* baisser:—*vi* baisser; se calmer.

abbey *n* abbaye *f*.

abbreviate *vt* abréger.

abbreviation *n* abréviation *f*.

abdicate *vt* abdiquer; renoncer à.

abdomen *n* abdomen *m*.

abduct *vt* kidnapper, enlever.

abeyance *n* suspension *f*.

abhor *vt* abhorrer, exécrer.

abhorrent *adj* exécrable.

abide *vt* supporter, souffrir.

ability *n* capacité, aptitude *f*.

abject *adj* misérable; abject.

able *adj* capable:—**to be ~** pouvoir.

abnegation *n* renoncement *m*.

abnormal *adj* anormal.

abnormality *n* anomalie *f*.

aboard *adv* à bord.

abode *n* domicile *m*.

abolish *vt* abolir, supprimer.

abolition *n* abolition.

abominable *adj* abominable.

aboriginal *adj* aborigène.

abort *vi* avorter.

abortion *n* avortement *m*.

abound *vi* abonder.

about *prep* au sujet de; vers:—*adv* çà et là:—**to be ~ to** être sur le point de.

above *prep* au-dessus de:—*adv* au-dessus:—**~ all** surtout, principalement.

abrasion *n* écorchure *f*.

abrasive *adj* abrasif.

abroad *adv* à l'étranger.

abrupt *adj* abrupt; brusque.

abscess *n* abcès *m*.

absence *n* absence *f*.

absent *adj* absent:—*vi* s'absenter.

absent-minded *adj* distrait.

absolute *adj* absolu.

absolve *vt* absoudre.

absorb *vt* absorber.

absorption *n* absorption *f*.

abstain *vi* s'abstenir.

abstinence *n* abstinence *f*.

abstinent *adj* abstinent.

abstract *adj* abstrait:—*n* abrégé *m*.

abstraction *n* abstraction *f*.

absurd *adj* absurde.

absurdity *n* absurdité *f*.

abundance *n* abondance *f*.

abundant *adj* abondant.

abuse *vt* abuser de:—*n* abus *m*.

abyss *n* abîme *m*.

academic *adj* universitaire; scolaire; théorique.

academy n académie f.

accelerate vt accélérer.

acceleration n accélération f.

accelerator n accélérateur m.

accent n accent m:—vt accentuer.

accept vt accepter.

acceptable adj acceptable.

acceptance n acceptation f.

access n accès m.

accessible adj accessible.

accident n accident m.

accidental adj accidentel.

acclaim vt acclamer.

accommodate vt loger; accommoder.

accommodation n logement m.

accompany vt accompagner.

accomplice n complice mf.

accomplish vt accomplir.

accomplishment n accomplissement m.

accord n accord m:—**of one's own ~** de son propre chef.

accordance n:—**in ~ with** conformément à.

according prep selon:—**~ as** selon que:—**~ly** adv en conséquence.

accost vt accoster.

account n compte m:—**on no ~** en aucun cas:—**on ~ of** en raison de:—vt **to ~ for** expliquer.

accountability n responsabilité f.

accountancy n comptabilité f.

accountant n comptable mf.

accumulate vt accumuler:—vi s'accumuler.

accumulation n accumulation f

accuracy n exactitude f.

accurate adj exact.

accusation n accusation f.

accuse vt accuser.

accused n accusé(e) m(f).

accustom vt accoutumer.

ace n as m.

ache n douleur f:—vi faire mal.

achieve vt réaliser; obtenir.

achievement n réalisation f.

acid adj acide:—n acide m.

acknowledge vt reconnaître.

acknowledgment n reconnaissance f.

acoustics n acoustique f.

acquaint vt informer, aviser.

acquaintance n connaissance f.

acquiesce vi acquiescer, consentir.

acquiescent adj consentant.

acquire vt acquérir.

acquisition n acquisition f.

acquit vt acquitter.

acrimonious adj acrimonieux.

across adv en travers:—prep à travers.

act vt jouer:—vi agir; jouer la comédie:—n acte m.

action n action f.

activate vt activer.

active adj actif.

activity n activité f.

actor n acteur m.

actress n actrice f.

actual adj réel; concret.

acute adj aigu; perspicace

ad lib vt improviser.

ad nauseam adv à satiété.

adamant adj inflexible.

adapt vt adapter, ajuster.

adaptable adj adaptable.

adaptation n adaptation f.

add vt ajouter.

addict n intoxiqué m, -e f.

addiction n dépendance f.

addition n addition f.
additional adj additionnel.
address vt adresser.
adept adj adroit.
adequate adj adéquat; suffisant.
adhere vi adhérer.
adhesion n adhésion f.
adhesive adj adhésif.
adjacent adj adjacent, contigu.
adjective n adjectif m.
adjoin vi être contigu.
adjourn vt reporter, remettre.
adjournment n ajournement m.
adjust vt ajuster, adapter.
adjustable adj ajustable.
adjustment n ajustement m; réglage m.
administer vt administrer.
administration n administration f.
administrative adj administratif.
admirable adj admirable.
admiral n amiral m.
admiration n admiration f.
admire vt admirer.
admirer n admirateur m, -trice f.
admission n admission, entrée f.
admit vt admettre:—**to ~ to** reconnaître.
admonish vt admonester.
admonition n admonestation f.
adolescence n adolescence f.
adopt vt adopter.
adoption n adoption f.
adoptive adj adoptif.
adorable adj adorable.
adore vt adorer.
adorn vt orner.
adrift adv à la dérive.
adroit adj adroit, habile.
adulation n adulation f.

adult adj adulte:—n adulte mf.
adultery n adultère m.
advance vt avancer:—vi avancer:—n avance f.
advantage n avantage m:—**to take ~ of** profiter de.
advantageous adj avantageux.
a.m. adv du matin.
adventure n aventure f.
adventurous adj aventureux.
adversary n adversaire mf.
adverse adj défavorable.
adversity n adversité f.
advertise vt faire de la publicité pour.
advertisement n publicité f; annonce f.
advice n conseil m; avis m.
advise vt conseiller; aviser.
advisory adj consultatif.
advocacy n plaidoyer m.
advocate n avocat m:—vt plaider pour.
aerial n antenne f.
aerobics npl aérobic m.
aeroplane n avion m.
aeroplane n avion m.
aerosol n aérosol m.
affability n affabilité f.
affable adj affable.
affair n affaire f.
affect vt toucher; affecter.
affection n affection f.
affectionate adj affectueux.
affiliate vt affilier.
affinity n affinité f.
affirm vt affirmer, déclarer.
affirmative adj affirmatif.
afflict vt affliger.
affluent adj riche; abondant.

afford *vt* fournir:—**to be able to ~** avoir les moyens d'acheter.

affront *n* affront *m*, injure *f*:—*vt* affronter; insulter.

afloat *adv* à flot.

afraid *adj* apeuré:—**I am ~** j'ai peur.

after *prep* après:—*adv* après:—**~ all** après tout.

afterbirth *n* placenta *m*.

aftermath *n* conséquences *fpl*.

afternoon *n* après-midi *mf*.

afterward(s) *adv* ensuite.

again *adv* à nouveau.

against *prep* contre.

age *n* âge *m*:—*vt* vieillir.

agency *n* agence *f*.

agenda *n* ordre du jour *m*.

agent *n* agent *m*.

aggravate *vt* aggraver; énerver.

aggravation *n* aggravation *f*.

aggression *n* agression *f*.

aggressive *adj* agressif.

aggressor *n* agresseur *m*.

agile *adj* agile; adroit.

agility *n* agilité *f*; adresse *f*.

agitate *vt* agiter.

agitation *n* agitation *f*.

ago *adv*:—**how long ~?** il y a combien de temps?

agony *n* agonie *f*.

agree *vt* convenir:—*vi* être d'accord.

agreeable *adj* agréable.

agreed *adj* convenu:—**~!** *adv* d'accord!

agreement *n* accord *m*.

agricultural *adj* agricole.

agriculture *n* agriculture *f*.

ahead *adv* en avant.

aid *vt* aider, secourir:—*n* aide *f*.

AIDS *n* SIDA *m*.

ailment *n* maladie *f*.

aim *vt* pointer; viser.

air *n* air *m*.

air terminal *n* aérogare *f*.

air-conditioned *adj* climatisé.

air-conditioning *n* climatisation *f*.

aircraft *n* avion *m*.

airiness *n* aération, ventilation *f*.

airlift *n* pont aérien *m*.

airline *n* ligne 8 34216rȷȷenne

airmail *n*:—**by ~** par avion.

airport *n* aéroport *m*.

airsick *adj*:—**to be ~** avoir le mal de l'air.

airtight *adj* hermétique.

aisle *n* nef d'église *f*.

ajar *adj* entrouvert.

akin *adj* ressemblant.

alarm bell *n* sonnette d'alarme *f*.

alarm *n* alarme *f*:—*vt* alarmer; inquiéter.

alarmist *n* alarmiste *mf*.

albeit *conj* bien que.

album *n* album *m*.

alcohol *n* alcool *m*.

alcoholic *adj* alcoolisé:—*n* alcoolique *mf*.

ale *n* bière *f*.

alert *adj* vigilant:—*n* alerte *f*.

alertness *n* vigilance *f*.

alien *adj* étranger:—*n* étranger *m*, -ère *f*; extra-terrestre *mf*.

alienate *vt* aliéner.

alight *vi* mettre pied à terre:—*adj* en feu.

alike *adj* semblable, égal:—*adv* de la même f8 34215on.

alimentation *n* alimentation *f*.

alive *adj* en vie, vivant; actif.

all *adj* tout:—*adv* totalement:—**~ the same** cependant:—**~ the better** tant mieux:—**not at ~!** pas du tout!:—*n* tout *m*.

allege *vt* alléguer.

allegiance *n* loyauté, fidélité *f*.

allergy *n* allergie *f*.

alley *n* ruelle *f*.

alliance *n* alliance *f*.

allocate *vt* allouer.

allocation *n* allocation *f*.

allot *vt* assigner.

allow *vt* permettre; accorder.

allowance *n* allocation *f*; concession *f*.

allude *vi* faire allusion à.

allure *n* charme, attrait *m*.

allusion *n* allusion *f*.

allusive *adj* allusif.

ally *n* allié *m*, -e *f*:—*vt* allier.

almost *adv* presque.

alone *adj* seul:—*adv* seul.

along *adv* le long (de):—**~side** à côté.

aloud *adj* à voix haute.

alphabet *n* alphabet *m*.

alphabetical *adj* alphabétique.

already *adv* déjà.

also *adv* aussi.

altar *n* autel *m*.

alter *vt* modifier.

alteration *n* modification *f*.

alternate *adj* alterné:—*vt* alterner.

alternation *n* alternance *f*.

alternative *n* alternative *f*:—*adj* alternatif:—**~ly** *adv* sinon.

although *conj* bien que, malgré.

altitude *n* altitude *f*.

always *adv* toujours.

amalgamate *vt* amalgamer; *vi* s'amalgamer.

amalgamation *n* amalgamation *f*.

amass *vt* accumuler, amasser.

amateur *n* amateur *m*.

amaze *vt* stupéfier.

amazement *n* stupéfaction *f*.

ambassador *n* ambassadeur *m*.

ambidextrous *adj* ambidextre.

ambiguity *n* ambiguïté *f*.

ambiguous *adj* ambigu.

ambition *n* ambition *f*.

ambitious *adj* ambitieux.

ambulance *n* ambulance *f*.

ambush *n* embuscade *f*:—*vt* tendre une embuscade à.

ameliorate *vt* améliorer.

amelioration *n* amélioration *f*.

amend *vt* modifier; amender.

amendment *n* amendement *m*.

amenities *npl* commodités *fpl*.

America *n* Amérique *f*.

American *adj* américain.

amiability *n* amabilité *f*.

amiable *adj* aimable.

amicable *adj* amical.

amid(st) *prep* entre, parmi.

ammunition *n* munitions *fpl*.

amnesia *n* amnésie *f*.

amnesty *n* amnistie *f*.

among(st) *prep* entre, parmi.

amorous *adj* amoureux

amount *n* montant *m*:—*vi* se monter.

amphibian *n* amphibie *m*.

amplify *vt* amplifier.

amplitude *n* amplitude *f*.

amputate *vt* amputer.

amputation *n* amputation *f*.

amuse *vt* distraire, divertir.

amusement *n* distraction *f*.

amusing *adj* divertissant.

an *art* un, une.

anachronism n anachronisme m.

anaemic adj (med) anémique.

anaesthetic n anesthésique m.

analogy n analogie f.

analyse vt analyser.

analysis n analyse f.

analytical adj analytique.

anarchic adj anarchique.

anarchy n anarchie f.

anatomical adj anatomique.

anatomy n anatomie f.

ancestor n ancêtre mf.

anchor n ancre f.

ancient adj ancien, antique.

and conj et.

anecdote n anecdote f.

angel n ange m.

anger n colère f:—vt irriter.

angle n angle m:—vi pêcher à la ligne.

angler n pêcheur à la ligne m.

angry adj en colère, irrité.

anguish n angoisse f.

angular adj angulaire.

animal n adj animal m.

animate vt animer:—adj vivant.

animation n animation f.

animosity n animosité f.

ankle n cheville f.

annex vt annexer:—n annexe f.

annihilate vt annihiler, anéantir.

anniversary n anniversaire m.

annotate vt annoter.

annotation n annotation f.

announce vt annoncer.

announcement n annonce f.

annoy vt ennuyer.

annoyance n ennui m.

annual adj annuel

annul vt annuler.

anomaly n anomalie.

anonymity n anonymat m.

anonymous adj anonyme.

another adj un autre:—**one ~** l'un l'autre.

answer vt répondre à:—n réponse f.

ant n fourmi f.

antagonise vt provoquer.

antagonism n antagonisme m.

antarctic adj antarctique.

antenna n antenne f.

anterior adj antérieur.

anthem n hymne m.

anthology n anthologie f.

anthropology n anthropologie f.

antibiotic n antibiotique m.

anticipate vt prévoir.

anticipation n attente f.

antidote n antidote m.

antipathy n antipathie f.

antiquarian n antiquaire mf.

antique n antiquité f.

antiquity n antiquité f.

antithesis n antithèse f.

antler n corne f.

anxiety n anxiété f; désir m.

anxious adj anxieux.

any adj pn n'importe quel, n'importe quelle; un, une; tout:—**~body** quelqu'un; n'importe qui; personne:—**~thing** quelque chose; n'importe quoi; rien.

apart adv séparément.

apartment n appartement m.

apathetic adj apathique.

apathy n apathie f.

aperture n ouverture f.

apex n sommet m; apex m.

apologise vt excuser.

apology n apologie, défense f.
apostle n apôtre m.
appall vt horrifier, atterrer.
apparatus n appareil m.
apparent adj évident, apparent.
apparition n apparition, vision f.
appeal vi faire appel:—n (law) appel m.
appear vi paraître.
appearance n apparence f.
appellant n (law) appelant m.
append vt annexer.
appetising adj appétissant.
appetite n appétit m.
applaud vt vi applaudir.
applause n applaudissements mpl.
apple n pomme f.
apple tree n pommier m.
appliance n appareil m.
applicable adj applicable.
applicant n candidat m, -e f.
application n application f.
apply vt appliquer:—vi s'adresser.
appoint vt nommer.
appointment n rendez-vous m; nomination f.
apportion vt répartir.
apposite adj adapté.
appraisal n estimation f.
appraise vt évaluer.
appreciate vt apprécier.
appreciation n appréciation f.
appreciative adj reconnaissant.
apprehend vt appréhender.
apprehension n appréhension f.
apprentice n apprenti m.
approach vi approcher (s'):—n approche f.
appropriate adj approprié, adéquat.
approval n approbation f.
approve (of) vt approuver.

approximate adj approximatif.
approximation n approximation f.
April n avril m.
apron n tablier m.
apt adj idéal.
aqualung n scaphandre autonome m.
aquarium n aquarium m.
aquatic adj aquatique.
arable adj arable.
arbiter n arbitre m.
arbitrary adj arbitraire.
arbitrate vt arbitrer.
arbitration n arbitrage m.
arcade n galerie f.
arch n arc m.
archbishopric n archevêché m.
archeological adj archéologique.
archeology n archéologie f.
architect n architecte mf.
architecture n architecture f.
archives npl archives fpl.
arctic adj arctique.
ardent adj ardent.
ardour n ardeur f.
area n région f; domaine m.
argue vi se disputer.
argument n argument m; dispute f.
argumentative adj raisonneur.
arid adj aride.
aridity n aridité f.
arise vi se lever; survenir.
aristocracy n aristocratie f.
aristocrat n aristocrate mf.
arithmetic n arithmétique f.
arm n bras m; arme f:—vt armer:—vi (s')armer.
armament n armement m.
armchair n fauteuil m.
armful n brassée f.

armistice n armistice m.

armour n armure f.

armpit n aisselle f.

army n armée f.

aroma n arôme m.

aromatic adj aromatique.

around prep autour de:—adv autour.

arouse vt éveiller; exciter.

arrange vt arranger, organiser.

arrangement n arrangement m.

array n série f.

arrest n arrestation f:—vt arrêter.

arrival n arrivée f.

arrive vi arriver.

arrogance n arrogance f.

arrogant adj arrogant.

arrow n flèche f.

arsenal n (mil) arsenal m.

art gallery n musée d'art m.

art n art m.

artery n artère f.

artful adj malin, astucieux.

article n article m.

articulate vt articuler.

articulation n articulation f.

artificial adj artificiel.

artillery n artillerie f.

artisan n artisan m.

artist n artiste mf.

artistry n habileté f.

as conj comme; pendant que; aussi:
—~ for, ~ to quant à.

ascend vi monter.

ascension n ascension f.

ascent n montée f.

ascertain vt établir.

ascetic adj ascétique:—n ascète mf.

ash n (bot) frêne m; cendre f.

ashamed adj honteux.

ashore adv à terre:—**to go** ~ débarquer.

ashtray n cendrier m.

aside adv de côté.

ask vt demander.

asleep adj endormi:—**to fall** ~
s'endormir.

aspect n aspect m.

aspersion n calomnie f.

asphyxiate vt asphyxier.

asphyxiation n asphyxie f.

aspirant n aspirant m, -e f.

aspiration n aspiration f.

aspire vi aspirer, désirer.

aspirin n aspirine f.

assail vt assaillir, attaquer.

assailant n assaillant.

assassin n assassin m.

assassinate vt assassiner.

assault n assaut m:—vt agresser.

assemble vt assembler:—vi s'assembler.

assembly n assemblée f.

assent n assentiment m:—vi donner
son assentiment.

assert vt soutenir; affirmer.

assertion n assertion f.

assess vt évaluer.

assessment n évaluation f.

assets npl biens mpl.

assign vt assigner.

assignment n allocation f.

assimilate vt assimiler.

assist vt assister, aider.

assistance n assistance, aide f.

assistant n aide mf.

associate vt associer:—adj associé:
—n associé m, -e f.

association n association f.

assortment n assortiment m.

assume vt assumer; supposer.

assumption *n* supposition *f*.

assurance *n* assurance *f*.

assure *vt* assurer.

asthma *n* asthme *m*.

asthmatic *adj* asthmatique.

astonish *vt* surprendre.

astonishment *n* surprise.

astound *vt* ébahir.

astrologer *n* astrologue *mf*.

astrology *n* astrologie *f*.

astronomer *n* astronome *mf*.

astronomy *n* astronomie *f*.

astute *adj* malin.

asylum *n* asile, refuge *m*.

at *prep* à; en.

atheist *n* athée *mf*.

athlete *n* athlète *mf*.

athletic *adj* athlétique.

atlas *n* atlas *m*.

atmosphere *n* atmosphère *f*.

atom *n* atome *m*.

atomic *adj* atomique.

atrocious *adj* atroce.

atrocity *n* atrocité, énormité *f*.

attach *vt* joindre.

attachment *n* attachement *m*.

attack *vt* attaquer:—*n* attaque *f*.

attacker *n* attaquant *m*, -e *f*.

attain *vt* atteindre, obtenir.

attempt *vt* essayer:—*n* essai *m*, tentative *f*.

attend *vt* servir; assister à.

attendance *n* service *m*; assistance *f*.

attention *n* attention *f*; soin *m*.

attentive *adj* attentif:—**~ly** *adv* attentivement.

attic *n* grenier *m*.

attitude *n* attitude *f*.

attract *vt* attirer.

attraction *n* attraction *f*; attrait *m*.

attractive *adj* attrayant.

attribute *vt* attribuer:—*n* attribut *m*.

auction *n* vente aux enchères *f*.

audacious *adj* audacieux.

audacity *n* audace, témérité *f*.

audible *adj* audible.

audience *n* audience *f*.

audit *n* audit *m*:—*vt* vérifier.

auditor *n* auditeur *m*, -trice *f*.

augment *vt vi* augmenter.

August *n* août *m*.

aunt *n* tante *f*.

auspicious *adj* favorable, propice.

austere *adj* austère, sévère.

authentic *adj* authentique

authenticity *n* authenticité *f*.

author *n* auteur *m*.

authorisation *n* autorisation *f*.

authorise *vt* autoriser.

authoritarian *adj* autoritaire.

authority *n* autorité *f*.

autograph *n* autographe *m*.

automatic *adj* automatique.

autonomy *n* autonomie *f*.

autopsy *n* autopsie *f*.

autumn *n* automne *m*.

auxiliary *adj* auxiliaire.

available *adj* disponible.

avalanche *n* avalanche *f*.

avarice *n* avarice *f*.

avenge *vt* venger.

avenue *n* avenue *f*.

average *n* moyenne *f*, moyen terme *m*.

aversion *n* aversion *f*, dégoût *m*.

avert *vt* détourner, écarter.

avoid *vt* éviter; échapper à.

await *vt* attendre.

awake *vt* réveiller:—*vi* se réveiller:— *adj* éveillé.

award *vt* attribuer:—*n* prix *m*; décision *f*.
aware *adj* conscient; au courant.
awareness *n* conscience *f*.
away *adv* absent; loin.
awe *n* peur, crainte *f*.

awful *adj* horrible, terrible.
awkward *adj* gauche, maladroit.
axe *n* hache *f*.
axis *n* axe *m*.
axle *n* axe *m*.

B

babble *vi* bavarder, babiller.
babe, baby *n* bébé *m*; nourrisson *m*.
babyhood *n* petite enfance *f*.
babyish *adj* enfantin; puéril.
bachelor *n* célibataire *m*.
back *n* dos *m*:—*adv* en arrière, à l'arrière:—*vt* soutenir.
backbone *n* colonne vertébrale.
backdate *vt* antidater.
backer *n* partisan *m*, -e *f*.
background *n* fond *m*.
backpack *n* sac à dos *m*.
back payment *n* rappel de salaire *m*.
backside *n* derrière *m*.
backward *adj* rétrograde:—*adv* en arrière.
bacon *n* lard *m*.
bad *adj* mauvais, de mauvaise qualité; méchant:—**~ly** *adv* mal.
badge *n* insigne *m*, badge *m*.
badness *n* mauvaise qualité *f*; méchanceté *f*.
baffle *vt* déconcerter, confondre.
bag *n* sac *m*; valise *f*.
baggage *n* bagages *mpl*; équipement *m*.
bait *vt* appâter:—*n* appât *m*.
bake *vt* faire cuire au four.
bakery *n* boulangerie *f*.
baker *n* boulanger *m*, -ère *f*.
baking *n* cuisson *f*; fournée *f*.
balance *n* balance *f*; équilibre *m*:—*vt* équilibrer.

balcony *n* balcon *m*.
bald *adj* chauve.
baldness *n* calvitie *f*.
ball *n* balle *f*; boule *f*; ballon *m*.
ballad *n* ballade *f*.
ballerina *n* ballerine *f*.
ballet *n* ballet *m*.
balloon *n* aérostat *m*.
bricklayer *n* maçon *m*.
bride *n* mariée *f*.
bridegroom *n* marié *m*.
bridge *n* pont *m*.
bridle *n* bride *f*; frein *m*.
brief *adj* bref, concis:—*n* résumé *m*.
briefcase *n* serviette *f*.
bright *adj* clair, brillant.
brighten *vt* faire briller:—*vi* s'éclairer.
brilliance *n* éclat *m*.
brilliant *adj* éclatant; génial.
bring *vt* apporter; amener.
brisk *adj* vif, rapide, frais.
bristle *n* poil *m*:—*vi* se hérisser.
brittle *adj* cassant, fragile.
broad *adj* large.
broadcast *n* émission *f*:—*vt vi* diffuser.
broaden *vt* élargir:—*vi* s'élargir.
broadness *n* largeur *f*.
broccoli *n* brocoli *m*.
brochure *n* brochure *f*, dépliant *m*.
broken *adj* cassé; interrompu.
broker *n* courtier *m*.
bronze *n* bronze *m*.

brooch n broche f.

brood vi couver; ruminerf.

broom n genêt m; balai m.

brother n frère m.

brother-in-law n beau-frère m.

brow n sourcil m; front m.

brown adj marron; brun:—n marron m:—vt brunir.

browse vt brouter:—vi paître.

bruise n bleu m, ecchymose f.

brush n brosse f; pinceau m.

brutal adj brutal.

brutality n brutalité f.

brute n brute f:—adj bestial.

bubble n bulle f:—vi bouillonner; pétiller.

bucket n seau m.

buckle n boucle f:—vt boucler:—vi se déformer.

budge vi bouger, remuer.

budget n budget m.

buffet n buffet m:—vt gifler.

bug n punaise f.

build vt construire, bâtir.

builder n constructeur m.

building n bâtiment m; immeuble, édifice m.

bulb n bulbe m; oignon m.

bulge vi se renfler:—n renflement m.

bulk n masse f; volume m.

bulky adj volumineux.

bull n taureau m.

bullet n balle f.

bulletproof adj pare-balles, blindé.

bullion n or en barre m.

bully n tyran m:—vt tyraniser.

bump n heurt m; bosse f:—vt heurter.

bumpy adj cahoteux, bosselé.

bun n petit pain m; chignon m.

bunch n botte f; groupe m.

bundle n paquet m, liasse f:—vt empaqueter.

bungle vt bousiller.

bunk n couchette f.

buoy n (mar) bouée f.

buoyancy n flottabilité f.

buoyant adj flottable; gai, enjoué.

burden n charge f:—vt charger.

bureau n commode f; bureau m.

bureaucrat n bureaucrate mf.

burial n enterrement m; obsèques fpl.

burly adj robuste.

burn vt vi brûler:—n brûlure f.

burning adj brûlant.

burst vi éclater:—**to ~ out laughing** éclater de rire.

bury vt enterrer, inhumer.

bus n (auto)bus m.

bush n buisson, taillis m.

business n entreprise f; commerce m.

businessman n homme d'affaires m.

businesswoman n femme d'affaires f.

bus-stop n arrêt d'autobus m.

busy adj occupé; actif.

but conj mais; sauf, excepté, seulement.

butcher n boucher m, -ère f:—vt abattre, massacrer.

butchery n boucherie f, carnage m.

butter n beurre m:—vt beurrer.

butterfly n papillon m.

button n bouton m:—vt boutonner.

buy vt acheter.

buyer n acheteur m, -euse f.

buzz n bourdonnement:—vi bourdonner.

by prep à côté de, près de; par.

bypass n route de contournement f.
by-product n sous-produit m.

by-road n chemin de traverse m
byte n (comput) octet m.

C

cabbage n chou m.
cabin n cabine f; cabane f.
cabinet n meuble de rangement m; console f.
cable n câble m.
cache n cachette f.
cackle vi caqueter, jacasser.
cafe n café m.
cafeteria n cafétéria f.
caffein(e) n caféine f.
cage n cage f:—vt mettre en cage.
cake n gâteau m.
calamity n calamité f, désastre m.
calculate vt calculer, compter.
calculation n calcul m.
calendar n calendrier m.
calf n veau m.
calibre n calibre m.
call vt appeler; convoquer:—n appel m; cri m.
calligraphy n calligraphie f.
calling n profession, vocation f.
callous adj dur; insensible.
calm n calme m:—adj calme:—vt calmer.
calorie n calorie f.
camera n caméra f.
camouflage n camouflage m.
camp n camp m:—vi camper.
campaign n campagne f.
camper n campeur m, -euse f.
camping n camping m.
campsite n camping m.
campus n campus m.
can v aux pouvoir:—n boîte de conserve f.
canal n conduit m; canal m.

cancel vt annuler.
cancer n cancer m.
candid adj candide, simple.
candidate n candidat(e) m(f).
candle n bougie f; cierge m.
candour n candeur f; sincérité f.
cane n canne f; bâton m.
cannon n canon m.
canoe n canoë m.
canon n canon m; règle f.
can opener n ouvre-boîte m.
canopy n baldaquin m.
cantankerous adj acariâtre.
canteen n cantine f.
canvas n toile f.
canvass vt sonder.
canvasser n prospecteur m, -trice f.
cap n casquette f.
capability n capacité, aptitude.
capable adj capable.
capacity n capacité; potentiel m.
cape n cap, promontoire m.
capital adj capital:—n capital m; capitale f.
capitalise vt capitaliser.
capitalist n capitaliste mf.
capital punishment n peine de mort.
capitulate vi capituler.
capitulation n capitulation f.
capricious adj capricieux.
capsize vt (mar) chavirer.
capsule n capsule f.
captain n capitaine m.
captivate vt captiver.
captivation n fascination f.

captive *n* captif *m*, -ive *f*, prisonnier *m*, -ière *f*.

captivity *n* captivité *f*.

capture *n* capture *f*:—*vt* capturer.

car *n* voiture *f*; wagon *m*.

caravan *n* caravane *f*.

carbohydrates *npl* hydrates de carbone *m pl*.

carcass *n* cadavre *m*.

card *n* carte *f*.

cardboard *n* carton *m*.

cardinal *adj* cardinal, principal:—*n* cardinal *m*.

card table *n* table de jeu *f*.

care *n* soin *m*; souci *m*:—*vi* se soucier de.

career *n* carrière *f*; cours *m*.

careful *adj* soigneux, consciencieux.

careless *adj* insouciant, négligent.

carelessness *n* négligence *f*.

caress *n* caresse *f*:—*vt* caresser.

caretaker *n* concierge *mf*.

cargo *n* cargaison *f*.

caricature *n* caricature *f*:—*vt* caricaturer.

carnage *n* carnage *m*.

carnal *adj* charnel; sensuel.

carnival *n* carnaval *m*.

carnivorous *adj* carnivore.

carpenter *n* charpentier *m*.

carpentry *n* charpenterie *f*.

carpet *n* tapis *m*.

carriage *n* port *m*; voiture *f*.

carrier *n* porteur, transporteur *m*.

carrion *n* charogne *f*.

carrot *n* carotte *f*.

carry *vt* porter:—*vi* porter.

cart *n* charrette *f*.

cartel *n* cartel *m*.

cartilage *n* cartilage *m*.

cartoon *n* dessin animé *m*.

cartridge *n* cartouche *f*.

carve *vt* tailler, sculpter.

carving *n* sculpture *f*.

case *n* cas *m*; boîte *f*, étui *m*; enveloppe *f*.

cash *n* espèces *fpl*:—*vt* encaisser.

cashier *n* caissier *m*, -ière *f*.

casing *n* chambranle *m*.

casino *n* casino *m*.

cask *n* tonneau, fût *m*.

casket *n* cercueil *m*.

casserole *n* cocotte *f*.

cassette *n* cassette *f*.

cassette player magnétophone *m*.

cast *vt* jeter, lancer:—*n* moule *m*.

caste *n* caste *f*.

castigate *vt* punir.

castle *n* château *m*.

castrate *vt* castrer.

castration *n* castration *f*.

casual *adj* accidentel, fortuit.

cat *n* chat *m*, chatte *f*.

catalogue *n* catalogue *m*.

catapult *n* catapulte *f*.

cataract *n* cascade *f*; déluge *m*.

catastrophe *n* catastrophe *f*.

catch *vt* attraper, saisir:—*n* prise *f*.

catchword *n* slogan *m*.

catechism *n* catéchisme *m*.

categorical *adj* catégorique.

category *n* catégorie *f*.

caterer *n* fournisseur, traiteur *m*.

catering *n* restauration *f*.

caterpillar *n* chenille *f*.

cathedral *n* cathédrale *f*.

catholic *adj n* catholique *mf*.

cattle *n* bétail *m*.

cauliflower *n* chou-fleur *m*.

cause n cause f; raison f:—vt causer.

cauterise vt cautériser.

caution n prudence, précaution:—vt avertir.

cautious adj prudent, circonspect.

cavalry n cavalerie f.

cave n grotte f, caverne f.

cavern n caverne f.

cavity n cavité f.

cease vt cesser, arrêter.

ceaseless adj incessant, continuel.

cede vt céder.

ceiling n plafond m.

celebrate vt célébrer, fêter.

celebration n fête f.

celibate adj célibataire.

cell n cellule f.

cellar n cave f; cellier m.

cement n ciment m:—vt cimenter.

cemetery n cimetière m.

censor n censeur m.

censorship n censure f.

censure n censure:—vt censurer.

census n recensement m.

centenary n centenaire m:—adj centenaire.

centigrade n centigrade m.

centimetre n centimètre m.

central adj central.

centralise vt centraliser.

centre n centre m:—vt centrer.

century n siècle m.

cereal n céréal f.

ceremonial adj n cérémonial m; rituel m.

ceremony n cérémonie f.

certain adj certain, sûr.

certainty n certitude f.

certificate n certificat, acte m.

certification n authentification f.

certify vt certifier, assurer.

cessation n cessation f.

chafe vt irriter; frotter.

chagrin n dépit m.

chain n chaîne f:—vt enchaîner.

chair n chaise f:—vt présider.

chairman n président m.

chalk n craie f.

challenge n défi m:—vt défier.

chamber n pièce f; chambre f.

champagne n champagne m.

champion n champion m, -ionne f:—vt défendre.

championship n championnat m.

chance n hasard m.

chancellor n chancelier m.

change vt changer:—vi changer, se transformer:—n modification f; change m.

changeable adj changeant.

channel n canal m:—vt canaliser.

chant n chant m.

chaotic adj chaotique.

chapel n chapelle f.

chapter n chapitre m.

character n caractère m; personnage m.

characteristic adj caractéristique.

charcoal n charbon de bois m.

charge vt charger; accuser:—n fardeau m; accusation f.

chargeable adj passible.

charitable adj caritatif.

charity n charité, bienfaisance f.

charm n charme m:—vt charmer.

chart n carte (marine) f; diagramme m.

charter n charte f; privilège m:—vt affréter.

chase vt poursuivre:—n chasse f.

chaste adj chaste; pur.

chastise vt châtier, punir.

chastisement n châtiment m.

chastity n chasteté, pureté f.

chat vi causer:—n bavardage m.

chatter vi jacasser.

chauffeur n chauffeur m.

chauvinist n chauvin m, -e f.

cheap adj bon marché.

cheapen vt baisser le prix de.

cheat vt tromper, frauder:—n tricheur m -euse f.

check vt vérifier; contrôler; réprimer, enrayer; stopper; enregistrer: —n contrôle m.

checkup n bilan de santé.

cheek n joue f.

cheer n gaieté f; applaudissement m: —vt réconforter.

cheerful adj gai, enjoué, joyeux.

cheerfulness n gaieté f; bonne humeur f.

cheese n fromage m.

chef n chef (de cuisine) m.

chemist n chimiste mf; pharmacien m, -ienne f.

chemistry n chimie f.

cheque n chèque m.

cherish vt chérir, aimer.

chess n échecs mpl.

chest n poitrine f.

chew vt mâcher, mastiquer.

chick n poussin m.

chicken n poulet m.

chief adj principal, en chef:—n chef m.

chieftain n chef m.

child n enfant m.

childbirth n accouchement m.

childhood n enfance f.

childish adj enfantin.

children npl de **child**, enfants mpl.

chill n froid m:—vt refroidir.

chilly adj froid, très frais.

chimney n cheminée f.

chin n menton m.

chip vt ébrécher:—n fragment, éclat m; frite f.

chisel n ciseau m:—vt ciseler.

chivalrous adj chevaleresque.

chocolate n chocolat m.

choice n choix m, préférence.

choir n chœur m.

choke vt étrangler; étouffer.

choose vt choisir, élire.

chop vt trancher, hacher:—n côtelette f.

chore n corvée f; travail routinier m.

chorus n chœur m.

christen vt baptiser.

christening n baptême m.

Christian adj chrétien m, -ne f.

Christmas n Noël f.

Christmas Eve n veille de Noël f.

chronic adj chronique.

chronicle n chronique f.

chronicler n chroniqueur m.

chronological adj chronologique

chronology n chronologie f.

chuckle vi rire, glousser.

chum n copain m, copine f.

church n église f.

cider n cidre m.

cigar n cigare m.

cigarette n cigarette f.

cinder n cendre f.

cinema n cinéma m.

circle n cercle m; groupe m:—vt encercler.

circuit n circuit m; tour m; tournée f.

circular adj circulaire:—n circulaire f.

circulate vi circuler.

circulation n circulation f.
circumference n circonférence f.
circumnavigation n circumnavigation f.
circumspect adj circonspect.
circumspection n circonspection f.
circumstance n circonstance, situation f.
circumvent vt circonvenir.
circus n cirque m.
citation n citation f.
cite vt citer.
citizen n citoyen m, -enne f.
city n ville f.
civic adj civique.
civil adj civil, courtois.
civilian n civil m, -e f.
civilisation n civilisation f.
civilise vt civiliser.
claim vt revendiquer, réclamer:—n demande f; réclamation f.
claimant n demandeur m.
clamour n clameur f.
clamp n attache f:—vt serrer.
clandestine adj clandestin.
clap vt vi applaudir.
clapping n applaudissements mpl.
clarification n clarification f.
clarify vt clarifier, éclaircir.
clarity n clarté f.
clash vi se heurter.
clasp n fermoir m; boucle f.
class n classe f; catégorie f:—vt classer.
classic(al) adj classique.
classification n classification f.
classify vt classifier.
classroom n salle de classe f.
clatter vi résonner; cliqueter.
claw n griffe f; serre f.
clean adj propre; net:—vt nettoyer.

cleaning n nettoyage m.
cleanliness n propreté, pureté f.
cleanse vt nettoyer.
clear adj clair; net:—vt clarifier.
cleft n fissure, crevasse f.
clemency n clémence f.
clement adj clément.
clergy n clergé m.
clergyman n ecclésiastique m.
clerical adj clérical.
clerk n employé m.
clever adj intelligent; habile.
click vt claquer.
client n client m, -e f.
cliff n falaise f.
climate n climat m.
climatic adj climatique.
climax n apogée a.
climb vt vi grimper, escalader.
climber n alpiniste mf.
cling vi s'accrocher (à).
clinic n clinique f.
clip vt couper:—n clip m.
cloak n cape f:—vt masquer.
cloakroom n vestiaire m.
clock n horloge f.
clog n sabot m:—vi se boucher.
close vt fermer:—n fin f; conclusion f:—adj proche:—adv de près.
closeness n proximité f.
closure n fermeture f; clôture f.
cloth n tissu m; toile f.
clothe vt habiller, vêtir.
clothes npl vêtements mpl.
cloud n nuage m; nuée f.
cloudiness n nébulosité f.
cloudy adj nuageux.
clover n trèfle m.
clown n clown m.

club n matraque f; club m.

clue n indice m, indication f.

clumsiness n gaucherie f.

clumsy adj gauche, maladroit.

cluster n grappe f:—vt grouper.

clutch n prise f; embrayage m:—vt empoigner.

coach n autocar m; wagon m; entraîneur m:—vt entraîner.

coal n charbon m.

coalesce vi s'unir.

coalition n coalition f.

coarse adj rude; grossier.

coast n côte f.

coastal adj côtier.

coastguard n gendarmerie maritime f.

coastline n littoral m.

coat n manteau m; couche f:—vt enduire.

coating n revêtement m.

coax vt cajôler.

cobweb n toile d'araignée f.

cock n coq m.

cockpit n cabine de pilotage f.

cocoa n cacao m.

coconut n noix de coco f.

cocoon n cocon m.

cod n morue f.

code n code m.

coercion n coercition.

coexistence n coexistence f.

coffee n café m.

coffeepot n cafetière f.

coffer n coffre m; caisse f.

coffin n cercueil m.

cog n dent d'engrenage f.

cogency n puissance, force f.

cogent adj convaincant, puissant.

cognac n cognac m.

cognisance n connaissance f; compétence f.

cogwheel n roue dentée f.

cohabit vi cohabiter.

cohabitation n cohabitation f.

cohere vi se tenir; être cohérent.

coherent adj cohérent; logique.

cohesive adj cohésif.

coil n rouleau m:—vt enrouler.

coin n pièce de monnaie f.

coincide vi coïncider.

coincidence n coïncidence f.

colander n passoire f.

cold adj froid; indifférent:—n froid m; rhume m.

coldness n froideur f.

collaborate vi collaborer.

collaboration n collaboration f.

collapse vi s'écrouler:—n écroulement.

collapsible adj pliant.

collar n col m.

collate vt collationner.

collateral adj concomitant:—n nantissement m.

collation n collation f.

colleague n collègue mf.

collect vt rassembler; collectionner.

collection n collection f.

collective adj collectif.

collector n collectionneur m, -euse f.

college n collège m.

collide vi se heurter.

collision n collision f, heurt m.

colloquial adj familier.

colloquialism n expression familière f.

collusion n collusion f.

colonial adj colonial.

colonise vt coloniser.

colonist *n* colon *m*.

colony *n* colonie *f*.

colour *n* couleur *f*:—*vt* colorer:—*vi* se colorer.

colourful *adj* coloré.

colouring *n* teint *m*.

column *n* colonne *f*.

columnist *n* chroniqueur *m*.

coma *n* coma *m*.

comatose *adj* comateux.

comb *n* peigne *m*:—*vt* peigner.

combat *n* combat *m*:—*vt* combattre.

combatant *n* combattant *m*, -e *f*.

combination *n* combinaison *f*.

combine *vt* combiner:—*vi* s'unir.

combustion *n* combustion *f*.

come *vi* venir:—**to ~ across, ~ upon** *vt* rencontrer par hasard:—**to ~ round, ~ to** *vi* revenir à soi.

comedian *n* comédien *m*; comique *m*.

comedy *n* comédie *f*.

comet *n* comète *f*.

comfort *n* confort *m*:—*vt* réconforter; soulager.

comfortable *adj* confortable.

comic(al) *adj* comique.

command *vt* ordonner, commander:—*n* ordre *m*.

commander *n* commandant *m*.

commemorate *vt* commémorer.

commemoration *n* commémoration *f*.

commence *vt vi* commencer.

commencement *n* commencement *m*.

commend *vt* recommander.

commendation *n* louange *f*; recommandation *f*.

commensurate *adj* proportionné.

comment *n* commentaire *m*:—*vt* commenter.

commentary *n* commentaire *m*; observation *f*.

commentator *n* commentateur *m*, -trice *f*.

commerce *n* commerce *m*.

commercial *adj* commercial.

commiserate *vt* compatir avec.

commiseration *n* commisération, pitié *f*.

commission *n* commission *f*:—*vt* commissionner.

commit *vt* commettre; confier à; engager.

commitment *n* engagement *m*.

committee *n* comité *m*.

common *adj* commun; ordinaire.

common sense *n* bon sens *m*.

commonly *adv* communément, généralement.

commotion *n* vacarme *m*.

communicable *adj* communicable

communicate *vt* communiquer:—*vi* communiquer.

communication *n* communication *f*.

communion *n* communion *f*.

communist *n* communiste *mf*.

community *n* communauté *f*.

commutable *adj* interchangeable, permutable.

commute *vt* échanger.

compact *adj* compact, serré.

compact disc *n* disque compact *m*.

companion *n* compagnon *m*, compagne *f*.

company *n* compagnie; société *f*.

comparable *adj* comparable.

comparative *adj* comparatif.

compare *vt* comparer.

comparison *n* comparaison *f*.

compartment *n* compartiment *m*.

compass *n* boussole *f*.

compassion n compassion f.
compassionate adj compatissant.
compatibility n compatibilité f.
compatible adj compatible.
compatriot n compatriote mf.
compel vt contraindre, obliger, forcer.
compensate vt compenser.
compensation n compensation f.
compete vi rivaliser (avec).
competence n compétence f; aptitude f.
competent adj compétent.
competition n compétition f; concurrence f.
competitive adj concurrentiel, compétitif.
competitor n concurrent m, -e f.
complacency n suffisance f.
complacent adj suffisant.
complain vi se plaindre.
complaint n plainte f; réclamation f.
complement n complément m.
complementary adj complémentaire.
complete adj complet; achevé:—vt achever.
completion n achèvement m.
complex adj complexe.
complexion n teint m; aspect m.
complexity n complexité f.
compliance n conformité f; soumission f.
complicate vt compliquer.
complication n complication f.
complicity n complicité f.
compliment n compliment m:—vt complimenter.
comply vi se conformer.
component adj composant.
compose vt composer.
composer n compositeur m, -trice f.

composition n composition f.
composure n maîtrise de soi f.
compound vt composer:—adj n composé m.
comprehend vt comprendre.
comprehensible adj compréhensible.
comprehension n compréhension f.
comprehensive adj global; compréhensif.
compress vt comprimer.
comprise vt comprendre, embrasser.
compromise n compromis m:—vt compromettre.
compulsion n compulsion f.
compulsory adj obligatoire.
computer n ordinateur m.
computerise vt traiter par ordinateur, informatiser.
computer science n informatique f.
comrade n camarade mf.
comradeship n camaraderie f.
conceal vt cacher.
concealment n dissimulation f.
concede vt concéder, accorder.
conceit n vanité f.
conceive vt vi concevoir.
concentrate vt concentrer.
concentration n concentration f.
concept n concept m.
conception n conception f.
concern vt concerner:—n affaire f; souci m.
concerning prep en ce qui concerne, concernant.
concert n concert m.
concession n concession f.
conciliate vt concilier.
conciliation n conciliation f.
concise adj concis, succinct.

conclude *vt* conclure.

conclusion *n* conclusion.

conclusive *adj* décisif, concluant.

concoct *vt* confectionner.

concord *n* entente, harmonie *f*.

concordance *n* accord *m*.

concrete *n* béton *m*:—*vt* bétonner.

concur *vi* coïncider; s'entendre.

concurrence *n* consentement *m*.

concussion *n* commotion *f*.

condemn *vt* condamner.

condemnation *n* condamnation *f*.

condensation *n* condensation *f*.

condense *vt* condenser.

condescend *vi* condescendre.

condescension *n* condescendance *f*.

condition *vt* conditionner:—*n* condition, situation *f*; état *m*.

conditional *adj* conditionnel.

condolences *npl* condoléances *fpl*.

condom *n* préservatif *m*.

conduct *n* conduite *f*:—*vt* conduire.

conduit *n* conduit *m*; tuyau *m*.

cone *n* cône *m*.

confectioner *n* confiseur *m*, -euse *f*.

confectionery *n* confiserie *f*.

confer *vt vi* conférer.

conference *n* conférence *f*.

confess *vt* confesser:—*vi* se confesser.

confession *n* confession *f*.

confidant *n* confident *m*, -e *f*.

confide *vt* confier:—~ **in** se confier à.

confidence *n* confiance *f*; assurance *f*.

confident *adj* confiant, sûr (de soi).

confidential *adj* confidentiel.

confine *vt* limiter.

confinement *n* détention *f*; alitement *m*.

confirm *vt* confirmer; ratifier.

confirmation *n* confirmation *f*.

confiscate *vt* confisquer.

confiscation *n* confiscation *f*.

conflict *n* conflit *m*; lutte *f*.

conflicting *adj* contradictoire.

conform *vi* se conformer (à).

conformity *n* conformité *f*.

confront *vt* confronter.

confrontation *n* confrontation *f*.

confuse *vt* confondre.

confusion *n* confusion *f*; désordre *m*.

congeal *vi* se congeler.

congenial *adj* sympathique.

congenital *adj* congénital.

congestion *n* congestion *f*.

congratulate *vt* complimenter, féliciter.

congratulations *npl* félicitations *fpl*.

congregate *vt* rassembler, réunir.

congregation *n* assemblée *f*.

congress *n* congrès *m*; conférence *f*.

congruity *n* congruence *f*.

congruous *adj* congru, approprié.

conifer *n* conifère *m*.

conjecture *n* conjecture.

conjugal *adj* conjugal.

conjunction *n* conjonction *f*.

conjuncture *n* conjoncture *f*.

connect *vt* relier, joindre.

connection *n* liaison, connexion *f*.

connoisseur *n* connaisseur *m* -euse *f*.

conquer *vt* conquérir.

conqueror *n* conquérant *m*.

conquest *n* conquête *f*.

conscience *n* conscience *f*.

conscientious *adj* consciencieux.

conscious *adj* conscient.

consciousness *n* conscience *f*.

consecrate *vt* consacrer.

consecration *n* consécration *f*.

consecutive *adj* consécutif.

consensus n consensus m.

consent n consentement:—vi consentir.

consequence n conséquence f; importance f.

consequent adj consécutif.

conservation n conservation f.

conservative adj conservateur.

conserve vt conserver:—n conserve f.

consider vt considérer.

considerable adj considérable.

considerate adj prévenant, attentionné.

consideration n considération f.

consign vt confier, remettre.

consignment n expédition f.

consist vi consister (en).

consistency n consistance f.

consistent adj constant; cohérent.

consolation n consolation f; réconfort m.

console vt consoler.

consolidate vt consolider.

consolidation n consolidation f.

conspicuous adj voyant, manifeste.

conspiracy n conspiration f.

conspire vi conspirer.

constancy n constance.

constant adj constant.

constellation n constellation f.

consternation n consternation f.

constitute vt constituer; établir.

constitution n constitution f.

constitutional adj constitutionnel.

constrain vt contraindre.

constraint n contrainte f.

constrict vt serrer; gêner.

construct vt construire, bâtir.

construction n construction f.

consulate n consulat m.

consult vt consulter.

consultation n consultation.

consume vt consommer.

consumer n consommateur m -trice f.

consumerism n consumérisme m.

consummate vt consommer:—adj accompli.

consummation n consommation f.

consumption n consommation f.

contact n contact m.

contagious adj contagieux.

contain vt contenir.

container n récipient m.

contaminate vt contaminer.

contamination n contamination f.

contemplate vt contempler.

contemplation n contemplation f.

contemporary adj contemporain.

contempt n mépris, dédain m.

contemptible adj méprisable.

contemptuous adj méprisant.

contend vi combattre.

content adj content, satisfait:—vt contenter, satisfaire:—n contentement m.

contention n querelle, altercation f.

contentment n contentement m, satisfaction f.

contest vt contester, discuter:—n concours m.

contestant n concurrent m, -e f.

context n contexte m.

continent n continent m.

continental adj continental.

contingency n contingence f.

contingent n contingent m:—adj contingent.

continual adj continuel.

continuation n continuation.

continue vt vi continuer.

continuous *adj* continu.
contort *vt* tordre, déformer.
contortion *n* contorsion *f*.
contour *n* contour *m*.
contraception *n* contraception *f*.
contraceptive *n* contraceptif *m*:—*adj* contraceptif.
contract *vt* contracter:—*n* contrat *m*.
contradict *vt* contredire.
contradiction *n* contradiction *f*.
contradictory *adj* contradictoire.
contraption *n* gadget, bidule (*fam*) *m*.
contrary *adj* contraire:—*n* contraire *m*.
contrast *n* contraste *m*:—*vt* contraster.
contravention *n* infraction *f*.
contribute *vt* contribuer.
contribution *n* contribution *f*.
contrite *adj* contrit, repentant.
contrivance *n* dispositif *m*; invention *f*.
control *n* contrôle *m*; maîtrise *f*:—*vt* maîtriser; contrôler.
controversial *adj* polémique.
controversy *n* polémique *f*.
contusion *n* contusion *f*.
conurbation *n* conurbation *f*.
convalescence *n* convalescence *f*.
convalescent *adj* convalescent.
convene *vt* convoquer.
convenience *n* commodité, convenance *f*.
convenient *adj* commode, pratique
convention *n* convention *f*.
conventional *adj* conventionnel.
converge *vi* converger.
convergence *n* convergence *f*.
convergent *adj* convergent.
conversant *adj* au courant; compétent.
conversation *n* conversation *f*.
converse *vi* converser.

conversion *n* conversion; transformation *f*.
convert *vt* convertir:—*n* converti *m*, -e *f*.
convey *vt* transporter.
conveyance *n* transport *m*; cession *f*.
convict *n* détenu *m*, -e *f*.
conviction *n* condamnation *f*; conviction *f*.
convince *vt* convaincre, persuader.
convivial *adj* jovial.
conviviality *n* jovialité *f*.
convoke *vt* convoquer.
convoy *n* convoi *m*.
convulse *vt* ébranler.
convulsion *n* convulsion *f*; bouleversement *m*.
convulsive *adj* convulsif.
cook *n* cuisinier *m*, -ière *f*:—*vt* cuire.
cooker *n* cuisinière *f*.
cookery *n* cuisine *f*.
cool *adj* frais:—*n* fraîcheur *f*:—*vt* rafraîchir.
coolness *n* fraîcheur *f*; sang-froid *m*.
cooperate *vi* coopérer.
cooperation *n* coopération *f*.
cooperative *adj* coopératif.
coordinate *vt* coordonner.
coordination *n* coordination *f*.
cope *vi* se débrouiller.
copious *adj* copieux.
copy *n* copie *f*:—*vt* copier.
copyright *n* droit d'auteur *m*.
coral *n* corail *m*.
cord *n* corde *f*, cordon *m*.
cordial *adj* cordial, chaleureux.
core *n* trognon *m*; noyau, centre, cœur *m*.
cork *n* bouchon *m*:—*vt* boucher.
corkscrew *n* tire-bouchon *m*.

corn *n* maïs *m*; grain *m*; blé *m*.

corner *n* coin *m*; angle *m*.

cornerstone *n* pierre angulaire *f*.

corollary *n* corollaire *m*.

coronation *n* couronnement *m*.

coroner *n* coroner *m*.

corporate *adj* en commun; d'entreprise.

corporation *n* corporation *f*; société par actions *f*.

corps *n* corps *m*.

corpse *n* cadavre *m*.

corpulent *adj* corpulent.

correct *vt* corriger; rectifier:—*adj* correct.

correction *n* correction *f*; rectification *f*.

corrective *adj* correcteur, correctif: —*n* correcteur *m*.

correctness *n* correction *f*.

correlation *n* corrélation *f*.

correlative *adj* corrélatif.

correspond *vi* correspondre.

correspondence *n* correspondance *f*.

correspondent *adj* correspondant: — *n* correspondant *m*, -e *f*.

corridor *n* couloir, corridor *m*.

corroborate *vt* corroborer.

corrode *vt* corroder.

corrosion *n* corrosion *f*.

corrosive *adj n* corrosif *m*.

corrupt *vt* corrompre:—*adj* corrompu.

corruption *n* corruption *f*; dépravation *f*.

cosmetic *adj n* cosmétique *m*.

cosmic *adj* cosmique.

cosmopolitan *adj* cosmopolite.

cost *n* prix, coût *m*:—*vi* coûter.

costly *adj* coûteux, cher.

costume *n* costume *m*.

cottage *n* cottage *m*.

cotton *n* coton *m*.

cotton wool *n* coton hydrophile *m*.

couch *n* canapé, divan *m*.

cough *n* toux *f*.—*vi* tousser.

council *n* conseil *m*.

counsel *n* conseil *m*; avocat *m*.

counsellor *n* conseiller *m*, -ère *f*.

count *vt* compter:—*n* compte *m*.

countenance *n* visage *m*.

counter *n* comptoir *m*; jeton *m*.

counteract *vt* contrecarrer.

counterbalance *vt* contrebalancer.

counterfeit *vt* contrefaire:—*adj* faux.

counterpart *n* contrepartie *f*.

countersign *vt* contresigner.

countified *adj* rustique; campagnard.

country *n* pays *m*; patrie *f*:—*adj* rustique; campagnard.

countryman *n* campagnard *m*; compatriote *m*.

county *n* comté *m*.

couple *n* couple *m*:—*vt* unir, associer.

coupon *n* coupon *m*.

courage *n* courage *m*.

courageous *adj* courageux.

courier *n* messager *m*; guide *m*.

course *n* cours *m*; route *f*; chemin *m*: —of ~ bien sûr.

court *n* cour *f*; tribunal *m*:—*vt* courtiser. *adj* courtois

courtesy *n* courtoisie *f*.

courthouse *n* palais de justice *m*.

courtroom *n* salle de tribunal *f*.

cousin *n* cousin *m*, -e *f*.

cover *n* couverture *f*:—*vt* (re)couvrir.

covert *adj* voilé; caché.

cover-up *n* dissimulation *f*.

covet *vt* convoiter.

cow *n* vache *f*.

coward *n* lâche *mf*.

cowardice n lâcheté f.
cowboy n cowboy m.
coy adj timide; coquet; évasif.
coyness n timidité f; modestie f.
crab n crabe m.
crack n craquement m; fente f:—vt fêler:—vi se fêler; craquer.
crackle vi crépiter, pétiller.
cradle n berceau m:—vt bercer.
craft n habileté f; barque f.
craftsman n artisan m.
crafty adj astucieux, rusé.
cram vt bourrer:—vi s'entasser.
cramp n crampe f:—vt entraver.
crane n grue f.
crash vi s'écraser:—n fracas m; collision f.
crate n caisse f; cageot m.
crater n cratère m.
crawl vi ramper.
crayon n crayon m.
craze n manie f, engouement m.
craziness n folie f.
crazy adj fou.
creak vi grincer, craquer.
cream n crème f:—adj crème.
crease n pli m:—vt froisser.
create vt créer; causer.
creation n création f.
creature n créature f.
credence n croyance; créance f.
credibility n crédibilité f.
credible adj crédible.
credit n crédit m; honneur m.
creditable adj estimable, honorable.
credit card n carte de crédit f.
creep vi ramper.
cremate vt incinérer.
cremation n incinération, crémation f.

crematorium n crématoire m.
crest n crête f.
crevice n fissure, lézarde f.
crew n bande, équipe f; équipage m.
crib n berceau m; mangeoire f.
crime n crime m; délit m.
criminal adj criminel:—n criminel m, -elle f.
cripple n, adj invalide mf:—vt paralyser.
crisis n crise f.
criterion n critère m.
critic n critique m.
critic(al) adj critique.
criticise vt critiquer.
criticism n critique f.
croak vi coasser, croasser.
crockery n poterie f.
crocodile n crocodile m.
crook n (fam) escroc m.
crop n culture f; récolte f.
cross n croix f; croisement m:—adj fâché:—vt traverser, croiscr.
crossbreed n hybride m.
crossing n traversée f; passage pour piétons m.
cross-reference n renvoi m, référence f.
crossroad n carrefour m.
crouch vi s'accroupir, se tapir.
crow n corbeau m.
crowd n foule f; monde m; vi s'entasser.
crown n couronne f:—vt couronner.
crucial adj crucial.
crucifix n crucifix m.
crude adj brut, grossier.
cruel adj cruel.
cruelty n cruauté f.
crumb n miette f.
crumble vt émietter; effriter:—vi s'émietter.

crunch *vt* croquer.
crush *vt* écraser; opprimer:—*n* cohue *f.*
crust *n* croûte *f.*
crutch *n* béquille *f.*
crux *n* cœur *m.*
cry *vt vi* crier; pleurer:—*n* cri *m*; sanglot *m.*
crystal *n* cristal *m.*
crystalline *adj* cristallin; pur.
crystallise *vi* se cristalliser.
cube *n* cube *m.*
cuddle *vt* embrasser.
cuff *n* manchette *f.*
culinary *adj* culinaire.
culminate *vi* culminer.
culpable *adj* coupable.
culprit *n* coupable *mf.*
cult *n* culte *m.*
cultivate *vt* cultiver.
cultivation *n* culture *f.*
culture *n* culture *f.*
cumbersome *adj* encombrant.
cumulative *adj* cumulatif.
cunning *adj* astucieux, rusé.
cup *n* tasse, coupe *f.*
cupboard *n* placard *m.*
curb *n* frein *m*:—*vt* freiner, juguler.
cure *n* remède *m*; cure *f*:—*vt* guérir.
curiosity *n* curiosité *f.*

curious *adj* curieux.
curl *n* boucle de cheveux *f*:—*vt* boucler.
curly *adj* frisé, bouclé.
currency *n* monnaie *f*; cours *m.*
current *adj* courant; actuel:—*n* courant *m.*
current affairs *npl* actualité *f.*
curse *vt* maudire.
curt *adj* succinct; sec.
curtain *n* rideau *m.*
curve *vt* courber:—*n* courbe *f.*
cushion *n* coussin *m.*
custodian *n* gardien *m*, -ienne *f.*
custom *n* coutume *f*, usage *m.*
customary *adj* habituel, coutumier.
customer *n* client *m*, -e *f.*
customs *npl* douane *f.*
customs officer *n* douanier *m.*
cut *vt* découper; couper:—*n* coup *m*; coupure *f.*
cutlery *n* couverts *mpl.*
cutting *n* coupure *f.*
cycle *n* cycle *m*; bicyclette *f*:—*vi* aller à bicyclette.
cycling *n* cyclisme *m.*
cyclist *n* cycliste *mf.*
cylinder *n* cylindre *m*; rouleau *m.*
cynic(al) *adj* cynique:—*n* cynique *mf.*

D

dad(dy) *n* papa *m.*
daily *adj* quotidien:—*adv* quotidiennement.
daintiness *n* élégance *f*; délicatesse *f.*
dainty *adj* délicat; élégant.
dairy *n* laiterie *f.*
dam *n* barrage *m*:—*vt* endiguer.

damage *n* dommage *m*; tort *m*:—*vt* endommager.
damnation *n* damnation *f.*
damp *adj* humide:—*vt* humidifier.
dampen *vt* humidifier.
dance *n* danse *f*; soirée dansante *f*:—*vi*, *vt* danser.
dancer *n* danseur *m*, -euse *f.*

danger n danger m.

dangerous adj dangereux.

dangle vi pendre.

dare vi oser:—vt défier.

daring n audace f:—adj audacieux.

dark adj sombre, obscur:—n obscurité f;
ignorance f.

darken vt assombrir:—vi s'assombrir.

darkness n obscurité f.

darling n, adj chéri m, -e f.

dart n dard m.

dash vi se dépêcher.

data n données fpl.

data processing n traitement de données m.

date n date f; rendez-vous m.

dated adj démodé.

daughter n fille f:—~ in-law belle-fille f.

dawn n aube f.

day n jour m, journée f:—~ by ~ de
jour en jour.

daylight n lumière du jour.

daze vt étourdir.

dazzle vt éblouir.

dead adj mort l.

deaden vt amortir.

deadline n date limite f.

deadlock n impasse f.

deadly adj mortel.

deaf adj sourd.

deafen vt assourdir.

deafness n surdité f.

deal n accord m; marché m:—a great
~ beaucoup:—vt distribuer.

dealer n commerçant m; trafiquant m.

dear adj ~ly adv cher.

dearness n cherté f.

death n mort f.

death certificate n acte de décès m.

death penalty n peine de mort f.

debar vt exclure.

debase vt dégrader.

debasement n dégradation f.

debatable adj discutable.

debate n débat m:—vt discuter, examiner.

debilitate vt débiliter.

debit n débit m:—vt débiter.

debt n dette f:—get into ~ s'endetter.

debtor n débiteur m, -trice f.

decade n décennie f.

decadence n décadence f.

decaffeinated adj décaféiné.

decay vi décliner; pourrir:—n pouris-
sement m.

deceased adj décédé.

deceit n tromperie f.

deceive vt tromper.

December n décembre m.

decency n décence f; pudeur f.

decent adj décent; bien, bon.

decide vt décider:—vi se décider.

decided adj décidé.

decimate vt décimer.

decipher vt déchiffrer.

decision n décision, détermination f.

decisive adj décisif.

deck n pont m:—vt orner.

declaration n déclaration f.

declare vt déclarer.

decode vt décoder.

decor n décor m; décoration f.

decorate vt décorer, orner.

decoration n décoration f.

decorative adj décoratif.

decoy n leurre m.

decrease vt diminuer:—n diminution f.

decree n décret m:—vt décréter; ordonner.

decrepit *adj* décrépit.
dedicate *vt* dédier; consacrer.
dedication *n* dédicace *f*; consacration *f*.
deduce *vt* déduire, conclure.
deduct *vt* déduire, soustraire.
deed *n* action *f*; exploit *m*.
deep *adj* profond.
deepen *vt* approfondir.
deepness *n* profondeur *f*.
default *n* défaut *m*:—*vi* manquer à ses engagements.
defeat *n* défaite *f*:—*vt* vaincre; frustrer.
defect *n* défaut *m*.
defective *adj* défectueux.
defend *vt* défendre; protéger.
defendant *n* accusé *m*, -e *f*.
defense *n* défense *f*; protection *f*.
defensive *adj* défensif.
defer *vt* déférer.
deference *n* déférence *f*.
defiance *n* défi *m*.
deficiency *n* défaut *m*; manque *m*.
deficient *adj* insuffisant.
define *vt* définir.
definite *adj* sûr; précis.
definition *n* définition *f*.
definitive *adj* définitif.
deflect *vt* dévier.
deform *vt* déformer.
deformity *n* déformité *f*.
defraud *vt* frauder.
deft *adj* habile.
degenerate *vi* dégénérer:—*adj* dégénéré.
degeneration *n* dégénération *f*.
degradation *n* dégradation *f*.
degrade *vt* dégrader.
degree *n* degré *m*; diplôme *m*.
dejected *adj* découragé.

dejection *n* découragement *m*.
delay *vt* retarder:—*n* retard *m*.
delegate *vt* déléguer:—*n* délégué *m*, -e *f*.
delegation *n* délégation *f*.
delete *vt* effacer.
deliberate *vt* examiner:—*adj* délibéré.
deliberation *n* délibération *f*.
delicacy *n* délicatesse *f*.
delicate *adj* délicat.
delicious *adj* délicieux.
delight *n* délice *m*:—*vt* enchanter.
delighted *adj* enchanté.
delightful *adj* charmant.
delinquency *n* délinquance *f*.
delinquent *n* délinquant *m*, -e *f*.
delirious *adj* délirant.
deliver *vt* livrer; délivrer.
delivery *n* livraison *f*.
delude *vt* tromper.
delusion *n* tromperie *f*; illusion *f*.
demand *n* demande *f*:—*vt* exiger; réclamer.
demanding *adj* exigeant.
demean *vi* s'abaisser.
demeanour *n* conduite *f*.
democracy *n* démocratie *f*.
democratic *adj* démocratique.
demolish *vt* démolir.
demolition *n* démolition *f*.
demonstrate *vt* démontrer, prouver:—*vi* manifester.
demonstration *n* démonstration *f*.
demonstrator *n* manifestant *m*, -e *f*.
demoralisation *n* démoralisation *f*.
demoralise *vt* démoraliser.
den *n* antre *m*.
denial *n* dénégation *f*.
denims *npl* jean *m*.

denomination n valeur f; dénomination f.

denote vt dénoter, indiquer.

denounce vt dénoncer.

dense adj dense, épais.

dentist n dentiste mf.

dentistry n dentisterie f.

denture n dentier m.

denunciation n dénonciation f.

deny vt nier.

deodorant n déodorant m.

depart vi partir.

department n département m; service m.

department store n grand magasin m.

departure n départ m.

depend vi dépendre.

dependable adj fiable; sûr.

dependent adj dépendant.

depict vt dépeindre, décrire.

deplorable adj déplorable.

deplore vt déplorer, lamenter.

depopulated adj dépeuplé.

deport vt déporter.

deportation n déportation f.

deportment n comportement m.

deposit vt déposer:—n dépôt m; caution f.

deposition n déposition f.

depot n dépôt m.

depreciate vi se déprécier.

depreciation n dépréciation f.

depress vt déprimer.

depression n dépression f.

deprivation n privation f.

deprive vt priver.

depth n profondeur f.

deputation n députation f.

depute vt députer, déléguer.

deputy n député m.

deranged adj dérangé.

derelict adj abandonné.

deride vt se moquer de.

derision n dérision f.

derivative n dérivé m.

derive vt vi dériver.

descend vi descendre.

descendant n descendant m, -e f.

descent n descente f.

describe vt décrire.

description n description f.

descriptive adj descriptif.

desert n désert m:—adj désert.

desert vt abandonner; déserter:—n mérite m.

desertion n désertion f.

deserve vt mériter.

design vt concevoir; dessiner:—n dessein m.

designate vt désigner.

desirable adj désirable.

desire n désir m:—vt désirer.

desist vi abandonner.

desk n bureau m.

desolate adj désert, désolé.

despair n désespoir m:—vi se désespérer.

desperate adj désespéré.

desperation n désespoir m.

despicable adj méprisable.

despise vt mépriser.

despite prep malgré.

despondency n abattement m.

despondent adj abattu.

dessert n dessert m.

destination n destination f.

destine vt destiner.

destiny n destin, sort m.

destitute adj indigent.

destitution n indigence f.

destroy vt détruire.

destruction n destruction f.

detach vt séparer, détacher.

detachable adj détachable.

detail n détail m:—**in ~** en détail:—vt détailler.

detain vt retenir; détenir.

detect vt détecter.

detection n détection f; découverte f.

detective n détective m.

detention n détention f.

deteriorate vt détériorer.

deterioration n détérioration f.

determination n détermination f.

determine vt déterminer, décider.

detest vt détester.

detestable adj détestable.

detour n déviation f.

detriment n détriment m.

devaluation n dévaluation f.

devastate vt dévaster.

devastation n dévastation f.

develop vt développer.

development n développement m.

deviate vi dévier.

deviation n déviation f.

device n mécanisme m.

devil n diable, démon m.

devise vt inventer; concevoir.

devoid adj dépourvu.

devote vt consacrer.

devoted adj dévoué.

devotion n dévotion f.

devour vt dévorer.

dew n rosée f.

dexterity n dextérité f.

diagnosis n (med) diagnostic m.

diagram n diagramme m.

dialect n dialecte m.

dialogue n dialogue m.

diamond n diamant m.

diary n journal m.

dictate vt dicter:—n ordre m.

dictionary n dictionnaire m.

die vi mourir.

diet n diète f; régime m:—vi être au régime.

differ vi différer.

difference n différence f.

different adj différent.

difficult adj difficile.

difficulty n difficulté f.

dig vt creuser.

digest vt digérer.

digestion n digestion f.

digestive adj digestif.

digit n chiffre m.

digital adj digital.

dignified adj digne.

dignity n dignité f.

digression n digression f.

dilemma n dilemme m.

diligence n assiduité f.

diligent adj assidu.

dilute vt diluer.

dim adj indistinct; faible; sombre.

dimension n dimension f.

diminish vt vi diminuer.

diminutive n diminutif m.

din n vacarme m.

dine vi dîner.

dinner n dîner m.

dint n:—**by ~ of** à force de.

dip vt tremper.

diploma n diplôme m.

diplomat n diplomate m.

diplomatic adj diplomatique.

dire adj atroce, affreux.

direct *adj* direct:—*vt* diriger.
direction *n* direction *f*; instruction *f*.
director *n* directeur *m*, -trice *f*.
directory *n* annuaire *m*.
dirt *n* saleté *f*.
dirty *adj* sale.
disability *n* incapacité *f*; infirmité *f*.
disabled *adj* infirme.
disadvantage *n* désavantage *m*:—*vt* désavantager.
disagree *vi* ne pas être d'accord.
disagreeable *adj* désagréable.
disagreement *n* désaccord *m*.
disallow *vt* rejeter.
disappear *vi* disparaître.
disappearance *n* disparition *f*.
disappoint *vt* décevoir.
disappointment *n* déception *f*.
disapproval *n* désapprobation *f*.
disapprove *vt* désapprouver.
disarm *vt* désarmer.
disaster *n* désastre *m*.
disastrous *adj* désastreux.
disbelief *n* incrédulité *f*.
discard *vt* jeter.
discern *vt* discerner, percevoir.
discerning *adj* perspicace.
disciple *n* disciple *m*.
discipline *n* discipline *f*:—*vt* discipliner.
disclose *vt* révéler.
disclosure *n* révélation *f*.
disco *n* discothèque *f*.
discomfort *n* incommodité *f*.
disconnect *vt* débrancher.
disconsolate *adj* inconsolable.
discontent *n* mécontentement *m*:—*adj* mécontent.
discontented *adj* mécontent.

discontinue *vt* interrompre.
discord *n* discorde *f*.
discount *n* escompte *m*:—*vt* escompter.
discourage *vt* décourager.
discouragement *n* découragement *m*.
discourse *n* discours *m*.
discourteous *adj* discourtois.
discover *vt* découvrir.
discovery *n* découverte *f*.
discredit *vt* discréditer.
discreet *adj* discret.
discrepancy *n* contradiction *f*.
discretion *n* discrétion *f*.
discretionary *adj* discrétionnaire.
discriminate *vt* distinguer; discriminer.
discrimination *n* discrimination *f*.
discuss *vt* discuter.
discussion *n* discussion *f*.
disdain *vt* dédaigner:—*n* dédain, mépris *m*.
disdainful *adj* dédaigneux.
disease *n* maladie *f*.
disembark *vt vi* débarquer.
disenchant *vt* désenchanter.
disenchanted *adj* désenchanté.
disengage *vt* dégager.
disfigure *vt* défigurer.
disgrace *n* honte *f*; scandale *m*:—*vt* déshonorer.
disgraceful *adj* honteux.
disguise *vt* déguiser:—*n* déguisement *m*.
disgust *n* dégoût *m*:—*vt* dégoûter.
dish *n* plat *m*; assiette *f*.
dishearten *vt* démoraliser.
dishonest *adj* malhonnête.
dishonesty *n* malhonnêteté *f*.
disillusion *vt* désillusionner.
disillusioned *adj* désillusionné.
disinfect *vt* désinfecter.

disinfectant *n* désinfectant *m*.
disinherit *vt* déshériter.
disintegrate *vi* se désintégrer.
disinterested *adj* désintéressé.
disk *n* disque *m*; disquette *f*.
dislike *n* aversion *f*:—*vt* ne pas aimer.
dislocate *vt* disloquer.
dislocation *n* dislocation *f*.
dislodge *vt* déloger.
disloyal *adj* déloyal.
dismantle *vt* démonter.
dismay *n* consternation *f*.
dismiss *vt* renvoyer; écarter.
dismissal *n* renvoi *m*; rejet *m*.
disobedience *n* désobéissance *f*.
disobedient *adj* désobéissant.
disobey *vt* désobéir.
disorder *n* désordre *m*.
disorderly *adj* en désordre, confus.
disorganization *n* désorganisation *f*.
disparage *vt* dénigrer.
disparity *n* disparité *f*.
dispatch *vt* envoyer:—*n* envoi *m*;
dépêche *f*.
dispel *vt* dissiper.
dispensary *n* dispensaire *m*.
dispense *vt* dispenser; distribuer.
disperse *vt* disperser.
displace *vt* déplacer.
display *vt* exposer:—*n* exposition *f*.
displeased *adj* mécontent.
displeasure *n* mécontentement *m*.
dispose *vt* disposer.
disposition *n* disposition *f*.
disprove *vt* réfuter.
dispute *n* dispute *f*; controverse *f*:—*vt*
mettre en cause.
disqualify *vt* rendre incapable.
dissatisfaction *n* mécontentement *m*.

dissatisfied *adj* mécontent.
disseminate *vt* disséminer.
dissension *n* dissension *f*.
dissent *n* dissension *f*.
dissertation *n* thèse *f*.
dissident *n* dissident *m*, -e *f*.
dissimilar *adj* dissemblable.
dissimilarity *n* dissemblance *f*.
dissipate *vt* dissiper.
dissipation *n* dissipation *f*.
dissolution *n* dissolution *f*.
dissolve *vt* dissoudre.
dissonance *n* dissonance *f*.
dissuade *vt* dissuader.
distance *n* distance *f*.
distant *adj* distant.
distaste *n* dégoût *m*.
distasteful *adj* désagréable.
distil *vt* distiller.
distinct *adj* distinct.
distinction *n* distinction *f*.
distinctive *adj* distinctif.
distinguish *vt* distinguer; discerner.
distort *vt* déformer.
distortion *n* distortion *f*.
distract *vt* distraire.
distracted *adj* distrait.
distraction *n* distraction *f*; confusion *f*.
distress *n* souffrance *f*:—*vt* désoler.
distribute *vt* distribuer, répartir.
distribution *n* distribution *f*.
district *n* district *m*.
disturb *vt* déranger.
disturbance *n* dérangement *m*;
trouble *m*.
disturbed *adj* troublé.
disturbing *adj* troublant.
disuse *n* désuétude *f*.
disused *adj* abandonné.

ditch n fossé m.

dive vi plonger.

diver n plongeur m, -euse f.

diverge vi diverger.

divergent adj divergent.

diverse adj divers, différent.

diversion n diversion f.

diversity n diversité f.

divert vt dévier; divertir.

divide vt diviser:—vi se diviser.

divine adj divin.

divinity n divinité f.

divisible adj divisible.

division n division f.

divorce n divorce m:—vi divorcer.

divorced adj divorcé.

divulge vt divulguer.

dizziness n vertige m.

dizzy adj pris de vertige.

do vt faire.

docile adj docile.

dock n dock m.

do-it-yourself n bricolage m.

doctor n docteur m.

doctrine n doctrine f.

document n document m.

documentary adj documentaire.

dodge vt esquiver.

dog n chien m.

dogmatic adj dogmatique.

doll n poupée f.

dolphin n dauphin m.

dome n dôme m.

domestic adj domestique.

domesticate vt domestiquer.

domesticity n domesticité f.

domicile n domicile m.

dominate vi dominer.

domination n domination f.

donate vt donner, faire don de.

donation n donation f.

donkey n âne m.

donor n donneur m; donateur m.

door n porte f.

doorway n entrée f.

dormant adj latent; dormant.

dormitory n dortoir m.

dosage n dose f; dosage m.

dose n dose f:—vt doser.

dossier n dossier m.

dot n point m.

double adj double:—vt doubler:—n double m.

double room n chambre pour deux f.

double-dealing n duplicité f.

doubt n doute m:—vt douter de.

doubtful adj douteux.

douse vt éteindre.

dove n colombe f.

down n duvet m:—prep en bas:—upside ~ à l'envers.

down-to-earth adj pratique; terre à terre.

downfall n ruine f.

downhearted adj découragé.

downhill adv en descendant, dans la descente.

downstairs adv en bas.

dowry n dot f.

doze vi somnoler.

dozen n douzaine f.

drab adj gris; morne.

drag vt tirer:—n drague f; ennui m.

drain vt drainer; vider:—n tuyau d'écoulement m.

drama n drame m.

dramatic adj dramatique.

dramatist n dramaturge mf.

draught *n* courant d'air *m*.
draw *vt* tirer; dessiner.
drawback *n* désavantage.
drawer *n* tiroir *m*.
drawing *n* dessin *m*.
drawing room *n* salon *m*.
dread *n* terreur *f*:—*vt* redouter.
dreadful *adj* horrible.
dream *n* rêve *m*:—*vi, vt* rêver.
dreary *adj* triste, morne.
dress *vi* s'habiller:—*n* robe *f*.
dressing *n* pansement *m*; sauce *f*.
dressy *adj* élégant.
drift *vi* aller à la dérive.
drill *n* perceuse *f*; *vt* percer.
drink *vt vi* boire:—*n* boisson *f*.
drinker *n* buveur *m*, -euse *f*.
drip *vi* goutter:—*n* goutte *f*.
drive *vt vi* conduire.
driver *n* conducteur *m*, -trice *f*; chauffeur *m*.
driving licence *n* permis *m* de conduire.
drizzle *vi* pleuvasser.
drop *n* goutte *f*:—*vt* laisser tomber.
drought *n* sécheresse *f*.
drown *vt* noyer:—*vi* se noyer.
drowsiness *n* somnolence *f*.
drug *n* drogue *f*:—*vt* droguer.
drum *n* tambour *m*:—*vi* jouer du tambour.

drunk *adj* ivre.
drunken *adj* ivre.
drunkenness *n* ivresse *f*.
dry *adj* sec:—*vt* faire sécher:—*vi* sécher.
dryness *n* sécheresse *f*.
dual *adj* double.
dub *adj* doubler.
due *adj* dû, *f* due *n* droit *m*.
duel *n* duel *m*.
dull *adj* terne; insipide.
duly *adv* dûment.
dumb *adj* muet.
dump *n* tas *m*:—*vt* jeter.
duplicate *vt* dupliquer.
duplicity *n* duplicité *f*.
durability *n* durabilité *f*.
durable *adj* durable.
duration *n* durée *f*.
during *prep* pendant.
dusk *n* crépuscule *m*.
dust *n* poussière *f*:—*vt* épousseter.
dutiful *adj* obéissant, soumis.
duty *n* devoir *m*; obligation *f*.
dwarf *n* nain *m*, naine *f*:—*vt* rapetisser.
dwell *vi* habiter, vivre.
dwelling *n* habitation *f*; domicile *m*.
dye *vt* teindre:—*n* teinture *f*.
dying *p, adj* mourant.
dynamic *adj* dynamique.
dynasty *n* dynastie *f*.

E

each *pn* chacun:—~ **other** les un(e)s les autres.
eager *adj* enthousiaste.
eagerness *n* enthousiasme *m*.
eagle *n* aigle *m*.
ear *n* oreille *f*; ouïe *f*.

early *adj* premier:—*adv* tôt.
earn *vt* gagner.
earnest *adj* sérieux
earth *n* terre *f*:—*vt* brancher à la terre.
earthquake *n* tremblement de terre *m*.
ease *n* aise *f*; facilité *f*.

easiness n facilité f.

east n est m; orient m.

Easter n Pâques fpl.

eastern adj de l'est, oriental.

easy adj facile.

eat vt vi manger.

ebb n reflux m:—vi refluer.

eccentric adj excentrique.

eccentricity n excentricité f.

echo n écho m:—vi résonner.

eclipse n éclipse f:—vt éclipser.

ecology n écologie f.

economic adj économique

economist n économiste mf.

economise vt économiser.

economy n économie f.

ecstasy n extase f.

ecstatic adj extatique.

edge n fil m; pointe f.

edible adj mangeable.

edifice n édifice m.

edit vt diriger; rédiger.

edition n édition f.

editor n rédacteur m, -trice f.

educate vt éduquer; instruire.

education n éducation f.

efface vt effacer.

effect n effet mf:—~s npl biens mpl:
—vt effectuer.

effective adj efficace; effectif.

effectiveness n efficacité f.

effectual adj efficace.

effeminate adj efféminé.

effervescence n effervescence f.

efficiency n efficacité f.

efficient adj efficace.

effort n effort m.

egg n œuf m.

ego(t)ist n égoïste mf.

ego(t)istical adj égoïste.

eight adj n huit m.

eighteen adj n dix-huit m.

eighteenth adj n dix-huitième mf.

eighth adj n huitième mf.

eightieth adj n quatre-vingtième mf.

eighty adj n quatre-vingt.

either pn n'importe lequel/laquelle:
—conj ou, soit.

eject vt éjecter, expulser.

ejection n éjection, expulsion f.

elaborate vt élaborer:—adj élaboré.

elapse vi passer.

elastic adj élastique.

elbow n coude m.

elder adj aîné.

eldest adj aîné.

elect vt élire; choisir.

election n élection f; choix m.

electoral adj électoral.

electorate n électorat m.

electric(al) adj électrique.

electrician n électricien m.

electricity n électricité f.

electrify vt électriser.

electronic adj électronique.

elegance n élégance f.

elegant adj élégant.

element n élément m.

elementary adj élémentaire.

elephant n éléphant m.

elevate vt élever, hausser.

elevation n élévation f; hauteur f.

eleven adj n onze m.

eleventh adj n onzième mf.

eligibility n éligibilité f.

eligible adj éligible.

eliminate vt éliminer.

elocution n élocution f.

eloquence *n* éloquence *f*.

eloquent *adj* éloquent.

else *pn* autre.

elsewhere *adv* ailleurs.

elude *vt* éluder; éviter.

emaciated *adj* émacié.

emancipate *vt* émanciper.

emancipation *n* émancipation *f*.

embargo *n* embargo *m*.

embark *vt* embarquer.

embarkation *n* embarcation *f*.

embarrass *vt* embarrasser.

embarrassment *n* embarras *m*.

embassy *n* ambassade *f*.

emblem *n* emblème *m*.

embody *vt* incorporer; incarner.

embrace *vt* étreindre; comprendre.

embryo *n* embryon *m*.

emerald *n* émeraude *f*.

emerge *vi* émerger; apparaître.

emergency *n* urgence *f*.

emergency exit *n* sortie de secours *f*.

emigrate *vi* émigrer.

emigration *n* émigration *f*.

emission *n* émission *f*.

emit *vt* émettre.

emotion *n* émotion *f*.

emotional *adj* émotionnel.

emphasise *vt* souligner, accentuer.

emphatic *adj* emphatique.

empire *n* empire *m*.

employ *vt* employer.

employee *n* employé *m*, -e *f*.

employer *n* employeur *m*.

employment *n* emploi, travail *m*.

emptiness *n* vide *m*.

empty *adj* vide; vain:—*vt* vider.

emulate *vt* imiter.

enable *vt* permettre.

enamour *vt* s'éprendre de.

encamp *vi* camper.

encampment *n* campement *m*.

encase *vt* entourer.

enchant *vt* enchanter.

enchantment *n* enchantement *m*.

encircle *vt* encercler.

enclose *vt* entourer.

enclosure *n* clôture *f*.

encompass *vt* comprendre.

encounter *n* rencontre *f*:—*vt* rencontrer.

encourage *vt* encourager.

encouragement *n* encouragement *m*.

encyclopedia *n* encyclopédie *f*.

end *n* fin *f*; extrémité *f*:—**to the ~ that** afin que:—*vt vi* terminer.

endanger *vt* mettre en danger.

endeavour *vi* s'efforcer:—*n* effort *m*.

endorse *vt* endosser; approuver.

endorsement *n* endos *m*; approbation *f*.

endurable *adj* supportable.

endurance *n* endurance *f*.

endure *vt* supporter:—*vi* durer.

enemy *n* ennemi *mf*.

energetic *adj* énergique.

energy *n* énergie, force *f*.

enfeeble *vt* affaiblir.

enfold *vt* envelopper.

enforce *vt* mettre en vigueur.

engage *vt* aborder.

engaged *adj* fiancé; occupé.

engagement *n* engagement *m*.

engender *vt* engendrer.

engine *n* moteur *m*; locomotive *f*.

engineer *n* ingénieur *m*; mécanicien *m*.

engineering *n* ingénierie *f*.

enigma *n* énigme *f*.

enjoy *vr*:—**to ~ oneself** s'amuser.

enjoyable *adj* agréable; amusant.

enjoyment *n* plaisir *m*; jouissance *f*.

enlarge *vt* agrandir; étendre.

enlargement *n* agrandissement *m*.

enlist *vt* recruter.

enliven *vt* animer; égayer.

enmity *n* inimitié *f*; haine *f*.

enormous *adj* énorme.

enough *adv* suffisamment; assez:—*n* assez *m*.

enrich *vt* enrichir; orner.

enrichment *n* enrichissement *m*.

enrol *vt* enrôler; inscrire.

ensue *vi* s'ensuivre.

ensure *vt* assurer.

entail *vt* impliquer, entraîner.

enter *vt* entrer dans; inscrire.

enterprise *n* entreprise *f*.

enterprising *adj* entreprenant.

entertain *vt* divertir.

entertaining *adj* divertissant, amusant.

enthusiasm *n* enthousiasme *m*.

enthusiast *n* enthousiaste *mf*.

enthusiastic *adj* enthousiaste.

entire *adj* entier, complet.

entitle *vt* intituler.

entity *n* entité *f*.

entrance *n* entrée *f*; admission *f*.

entrant *n* participant *m*, -e *f*.

entreat *vt* implorer.

entrust *vt* confier.

entry *n* entrée *f*.

enumerate *vt* énumérer.

envelop *vt* envelopper.

envelope *n* enveloppe *f*.

envious *adj* envieux.

environment *n* environnement *m*.

environmental *adj* relatif à l'environnement.

envisage *vt* envisager.

envy *n* envie *f*:—*vt* envier.

epidemic *adj* épidémique:—*n* épidémie *f*.

episode *n* épisode *m*.

epitomise *vt* incarner; résumer.

equable *adj* uniforme.

equal *adj* égal; semblable:—*n* égal *m*, -e *f*:—*vt* égaler.

equalise *vt* égaliser.

equality *n* égalité *f*.

equanimity *n* équanimité *f*.

equate *vt* égaliser.

equator *n* équateur *m*.

equilibrium *n* équilibre *m*.

equip *vt* équiper.

equipment *n* équipement *m*.

equivalent *adj n* équivalent *m*.

equivocal *adj* équivoque.

equivocate *vt* équivoquer.

era *n* ère *f*.

eradicate *vt* supprimer.

eradication *n* suppression *f*.

erase *vt* effacer.

eraser *n* gomme *f*.

erect *vt* ériger:—*adj* droit, debout.

erode *vt* éroder; ronger.

erotic *adj* érotique.

err *vi* se tromper.

errand *n* message *m*.

erratic *adj* changeant; irrégulier.

erroneous *adj* erroné.

error *n* erreur *f*.

erudite *adj* érudit.

eruption *n* éruption *f*.

escalate *vi* monter en flèche.

escape *vt* éviter:—*vi* s'évader, s'échapper:—*n* évasion *f*.

escort *n* escorte *f*:—*vt* escorter.

especial *adj* spécial.

essay n essai m.

essence n essence f.

essential n essentiel m:—adj essentiel.

establish vt établir.

establishment n établissement m.

estate n état m; biens mpl.

esteem vt estimer:—n estime f.

esthetic adj esthétique f.

estimate vt estimer; évaluer.

estimation n estimation.

estuary n estuaire m.

eternal adj éternel.

eternity n éternité f.

ethical adj éthique.

ethics npl éthique f.

ethnic adj ethnique.

etiquette n étiquette f.

evacuate vt évacuer.

evacuation n évacuation f.

evade vt éviter; échapper à.

evaluate vt évaluer.

evaporate vi s'évaporer.

evaporation n évaporation f.

evasion n dérobade f.

evasive adj évasif.

eve n veille f.

even adj pair:—adv même:—vt égaliser.

evening n soir m, soirée f.

evenness n égalité f; impartialité f.

event n événement m.

eventual adj final:—~ly adv finalement, en fin de comptes.

eventuality n éventualité f.

ever adv toujours; jamais.

everlasting adj éternel.

every adj chacun, chacune:—~where partout:—~thing tout:—~one, ~body tout le monde.

evict vt expulser.

eviction n expulsion f.

evidence n évidence f.

evident adj évident.

evil adj malveillant:—n mal m.

evocative adj évocateur.

evoke vt évoquer.

evolution n évolution f.

evolve vi évoluer.

exacerbate vt exacerber.

exact adj exact:—vt exiger.

exacting adj exigeant.

exaction n exaction f; extorsion f.

exactness n exactitude f.

exaggerate vt exagérer.

exaggeration n exagération f.

exalt vt exalter; élever.

examination n examen m.

examine vt examiner.

example n exemple m.

exasperate vt exaspérer.

exasperation n exaspération f.

excavate vt excaver, creuser.

excavation n excavation f.

exceed vt excéder, dépasser.

excel vt surpasser; vi exceller.

excellence n excellence f.

excellent adj excellent.

except vt excepter:—~(ing) prep excepté, à l'exception de.

exception n exception f.

exceptional adj exceptionnel.

excess n excès m.

excessive adj excessif.

exchange vt échanger:—n échange m.

exchange rate n taux de change m.

excise n impôt m.

excitable adj excitable.

excite vt exciter; animer.

excited *adj* animé, enthousiaste.

excitement *n* animation *f*.

exciting *adj* passionnant; stimulant.

exclaim *vi* s'exclamer.

exclamation *n* exclamation *f*.

exclude *vt* exclure.

exclusion *n* exclusion *f*, exception *f*.

exclusive *adj* exclusif.

excommunicate *vt* excommunier.

exculpate *vt* disculper; justifier.

excursion *n* excursion *f*; digression *f*.

excusable *adj* excusable.

excuse *vt* excuser:—*n* excuse *f*.

execute *vt* exécuter.

execution *n* exécution *f*.

executive *adj* exécutif.

exemplary *adj* exemplaire.

exemplify *vt* exemplifier.

exempt *adj* exempt.

exemption *n* exemption *f*.

exercise *n* exercice *m*:—*vt* exercer.

exert *vt* employer, exercer.

exertion *n* effort *m*.

exhale *vt* exhaler.

exhaust *n vt* épuiser.

exhaustion *n* épuisement *m*.

exhaustive *adj* exhaustif.

exhibit *vt* exhiber.

exhibition *n* exposition, présentation *f*.

exhilarating *adj* stimulant.

exhilaration *n* joie *f*, stimulation *f*.

exhume *vt* exhumer, déterrer.

exile *n* exil *m*:—*vt* exiler, déporter.

exist *vi* exister.

existence *n* existence *f*.

existent *adj* existant.

exit *n* sortie *f*:—*vi* sortir.

exonerate *vt* disculper.

exoneration *n* disculpation *f*.

exorbitant *adj* exorbitant, excessif.

exotic *adj* exotique.

expand *vt* étendre.

expanse *n* étendue *f*.

expansion *n* expansion *f*.

expect *vt* attendre; espérer.

expectancy *n* attente *f*, espoir *m*.

expectation *n* expectative *f*; attente *f*.

expediency *n* convenance *f*; opportunité *f*.

expedient *adj* opportun.

expedite *vt* accélérer; expédier.

expedition *n* expédition *f*.

expel *vt* expulser.

expend *vt* dépenser; utiliser.

expense *n* dépense *f*; coût *m*.

expensive *adj* cher; coûteux.

experience *n* expérience *f*; pratique *f*:—*vt* ressentir; connaître.

experienced *adj* expérimenté.

experiment *n* expérience *f*:—*vi* expérimenter.

experimental *adj* expérimental.

expert *adj* expert.

expertise *n* habileté *f*.

explain *vt* expliquer.

explanation *n* explication *f*.

explanatory *adj* explicatif.

explicit *adj* explicite.

explode *vt* faire exploser:—*vi* exploser.

exploit *vt* exploiter:—*n* exploit *m*.

exploitation *n* exploitation *f*.

exploration *n* exploration *f*.

explore *vt* explorer; sonder.

explorer *n* explorateur *m*, -trice *f*.

explosion *n* explosion *f*.

explosive *adj n* explosif *m*.

export *vt* exporter.

exportation n exportation f.

exporter n exportateur m, -trice f.

expose vt exposer; dévoiler.

exposition n exposition f.

exposure n exposition f; temps de pose m.

expound vt exposer; interpréter.

express vt exprimer:—adj exprès:—
n exprès m; (rail) rapide m.

expression n expression f.

expressive adj expressif.

expropriate vt exproprier.

expulsion n expulsion f.

exquisite adj exquis.

extemporise vi improviser.

extend vt étendre:—vi s'étendre.

extension n extension f.

extensive adj étendu.

extent n extension f.

extenuate vt atténuer.

exterior adj n extérieur m.

exterminate vt exterminer.

external adj externe.

extinct adj disparu; éteint.

extinction n extinction f.

extinguish vt éteindre.

extinguisher n extincteur m.

extort vt extorquer.

extortion n extorsion f.

extra adv particulièrement; n supplément m.

extract vt extraire:—n extrait m.

extraction n extraction f; origine f.

extraneous adj superflu; sans rapport.

extraordinary adj extraordinaire.

extravagance n extravagance f.

extravagant adj extravagant.

extreme adj extrême.

extremist adj n extrémiste mf.

extricate vt extirper, démêler.

extrovert adj n extraverti m, -e f.

exuberance n exubérance f.

exuberant adj exubérant.

eye n œil m:—vt regarder; lorgner.

eyebrow n sourcil m.

eyelash n cil m.

eyelid n paupière f.

eyesight n vue f.

F

fabric n tissu m.

fabricate vt fabriquer; inventer.

fabrication n fabrication f.

fabulous adj fabuleux.

face n visage m; mine f; apparence f:
—vt faire face à.

facet n facette f.

facile adj facile.

facilitate vt faciliter.

facility n facilité f; équipement m.

facing n revers m:—prep en face de.

fact n fait m; réalité f:—**in ~** en fait.

factory n usine f.

factual adj factuel.

faculty n faculté f.

fail vt échouer à; omettre:—vi
échouer; faiblir; manquer.

failure n faillite f; manquement m.

faint vi s'évanouir, défaillir:—n
évanouissement m:—adj faible.

fair adj beau; blond; équitable; considérable:—n foire f.

fairness n beauté f; justice f.

fair play n fair-play.

faith n foi f; croyance f; fidélité f.

faithful adj fidèle, loyal.

fake n falsification f:—adj faux:—vt falsifier.

fall vi tomber; baisser:—n chute f; automne m.

fallacy n erreur f; tromperie f.

fallibility n faillibilité f.

fallible adj faillible.

false adj faux.

false alarm n fausse alerte f.

falsify vt falsifier.

falter vi vaciller.

fame n réputation f; renommée.

familiar adj familier.

familiarise vt familiariser.

familiarity n familiarité f.

family n famille f.

famine n famine f.

famous adj célèbre, fameux.

fan n éventail m; ventilateur m:—vt éventer.

fancy n caprice m:—vt avoir envie de; s'imaginer.

fantastic adj fantastique; excentrique.

fantasy n fantaisie f.

far adv loin:—adj lointain, éloigné.

fare n prix (du voyage) m; tarif m; régime alimentaire m.

farewell n adieu m.

farm n ferme f:—vt cultiver.

farmer n fermier m; agriculteur m.

farming n agriculture f.

fascinate vt fasciner, captiver.

fascination n fascination f; charme m.

fashion n manière, façon f; mode f:— vt façonner.

fashionable adj à la mode; chic.

fast vi jeûner:—n jeûne m:—adj rapide:—adv rapidement.

fasten vt attacher; fixer.

fast food n restauration rapide f.

fat adj gros, gras:—n graisse f.

fatal adj mortel.

fatality n fatalité f.

fate n destin, sort m.

father n père m.

fatherhood n paternité f.

fatigue n fatigue f:—vt fatiguer.

fatuous adj imbécile.

fault n défaut m, faute f; délit m.

faulty adj défectueux.

favour n faveur f:—vt favoriser.

favourable adj favorable.

favourite n favori m:—adj favori.

fax n fax m:—vt envoyer par fax.

fear vt craindre:—n crainte f.

fearful adj effrayant; craintif.

fearless adj intrépide, courageux.

feasibility n faisabilité f.

feasible adj faisable.

feast n banquet m; fête f.

feat n exploit m; prouesse f.

feather n plume f.

feature n trait m:—vi figurer.

February n février m.

fed-up adj:—**to be ~** en avoir marre.

fee n honoraires mpl.

feeble adj faible, frêle.

feebleness n faiblesse f.

feed vt nourrir:—vi manger; se nourrir.

feel vt sentir; toucher:—n sensation f.

feeling n sensation f; sentiment m.

feign vt feindre, simuler.

fellow n homme, type m.

female n femelle f:—adj femelle.

feminine adj féminin.

feminist n féministe mf.

fence n barrière f; clôture f.

ferment n agitation f:—vi fermenter.

ferocious *adj* féroce.

ferocity *n* férocité *f*.

ferry *n* bac *m*; ferry *m*:—*vt* transporter.

fertile *adj* fertile, fécond.

fertility *n* fertilité, fécondité *f*.

fervent *adj* fervent; ardent.

fervour *n* ferveur *f*.

festival *n* fête *f*; festival *m*.

festive *adj* de fête.

fetch *vt* aller chercher.

fetching *adj* charmant, séduisant.

feud *n* rivalité *f*.

fever *n* fièvre *f*.

feverish *adj* fiévreux.

few *adj* peu:—**a ~** quelques.

fibre *n* fibre *f*.

fickle *adj* volage, inconstant.

fiction *n* fiction *f*; invention *f*.

fictional *adj* fictif.

fictitious *adj* fictif, imaginaire.

fidelity *n* fidélité, loyauté *f*.

fidget *vi* s'agiter, remuer.

fidgety *adj* agité, remuant.

field *n* champ *m*; domaine *m*.

fiend *n* démon *m*.

fiendish *adj* diabolique.

fierce *adj* féroce; acharné.

fierceness *n* férocité, fureur *f*.

fifteen *adj n* quinze *m*.

fifteenth *adj n* quinzième *mf*.

fifth *adj n* cinquième *mf*.

fiftieth *adj n* cinquantième *mf*.

fifty *adj n* cinquante *m*.

fight *vt vi* combattre; lutter:—*n* combat *m*.

fighter *n* combattant *m*.

figure *n* figure *f*; image *f*; chiffre *m*.

file *n* file *f*; liste *f*; dossier *m*; fichier *m*:—*vt* enregistrer; classer.

fill *vt* remplir.

fillet *n* filet *m*.

film *n* pellicule *f*; film *f*:—*vt* filmer:—*vi* s'embuer.

filter *n* filtre *m*:—*vt* filtrer.

filth *n* immondice, ordure *f*.

filthy *adj* crasseux, dégoûtant.

fin *n* nageoire *f*.

final *adj* dernier; définitif.

finalise *vt* parachever.

finance *n* finance *f*.

financial *adj* financier.

financier *n* financier *m*.

find *vt* trouver:—*n* trouvaille *f*.

findings *npl* résultats *mpl*.

fine *adj* fin; pur; délicat:—*n* amende *f*.

finesse *n* finesse, subtilité *f*.

finger *n* doigt *m*:—*vt* manier.

fingernail *n* ongle *m*.

finish *vt* finir, terminer.

fir (tree) *n* sapin *m*

fire *n* feu *m*; incendie *m*:—*vt* incendier:—*vi* s'enflammer.

firearm *n* arme à feu *f*.

fire engine *n* voiture de pompiers *f*.

fire extinguisher *n* extincteur *m*.

fireman *n* pompier *m*.

fireplace *n* cheminée *f*, foyer *m*.

fireproof *adj* ignifugé.

fire station *n* caserne de pompiers *f*.

fireworks *npl* feu d'artifice *m*.

firm *adj* ferme:—*n* (*com*) compagnie *f*.

firmness *n* fermeté *f*; résolution *f*.

first *adj* premier:—*adv* premièrement.

first aid *n* premiers secours *mpl*.

first name *n* prénom *m*.

first-class *adj* de première classe.

first-hand *adj* de première main.

first-rate *adj* de première qualité.

fish *n* poisson *m*:—*vi* pêcher.

fisherman *n* pêcheur *m*.

fishing *n* pêche *f*.

fissure *n* fissure, crevasse *f*.

fist *n* poing *m*.

fit *n* accès *m*:—*adj* en forme; capable:—*vt* adapter:—*vi* (bien) aller.

fitness *n* forme physique *f*.

fitting *adj* qui convient, approprié:—*n* accessoire *ml*.

five *adj n* cinq *m*.

fix *vt* fixer, établir.

fixation *n* obsession *f*.

fixed *adj* fixe.

fizz(le) *vi* pétiller.

fizzy *adj* gazeux.

flabby *adj* mou, *f* molle, flasque.

flag *n* drapeau *m*:—*vi* s'affaiblir.

flagrant *adj* flagrant.

flair *n* flair *m*; talent *m*.

flake *n* flocon *m*:—*vi* s'effriter.

flamboyant *adj* flamboyant.

flame *n* flamme *f*; ardeur *f*.

flammable *adj* inflammable.

flank *n* flanc *m*.

flap *n* battement *m*; rabat *m*.

flare *vi* luire, briller:—*n* flamme *f*.

flash *n* éclat *m*:—*vt* allumer.

flask *n* flasque *f*, flacon *m*.

flat *adj* plat; insipide.

flatten *vt* aplanir; aplatir.

flatter *vt* flatter.

flattery *n* flatterie *f*.

flaunt *vt* étaler, afficher.

flavour *n* saveur *m*:—*vt* assaisonner.

flaw *n* défaut *m*; imperfection *f*.

fleck *n* petite tache *f*; particule *f*.

flee *vt* fuir de:—*vi* s'enfuir.

fleece *n* toison *f*.

fleet *n* flotte *f*; parc *m*.

fleeting *adj* fugace, fugitif.

flesh *n* chair *f*.

flex *n* cordon *m*:—*vt* fléchir.

flexibility *n* flexibilité *f*.

flexible *adj* flexible, souple.

flicker *vt* vaciller; trembloter.

flier *n* aviateur *m*, -trice *f*.

flight *n* vol *m*; fuite *f*; volée *f*.

flight attendant *n* steward *m*, hôtesse de l'air *f*.

flimsy *adj* léger; fragile.

flinch *vi* sourciller.

fling *vt* lancer, jeter.

flip *vt* lancer.

flippant *adj* désinvolte, cavalier.

flipper *n* nageoire *f*.

flirt *vi* flirter:—*n* charmeur *m*, -euse *f*.

flirtation *n* flirt *f*.

float *vt* faire flotter:—*vi* flotter:—*n* flotteur *m*; char (de carnaval) *m*.

flock *n* troupeau *m*; foule *f*:—*vi* affluer.

flood *n* inondation *f*; déluge *m*:—*vt* inonder.

floodlight *n* projecteur *m*.

floor *n* sol *m*; plancher *m*; étage *m*:—*vt* parqueter.

flop *n* four, fiasco *m*.

floppy *adj* lâche:—*n* disquette *f*.

flora *n* flore *f*.

floral *adj* floral.

florid *adj* fleuri.

florist *n* fleuriste *mf*.

flounder *n* flet *m*:—*vi* patauger.

flour *n* farine *f*.

flourish *vi* fleurir; prospérer.

flourishing *adj* florissant.

flout *vt* mépriser.

flow vi couler; circuler:—n flux m; écoulement m; flot m.

flower n fleur f:—vi fleurir.

flowery adj fleuri.

fluctuate vi fluctuer.

fluctuation n fluctuation f.

fluency n aisance f.

fluent adj coulant; facile.

fluff n peluche f.

fluid adj n fluide m.

fluke n veine f.

flurry n rafale f; agitation f.

flush vi rougir:—n rougeur f; éclat m.

flushed adj rouge.

fluster vt énerver.

flute n flûte f.

flutter vi voleter; s'agiter.

fly vt piloter:—vi voler; fuir:—n mouche f; braguette f.

flying n aviation f.

foam n écume f:—vi écumer.

foamy adj écumeux.

focus n foyer m; centre m.

foe n ennemi m, -e f.

fog n brouillard m.

foggy adj brumeux.

fold n pli m:—vt plier.

folder n chemise f; dépliant m.

folding adj pliant.

foliage n feuillage m.

folio n folio m.

folk n gens mpl.

folklore n folklore m.

follow vt suivre:—vi suivre, s'ensuivre.

follower n partisan m, -e f; adhérent m, -e f.

folly n folie, extravagance f.

fond adj affectueux:—**to be ~ of** aimer.

fondle vt caresser.

fondness n prédilection f; affection f.

food n nourriture f.

food processor n robot m.

foodstuffs npl denrées alimentaires fpl.

fool n imbécile mf:—vt duper.

foolhardy adj téméraire.

foolish adj idiot, insensé.

foolproof adj infaillible.

foolscap n papier ministre m.

foot n pied m.

football n football m; ballon de football m.

footballer n footballeur m, -euse f.

footbridge n passerelle f.

footnote n note (de bas de page) f.

footpath n sentier m.

footprint n empreinte (de pas) f.

footstep n pas m.

for prep pour; en raison de; pendant:—conj car:—**as ~ me** quant à moi.

foray n incursion f.

forbid vt interdire, défendre.

forbidding adj menaçant; sévère.

force n force f; puissance:—vt forcer, contraindre.

forceful adj énergique.

forceps n forceps m.

forcible adj énergique, vigoureux.

forearm n avant-bras m.

foreboding n pressentiment m.

forecast vt prévoir:—n prévision f.

forefinger n index m.

foregone adj passé; anticipé.

foreground n premier plan m.

forehead n front m.

foreign adj étranger.

foreigner n étranger m, -ère f.

foreman n contremaître m.

foremost *adj* principal.

forensic *adj* judiciaire.

forerunner *n* précurseur *m*.

foresee *vt* prévoir.

foresight *n* prévoyance *f*; prescience *f*.

forest *n* forêt *f*.

foretaste *n* avant-goût *m*.

foretell *vt* prédire.

forever *adv* toujours; un temps infini.

forewarn *vt* prévenir à l'avance.

foreword *n* préface *f*.

forfeit *n* amende *f*:—*vt* perdre.

forge *n* forge *f*:—*vt* forger.

forger *n* faussaire *mf*.

forgery *n* contrefaçon *f*.

forget *vt vi* oublier.

forgetful *adj* étourdi; négligent.

forgive *vt* pardonner.

forgiveness *n* pardon *m*.

fork *n* fourchette *f*; fourche *f*:—*vi* bifurquer.

forked *adj* fourchu.

form *n* forme *f*; formalité *f*; moule *m*:—*vt* former.

formal *adj* formel.

formality *n* formalité *f*.

format *n* format *m*:—*vt* formater.

formation *n* formation *f*.

formative *adj* formateur *m*, -trice *f*.

former *adj* précédent, ancien:—**~ly** *adv* autrefois, jadis.

formula *n* formule *f*.

forsake *vt* abandonner, renoncer à.

fort *n* fort *m*.

forthcoming *adj* prochain; sociable.

forthwith *adv* immédiatement, tout de suite.

fortieth *adj n* quarantième *mf*.

fortification *n* fortification *f*.

fortify *vt* fortifier, renforcer.

fortnight *n* quinze jours *mpl*:—*adj* **~ly** bimensuel:—*adv* **~ly** tous les quinze jours.

fortuitous *adj* fortuit; imprévu.

fortunate *adj* chanceux.

fortune *n* chance *f*, sort *m*; fortune *f*.

forty *adj n* quarante *m*.

forward *adj* avancé; précoce; présomptueux:—**~(s)** *adv* en avant:—*vt* transmettre.

forwardness *n* précocité *f*.

fossil *n* fossile *m*.

foster *vt* élever.

foster child *n* enfant adoptif *m*.

foul *adj* infect:—*vt* polluer.

found *vt* fonder, créer; établir.

foundation *n* foundation *f*; fondement *m*.

foundry *n* fonderie *f*.

fountain *n* fontaine *f*.

four *adj n* quatre *m*.

fourfold *adj* quadruple.

fourteen *adj n* quatorze *m*.

fourteenth *adj n* quatorzième *mf*.

fourth *adj n* quatrième *mf*:—*n* quart *m*.

fowl *n* volaille *f*.

fox *n* renard *f*.

foyer *n* vestibule *m*.

fracas *n* rixe *f*.

fraction *n* fraction *f*.

fracture *n* fracture *f*:—*vt* fracturer.

fragile *adj* fragile.

fragility *n* fragilité *f*.

fragment *n* fragment *m*.

fragmentary *adj* fragmentaire.

fragrance *n* parfum *m*.

fragrant *adj* parfumé, odorant.

frail adj frêle, fragile.

frailty n fragilité f; faiblesse f.

frame n charpente f; cadre m:—vt encadrer.

franchise n droit de vote m; franchise f.

frank adj franc, direct.

frankness n franchise f.

frantic adj frénétique.

fraternal adv fraternel.

fraternise vi fraterniser.

fratricide n fratricide mf.

fraud n fraude, tromperie f.

fraudulent adj frauduleux.

free adj libre; autonome; gratuit; dégagé:—vt affranchir; libérer; débarrasser.

freedom n liberté f.

freelance adj indépendant:—adv en indépendant.

freely adv librement; libéralement.

freewheel vi rouler au point mort.

free will n libre arbitre m.

freeze vi geler:—vt congeler; geler.

freezer n congélateur m.

freezing adj gelé.

freight n cargaison f; fret m.

freighter n affréteur m.

French fries npl frites fpl.

French window n porte-fenêtre f.

frenzied adj fou, frénétique.

frenzy n frénésie f; folie f.

frequency n fréquence f.

frequent adj fréquent:—vt fréquenter.

fresco n fresque f.

fresh adj frais; nouveau, récent.

freshen vt rafraîchir:—vi se rafraîchir.

freshly adv récemment.

freshness n fraîcheur f.

freshwater adj d'eau douce.

fret vi s'agiter, se tracasser.

friction n friction f.

Friday n vendredi m:—**Good ~** Vendredi Saint m.

friend n ami m, -e f.

friendliness n amitié, bienveillance f.

friendly adj amical.

friendship n amitié f.

fright n peur, frayeur f.

frighten vt effrayer.

frightened adj effrayé, apeuré.

frightful adj épouvantable.

frigid adj glacé; frigide.

fringe n frange f.

frisk vt fouiller.

frivolity n frivolité f.

frivolous adj frivole.

fro adv:—**to go to and ~** aller et venir.

frock n robe f.

frog n grenouille f.

frolic vi folâtrer.

from prep de; depuis; à partir de.

front n avant, devant m; front m:—adj de devant; premier.

front door n porte d'entrée f.

frontier n frontière f.

front-wheel drive n (auto) traction avant f.

frost n gel m; gelée f:—vt geler.

frostbite n engelure f.

frostbitten adj gelé.

frosty adj glacial; givré.

froth n écume f:—vi écumer.

frothy adj mousseux, écumeux.

frown vt froncer les sourcils.

frozen adj gelé.

frugal *adj* frugal; économique.
fruit *n* fruit *m*.
fruiterer *n* fruitier *m*, -ière *f*.
fruitful *adj* fécond, fertile; fructueux.
fruition *n* réalisation *f*.
fruitless *adj* stérile.
frustrate *vt* contrecarrer; annuler.
frustrated *adj* frustré.
frustration *n* frustration *f*.
fry *vt* frire.
frying pan *n* poêle *f*.
fudge *n* caramel *m*.
fuel *n* combustible, carburant *m*.
fuel tank *n* réservoir à carburant *m*.
fugitive *adj* fugitif *m*, -ive *f*.
fulfil *vt* accomplir; réaliser.
fulfilment *n* accomplissement *m*.
full *adj* plein, rempli; complet:—*adv* pleinement, entièrement.
full moon *n* pleine lune *f*.
fullness *n* plénitude *f*; abondance *f*.
full-time *adj* à plein temps.
fully *adv* pleinement, entièrement.
fumble *vi* farfouiller.
fume *vi* rager, fumer.
fumigate *vt* fumiger.
fun *n* amusement *m*:—**to have ~** (bien) s'amuser.
function *n* fonction *f*.
functional *adj* fonctionnel.
fund *n* fonds *m*:—*vt* financer.

fundamental *adj* fondamental.
funeral service *n* office des morts *m*.
funeral *n* enterrement *m*.
funnel *n* entonnoir *m*; cheminée *f*.
funny *adj* amusant; curieux.
fur *n* fourrure *f*.
furious *adj* furieux; déchaîné.
furnace *n* fourneau *m*; chaudière *f*.
furnish *vt* meubler; fournir.
furniture *n* meubles *mpl*.
furrow *n* sillon *m*:—*vt* sillonner.
furry *adj* à poil.
further *adj* supplémentaire; plus lointain:—*adv* plus loin; en outre; de plus:—*vt* favoriser; promouvoir.
further education *n* formation continue *f*.
furthermore *adv* de plus.
furtive *adj* furtif; secret.
fury *n* fureur *f*; colère *f*.
fuse *vi* fondre, sauter:—*n* fusible *m*; amorce *f*.
fuse box *n* boîte à fusibles *f*.
fusion *n* fusion *f*.
fuss *n* tapage *m*.
fussy *adj* tatillon, chipoteur.
futile *adj* futile, vain.
futility *n* futilité *f*.
future *adj* futur:—*n* futur *m*; avenir *m*.
fuzzy *adj* flou, confus.

G

gabble *vi* baragouiner:—*n* charabia *m*.
gadget *n* gadget *m*.
gaiety *n* gaieté *f*.
gain *n* gain *m*; bénéfice *m*:—*vt* gagner.
gait *n* démarche *f*; maintien *m*.

galaxy *n* galaxie *f*.
gale *n* grand vent *m*.
gallant *adj* galant.
gallery *n* galerie *f*.
gallop *n* galop *m*:—*vi* galoper.
galore *adv* en abondance.

galvanise *vt* galvaniser.

gamble *vi* jouer; spéculer:—*n* risque *m*; pari *m*.

gambler *n* joueur *m*, -euse *f*.

gambling *n* jeu *m*.

game *n* jeu *m*; divertissement *m*:—*vi* jouer.

gang *n* gang *m*, bande *f*.

gangway *n* passerelle *f*.

gap *n* vide *m*; écart *m*.

garage *n* garage *m*.

garbage *n* ordures *fpl*.

garbage can *n* poubelle *f*.

garden *n* jardin *m*.

gardener *n* jardinier *m*, -ière *f*.

gardening *n* jardinage *m*.

garlic *n* ail *m*.

garment *n* vêtement *m*.

garnish *vt* garnir:—*n* garniture *f*.

garret *n* mansarde *f*.

garrulous *adj* locace, bavard.

garter *n* jarretelle *f*.

gas *n* gaz *m*; essence *f*.

gas cylinder *n* bouteille de gaz *f*.

gaseous *adj* gazeux.

gash *n* entaille *f*:—*vt* entailler.

gasoline *n* essence *f*.

gasp *vi* haleter.

gas station *n* poste d'essence *m*.

gassy *adj* gazeux.

gastronomic *adj* gastronomique.

gate *n* porte *f*; portail *m*.

gather *vt* rassembler; ramasser:—*vi* se rassembler.

gaudy *adj* criard.

gauge *n* calibre *m*:—*vt* calibrer.

gaunt *adj n* maigre *mf*.

gay *adj* gai; vif.

gaze *vi* contempler:—*n* regard *m*.

gear *n* équipement *m*, matériel *m*; vitesse *f*.

gearbox *n* boîte de vitesses *f*.

gem *n* pierre précieuse *f*; perle *f*.

gender *n* genre *m*.

gene *n* gène *m*.

genealogical *adj* généalogique.

genealogy *n* généalogie *f*.

general *adj* général:—**in** ~ en général:—*n* général *m*.

generalisation *n* généralisation *f*.

generalise *vt* généraliser.

generation *n* génération *f*.

generator *n* générateur *m*.

generosity *n* générosité, libéralité *f*.

generous *adj* généreux.

genial *adj* bienveillant; doux.

genitals *npl* organes génitaux *mpl*.

genius *n* génie *m*.

gentle *adj* doux, *f* douce, modéré.

gentleman *n* gentleman *m*.

gentleness *n* douceur *f*.

genuine *adj* authentique; sincère.

genus *n* genre *m*.

geographer *n* géographe *mf*.

geography *n* géographie *f*.

geologist *n* géologue *mf*.

geology *n* géologie *f*.

geometry *n* géométrie *f*.

germinate *vi* germer.

gesticulate *vi* gesticuler.

gesture *n* geste *m*.

get *vt* avoir; obtenir:—*vi* devenir.

geyser *n* geyser *m*; chauffe-eau *m invar*.

ghost *n* fantôme, spectre *m*.

giant *n* géant *m*, -e *f*.

gibe *vi* se moquer:—*n* moquerie *f*.

giddiness *n* vertige *m*.

giddy *adj* vertigineux.

gift *n* cadeau *m*.
gifted *adj* talentueux; doué.
gigantic *adj* gigantesque.
gild *vt* dorer.
gills *pl* branchies *fpl*.
ginger *n* gingembre *m*.
ginger-haired *adj* roux, *f* rousse.
girl *n* fille *f*.
girlfriend *n* amie *f*; petite amie *f*.
gist *n* essence *f*.
give *vt* donner; remettre.
gizzard *n* gésier *m*.
glacial *adj* glacial.
glacier *n* glacier *m*.
glad *adj* joyeux, content.
gladden *vt* réjouir.
glamour *n* attrait *m*, séduction *f*.
glamorous *adj* attrayant, séduisant.
glance *vi* jeter un coup d'œil.
glare *n* éclat *m*:—*vi* éblouir.
glass *n* verre *m*:—**es** *pl* lunettes *fpl*.
glaze *vt* vitrer.
gleam *n* rayon *m*.
glee *n* joie *f*; exultation *f*.
glide *vi* glisser; planer.
glimmer *n* lueur *f*:—*vi* luire.
glimpse *n* aperçu *m*:—*vt* entrevoir.
glint *vi* briller, scintiller.
glitter *vi* luire, briller.
global *adj* global; mondial.
globe *n* globe *m*; sphère *f*.
gloom *n* obscurité *f*; mélancolie.
gloomy *adj* sombre, mélancolique.
glorious *adj* glorieux, illustre.
glory *n* gloire, célébrité *f*.
glove *n* gant *m*.
glow *vi* rougeoyer:—*n* rougeoiement *m*.
glue *n* colle *f*:—*vt* coller.
glum *adj* abattu, triste.

glutton *n* glouton *m*, -onne *f*.
gnome *n* gnome *m*.
go *vi* aller:—**away** s'en aller.
goal *n* but, objectif *m*.
gobble *vt* engloutir.
God *n* Dieu *m*.
godfather *n* parrain *m*.
godlike *adj* divin.
godmother *n* marraine *f*.
gold *n* or *m*.
golden *adj* doré; d'or.
goldsmith *n* orfèvre *m*.
golf *n* golf *m*.
golfer *n* golfeur *m*, -euse *f*.
gong *n* gong *m*.
good *adj* bon; valable:—*n* bien *m*:—**s** *pl* biens *mpl*.
goodbye! *excl* au revoir!
good-looking *adj* beau.
goodness *n* bonté *f*; qualité *f*.
goodwill *n* bienveillance *f*.
goose *n* oie *f*.
gorge *n* gorge *f*:—*vt* engloutir, avaler.
gorgeous *adj* merveilleux.
gory *adj* sanglant.
gossip *n* potins *mpl*:—*vi* potiner.
govern *vt* gouverner, diriger.
government *n* gouvernement *m*.
governor *n* gouverneur *m*.
gown *n* toge *f*; robe *f*.
grab *vt* saisir.
grace *n* grâce *f*:—*vt* honorer.
graceful *adj* gracieux.
gradation *n* gradation *f*.
grade *n* grade *m*.
gradual *adj* graduel.
graduate *vi* obtenir son diplôme.
graft *n* greffe *f*:—*vt* greffer.

grain n grain m.

grammar n grammaire f.

grammatical adj grammatical.

grand adj grandiose; magnifique.

grandchild n petit-fils m; petite-fille f:—**grandchildren** pl petits-enfants m pl.

grandad n pépé m.

granddaughter n petite-fille f.

grandeur n grandeur f; pompe f.

grandfather n grand-père m.

grandma n mémé f.

grandmother n grand-mère f.

grandparents npl grands-parents mpl.

grandson n petit-fils m.

grandstand n tribune f.

granny n mémé f.

grant vt accorder:—n bourse f.

granulate vt granuler.

granule n granule m.

grape n raisin m.

grapefruit n pamplemousse m.

graph n graphe, graphique m.

graphic(al) adj graphique.

grasp vt saisir, empoigner; comprendre.

grass n herbe f.

grasshopper n sauterelle f.

grassy adj herbeux.

grate n grille f:—vt râper:—vi grincer.

grateful adj reconnaissant.

gratification n satisfaction f.

gratify vt satisfaire.

gratifying adj réjouissant.

gratis adv gratis, gratuitement.

gratitude n gratitude, reconnaissance f.

gratuitous adj gratuit; volontaire.

gratuity n gratification f.

grave n tombe f:—adj grave.

graveyard n cimetière m.

gravity n gravité f.

gravy n jus de viande m; sauce f.

graze vt paître:—vi paître.

grease n graisse f:—vt graisser.

great adj grand; important.

greatness n grandeur f; importance f.

greed n avidité f; gloutonnerie f.

greedy adj avide; glouton.

green adj vert:—n vert m; verdure f.

greenery n verdure f.

greenhouse n serre f.

greenish adj verdâtre.

greet vt saluer; accueillir.

greeting n salutation f; accueil m.

grey adj gris:—n gris m.

greyish adj grisâtre; grisonnant.

grid n grille f; réseau m.

grief n chagrin m, douleur.

grievance n grief m; doléance f.

grieve vt peiner:—vi se chagriner.

grievous adj douloureux; grave.

grill n gril m:—vt faire griller.

grim adj peu engageant.

grimace n grimace f; moue f.

grime n saleté f.

grind vt moudre.

grip n prise f; poignée f:—vt saisir, agripper.

groan vi gémir; grogner:—n gémissement m.

grocer n épicier m, -ière f.

groom n valet m; marié m:—vt panser; préparer.

groove n rainure f.

grope vt chercher à tâtons:—vi tâtonner.

gross adj gros; grossier.

grotesque adj grotesque.

ground n terre f, sol m; terrain:—vt fonder.

ground floor n rez-de-chaussée m.

groundless adj sans fondement.

group n groupe m:—vt regrouper.

grove n bosquet m.

grovel vi se traîner; ramper.

grow vt cultiver:—vi pousser.

grower n cultivateur m, -trice f.

growl vi grogner.

growth n croissance f.

grudge n rancune f.

gruelling adj difficile, pénible.

gruesome adj horrible.

grumble vi grogner; grommeler.

guarantee n garantie f:—vt garantir.

guard n garde f:—vt garder.

guardian n tuteur m, -trice f.

guardianship n tutelle f.

guess vt deviner:—vi deviner:—n conjecture f.

guest n invité m, invitée f.

guidance n guidage m; direction f.

guide vt guider, diriger:—n guide m.

guidebook n guide m.

guild n association f; corporation f.

guile n astuce f.

guilt n culpabilité f.

guilty adj coupable.

guise n apparence f.

guitar n guitare f.

gullibility n crédulité f.

gullible adj crédule.

gulp n gorgée f:—vi, vt avaler.

gum n gomme f:—vt coller.

gun n pistolet m; fusil m.

gunpowder n poudre à canon f.

gunshot n coup de feu m.

gurgle vi gargouiller.

gush vi jaillir; bouillonner:—n jaillissement m.

gust n rafale f; bouffée f.

gusto n plaisir m, délectation f.

gusty adj venteux.

gut n intestin m:—vt vider.

gutter n gouttière f; caniveau m.

guy n mec, type m.

guzzle vt bouffer, engloutir.

gymnasium n gymnase m.

gymnast n gymnaste mf.

gymnastic adj gymnastique:—~s npl gymnastique f.

gynecologist n gynécologue mf.

gypsy n gitan m, -e f.

H

habit n habitude f.

habitable adj habitable.

habitat n habitat m.

habitual adj habituel.

haemorrhage n hémorragie f.

haggard adj décharné hagard.

haggle vi marchander.

hail n grêle f:—vt saluer:—vi grêler.

hair n cheveu m; poil m.

haircut n coupe de cheveux f.

hairless adj chauve; sans poils.

hairstyle n coiffure f.

hairy adj chevelu; poilu.

hale adj vigoureux.

half n moitié f:—adj demi:—adv à moitié.

half-hearted adj peu enthousiaste.

half-hour n demi-heure f.

half-moon n demi-lune f.

halfway adv à mi-chemin.

hall n vestibule m.

hallow vt consacrer, sanctifier.

hallucination n hallucination f.

halt vi s'arrêter:—n arrêt m; halte f.

ham n jambon m.

hammer n marteau m:—vt marteler.

hammock n hamac m.

hamper n panier m:—vt entraver.

hand n main f:—vt donner, passer.

handbag n sac à main m.

handbrake n frein à main m.

handful n poignée f.

handicap n handicap m.

handicapped adj handicapé.

handkerchief n mouchoir m.

handle n manche m:—vt manier.

handlebars npl guidon m.

handrail n garde-fou m.

handsome adj beau.

handwriting n écriture f.

hang vt accrocher; pendre:—vi pendre.

hangover n gueule de bois f.

haphazard adj fortuit.

hapless adj malheureux.

happen vi se passer.

happening n événement m.

happily adv heureusement.

happiness n bonheur m.

happy adj heureux.

harass vt harceler.

harbour n port m:—vt héberger.

hard adj dur; pénible; sévère.

harden vt vi durcir.

hardiness n robustesse f.

hardly adv à peine:—~ ever presque jamais.

hardness n dureté f; difficulté f.

hard-up adj fauché.

hardy adj fort, robuste.

hare n lièvre m.

harm n mal m; tort m:—vt nuire à.

harmful adj nuisible.

harmonious adj harmonieux.

harmony n harmonie f.

harp n harpe f.

harsh adj dur; austère; rude.

harshness n aspérité, dureté f; austérité f.

harvest n moisson f:—vt moissonner.

harvester n moissonneur m, -euse f.

haste n hâte f.

hasten vt accélérer:—vi se dépêcher.

hasty adj hâtif; irréfléchi.

hat n chapeau m.

hatch vt couver; faire éclore:—n écoutille f.

hatchet n hachette f.

hate n haine f:—vt haïr, détester.

hatred n haine f.

haughtiness n orgueil m.

haughty adj orgueilleux.

haul vt tirer:—n prise f.

haunt vt hanter:—n repaire m.

have vt avoir; posséder.

haversack n sac à dos m.

havoc n ravages mpl.

hay n foin m.

hay fever n rhume des foins m.

hazard n risque, danger m:—vt risquer.

hazardous adj risqué, dangereux.

haze n brume f.

hazelnut n noisette f.

hazy adj brumeux.

he pn il.

head n tête f; chef m:—vt conduire.

headache n mal de tête m.

headland n promontoire m.

headlight n phare m.

headline n titre m.

headlong *adv* à toute allure.
headstrong *adj* têtu.
headwaiter *n* maître d'hôtel *m*.
heady *adj* capiteux.
heal *vt vi* guérir.
health *n* santé *f*.
healthiness *n* bonne santé *f*.
healthy *adj* en bonne santé; sain.
heap *n* tas *m*:—*vt* entasser.
hear *vt* entendre; écouter:—*vi* entendre.
hearing *n* ouïe *f*.
heart *n* cœur *m*.
heart failure *n* arrêt cardiaque *m*.
hearth *n* foyer *m*.
heartless *adj* cruel.
hearty *adj* cordial.
heat *n* chaleur *f*:—*vt* chauffer.
heater *n* radiateur *m*.
heathen *n* païen *m*, païenne *f*.
heating *n* chauffage *m*.
heatwave *n* onde de chaleur *f*.
heave *vt* lever; tirer.
heaven *n* ciel *m*.
heaviness *n* lourdeur *f*.
heavy *adj* lourd, pesant.
hectic *adj* agité.
hedge *n* haie *f*.
hedgehog *n* hérisson *m*.
heed *vt* tenir compte de:—*n* attention *f*.
heedless *adj* inattentif, étourdi.
heel *n* talon *m*.
hefty *adj* fort; gros.
height *n* hauteur *f*; altitude *f*.
heighten *vt* rehausser.
heinous *adj* atroce.
heir *n* héritier *m*.
helicopter *n* hélicoptère *m*.
hell *n* enfer *m*.
helmet *n* casque *m*.

help *vt* aider, secourir:—*n* aide *f*; secours *m*.
helper *n* aide *mf*.
helpful *adj* utile.
helpless *adj* impuissant.
hemisphere *n* hémisphère *m*.
hen *n* poule *f*.
henceforward *adv* dorénavant.
hen-house *n* poulailler *m*.
hepatitis *n* hépatite *f*.
her *pn* son, sa, ses; elle; la; lui.
herb *n* herbe *f*.
herbalist *n* herboriste *mf*.
herd *n* troupeau *m*.
here *adv* ici.
hereby *adv* par la présente.
hereditary *adj* héréditaire.
heredity *n* hérédité *f*.
heritage *n* patrimoine, héritage *m*.
hermit *n* ermite *m*.
hernia *n* hernie *f*.
hero *n* héros *m*.
heroic *adj* héroïque.
hers *pn* le sien, la sienne, le(s) sien(ne)s, à elle.
herself *pn* elle-même.
hesitate *vi* hésiter.
hesitation *n* hésitation *f*.
heterogeneous *adj* hétérogène.
heterosexual *adj n* hétérosexuel *m*, -elle *f*.
hiatus *n* (*gr*) hiatus *m*.
hiccup *n* hoquet *m*:—*vi* avoir le hoquet.
hide *vt* cacher:—*n* cuir *m*; peau *f*.
hideaway *n* cachette *f*.
hideous *adj* hideux; horrible.
hierarchy *n* hiérarchie *f*.
hi-fi *n* hi-fi *f invar*.
high *adj* haut; élevé.

highlight n point fort m.

highness n hauteur f; altesse f.

hike vi faire une randonnée.

hilarious adj hilarant; hilare.

hill n colline f.

hillside n coteau m.

hilly adj montagneux.

him pn lui; le.

himself pn lui-même; soi.

hinder vt gêner, entraver.

hindrance n gêne f, obstacle m.

hindsight n:—**with ~** rétrospectivement.

hint n allusion f:—vt insinuer; suggérer.

hip n hanche f.

hire vt louer:—n location f.

his poss adj son, sa, ses; poss pn le sien, la sienne, les sien(ne)s; à lui.

hiss vt vi siffler.

historian n historien m, -ienne f.

historic(al) adj historique.

history n histoire f.

hit vt frapper; atteindre.

hitch-hike vi faire du stop.

hoard n stock m; trésor caché m:—vt accumuler.

hoarse adj rauque.

hoarseness n voix rauque f.

hobby n passe-temps m invar.

hoist vt hisser:—n grue f.

hold vt tenir; détenir:—n prise f; pouvoir m.

holder n détenteur m, -trice f.

holdup n hold-up m.

hole n trou m.

holiday n jour de congé m:—**~s** pl vacances fpl.

hollow adj creux:—n creux m:—vt creuser.

holocaust n holocauste m.

holy adj saint; bénit.

homage n hommage m.

home n maison f; domicile m.

homeless adj sans abri.

homely adj simple.

homesick adj nostalgique.

homesickness n nostalgie f.

homework n devoirs mpl.

homicide n homicide m; homicide mf.

homogeneous adj homogène.

homosexual adj n homosexuel m, -elle f.

honest adj honnête.

honesty n honnêteté f.

honey n miel m.

honor n honneur m:—vt honorer.

honorable adj honorable.

honorary adj honoraire.

hood n capot m; capuche f.

hoof n sabot m.

hook n crochet m; hameçon m:—vt accrocher.

hoop n cerceau m.

hooter n sirène f.

hop n saut m:—vi sauter.

hope n espoir m, espérance f:—vi espérer.

hopeful adj plein d'espoir; prometteur.

horizon n horizon m.

horizontal adj horizontal.

hormone n hormone f.

horn n corne f.

horoscope n horoscope m.

horrible adj horrible.

horrific adj horrible, affreux.

horrify vt horrifier.

horror n horreur f.

hors d'œuvre n hors-d'œuvre m invar.

horse n cheval m.

horseback adv:—**on ~** à cheval.

horseman n cavalier m.

horsepower n cheval-vapeur m; puissance en chevaux f.

horseshoe n fer à cheval m.

horticulture n horticulture f.

horticulturist n horticulteur m, -trice f.

hospitable adj hospitalier.

hospital n hôpital m.

hospitality n hospitalité f.

host n hôte m; hostie f.

hostage n otage m.

hostess n hôtesse f.

hostile adj hostile.

hostility n hostilité f.

hot adj chaud; épicé.

hotel n hôtel m.

hotelier n hôtelier m, -ière f.

hotheaded adj exalté.

hotplate n plaque chauffante f.

hour n heure f.

hour-glass n sablier m.

hourly adv toutes les heures.

house n maison f; maisonnée f:—vt loger.

houseboat n péniche f.

household n famille f, ménage m.

householder n propriétaire mf; chef de famille m.

housekeeper n gouvernante f.

housewife n ménagère f.

housework n travaux ménagers mpl.

housing n logement m.

hovel n taudis m.

hover vi planer.

how adv comme; comment:—~ do you do! enchanté.

however adv de quelque manière que; cependant, néanmoins.

howl vi hurler:—n hurlement m.

hub n centre m; moyeu m.

hue n teinte f; nuance f.

hug vt étreindre:—n étreinte f.

huge adj énorme.

hull n (mar) coque f.

hum vi chantonner.

human adj humain.

humane adj humain.

humanise vt humaniser.

humanist n humaniste mf.

humanity n humanité f.

humble adj humble:—vt humilier.

humdrum adj monotone.

humid adj humide.

humiliate vt humilier.

humiliation n humiliation f.

humility n humilité f.

humorous adj humoristique.

humour n sens de l'humour m, humour m.

hump n bosse f.

hundred adj cent:—n centaine f.

hundredth adj centième.

hunger n faim f:—vi avoir faim.

hungry adj affamé.

hunt vt chasser:—n chasse f.

hunter n chasseur m.

hurdle n haie f.

hurl vt jeter.

hurricane n ouragan m.

hurry vt presser:—vi se presser:—n hâte f.

hurt vt faire mal à; blesser:—n mal m.

hurtful adj blessant.

husband n mari m.

hut n cabane, hutte f.

hydrant n bouche d'incendie f.

hydraulic adj hydraulique.

hydroelectric adj hydroélectrique.

hygiene n hygiène f.

hygienic adj hygiénique.

hypochondriac adj n hypocondriaque mf.
hypocrisy n hypocrisie f.
hypocritical adj hypocrite.

hypothesis n hypothèse f.
hypothetical adj hypothétique.
hysterical adj hystérique.
hysterics npl hystérie f.

I

I pn je, j'; moi
ice n glace f:—vt glacer.
ice cream n glace f.
ice rink n patinoire f.
ice skating n patinage sur glace m.
icy adj glacé.
idea n idée f.
ideal adj idéal.
identical adj identique.
identification n identification f.
identify vt identifier.
identity n identité f.
idiot n imbécile mf.
idiotic adj idiot, bête.
idle adj désœuvré; au repos.
idleness n paresse f.
idler n paresseux m, -euse f.
idol n idole f.
idolise vt idôlatrer.
idyllic adj idyllique.
if conj si:—— **not** sinon.
ignite vt allumer, enflammer.
ignoble adj ignoble; bas.
ignominious adj ignominieux.
ignorance n ignorance f.
ignorant adj ignorant.
ignore vt ne pas tenir compte de.
ill adj malade:—n mal m.
illegal adj illégal.
illegality n illégalité f.
illegible adj illisible.
illegitimacy n illégitimité f.
illegitimate adj illégitime.

illicit adj illicite.
illiterate adj analphabète.
illness n maladie f.
illogical adj illogique.
illuminate vt illuminer.
illusion n illusion f.
illusory adj illusoire.
illustrate vt illustrer.
illustration n illustration f.
illustrious adj illustre.
image n image f.
imaginary adj imaginaire.
imagination n imagination f.
imagine vt imaginer.
imbecile adj imbécile, idiot.
imitate vt imiter.
imitation n imitation f.
immaterial adj insignifiant.
immeasurable adj incommensurable.
immediate adj immédiat.
immense adj immense.
immigrant n immigrant m, -e f.
immigration n immigration f.
imminent adj imminent.
immobile adj immobile.
immobility n immobilité f.
immoderate adj immodéré.
immoral adj immoral.
immorality n immoralité f.
immortal adj immortel.
immune adj immunisé.
immunise vt immuniser.
immutable adj immuable.

impact n impact m.
impalpable adj impalpable.
impart vt communiquer.
impartial adj impartial.
impartiality n impartialité f.
impassive adj impassible.
impatience n impatience f.
impatient adj impatient.
impeccable adj impeccable.
impede vt empêcher; entraver.
impending adj imminent.
impenetrable adj impénétrable.
imperceptible adj imperceptible.
imperfect adj imparfait.
imperfection n imperfection f; défaut m.
impermeable adj imperméable.
impersonal adj impersonel.
impertinence n impertinence f.
impertinent adj impertinent.
impetuosity n impétuosité f.
impetuous adj impétueux.
implement n outil m; ustensile m.
implicate vt impliquer.
implication n implication f.
implicit adj implicite.
implore vt supplier.
imply vt supposer.
impolite adj impoli.
import vt importer:—n importation f.
importance n importance f.
important adj important.
impose vt imposer.
imposition n imposition f.
impossibility n impossibilité f.
impossible adj impossible.
impostor n imposteur m.
impotence n impotence f.
impotent adj impotent.
impoverish vt appauvrir.

impoverishment n appauvrissement m.
impracticable adj impraticable.
imprecise adj imprécis.
impress vt impressionner.
impression n impression f; édition f.
impressionable adj impressionnable.
impressive adj impressionnant.
imprint n empreinte f:—vt imprimer.
imprison vt emprisonner.
imprisonment n emprisonnement m.
improbability n improbabilité f.
improbable adj improbable.
improper adj indécent; impropre.
improve vt améliorer:—vi s'améliorer.
improvement n amélioration f.
improvise vt improviser.
imprudent adj imprudent.
impudent adj impudent.
impulse n impulsion f.
impulsive adj impulsif.
impunity n impunité f.
in prep dans; en.
inability n incapacité f.
inaccurate adj inexact.
inactive adj inactif.
inadequate adj inadéquat.
inadmissible adj inadmissible.
inane adj inepte.
inanimate adj inanimé.
inapplicable adj inapplicable.
inaudible adj inaudible.
incalculable adj incalculable.
incapable adj incapable.
incapacitate vt mettre dans l'incapacité.
incapacity n incapacité f.
incarcerate vt incarcérer.
incautious adj imprudent.
incentive n prime, aide f
inception n commencement m.

incessant *adj* incessant, continuel.
incidence *n* fréquence *f*.
incident *n* incident *m*.
incidental *adj* fortuit.
incisive *adj* incisif.
incite *vt* inciter, encourager.
inclination *n* inclination, propension *f*.
incline *vt* incliner:—*vi* s'incliner.
include *vt* inclure, comprendre.
including *prep* inclus, y compris.
incoherence *n* incohérence *f*.
incoherent *adj* incohérent.
income *n* revenu *m*; recettes *fpl*.
incomparable *adj* incomparable.
incompetence *n* incompétence *f*.
incompetent *adj* incompétent.
incomplete *adj* incomplet.
incomprehensible *adj* incompréhensible.
inconceivable *adj* inconcevable.
incongruity *n* incongruité *f*.
incongruous *adj* incongru.
inconsiderate *adj* inconsidéré.
inconsistent *adj* inconsistant.
inconspicuous *adj* discret.
incontrovertible *adj* incontestable.
inconvenience *n* inconvénient:—*vt* incommoder.
inconvenient *adj* incommode.
incorporate *vt* incorporer:—*vi* s'incorporer.
incorporation *n* incorporation *f*.
incorrect *adj* incorrect.
increase *vt vi* augmenter:—*n* augmentation *f*.
increasing *adj* croissant.
incredible *adj* incroyable.
incredulous *adj* incrédule.
incriminate *vt* incriminer.

incur *vt* encourir.
incurable *adj* incurable.
incursion *n* incursion *f*.
indebted *adj* endetté; redevable.
indecent *adj* indécent.
indecision *n* indécision, irrésolution *f*.
indecisive *adj* indécis, irrésolu.
indefatigable *adj* infatigable.
indefinite *adj* indéfini.
indemnify *vt* indemniser.
indemnity *n* indemnité *f*.
independence *n* indépendance *f*.
independent *adj* indépendant.
indeterminate *adj* indéterminé.
index *n* indice *m*.
indicate *vt* indiquer.
indication *n* indication *f*; indice *m*.
indifference *n* indifférence *f*.
indifferent *adj* indifférent.
indigenous *adj* indigène.
indigent *adj* indigent.
indigestion *n* indigestion *f*.
indignant *adj* indigné.
indignation *n* indignation *f*.
indirect *adj* indirect.
indiscreet *adj* indiscret.
indiscretion *n* indiscrétion *f*.
indispensable *adj* indispensable.
indisputable *adj* indiscutable.
indistinct *adj* indistinct.
indistinguishable *adj* indistinctible.
individual *adj* individuel:—*n* individu *m*.
individuality *n* individualité *f*.
indolence *n* indolence *f*.
indolent *adj* indolent.
indoors *adv* à l'intérieur.
induce *vt* persuader; provoquer.

inducement *n* encouragement *m*; incitation *f*.

indulge *vt* céder à; *vi* se permettre.

indulgent *adj* indulgent.

industrial *adj* industriel.

industrialise *vt* industrialiser.

industrious *adj* travailleur.

industry *n* industrie *f*.

inebriated *vt* ivre.

inedible *adj* non comestible.

inefficiency *n* inefficacité *f*.

inefficient *adj* inefficace.

ineligible *adj* inéligible.

inept *adj* inepte; déplacé.

inequality *n* inégalité *f*.

inertia *n* inertie *f*.

inestimable *adj* inestimable.

inevitable *adj* inévitable.

inexhaustible *adj* inépuisable.

inexpedient *adj* imprudent, inopportun.

inexpensive *adj* bon marché.

inexplicable *adj* inexplicable.

infallible *adj* infaillible.

infamous *adj* vil, infâme.

infancy *n* enfance *f*.

infant *n* bébé *m*; enfant *mf*.

infantile *adj* infantile.

infatuated *adj* fou.

infatuation *n* folie *f*; obsession *f*.

infect *vt* infecter.

infectious *adj* infectieux.

infer *vt* inférer.

inference *n* inférence *f*.

inferior *adj* inférieur.

inferiority *n* infériorité *f*.

infernal *adj* infernal.

infest *vt* infester.

infidelity *n* infidélité *f*.

infiltrate *vi* s'infiltrer.

infinite *adj* infini.

infinity *n* infini *m*; infinité *f*.

infirm *adj* infirme.

infirmity *n* infirmité *f*.

inflame *vt* enflammer:—*vi* s'enflammer.

inflammation *n* inflammation *f*.

inflatable *adj* gonflable.

inflate *vt* gonfler.

inflation *n* inflation *f*.

inflict *vt* infliger.

influence *n* influence *f*:—*vt* influencer.

influential *adj* influent.

influenza *n* grippe *f*.

inform *vt* informer.

informal *adj* informel.

informality *n* simplicité *f*.

information *n* information *f*.

infrequent *adj* rare.

infringe *vt* enfreindre.

infringement *n* infraction *f*.

infuriate *vt* rendre furieux.

ingenious *adj* ingénieux.

ingenuity *n* ingéniosité *f*.

ingenuous *adj* ingénu.

inglorious *adj* honteux.

ingot *n* lingot *m*.

ingratitude *n* ingratitude *f*.

ingredient *n* ingrédient *m*.

inhabit *vt vi* habiter.

inhabitable *adj* habitable.

inhabitant *n* habitant *m*, -e *f*.

inhale *vt* inhaler.

inherit *vt* hériter.

inheritance *n* héritage *m*.

inhibit *vt* inhiber.

inhibition *n* inhibition *f*.

inhospitable *adj* inhospitalier.

inhuman *adj* inhumain.

inhumanity *n* inhumanité.

inimical *adj* hostile, ennemi.

inimitable *adj* inimitable.

initial *adj* initial:—*n* initiale *f*.

initiate *vt* commencer; initier.

initiation *n* initiation *f*.

initiative *n* initiative *f*.

inject *vt* injecter.

injection *n* injection *f*.

injunction *n* injonction *f*.

injure *vt* blesser.

injury *n* blessure *f*; tort *m*.

injustice *n* injustice *f*.

ink *n* encre *f*.

inlet *n* entrée *f*; bras de mer *m*.

inn *n* auberge *f*; hôtel *m*.

innate *adj* inné.

inner *adj* intérieur.

innkeeper *n* aubergiste *mf*.

innocence *n* innocence *f*.

innocent *adj* innocent.

innocuous *adj* inoffensif.

innovate *vt* innover.

innuendo *n* allusion *f*; insinuation *f*.

innumerable *adj* innombrable.

inoculate *vt* inoculer.

inoffensive *adj* inoffensif.

inopportune *adj* inopportun.

inquest *n* enquête *f*.

inquire *vt vi* demander.

inquiry *n* enquête *f*.

inquisition *n* investigation *f*.

inquisitive *adj* curieux.

insane *adj* fou, *f* folle.

insanity *n* folie *f*.

insatiable *adj* insatiable.

inscribe *vt* inscrire.

inscription *n* inscription *f*.

inscrutable *adj* impénétrable.

insect *n* insecte *m*.

insecure *adj* peu assuré.

insecurity *n* insécurité *f*.

insemination *n* insémination *f*.

insensible *adj* inconscient.

insensitive *adj* insensible.

inseparable *adj* inséparable.

insert *vt* introduire, insérer.

insertion *n* insertion *f*.

inside *n* intérieur *m*:—*adv* à l'intérieur.

inside out *adv* à l'envers.

insidious *adj* insidieux.

insight *n* perspicacité *f*.

insignificant *adj* insignifiant.

insinuate *vt* insinuer.

insinuation *n* insinuation *f*.

insipid *adj* insipide.

insist *vi* insister.

insistence *n* insistance *f*.

insistent *adj* insistant.

insolence *n* insolence *f*.

insolent *adj* insolent.

inspect *vt* examiner, inspecter.

inspection *n* inspection *f*.

inspector *n* inspecteur *m*, -trice *f*.

instability *n* instabilité *f*.

instal *vt* installer.

installation *n* installation *f*.

instalment *n* installation *f*.

instance *n* exemple *m*.

instant *adj* instantané:—*n* instant.

instead (of) *pr* au lieu.

instigate *vt* inciter; susciter.

instinct *n* instinct *m*.

instinctive *adj* instinctif.

institute *vt* instituer.

institution *n* institution *f*.

instruct *vt* instruire.

instrument *n* instrument *m*.

insufficiency *n* insuffisance *f*.

insufficient *adj* insuffisant.
insular *adj* insulaire.
insulate *vt* isoler.
insulation *n* isolation *f*.
insult *vt* insulter:—*n* insulte *f*.
insurance *n* (*com*) assurance *f*.
insure *vt* assurer.
intact *adj* intact.
integrate *vt* intégrer.
integration *n* intégration *f*.
integrity *n* intégrité *f*.
intellect *n* intellect *m*.
intellectual *adj* intellectuel.
intelligence *n* intelligence *f*.
intelligent *adj* intelligent.
intelligible *adj* intelligible.
intend *vt* avoir l'intention de.
intense *adj* intense.
intensify *vt* intensifier.
intensity *n* intensité *f*.
intensive *adj* intensif.
intention *n* intention *f*, dessein *m*.
intentional *adj* intentionnel:—**~ly** *adv* à dessein, intentionnellement.
intercede *vi* intercéder.
intercept *vt* intercepter.
interest *vt* intéresser:—*n* intérêt *m*.
interesting *adj* intéressant.
interfere *vi* s'ingérer.
interior *adj* intérieur.
interlock *vi* s'entremêler.
interlude *n* intermède *m*.
intermediary *n* intermédiaire *mf*.
intermediate *adj* intermédiaire.
interminable *adj* interminable.
intermingle *vt* entremêler:—*vi* s'entremêler.
intermittent *adj* intermittent.
intern *n* interne *mf*.

internal *adj* intérieur; interne.
international *adj* international.
interpret *vt* interpréter.
interpretation *n* interprétation *f*.
interpreter *n* interprète *mf*.
interrogate *vt* interroger.
interrogation *n* interrogatoire *m*.
interrupt *vt* interrompre.
interruption *n* interruption *f*.
intersect *vi* se croiser.
intersection *n* croisement *m*.
intertwine *vt* entrelacer.
interval *n* intervalle *m*; mi-temps *f*.
intervene *vi* intervenir.
intervention *n* intervention *f*.
interview *n* entrevue *f*; interview *f*.
interviewer *n* interviewer *m*.
intestine *n* intestin *m*.
intimacy *n* intimité *f*.
intimate *adj* intime *vt* insinuer.
intimidate *vt* intimider.
into *prep* dans, en.
intolerable *adj* intolérable.
intolerant *adj* intolérant.
intonation *n* intonation *f*.
intoxicate *vt* enivrer.
intoxication *n* ivresse *f*.
intricacy *n* complexité *f*.
intricate *adj* complexe.
intrigue *n* intrigue *f*:—*vi* intriguer.
intriguing *adj* intrigant.
intrinsic *adj* intrinsèque.
introduce *vt* introduire.
introduction *n* introduction *f*.
introvert *n* introverti *m*, -ie *f*.
intruder *n* intrus *m*, -e *f*.
intuition *n* intuition *f*.
intuitive *adj* intuitif.
inundate *vt* inonder.

invade vt envahir.

invader n envahisseur m, -euse f.

invalid n invalide mf.

invalidate vt invalider.

invaluable adj inappréciable.

invasion n invasion f.

invent vt inventer.

invention n invention f.

inventor n inventeur m, -trice f.

investigation n investigation f.

investigator n investigateur m, -trice f.

invincible adj invincible.

inviolable adj inviolable.

invisible adj invisible.

invitation n invitation f.

invite vt inviter.

invoice n facture f.

invoke vt invoquer.

involuntary adj involontaire.

involve vt impliquer, entraîner.

involvement n implication f.

irascible adj irascible.

irate adj irrité.

iron n fer m:—adj de fer.

ironic adj ironique.

irony n ironie f.

irrational adj irrationnel.

irreconcilable adj irréconciliable.

irregular adj irrégulier.

irregularity n irrégularité f.

irreparable adj irréparable.

irreplaceable adj irremplaçable.

irresistible adj irrésistible.

irresponsible adj irresponsable.

irreverence n irrévérence f.

irrigate vt irriguer.

irrigation n irrigation f.

irritability n irritabilité f.

irritable adj irritable.

irritate vt irriter.

irritation n irritation f.

island n île f.

isle n île f.

isolate vt isoler.

isolation n isolement m.

issue n sujet m, question f:—vt publier.

it pn il, elle; le, la; cela, ça, ce, c'.

itch n démangeaison f:—vi avoir des démangeaisons.

item n article m.

itinerant adj itinérant.

itinerary n itinéraire m.

its pn son, sa, ses.

itself pn lui-même, elle-même.

ivory n ivoire m.

ivy n lierre m.

J

jabber vi bafouiller.

jack n cric m; valet m.

jacket n veste f; couverture f.

jackpot n gros lot m.

jagged adj dentelé.

jail n prison f.

jailer n geôlier m, -ière f.

jam n confiture f; embouteillage m.

January n janvier m.

jar vi (mus) détonner:—n pot m.

jargon n jargon m.

jaw n mâchoire f.

jazz n jazz m.

jealous adj jaloux.

jealousy n jalousie f.

jeans npl jean m.

jeer vi railler:—n raillerie.

jelly n gelée f.

jeopardise vt mettre en péril.

jerk n secousse f.

jersey n jersey m.

jest n blague.

jester n bouffon m.

jet n avion à réaction m; jet m.

jettison vt se défaire de.

jewel n bijou m.

jewellery n bijouterie f.

Jewish adj juif.

jibe n raillerie, moquerie f.

jigsaw n puzzle m.

jinx n porte-malheur m invar.

job n travail m.

jockey n jockey m.

jocular adj joyeux; facétieux.

jog vi faire du jogging.

join vt joindre, unir.

joint n articulation f:—adj commun.

joke n blague:—vi blaguer.

joker n blagueur m, -euse f.

jolly adj gai, joyeux.

jostle vt bousculer.

journal n revue f.

journalism n journalisme m.

journalist n journaliste mf.

journey n voyage m:—vi voyager.

joy n joie f.

joyful adj joyeux.

jubilation n jubilation f.

jubilee n jubilé m.

Judaism n judaïsme m.

judge n juge m:—vt juger.

judgment n jugement m.

judicious adj judicieux.

judo n judo m.

jug n cruche f.

juggle vi jongler.

juice n jus m; suc m.

juicy adj juteux.

July n juillet m.

jumble vt mélanger:—n mélange m.

jump vi sauter:—n saut m.

June n juin m.

jungle n jungle f.

junior adj plus jeune.

jurisdiction n juridiction f.

juror n juré m.

jury n jury m.

just adj juste:—adv justement, exactement.

justice n justice f.

justification n justification f.

justify vt justifier.

juvenile adj juvénile.

juxtaposition n juxtaposition f.

K

kaleidoscope n kaléidoscope m.

kangaroo n kangourou m.

keen adj enthousiaste; vif.

keenness n enthousiasme m.

keep vt garder, conserver.

kernel n amande f; noyau m.

kettle n bouilloire f.

key n clé, clef f; (mus) ton m; touche f.

keyboard n clavier m.

key ring n porte-clefs m invar.

keystone n clef de voûte f.

kick vi (vt) donner un coup de pied (à).

kidnap vt kidnapper.

kidney n rein m; rognon m.

killer n assassin m.

killing n assassinat m.

kiln n four m.

kilo n kilo m.
kilogram n kilogramme m.
kilometre n kilomètre m.
kin n parents mpl.
kind adj gentil:—n genre m.
kindle vt allumer:—vi s'allumer.
kindliness n gentillesse, bonté f.
kindly adj bon, bienveillant.
kindness n bonté f.
king n roi m.
kingdom n royaume m.
kiss n baiser m:—vt embrasser.
kit n équipement m.
kitchen n cuisine f.
kitten n chaton m.
knack n don, chic m.

knead vt pétrir.
knee n genou m.
kneel vi s'agenouiller.
knife n couteau m.
knight n chevalier m.
knit vt vi tricoter.
knob n bouton m.
knock vt vi cogner, frapper:—n coup m.
knot n nœud m:—vt nouer.
know vt vi savoir; connaître.
know-how n savoir-faire m.
knowledge n connaissances fpl.
knowledgeable adj bien informé.
knuckle n articulation f.

L

label n étiquette f.
laboratory n laboratoire m.
laborious adj laborieux.
labour n travail m:—vi travailler.
labourer n ouvrier m.
lace vt lacer.
lacerate vt lacérer.
lack vt manquer de:—vi manquer:—n manque m.
lad n garçon m.
ladder n échelle f.
lady n dame f.
lag vi se laisser distancer.
lagoon n lagune f.
lair n repaire m.
lake n lac m.
lame adj boiteux.
lament vt se lamenter sur:—n lamentation f.
lamentable adj lamentable.
lamentation n lamentation f.

lamp n lampe f.
lance n lance f:—vt inciser.
lancet n bistouri m.
land n pays m; terre f:—vi atterrir.
landlord n propriétaire m.
landmark n point de repère m.
landscape n paysage m.
landslide n glissement de terrain m.
lane n allée, ruelle f; file f.
language n langue f; langage m.
languish vi languir.
lantern n lanterne f.
lapel n revers m.
lapse n laps m; défaillance f:—vi expirer.
larder n garde-manger m invar.
large adj grand:—at ~ en liberté.
larva n larve f.
lascivious adj lascif.
lash n coup de fouet m:—vt fouetter
last adj dernier:—vi durer.

last-minute *adj* de dernière minute.
late *adj* en retard; défunt:—*adv* tard:
—**~ly** *adv* récemment.
latent *adj* latent.
lateral *ad* latérale.
lather *n* mousse *f*.
latitude *n* latitude *f*.
laudable *adj* louable.
laugh *vi* rire:—**to ~ at** *vt* rire de:—*n* rire *m*.
laughter *n* rires *mpl*.
launch *vt* lancer:—*vi* se lancer.
laundry *n* lessive *f*.
lava *n* lave *f*.
lavatory *n* toilettes *fpl*.
lavish *adj* prodigue:—*vt* prodiguer.
law *n* loi *f*; droit *m*.
lawful *adj* légal; légitime.
lawmaker *n* législateur *m*, -trice *f*.
lawn *n* pelouse *f*, gazon *m*.
lawyer *n* avocat *m*; notaire *m*.
lax *adj* relâché.
laxative *n* laxatif *m*.
lay *vt* mettre; pondre.
layer *n* couche *f*.
laziness *n* paresse *f*.
lazy *adj* paresseux.
lead *n* plomb *m*:—*vt vi* conduire, mener.
leader *n* chef *m*.
leadership *n* direction *f*.
leading *adj* principal; premier.
leaf *n* feuille *f*.
leaflet *n* feuillet *m*.
league *n* ligue *f*; lieue *f*.
leak *n* fuite *f*:—*vi* (*mar*) faire eau.
lean *vi* s'appuyer:—*adj* maigre.
leap *vi* sauter:—*n* saut *m*.
learn *vt vi* apprendre.

learning *n* érudition *f*.
lease *n* bail *m*:—*vt* louer.
leash *n* laisse *f*.
least *adj* moindre:—**at ~** au moins.
leather *n* cuir *m*.
leave *n* permission *f*; congé *m*:—*vt* laisser.
lecture *n* conférence *f*:—*vi* faire une conférence.
lecturer *n* conférencier *m*, -ière *f*.
leeway *n* liberté d'action *f*.
left *adj* gauche.
left-handed *adj* gaucher.
left-luggage office *n* consigne *f*.
leftovers *npl* restes *mpl*.
leg *n* jambe *f*; patte *f*.
legal *adj* légal, légitime.
legalise *vt* légaliser.
legality *n* légalité, légitimité *f*.
legend *n* légende *f*.
legendary *adj* légendaire.
legible *adj* lisible.
legion *n* légion *f*.
legislate *vi, vt* légiférer.
legislation *n* législation *f*.
legislative *adj* législatif.
legislature *n* corps législatif *m*.
legitimacy *n* légitimité *f*.
legitimate *adj* légitime:—*vt* légitimer.
leisure *n* loisir *m*:—**~ly** *adj* tranquille.
lemon *n* citron *m*.
lemonade *n* limonade *f*.
lend *vt* prêter.
length *n* longueur *f*; durée *f*:—**at ~** longuement.
lengthen *vt* allonger:—*vi* s'allonger.
lengthy *adj* long.
lenient *adj* indulgent.
lens *n* lentille *f*.

leotard n justaucorps m.

lesbian n lesbienne f.

less adj moins:—adv moins.

lessen vt vi diminuer.

lesser adj moindre.

lesson n leçon f.

let vt laisser, permettre.

lethal adj mortel.

lethargic adj léthargique.

lethargy n léthargie f.

letter n lettre f.

lettering n inscription f.

lettuce n salade f.

level adj plat, égal:—n niveau m:—vt niveler.

lever n levier m.

levity n légèreté f.

liability n responsabilité f.

liable adj sujet (à); responsable.

liaise vi effectuer une liaison.

liaison n liaison f.

liar n menteur m, -euse f.

liberal adj libéral; généreux.

liberate vt libérer.

liberation n libération f.

liberty n liberté f.

librarian n bibliothécaire mf.

library n bibliothèque f.

licence n licence f; permis m.

lick vt lécher.

lid n couvercle m.

lie n mensonge m:—vi mentir; être allongé.

lieu n:—**in ~ of** au lieu de.

life n vie f.

life jacket n gilet de sauvetage m.

lifeless adj mort; sans vie.

life sentence n condamnation à perpétuité f.

life-sized adj grandeur nature.

lift vt lever.

ligament n ligament m.

light n lumière f:—adj léger; clair: —vt allumer.

lighten vi s'éclaircir:—vt éclairer; éclaircir.

lighthouse n (mar) phare m.

lighting n éclairage m.

lightning n éclair m.

light year n année-lumière f.

like adj pareil:—adv comme:—vt vi aimer.

likelihood n probabilité f.

likely adj probable, vraisemblable.

liken vt comparer.

likeness n ressemblance f.

likewise adv pareillement.

liking n goût m.

limb n membre m.

limit n limite f:—vt limiter.

limitation n limitation f; restriction f.

limp vi boiter:—n boitement m:—adj mou.

line n ligne f; ride f:—vt rayer; rider.

linear adj linéaire.

liner n transatlantique m.

linger vi traîner.

linguist n linguiste mf.

linguistic adj linguistique.

link n chaînon m:—vt relier.

lion n lion m.

lip n lèvre f; bord m.

lip-read vi lire sur les lèvres.

lipstick n rouge à lèvres m.

liqueur n liqueur f.

liquid adj liquide:—n liquide m.

liquidise vt liquéfier.

liquor n spiritueux m.

lisp vi zézayer:—n zézaiement m.

list n liste f:—vt faire une liste de.

listen vi écouter.

literal adj littéral.

literary adj littéraire.

literature n littérature f.

litigation n litige m.

litigious adj litigieux.

litre n litre m.

litter n litière f, ordures fpl:-vt recouvrir.

little adj petit:—n peu m.

live vi vivre; habiter:—adj vivant.

livelihood n moyens de subsistance mpl.

liveliness n vivacité f.

lively adj vif.

liver n foie m.

livid adj livide; furieux.

living n vie f:—adj vivant.

living room n salle de séjour f.

load vt charger:—n charge f.

loaf n pain m.

loan n prêt m.

loathe vt détester.

loathing n aversion f.

lobster n langouste f.

local adj local.

locate vt localiser.

location n situation f.

lock n serrure f:—vt fermer à clé.

locker n casier m.

lockout n grève patronale f.

locomotive n locomotive f.

lodge vi se loger.

lodger n locataire mf.

log n bûche f.

logic n logique f.

logical adj logique.

loiter vi s'attarder.

lollipop n sucette f.

lonely adj seul, solitaire.

loneliness n solitude f.

long adj long, f longue:—vi désirer.

longevity n longévité f.

longing n désir m.

long-range adj à longue portée.

long-term adj à long terme.

look vi regarder; sembler:—n aspect m; regard m.

loop n boucle f.

loose adj lâché; desserré

loosen vt lâcher; desserrer.

loot vt piller:—n butin m.

loquacious adj loquace.

loquacity n loquacité f.

lose vt vi perdre.

loss n perte f.

lot n sort f; lot m:—**a ~** beaucoup.

lotion n lotion f.

loud adj fort, bruyant.

loudspeaker n haut-parleur m.

lounge n salon m.

lovable adj sympathique.

love n amour m:—vt aimer.

loveliness n beauté f.

lovely adj beau.

lover n amant m.

loving adj affectueux.

low adj bas:—vi meugler.

lower vt baisser.

lowly adj humble.

loyal adj loyal, fidèle.

loyalty n loyauté f; fidélité f.

lucid adj lucide.

luck n chance f.

luckless adj malchanceux.

lucky adj chanceux.

lucrative *adj* lucratif.
ludricrous *adj* absurde.
luggage *n* bagages *mpl*.
lukewarm *adj* tiède.
lull *vt* bercer:—*n* répit *m*.
luminous *adj* lumineux.
lump *n* bosse *f*; grosseur *f*.
lunch *n* déjeuner *m*.
lungs *npl* poumons *mpl*.
lure *n* leurre *m*; attrait *m*:—*vt* séduire, attirer.

lurk *vi* se cacher.
lush *adj* luxuriant.
lust *n* luxure *f*:—*vi* désirer.
lustre *n* lustre *m*.
luxuriance *n* luxuriance *f*.
luxuriant *adj* luxuriant.
luxurious *adj* luxueux.
luxury *n* luxe *m*.
lyrical *adj* lyrique.
lyrics *npl* paroles *fpl*.

M

macerate *vt* macérer.
machination *n* machination *f*.
machine *n* machine *f*.
machinery *n* machinerie *f*; mécanisme *m*.
mad *adj* fou; folle; insensé.
madam *n* madame *f*.
madden *vt* rendre fou; rendre furieux.
madman *n* fou *m*.
madness *n* folie *f*.
magazine *n* magazine *m*, revue *f*; magasin *m*.
magic *n* magie *f*:—*adj* magique.
magnanimous *adj* magnanime.
magnet *n* aimant *m*.
magnetic *adj* magnétique.
magnetism *n* magnétisme *m*.
magnificence *n* magnificence *f*.
magnificent *ad* magnifique.
magnify *vt* grossir; exagérer.
magnitude *n* magnitude *f*.
maid *n* bonne *f*.
mail *n* courrier *m*.
mail train *n* (*rail*) train-poste *m*.
maim *vt* mutiler.
main *adj* principal; essentiel:—**in the** ~ en général.

mainland *n* continent *m*.
main line *n* (*rail*) grande ligne *f*.
main street *n* rue principale *f*.
maintain *vt* maintenir; soutenir.
maintenance *n* entretien *m*.
majestic *adj* majestueux.
majesty *n* majesté *f*.
major *adj* majeur.
majority *n* majorité *f*.
make *vt* faire *n* marque *f*.
make-up *n* maquillage *m*.
malady *n* maladie *f*.
malaise *n* malaise *m*.
malaria *n* malaria *f*.
malcontent *adj n* mécontent *m*, -e *f*.
male *adj* mâle; masculin:—*n* mâle *m*.
malevolence *n* malveillance *f*.
malevolent *adj* malveillant.
malice *n* malice *f*.
malicious *adj* méchant.
malign *adj* nocif:—*vt* calomnier.
malleable *adj* malléable.
malnutrition *n* malnutrition *f*.
malpractice *n* négligence *f*.
maltreat *vt* maltraiter.
mammal *n* mammifère *m*.

man *n* homme *m*.

manage *vt* diriger; réussir:—*vi* réussir.

management *n* direction *f*.

manager *n* directeur *m*.

managing director *n* directeur général *m*.

mandate *n* mandat *m*.

mandatory *n* obligatoire.

manhandle *vt* maltraiter; manutentionner.

maniac *n* maniaque *mf*.

manic *adj* maniaque.

manifest *adj* manifeste:—*vt* manifester.

manifestation *n* manifestation *f*.

manipulate *vt* manipuler.

manipulation *n* manipulation *f*.

mankind *n* humanité *f*.

manliness *n* virilité *f*.

manly *adj* viril.

man-made *n* artificiel.

manner *n* manière *f*.

manoeuvre *n* manœuvre *f*.

manual *adj n* manuel *m*.

manufacture *n* fabrication *f*.

manufacturer *n* fabricant *m*.

manuscript *n* manuscrit *m*.

many *adj* beaucoup de:—**how ~?** combien?

map *n* carte *f*; plan *m*.

mar *vt* gâter, gâcher.

marble *n* marbre *m*:—*adj* marbré.

March *n* mars *m*.

march *n* marche *f*:—*vi* marcher.

margarine *n* margarine *f*.

margin *n* marge *f*; bord *m*.

marginal *adj* marginal.

marine *adj* marin.

maritime *adj* maritime.

mark *n* marque *f*; signe *m*:—*vt* marquer.

marker *n* marque *f*; marqueur *m*.

market *n* marché *m*.

marketable *adj* vendable.

marmalade *n* confiture d'oranges *f*.

marriage *n* mariage *m*.

marriageable *adj* mariable.

married *adj* marié; conjugal.

marry *vi* se marier.

marsh *n* marécage *m*.

marshy *adj* marécageux.

martial *adj* martial.

martyr *n* martyr *m*, -e *f*.

marvel *n* merveille *f*:—*vi* s'émerveiller.

marvellous *adj* merveilleux.

masculine *adj* masculin, viril.

mask *n* masque *m*:—*vt* masquer.

mason *n* maçon *m*.

mass *n* masse *f*; messe *f*; multitude *f*.

massacre *n* massacre *m*:—*vt* massacrer.

massage *n* massage *m*.

massive *adj* énorme.

mast *n* mât *m*.

master *n* maître *m*:—*vt* maîtriser.

mastermind *vt* diriger.

mastery *n* maîtrise *f*.

match *n* allumette *f*:—*vt* égaler.

matchless *adj* incomparable, sans pareil.

mate *n* camarade *mf*:—*vt* accoupler.

material *adj* matériel.

maternal *adj* maternel.

maternity hospital *n* maternité *f*.

mathematical *adj* mathématique.

mathematics *npl* mathématiques *fpl*.

matrimonial *adj* matrimonial.

matted *adj* emmêlé.

matter n matière, substance f:—vi importer.

mattress n matelas m.

mature adj mûr:—vi mûrir.

maturity n maturité f.

maximum n maximum m.

may v aux pouvoir:—**be** peut-être.

May n mai m.

mayor n maire m.

maze n labyrinthe m.

me pn moi; me.

meadow n prairie f, pré m.

meagre adj pauvre.

meal n repas m.

mean adj avare, mesquin; moyen:— ~**s** npl moyens mpl:—vt vi signifier.

meander vi serpenter.

meaning n sens m.

meanness n avarice, mesquinerie f.

meantime adv pendant ce temps-là.

measure n mesure f:—vt mesurer.

measurement n mesure f.

meat n viande f.

mechanic n mécanicien m.

mechanical adj mécanique.

mechanism n mécanisme m.

medal n médaille f.

media npl média mpl.

mediate vi agir en tant que médiateur.

mediator n médiateur m, -trice f.

medical adj médical.

medicinal adj médicinal.

medicine n médecine f.

mediocre adj médiocre.

meditate vi méditer.

meditation n méditation f.

meditative adj méditatif.

Mediterranean adj méditerranéen.

medium n milieu m; médium m:—adj moyen.

medium wave n ondes moyennes fpl.

meek adj doux.

meekness n douceur f.

meet vt rencontrer:—vi se rencontrer.

meeting n réunion f; congrès m.

melancholy n mélancolie f:—adj mélancolique.

mellow adj mûr; doux:—vi mûrir.

melody n mélodie f.

melon n melon m.

melt vt faire fondre:—vi fondre.

member n membre m.

memorable adj mémorable.

memorandum n mémorandum m.

memorise vt mémoriser.

memory n mémoire f; souvenir m.

menace n menace f.

mend vt réparer; raccommoder.

menial adj vil.

menstruation n menstruation f.

mental adj mental.

mentality n mentalité f.

mention n mention f:—vt mentionner.

menu n menu m.

mercantile adj commercial.

mercenary adj n mercenaire m.

merchandise n marchandise f.

merchant n négociant m, -e f.

merciful adj miséricordieux.

mercy n pitié f.

mere adj simple.

merge vt vi fusionner.

merger n fusion f.

merit n mérite m:—vt mériter.

merry adj joyeux.

mesh *n* maille *f*.

mesmerise *vt* hypnotiser.

mess *n* désordre *m*; confusion *f*.

message *n* message *m*.

messenger *n* messager *m*, -ère *f*.

metal *n* métal *m*.

metallic *adj* métallique.

meteorological *adj* météorologique.

meteorology *n* météorologie *f*.

meter *n* compteur *m*; mètre *m*.

method *n* méthode *f*.

methodical *adj*, **~ly** *adv* méthodique(ment).

metropolitan *adj* métropolitain.

mew *vi* miauler.

microphone *n* microphone *m*.

microscope *n* microscope *m*.

mid *adj* demi; mi-.

midday *n* midi *m*.

middle *adj* moyen; du milieu:—*n* milieu *m*.

middling *adj* moyen.

midnight *n* minuit *m*.

midway *adv* à mi-chemin.

midwife *n* sage-femme *f*.

might *n* force *f*.

mighty *adj* fort, puissant.

migrate *vi* émigrer.

migration *n* émigration *f*.

mild *adj* doux; modéré.

mildness *n* douceur *f*.

mile *n* mille *m*.

militant *adj* militant.

militate *vi* militer.

milk *n* lait *m*:—*vt* traire.

milky *adj* laiteux.

mill *n* moulin *m*:—*vt* moudre.

millimetre *n* millimètre *m*.

million *n* million *m*.

millionaire *n* millionaire *mf*.

millionth *adj n* millionième *mf*.

mime *n* mime *m*.

mimic *vt* mimer.

mimicry *n* mimique *f*.

mince *vt* hacher.

mind *n* esprit *m*:—*vt* prendre soin de.

minded *adj* disposé.

mindful *adj* conscient; attentif.

mine *pn* le mien, la mienne, les mien(ne)s; à moi:—*n* mine *f*.

miner *n* mineur *m*.

mineral *adj n* minéral *m*.

mingle *vt* mêler.

miniature *n* miniature *f*.

minimise *vt* minimiser.

minimum *n* minimum *m*.

minister *n* ministre *m*:—*vt* servir.

ministry *n* ministère *m*.

minor *adj* mineur:—*n* mineur *m*, -e *f*.

minority *n* minorité *f*.

minus *adv* moins.

minute *adj* minuscule.

minute *n* minute *f*.

miracle *n* miracle *m*.

miraculous *adj* miraculeux.

mirage *n* mirage *m*.

mirror *n* miroir *m*.

misadventure *n* mésaventure *f*.

misbehave *vi* se conduire mal.

misbehaviour *n* mauvaise conduite *f*.

miscarriage *n* fausse couche *f*.

miscellaneous *adj* divers, varié.

miscellany *n* mélange, assortiment *m*.

mischief *n* mal, tort *m*.

mischievous *adj* mauvais; espiègle.

misconception *n* méprise *f*.

misconduct *n* mauvaise conduite *f*.

misdeed *n* méfait *m*.

misdemeanour n délit m.

miser n avare mf.

miserable adj malheureux.

misery n malheur m; misère f.

misfortune n infortune f.

misgovern vt mal gouverner.

mishap n mésaventure f.

misjudge vt méjuger.

mislead vt induire en erreur.

misogynist n misogyne mf.

misprint n coquille f.

Miss n Mlle, Mademoiselle f.

miss vt rater; s'ennuyer de.

missing adj perdu; absent.

mission n mission f.

mist n brouillard m.

mistake vt confondre:—vi se tromper:—n erreur f.

Mister n Monsieur m.

mistress n maîtresse f.

mistrust vt se méfier de:—n méfiance f.

misty adj brumeux.

misunderstanding n malentendu m.

misuse vt faire un mauvais usage de.

mitigate vt atténuer.

mitigation n atténuation f.

mix vt mélanger.

mixed adj mélangé; mixte.

mixture n mélange m.

moan n gémissement m:—vi gémir.

moat n fossé m.

mob n foule f; masse f.

mobile adj mobile.

mobilise vt mobiliser.

mobility n mobilité f.

mock vt se moquer de.

mockery n moquerie f.

mode n mode m.

model n modèle m:—vt modeler.

moderate adj modéré:—vt modérer.

moderation n modération f.

modern adj moderne.

modernise vt moderniser.

modest adj modeste.

modesty n modestie f.

modification n modification f.

modify vt modifier.

moist adj humide.

moisten vt humidifier.

moisture n humidité f.

molest vt importuner.

molten adj fondu.

moment n moment m.

momentary adj momentané.

monastery n monastère m.

monastic adj monastique.

Monday n lundi m.

monetary adj monétaire.

money n argent m; pièce de monnaie f.

monk n moine m.

monkey n singe m.

monopolise vt monopoliser.

monopoly n monopole m.

monotonous adj monotone.

monotony n monotonie f.

monster n monstre m.

monstrous adj monstrueux.

month n mois m.

monthly adj mensuel; adv mensuellement.

mood n humeur f.

moon n lune f.

moonlight n clair de lune m.

moped n vélomoteur m.

moral adj moral:—~s npl moralité f.

morale n moral m.

morality n moralité f.

morbid adj morbide.

more *adj adv* plus:—~ **and** ~ de plus en plus.

moreover *adv* de plus, en outre.

morning *n* matin *m*:—**good** ~ bonjour.

morsel *n* bouchée *f*; morceau *m*.

mortal *adj* mortel:—*n* mortel *m*, -elle *f*.

mortality *n* mortalité *f*.

mortgage *n* hypothèque *f*:—*vt* hypothéquer.

mortuary *n* morgue *f*.

mosque *n* mosquée *f*.

most *adj pn* la plupart de:—**ly** *adv* surtout, essentiellement.

mother *n* mère *f*.

motherhood *n* maternité *f*.

mother-in-law *n* belle-mère *f*.

motherly *adj* maternel.

mother tongue *n* langue maternelle *f*.

motif *n* motif *m*.

motion *n* mouvement *m*.

motionless *adj* immobile.

motivated *adj* motivé.

motive *n* motif *m*.

motor *n* moteur *m*.

motorbike *n* moto *f*.

motor vehicle *n* automobile *f*.

motto *n* devise *f*.

mould *n* moule *m*:—*vt* mouler.

mound *n* monticule *m*.

mount *n* mont *m*:—*vt* gravir.

mountain *n* montagne *f*.

mountaineer *n* alpiniste *mf*.

mountainous *adj* montagneux.

mourn *vt* pleurer.

mourning *n* deuil *m*.

mouse *n* (*pl* mice) souris *f*.

moustache *n* moustache *f*.

mouth *n* bouche *f*; embouchure *f*.

mouthful *n* bouchée *f*.

movable *adj* mobile.

move *vt* déplacer:—*vi* bouger:—*n* mouvement *m*.

movement *n* mouvement *m*.

moving *adj* touchant, émouvant.

mow *vt* tondre.

Mrs *n* Mme, Madame *f*.

much *adj pn* beaucoup:—*adv* beaucoup, très.

mud *n* boue *f*.

muddy *adj* boueux.

multiple *adj* multiple.

multiplication *n* multiplication *f*.

multiply *vt* multiplier.

multitude *n* multitude *f*.

mumble *vt vi* grommeler.

munch *vt* mâcher.

mundane *adj* banal.

municipal *adj* municipal.

mural *n* mural *m*.

murder *n* meurtre *m*:—*vt* assassiner.

murderer *n* assassin, meurtrier *m*.

murky *adj* obscur.

murmur *n* murmure *m*:—*vt vi* murmurer.

muscle *n* muscle *m*.

muscular *adj* musculaire.

museum *n* musée *m*.

music *n* musique *f*.

musical *adj* musical; mélodieux.

musician *n* musicien *m*, -ienne *f*.

must *v aux* devoir.

musty *adj* moisi.

mute *adj* muet, silencieux.

mutilate *vt* mutiler.

mutilation *n* mutilation *f*.

mutter *vt vi* grommeler:—*n* grommellement *m*.

mutual *adj* mutuel, réciproque.
my *pn* mon, ma, mes.
myself *pn* moi-même.
mysterious *adj* mystérieux.

mystery *n* mystère *m*.
myth *n* mythe *m*.
mythology *n* mythologie *f*.

N

nag *vt* harceler.
nail *n* ongle *m*; clou *m*:—*vt* clouer.
naive *adj* naïf.
naked *adj* nu; dénudé; pur.
name *n* nom *m*:—*vt* nommer.
nap *n* sieste *f*, somme *m*.
nape *n* nuque *f*.
napkin *n* serviette *f*.
narrate *vt* narrer, raconter.
narrative *adj* narratif:—*n* narration *f*.
narrow *adj* étroit.
nasty *adj* méchant; mauvais.
nation *n* nation *f*.
national *adj* national.
nationalist *adj n* nationaliste *mf*.
nationality *n* nationalité *f*.
native *adj* natal:—*n* autochtone *mf*.
natural *adj* naturel.
naturalist *n* naturaliste *mf*.
nature *n* nature *f*; sorte *f*.
naughty *adj* méchant.
nausea *n* nausée.
nauseous *adj* écœurant.
navel *n* nombril *m*.
navigate *vi* naviguer.
navigation *n* navigation *f*.
navy *n* marine *f*.
near *prep* près de:—*adv* près; à côté:—*adj* proche.
nearly *adv* presque.
neat *adj* soigné; net.
necessary *adj* nécessaire.
necessitate *vt* nécessiter.

necessity *n* nécessité *f*.
neck *n* cou *m*.
necklace *n* collier *m*.
need *n* besoin *m*:—*vt* avoir besoin de.
needle *n* aiguille *f*.
needy *adj* nécessiteux.
negation *n* négation *f*.
negative *adj* négatif:—*n* négative *f*.
neglect *vt* négliger:—*n* négligence *f*.
negligence *n* négligence *f*.
negligent *adj* négligent.
negotiate *vt vi* négocier.
negotiation *n* négociation *f*.
Negro *adj* noir:—*n* Noire *m*.
neighbour *n* voisin *m*, -e *f*.
neighbouring *adj* voisin.
neither *conj* ni:—*pn* aucun(e), ni l'un(e) ni l'autre.
nephew *n* neveu *m*.
nerve *n* nerf *m*; courage *m*.
nervous *adj* nerveux.
nest *n* nid *m*; nichée *f*.
net *n* filet *m*.
net curtain *n* voile *m*.
nettle *n* ortie *f*.
network *n* réseau *f*.
neutral *adj* neutre.
neutrality *n* neutralité *f*.
never *adv* jamais.
nevertheless *adv* cependant, néanmoins.
new *adj* neuf; nouveau.

newborn adj nouveau-né, f nouveau-née.

news npl nouvelles, informations fpl.

newspaper n journal m.

New Year n Nouvel An m:—~'s Day n Jour du Nouvel An m:—~'s Eve Saint-Sylvestre f.

next adj prochain:—adv ensuite, après.

nibble vt mordiller.

nice adj gentil, f gentille; agréable.

niche n niche f.

nickname n surnom m:—vt surnommer.

niece n nièce f.

night n nuit f:—**good ~** bonne nuit.

nightly adv toutes les nuits:—adj nocturne.

nightmare n cauchemar m.

nimble adj léger; agile.

nine adj n neuf m.

nineteen adj n dix-neuf m.

nineteenth adj n dix-neuvième mf.

ninetieth adj n quatre-vingt-dixième mf.

ninety adj n quatre-vingt-dix m.

ninth adj n neuvième mf.

no adv non:—adj aucun; pas de.

noble adj noble:—n noble mf.

nobody pn personne.

nocturnal adj nocturne.

nod n signe de tête m:—vi faire un signe de la tête.

noise n bruit m.

noisiness n bruit, tapage m.

nominal adj nominal.

nominate vt nommer.

nomination n nomination f.

nonchalant adj nonchalant.

none pn aucun; personne.

nonentity n nullité f.

nonetheless adv cependant.

nonplussed adj perplexe.

nonsense n absurdité f.

nonsensical adj absurde.

nonstop adj direct.

noon n midi m.

nor conj ni.

normal adj normal.

north n nord m:—adj du nord.

northeast n nord-est m.

northern adj du nord.

northwest n nord-ouest m.

nose n nez m.

nostalgia n nostalgie f.

nostril n narine f.

not adv pas; non.

notable adj notable.

note n note f; billet m:—vt noter, marquer.

notebook n carnet m.

nothing n rien m.

notice n notice f; avis m:—vt remarquer.

noticeable adj visible.

notify vt notifier.

notion n notion f; idée f.

notoriety n notoriété f.

notorious adj notoire.

nourish vt nourrir, alimenter.

nourishment n nourriture f, aliments mpl.

novel n roman m.

novelty n nouveauté f.

November n novembre m.

novice n novice mf.

now adv maintenant.

nowadays adv de nos jours.

nowhere adv nulle part.

nuance *n* nuance *f.*
nuclear *adj* nucléaire.
nude *adj* nu.
nudity *n* nudité *f.*
nuisance *n* ennui *m*; gêne *f.*
null *adj* nul.
numb *adj* engourdi:—*vt* engourdir.
number *n* numéro, nombre *m*:—*vt* numéroter.

numbness *n* engourdissement *m.*
numeral *n* chiffre *m.*
numerical *adj* numérique.
nurse *n* infirmière *f*:—*vt* soigner.
nursery *n* crèche *f.*
nurture *vt* élever.
nut *n* noix *f.*
nutritious *adj* nutritif.
nylon *n* nylon *m.*

O

oak *n* chêne *m.*
oar *n* rame *f.*
oath *n* serment *m.*
obedience *n* obéissance *f.*
obedient *adj* obéissant.
obese *adj* obèse.
obesity *n* obésité *f.*
obey *vt* obéir à.
object *n* objet *m*:—*vt* objecter.
objection *n* objection *f.*
objective *adj n* objectif *m.*
obligation *n* obligation *f.*
obligatory *adj* obligatoire.
oblige *vt* obliger.
obliging *adj* obligeant.
oblique *adj* oblique.
oblivious *adj* oublieux.
obnoxious *adj* odieux.
obscene *adj* obscène.
obscure *adj* obscur:—*vt* obscurcir.
obscurity *n* obscurité *f.*
observant *adj* observateur.
observation *n* observation *f.*
observatory *n* observatoire *m.*
observe *vt* observer.
obsess *vt* obséder.
obsessive *adj* obsédant.
obsolete *adj* désuet.

obstacle *n* obstacle *m.*
obstinate *adj* obstiné.
obstruct *vt* obstruer; entraver.
obstruction *n* obstruction *f*, encombrement *m.*
obtain *vt* obtenir.
obtainable *adj* disponible.
obvious *adj* évident.
occasion *n* occasion *f*:—*vt* occasionner.
occasional *adj* occasionnel.
occupant *n* occupant *m*, -e *f.*
occupation *n* occupation *f*, emploi *m.*
occupy *vt* occuper.
occur *vi* se produire, arriver.
occurrence *n* incident *m.*
ocean *n* océan *m.*
oceanic *adj* océanique.
October *n* octobre *m.*
odd *adj* impair; étrange.
odious *adj* odieux.
odour *n* odeur *f*, parfum *m.*
of *prep* de; à.
off *adj* éteint; fermé; annulé.
offend *vt* offenser, blesser.
offense *n* offense *f*; injure *f.*
offensive *adj* offensant.
offer *vt* offrir:—*n* offre *f.*
office *n* bureau *m*; poste *m.*

officer n officier m; fonctionnaire mf.

official adj officiel:—n employé m, -e f.

officiate vi officier.

offset vt compenser; décaler.

offshore adj côtier.

offspring n progéniture f.

oil n huile f:—vt huiler.

oil painting n peinture à l'huile f.

oil tanker n pétrolier m.

ointment n onguent m.

OK, okay excl OK, d'accord.

old adj vieux, f vieille.

old age n vieillesse f.

olive n olivier m; olive f.

olive oil n huile d'olive f.

omelette n omelette f.

omission n omission f; négligence f.

omit vt omettre.

on prep sur, dessus; en; pour:—adj allumé, branché.

once adv une fois:—~ more encore une fois.

one adj un, une.

onerous adj lourd; onéreux.

oneself pn soi-même.

one-sided adj partial.

onion n oignon m.

onlooker n spectateur m, -trice f.

only adj seul, unique:—adv seulement.

onus n responsabilité f.

opaque adj opaque.

open adj ouvert; sincère, franc:—vt ouvrir; vi s'ouvrir.

opening n ouverture f.

openness n clareté f.

opera n opéra m.

operate vi fonctionner; opérer.

operation n fonctionnement m; opération f.

operator n opérateur m, -trice f.

opine vt être d'avis (que).

opinion n opinion f; jugement m.

opinion poll n sondage m.

opponent n opposant m, -e f.

opportune adj opportun.

opportunity n occasion f.

oppose vt s'opposer à.

opposing adj opposé.

opposite adj opposé:—adv en face: —prep en face de:—n contraire m.

opposition n opposition f.

oppress vt opprimer.

oppressive adj oppressif.

optimist n optimiste mf.

optimistic adj optimiste.

optimum adj optimum.

option n option f.

optional adj optionnel.

opulent adj opulent.

or conj ou.

oral adj oral, verbal.

orange n orange f.

orbit n orbite f.

orchestra n orchestre m.

ordain vt ordonner.

order n ordre m; commande f:—vt ordonner.

orderly adj ordonné; réglé.

ordinary adj ordinaire.

ore n minerai m.

organ n organe m.

organic adj organique.

organisation n organisation f.

organise vt organiser.

organism n organisme m.

oriental adj oriental.

orifice n orifice m.

origin n origine f.

original adj original.

originality n originalité f.

ornament n ornement m:—vt ornementer.

ornate adj ornementé.

orphan adj n orphelin m, -e f.

orthodox adj orthodoxe.

oscillate vi osciller.

other pn autre.

otherwise adv autrement.

ought v aux devoir; falloir.

our pn notre, pl nos.

ours pn le nôtre, la nôtre, les nôtres; à nous.

ourselves pn pl nous-mêmes.

out adv dehors; éteint.

outburst n explosion f.

outcome n résultat m.

outdo vt surpasser.

outdoor adj de plein air:—~s adv à l'extérieur.

outer adj extérieur.

outfit n tenue f; équipement m.

outgoing adj extroverti; sortant.

outlay n dépenses fpl, frais mpl.

outline n contour m; grandes lignes fpl.

outlook n perspective f.

output n rendement m; sortie f.

outrage n outrage m:—vt outrager.

outright adv absolument:—adj absolu.

outset n commencement m.

outside n surface f; extérieur m:—adv dehors:—prep en dehors de.

outstrip vt devancer; surpasser.

oval n, adj ovale m.

ovary n ovaire m.

oven n four m.

over prep sur, dessus; plus de; pendant:—adj fini.

overall adj total:—~s npl salopette f.

overbalance vi perdre l'équilibre.

overcast adj couvert.

overcharge vt surcharger.

overcoat n pardessus m.

overcome vt vaincre.

overdo vi exagérer.

overdraft n découvert m.

overdue adj en retard; arriéré.

overestimate vt surestimer.

overflow vi déborder:—n surplus m.

overhaul vt réviser:—n révision f.

overland adj adv par voie de terre.

overlap vi se chevaucher.

overlook vt donner sur; oublier; tolérer; négliger.

overnight adv pendant la nuit:—adj de nuit.

overpower vt dominer, écraser.

overrate vt surévaluer.

overrun vt envahir; infester; dépasser.

overseas adv à l'étranger; outremer:—adj étranger.

oversee vt inspecter, surveiller.

oversight n oubli m; erreur f.

oversleep vi se réveiller en retard.

overtake vt doubler.

overthrow vt renverser:—n renversement m.

overtime n heures supplémentaires fpl.

overturn vt renverser.

overwhelm vt écraser.

overwhelming adj écrasant.

overwork vi se surmener.

owe vt devoir.

owing adj dû:—~ **to** en raison de.

owl n chouette f.

own adj propre:—vt posséder.

owner n propriétaire mf.

ox n bœuf m.

oxygen n oxygène m.

oyster n huître f.

ozone n ozone m.

P

pace n pas m; allure f:—vi marcher.

pacific adj pacifique.

pacification n pacification f.

pacify vt pacifier.

pack n paquet m; bande f:—vt empaqueter:—vi faire ses valises.

package n paquet m.

packet n paquet m.

pact n pacte m.

pad n bloc m; tampon m; (sl) piaule f:—vt rembourrer.

paddle vi ramer:—n pagaie f.

pagan adj n païen m, païenne f.

page n page f; page m.

pail n seau m.

pain n douleur f; peine f:—vt peiner.

pained adj peiné.

painful adj douloureux; pénible.

painstaking adj soigneux.

paint vt peindre.

painter n peintre m.

painting n peinture f; tableau m.

pair n pair m.

palatable adj savoureux.

palate n palais m.

pale adj pâle; clair.

palette n palette f.

pallet n palette f.

pallid adj pâle.

palpable adj palpable; évident.

palpitation n palpitation f.

pamper vt gâter, dorloter.

pamphlet n pamphlet m; brochure f.

pan n casserole f; poêle f.

panache n panache m.

pane n vitre f.

panel n panneau m; comité m.

pang n angoisse f, tourment m.

panic adj n (de) panique f.

pant vi haleter.

panther n panthère f.

pantry n placard m.

pants npl slip m; pantalon m.

paper n papier m; journal m:—adj en papier:—vt tapisser.

paperweight n presse-papiers m.

par n équivalence f; pair m.

parachute n parachute m.

parade n parade f.

paradise n paradis m.

paradox n paradoxe m.

paragraph n paragraphe m.

parallel adj parallèle:—n parallèle f.

paralyse vt paralyser.

paralysis n paralysie f.

paramount adj suprême, supérieur.

paranoid adj paranoïaque.

parasite n parasite m.

parcel n paquet m; parcelle f:—vt empaqueter.

parch vt dessécher.

pardon n pardon m:—vt pardonner.

parent *n* père *m*; mère *f*:—**s** parents *mpl*.

park *n* parc *m*:—*vt* garer; *vi* se garer.

parking *n* stationnement *m*.

parking lot *n* parking *m*.

parliament *n* parlement *m*.

parody *n* parodie *f*:—*vt* parodier.

parry *vt* parer.

part *n* partie *f*; part *f*; rôle (d'acteur) *m*:—*vt* séparer; diviser:—*vi* se séparer; se diviser:—**ly** *adv* en partie.

partial *adj* partial.

participate *vi* participer (à).

participation *n* participation *f*.

particle *n* particule *f*.

particular *adj* particulier:—*n* particulier *m*; particularité *f*.

partition *n* partition, séparation *f*:—*vt* partager.

partner *n* associé *m*, -e *f*.

party *n* parti *m*; fête *f*.

pass *vt* passer; dépasser:—*vi* passer:—*n* permis *m*; passage *m*.

passage *n* passage *m*.

passenger *n* passager *m*, -ère *f*.

passer-by *n* passant *m*, -e *f*.

passion *n* passion *f*; amour *m*.

passionate *adj* passionné.

passive *adj* passif.

passport *n* passeport *m*.

past *adj* passé:—*n* passé *m*:—*prep* au-delà de; après.

paste *n* pâte *f*, colle *f*:—*vt* coller.

pastime *n* passe-temps *m invar*.

pastry *n* pâtisserie *f*.

pasture *n* pâture *f*.

patch *n* pièce *f*; terrain *m*:—*vt* rapiécer.

patent *adj* évident:—*n* brevet *m*:—*vt* faire breveter.

patentee *n* détenteur d'un brevet *m*.

paternal *adj* paternel.

paternity *n* paternité *f*.

path *n* chemin, sentier *m*.

pathetic *adj* pathétique.

patience *n* patience *f*.

patient *adj* patient:—**ly** *adv* patiemment:—*n* patient *m*, -e *f*.

patrol *n* patrouille *f*:—*vi* patrouiller.

patron *n* protecteur *m*; client *m*, -e *f*.

patronise *vt* patronner, protéger.

pattern *n* motif *m*; modèle *m*.

pause *n* pause *f*:—*vi* faire une pause; hésiter.

pave *vt* paver; carreler.

pavement *n* trottoir *m*.

paw *n* patte *f*:—*vt* tripoter.

pay *vt* payer:—**to ~ back** *vt* rembourser:—*n* paie *f*; salaire *m*.

payable *adj* payable.

payment *n* paiement *m*.

pea *n* pois *m*.

peace *n* paix *f*.

peaceful *adj* paisible; pacifique.

peak *n* pic *m*; maximum *m*.

pear *n* poire *f*.

pearl *n* perle *f*.

peasant *n* paysan *m*, -anne *f*.

pebble *n* caillou *m*; galet *m*.

peculiar *adj* étrange, singulier.

peculiarity *n* particularité, singularité *f*.

pedal *n* pédale *f*:—*vi* pédaler.

pedestrian *n* piéton *m*, -onne *f*:—*adj* pédestre.

peel *vt* peler:—*n* peau *f*; pelure *f*.

peer *n* pair *m*.

peerless *adj* incomparable.

pelt *n* fourrure *f*.

pen n stylo m; plume f.

penalty n peine f; sanction f; amende f.

pencil n crayon m.

pendulum n pendule m.

penetrate vt pénétrer dans.

peninsula n péninsule f.

penitentiary n pénitencier m.

penknife n canif m.

penpal n correspondant m, -e f.

pension n pension f:—vt pensionner.

pensive adj pensif.

penultimate adj pénultième.

people n peuple m; nation f; gens mpl:—vt peupler.

pepper n poivre m:—vt poivrer.

per prep par.

per annum adv par an.

perceive vt percevoir.

percentage n pourcentage m.

perception n perception f; notion f.

perch n perche f.

percussion n percussion f.

perdition n perte, ruine f.

perennial adj perpétuel.

perfect adj parfait; idéal:—vt parfaire, perfectionner.

perfection n perfection f.

perform vt exécuter:—vi donner une représentation.

performance n exécution f; accomplissement m.

performer n exécutant m, -e f; acteur m, -trice f.

perfume n parfum m:—vt parfumer.

perhaps adv peut-être.

peril n péril, danger m.

perilous adj dangereux.

perimeter n périmètre m.

period n période f; époque f.

periodic adj périodique.

perish vi périr.

perishable adj périssable.

permanent adj permanent.

permissible adj permis.

permission n permission f.

permissive adj permissif.

permit vt permettre:—n permis m.

perpetrate vt perpétrer, commettre.

perpetual adj perpétuel.

perplex vt confondre, laisser perplexe.

persecute vt persécuter; importuner.

persecution n persécution f.

persevere vi persévérer.

persist vi persister.

persistence adj persistance f.

persistent adj persistant.

person n personne f.

personage n personnage m.

personal adv personnel.

personal computer n ordinateur individuel m.

personality n personnalité f.

personnel n personnel m.

perspective n perspective f.

perspiration n transpiration f.

perspire vi transpirer.

persuade vt persuader.

persuasion n persuasion f.

persuasive adj persuasif.

pertaining:—~ **to** prep relatif à.

pertinent adj pertinent.

perturb vt perturber.

peruse vt lire; examiner attentivement.

perverse adj pervers, dépravé.

pessimist n pessimiste mf.

pest n insecte nuisible m; casse-pieds (fam) mf invar.

pester vt importuner, fatiguer.
pestilence n peste f.
pet n animal domestique m:—vt gâter.
petal n (bot) pétale m.
petition n pétition f.
petticoat n jupon m.
pettiness n insignifiance f.
petty adj mesquin; insignifiant.
phantom n fantôme m.
pharmacist n pharmacien m, -ienne f.
pharmacy n pharmacie f.
phase n phase f.
phenomenal adj phénoménal.
phenomenon n phénomène m.
philosopher n philosophe mf.
philosophical adj philosophique.
philosophise vi philosopher.
philosophy n philosophie f.
phobia n phobie f.
phone n téléphone m:—vt téléphoner à.
phone book n annuaire m.
phone call n coup de téléphone m.
photograph n photo(graphie) f:—vt photographier.
photographer n photographe mf.
photography n photographie f.
phrase n phrase f:—vt exprimer.
phrase book n guide de conversation m.
physical adv physique.
physician n médecin m.
physicist n physicien m, -ienne f.
physiotherapy n physiothérapie f.
physique n physique m.
pianist n pianiste mf.
piano n piano m.
pick vt choisir; cueillir:—n pic m; choix m.
picnic n pique-nique m.

pictorial adj pictural; illustré.
picture n image f; peinture f:—vt dépeindre.
pie n gâteau m; tarte f; pâté en croûte m.
piece n morceau m; pièce f.
pierce vt percer, transpercer.
piercing adj perçant.
pig n cochon m.
pigeon n pigeon m.
pile n tas m; pile f; amas m:—vt entasser.
pilgrim n pèlerin m.
pill n pilule f.
pillar n pilier m.
pillow n oreiller m.
pilot n pilote m:—vt piloter; (fig) mener.
pin n épingle f:—vt épingler.
pincers n pinces, tenailles fpl.
pine n (bot) pin m:—vi languir.
pineapple n ananas m.
pink n, adj rose m.
pint n pinte f.
pioneer n pionnier m.
pious adj pieux, dévot.
pipe n tube, tuyau m; pipe f.
pipeline n canalisation f.
piracy n piraterie f.
pirate n pirate m.
pistol n pistolet m.
pitch n lancement m:—vt lancer, jeter.
pitcher n cruche f.
pitiable adj pitoyable.
pitiful adj pitoyable.
pity n pitié f:—vt avoir pitié de.
placard n affiche f.
placate vt apaiser.
place n endroit, lieu m:—vt placer.

placid *adj* placide, calme.

plague *n* peste *f*:—*vt* tourmenter.

plain *adj* uni; simple; évident:—*n* plaine *f*.

plait *n* pli *m*; tresse *f*:—*vt* plier.

plan *n* plan *m*:—*vt* projeter.

plane *n* avion *m*; plan *m*:—*vt* aplanir.

planet *n* planète *f*.

plank *n* planche *f*.

planner *n* planificateur *m*, -trice *f*.

plant *n* plante *f*; usine *f*:—*vt* planter.

plantation *n* plantation *f*.

plaster *n* plâtre *m*; emplâtre *m*:—*vt* plâtrer.

plastic *adj* plastique.

plate *n* assiette *f*; plaque *f*; lame *f*.

platform *n* plateforme *f*.

platter *n* écuelle *f*; plat *m*.

plausible *adj* plausible.

play *n* jeu *m*; pièce *f* de théâtre:—*vt vi* jouer.

player *n* joueur *m*, -euse *f*; acteur *m*, -trice *f*.

playful *adj* enjoué, amusé.

playwright *n* dramaturge *mf*.

plea *n* appel *m*; excuse *f*, prétexte *m*.

plead *vt* plaider; prétexter.

pleasant *adj* agréable; plaisant.

please *vt* faire plaisir à.

pleased *adj* content.

pleasure *n* plaisir *m*; gré *m*.

pledge *n* promesse *f*; gage *m*:—*vt* engager.

plentiful *adj* copieux; abondant.

plenty *n* abondance *f*.

pliable *adj* pliant; souple.

pliers *npl* tenailles *fpl*.

plot *n* complot *m*; intrigue *f*:—*vt* tracer.

plough *n* charrue *f*:—*vt* labourer.

pluck *vt* tirer; arracher:—*n* courage *m*.

plug *n* bougie *f*; prise *f*:—*vt* boucher.

plumber *n* plombier *m*.

plump *adj* rondouillet, dodu.

plunge *vi* plonger; s'élancer.

plural *adj n* pluriel *m*.

plus *prep* plus.

pneumonia *n* pneumonie *f*.

poach *vt* pocher; braconner.

poacher *n* braconnier *m*.

pocket *n* poche *f*:—*vt* empocher.

poem *n* poème *m*.

poet *n* poète *m*.

poetry *n* poésie *f*.

poignant *adj* poignant.

point *n* pointe *f*; point *m*:—*vt* pointer.

pointed *adj* pointu; acéré.

poise *n* attitude *f*; équilibre *m*.

poison *n* poison *m*:—*vt* empoisonner.

poisonous *adj* vénéneux.

poke *vt* attiser.

poker-faced *adj* au visage impassible.

pole *n* pôle *m*; mât *m*; perche *f*.

police *n* police *f*.

policeman *n* agent de police *m*.

police station *n* commissariat *m*.

policy *n* politique *f*.

polish *vt* polir; cirer:—*n* poli *m*.

polished *adj* poli; ciré; élégant.

polite *adj* poli.

politeness *n* politesse.

political *adj* politique.

politician *n* homme (femme) politique *m(f)*.

politics *npl* politique *f*.

pollute *vt* polluer.

pollution n pollution.
polytechnic n école d'enseignement technique f.
pompous adj pompeux.
pond n mare f; étang m.
ponder vt considérer.
pony n poney m.
pool n piscine f.
poor adj pauvre; mauvais.
populace n populace f.
popular adj populaire.
popularity n popularité f.
populate vi peupler.
population n population f.
porch n porche m.
pork n porc m.
port n port m.
portable adj portable, portatif.
portion n portion, part f.
portrait n portrait m.
portray vt faire le portrait de; dépeindre.
pose n posture f; pose f:—vi, vt poser.
position n position f:—vt mettre en position.
positive adj positif; réel.
possess vt posséder.
possession n possession f.
possibility n possibilité f.
possible adj possible:—~ly adv peut-être.
post n courrier m; poste f; emploi m.
postage stamp n timbre m.
postcard n carte postale f.
poster n poster m.
posterior n postérieur m.
posthumous adj posthume.
postman n facteur m.

post office n poste f, bureau de poste m.
postpone vt remettre; différer.
posture n posture f.
pot n pot m; marmite f:—vt empoter.
potato n pomme de terre.
potent adj puissant.
potential adj potentiel.
potion n potion f.
pouch n sac m.
poultry n volaille f.
pound n livre f; livre sterling f:—vt concasser.
pour vt verser; servir:—vi couler; pleuvoir à verse.
poverty n pauvreté f.
powder n poudre f:—vt poudrer.
powdery adj poudreux.
power n pouvoir m; puissance f; force f:—vt propulser.
powerful adj puissant.
powerless adj impotent.
practicable adj praticable; faisable.
practical adj pratique.
practicality n faisabilité f.
practice n pratique f; usage m; entraînement m.
practise vt pratiquer:—vi s'exercer.
pragmatic adj pragmatique.
praise n louange f:—vt louer.
prance vi cabrioler.
prattle vi jacasser:—n jacasserie f.
prawn n crevette f.
pray vi prier.
prayer n prière f.
preach vt prêcher.
preacher n prédicateur m.
precarious adj précaire, incertain.
precaution n précaution f.

precede *vt* précéder.

precedent *adj n* précédent *m*.

precinct *n* limite *f*; enceinte *f*.

precious *adj* précieux.

precipitate *vt* précipiter:—*adj* précipité.

precise *n* précis, exact.

precision *n* précision, exactitude *f*.

precocious *adj* précoce, prématuré.

preconceive *vt* préconcevoir.

preconception *n* préjugé *m*; idée préconçue *f*.

predator *n* prédateur *m*.

predecessor *n* prédécesseur *m*.

predict *vt* prédire.

predictable *adj* prévisible.

prediction *n* prédiction *f*.

predominant *adj* prédominant.

predominate *vt* prédominer.

preface *n* préface *f*.

prefer *vt* préférer.

preferable *adj* préférable.

preference *n* préférence *f*.

preferential *adj* préférentiel.

prefix *vt* préfixer.

pregnancy *n* grossesse *f*.

pregnant *adj* enceinte.

prehistoric *adj* préhistorique.

prejudice *n* préjudice *m*; préjugé *m*:—*vt* préjudicier à.

prejudiced *adj* qui a des préjugés; partial.

prejudicial *adj* préjudiciable.

preliminary *adj* préliminaire.

premature *adj* prématuré.

premeditation *n* préméditation *f*.

premises *npl* locaux *mpl*.

premium *n* prix *m*; prime *f*.

premonition *n* prémonition *f*.

preparation *n* préparation *f*.

preparatory *adj* préparatoire.

prepare *vt* préparer:—*vi* se préparer.

preposterous *adj* ridicule, absurde.

prerogative *n* prérogative *f*.

prescribe *vt* prescrire.

prescription *n* prescription *f*.

presence *n* présence *f*.

present *n* cadeau *m*:—*adj* présent; actuel:—**~ly** *adv* actuellement:—*vt* présenter.

presentable *adj* présentable.

presenter *n* présentateur *m*, -trice *f*.

preservation *n* préservation *f*.

preserve *vt* préserver:—*n* conserve *f*; confiture *f*.

preside *vi* présider; diriger.

president *n* président *m*.

press *vt* appuyer sur:—*vi* se presser:—*n* presse *f*; pressoir *m*.

pressing *adj* pressant; urgent.

pressure *n* pression *f*.

prestige *n* prestige *m*.

presumable *adj* vraisemblable.

presume *vt* présumer, supposer.

presumption *n* présomption *f*.

pretence *n* prétexte *m*; simulation *f*.

pretend *vi* prétendre; faire semblant.

pretext *n* prétexte *m*.

pretty *adj* joli, mignon.

prevail *vi* prévaloir; prédominer.

prevalent *adj* prédominant.

prevent *vt* prévenir; empêcher.

prevention *n* prévention *f*.

previous *adj* précédent; antérieur:—**~ly** *adv* auparavant.

prey *n* proie *f*.

price *n* prix *m*.

prick *vt* piquer:—*n* piqûre *f*; pointe *f*.

pride *n* orgueil *m*; vanité *f*; fierté *f*.

priest n prêtre m.

priesthood n sacerdoce m, prêtrise f.

primacy n primauté f.

primarily adv principalement, surtout.

primary adj primaire; principal, premier.

primate n primate m.

prime n (fig) fleur f; commencement m:—adj premier; principal.

prime minister n premier ministre m.

primitive adj primitif.

prince n prince m.

princess n princesse f.

principal adj principal:—n principal m.

principle n principe m.

print vt imprimer:—n impression f; estampe f.

printer n imprimeur m; imprimante f.

prior adj antérieur, précédent.

priority n priorité f.

prison n prison f.

prisoner n prisonnier m, -ière f.

privacy n intimité f.

private adj privé; secret; particulier:—~ly adv en privé.

privilege n privilège m.

prize n prix m:—vt apprécier, évaluer.

pro prep pour.

probability n probabilité f; vraisemblance f.

probable adj probable, vraisemblable.

probation n essai m; probation f.

probationary adj d'essai.

probe n sonde f:—vt sonder.

problem n problème m.

problematical adj problématique.

procedure n procédure f.

proceed vi procéder; provenir.

process n processus m; procédé m.

procession n procession f.

proclaim vt proclamer; promulguer.

proclamation n proclamation f; décret m.

procure vt procurer.

procurement n obtention f.

prod vt pousser.

prodigious adj prodigieux.

prodigy n prodige m.

produce vt produire; créer.

producer n producteur m, -trice f.

product n produit m; œuvre f; fruit m.

production n production f; produit m.

productive adj productif.

profess vt professer; déclarer.

profession n profession f.

professional adj professionnel.

professor n professeur m.

proficiency n capacité f.

proficient adj compétent.

profile n profil m.

profit n bénéfice, profit m:—vi profiter (de).

profitability n rentabilité f.

profitable adj profitable, avantageux.

profound adj profond.

program(me) n programme m.

programmer n programmeur m, -euse f.

progress n progrès m; cours m:—vi progresser.

progression n progression f; avance f.

progressive adj progressif.

prohibit vt prohiber; défendre.

project vt projeter:—n projet m.

projection n projection f.

prolific adj prolifique, fécond.

prolong vt prolonger.

promenade *n* promenade *f*.
prominence *n* proéminence *f*.
prominent *adj* proéminent.
promise *n* promesse *f*:—*vt* promettre.
promising *adj* prometteur.
promote *vt* promouvoir.
promoter *n* promoteur *m*.
promotion *n* promotion *f*.
prompt *adj* prompt:—*vt* suggérer.
prone *adj* enclin (à).
pronounce *vt* prononcer; déclarer.
pronounced *adj* marqué, prononcé.
pronouncement *n* déclaration *f*.
pronunciation *n* prononciation *f*.
proof *n* preuve *f*:—*adj* imperméable; résistant.
prop *vt* soutenir:—*n* appui, soutien *m*.
propaganda *n* propagande *f*.
propel *vt* propulser.
propeller *n* hélice *f*.
propensity *n* propension, tendance *f*.
proper *adj* propre; convenable.
property *n* propriété *f*.
prophecy *n* prophétie *f*.
prophet *n* prophète *m*.
proportion *n* proportion *f*.
proportional *adj* proportionnel.
proposal *n* proposition *f*; offre *f*.
propose *vt* proposer.
proposition *n* proposition *f*.
proprietor *n* propriétaire *mf*.
prosecute *vt* poursuivre en justice.
prosecution *n* poursuites *fpl*; accusation *f*.
prospect *n* perspective *f*:—*vt vi* prospecter.
prospective *adj* probable; futur.
prosper *vi* prospérer.

prosperity *n* prospérité *f*.
prosperous *adj* prospère.
prostitute *n* prostituée *f*.
protagonist *n* protagoniste *mf*.
protect *vt* protéger; abriter.
protection *n* protection *f*.
protective *adj* protecteur.
protein *n* protéine *f*.
protest *vi* protester:—*n* protestation *f*.
Protestant *n* protestant *m*, -e *f*.
protester *n* protestataire *mf*.
prototype *n* prototype *m*.
proud *adj* fier, orgueilleux.
prove *vt* prouver; justifier:—*vi* s'avérer; se révéler.
proverb *n* proverbe *m*.
provide *vt* fournir.
provided *conj*:—~ **that** pourvu que.
providence *n* providence *f*.
province *n* province *f*.
provincial *adj n* provincial *m*, -e *f*.
provision *n* provision *f*; disposition *f*.
provisional *adj* provisoire.
provocation *n* provocation *f*.
provocative *adj* provocateur.
provoke *vt* provoquer.
prowess *n* prouesse *f*.
prowl *vi* rôder.
prowler *n* rôdeur *m*, -euse *f*.
proximity *n* proximité *f*.
prudence *n* prudence *f*.
prudent *adj* prudent.
pry *vi* espionner.
pseudonym *n* pseudonyme *m*.
psychiatric *adj* psychiatrique.
psychiatrist *n* psychiatre *mf*.
psychic *adj* psychique.
psychoanalyst *n* psychanaliste *mf*.
psychologist *n* psychologue *mf*.

psychology *n* psychologie *f*.
puberty *n* puberté *f*.
public *adj* public; commun:—*n* public *m*.
publication *n* publication *f*; édition *f*.
publicity *n* publicité *f*.
publish *vt* publier.
publisher *n* éditeur *m*, -trice *f*.
publishing *n* édition *f*.
pudding *n* pudding *m*; dessert *m*.
puddle *n* flaque d'eau *f*.
puff *n* souple *m*; bouffée *f*:—*vt* souffler; dégager.
pull *vt* tirer; arracher:—*n* tirage *m*; secousse *f*.
pulley *n* poulie *f*.
pulsate *vi* battre.
pulse *n* pouls *m*.
pulverise *vt* pulvériser.
pump *n* pompe *f*:—*vt* pomper; puiser.
punch *n* coup de poing *m*:—*vt* cogner.
punctual *adj* ponctuel, exact.
punctuate *vt* ponctuer.
punctuation *n* ponctuation *f*.
punish *vt* punir.
punishment *n* châtiment *m*, punition *f*; peine *f*.
puny *adj* chétif, maigrelet.

pupil *n* élève *mf*; pupille *mf*.
puppet *n* marionnette *f*.
puppy *n* chiot *m*.
purchase *vt* acheter:—*n* achat *m*; acquisition *f*.
purchaser *n* acheteur *m*, -euse *f*.
pure *adj* pur.
purification *n* purification *f*.
purify *vt* purifier.
purity *n* pureté *f*.
purple *adj n* pourpre, violet *m*.
purpose *n* intention *f*; but, dessein *m*:—**on ~** exprès, à dessein.
purse *n* sac à main *m*; porte-monnaie *m invar*.
pursue *vi* poursuivre; suivre.
pursuit *n* poursuite *f*; occupation *f*.
push *vt* pousser; presser:—*n* poussée *f*; impulsion *f*.
put *vt* mettre, poser.
putrid *adj* putride.
putty *n* mastic *m*.
puzzle *n* énigme *f*; casse-tête *m invar*.
puzzling *adj* curieux; inexplicable.
pyjamas *npl* pyjama *m*.
pylon *n* pylône *m*.
pyramid *n* pyramide *f*.
python *n* python *m*.

Q

quack *vi* cancaner:—*n* (*sl*) charlatan *m*.
quagmire *n* marécage *m*.
quaint *adj* désuet; bizarre.
quake *vi* trembler.
qualification *n* qualification *f*.
qualified *adj* qualifié.
qualify *vt* qualifier:—*vi* se qualifier.
quality *n* qualité *f*.
qualm *n* scrupule *m*.

quantity *n* quantité *f*.
quarantine *n* quarantaine *f*.
quarrel *n* querelle *f*:—*vi* se quereller.
quarrelsome *adj* querelleur.
quarry *n* carrière *f*.
quarter *n* quart *m*:—*vt* diviser en quatre.
quarterly *adj* trimestriel:—*adv* tous les trimestres.

quash vt écraser; annuler.

quay n quai m.

queen n reine f; femme f.

queer adj extrange:—n (sl) pédale f.

quell vt étouffer.

quench vt assouvir.

query n question f:—vt demander.

quest n recherche f.

question n question f:—vt questionner.

questionable adj discutable; douteux.

questioner n interrogateur m.

questionnaire n questionnaire m.

quibble vi chicaner.

quick adj rapide; vif.

quicken vt accélérer:—vi s'accélérer.

quiet adj calme; silencieux.

quietness n calme m, tranquillité f; silence m.

quip n sarcasme m:—vt railler.

quit vt arrêter de:—vi abandonner.

quite adv assez; complètement, absolument.

quiver vi trembler.

quiz n concours m; examen m:—vt interroger.

quota n quota m.

quotation n citation f.

quote vt citer.

R

rabbit n lapin m.

rabble n cohue f.

rabies n rage f.

race n course f; race f:—vi courir; foncer.

racial adj racial:—~ist adj n raciste mf.

rack n casier m; étagère f.

racket n vacarme m; raquette f.

radiant adj rayonnant, radieux.

radiate vt vi rayonner, irradier.

radiation n irradiation f.

radiator n radiateur m.

radical adj radical.

radio n radio f.

radioactive adj radioactif.

raft n radeau.

rag n lambeau m, loque f.

rage n rage f; fureur f:—vi faire rage.

ragged adj déguenillé.

raging adj furieux, enragé.

raid n raid m:—vt faire un raid sur.

rail n rambarde f; (rail) rail, chemin de fer m.

railway n chemin de fer m.

rain n pluie f:—vi pleuvoir.

rainbow n arc-en-ciel m.

rainy adj pluvieux.

raise vt lever, soulever.

raisin n raisin sec m.

rally vt (mil) rallier:—vi se rallier.

ramble vi errer; faire une randonnée.

ramp n rampe f.

ramshackle adj délabré.

rancid adj rance.

rancour n rancœur f.

random adj fortuit, fait au hasard.

range vt ranger:—vi s'étendre:—n rangée f; chaîne f; fourneau de cuisine m.

rank n rang m, classe f, grade m.

ransack vt saccager, piller.

ransom n rançon f.

rape n viol m:—vt violer.

rapid adj rapide.

rapidity n rapidité f.

rapist n violeur m.

rapt adj extasié; absorbé.

rapture n ravissement m; extase f.

rare adj rare.

rarity n rareté f.

rash adj imprudent:—n éruption (cutanée) f.

rashness n imprudence f.

rat n rat m.

rate n taux, prix m; vitesse f:—vt estimer, évaluer.

rather adv plutôt.

ratification n ratification f.

ratify vt ratifier.

ration n ration f.

rational adj rationnel.

rattle vi s'entrechoquer:—n hochet m; cliquetis m.

ravage vt ravager:—n ravage m.

rave vi délirer.

ravenous adj vorace.

ravine n ravin m.

raw adj cru; brut.

rawness n crudité f; inexpérience f.

ray n rayon m.

raze vt raser.

razor n rasoir m.

reach vt atteindre:—vi porter:—n portée f.

react vi réagir.

reaction n réaction f.

read vt vi lire.

reader n lecteur m, -trice f.

readily adv volontiers.

readiness n bonne volonté f.

reading n lecture f.

readjust vt réajuster.

ready adj prêt; enclin.

real adj réel, vrai.

realisation n réalisation f.

realise vt se rendre compte de; réaliser.

reality n réalité f.

reappear vi réapparaître.

rear n arrière m; derrière m:—vt élever.

reason n raison f; cause f:—vt vi raisonner.

reasonable adj raisonnable.

reasoning n raisonnement m.

reassure vt rassurer.

rebel n rebelle mf:—vi se rebeller.

rebellion n rébellion f.

rebound vi rebondir.

rebuild vt reconstruire.

rebuke vt réprimander:—n réprimande f.

recall vt (se) rappeler.

recapture n reprise f.

recede vi reculer.

receipt n reçu m; réception f.

receivable adj recevable.

receive vt recevoir; accueillir.

recent adj récent, neuf.

receptacle n récipient m.

reception n réception f.

recession n récession f.

recipe n recette f.

recipient n destinataire mf.

reciprocal adj ~ly adv réciproque-(ment).

recital n récit m.

recite vt réciter.

reckless adj téméraire.

reckon vt compter:—vi calculer.

reclaim vt assainir; récupérer.

recline vt reposer:—vi être allongé.

recognise vt reconnaître.

recognition n reconnaissance f.
recoil vi reculer.
recollect vt se rappeler.
recollection n souvenir m.
recommend vt recommander.
recompense n récompense f:—vt récompenser.
reconcile vt réconcilier.
reconciliation n réconciliation f.
reconsider vt reconsidérer.
record vt enregistrer:—n rapport m, registre m; disque m; record m.
recount vt raconter.
recourse n recours m.
recover vt retrouver:—vi se remettre.
recovery n guérison f; reprise f.
recreation n détente f; récréation f.
recriminate vi récriminer.
recrimination n récrimination f.
recruit vt recruter:—n (mil) recrue f.
rectangle n rectangle m.
rectification n rectification f.
rectify vt rectifier.
recumbent adj couché, étendu.
recur vi se reproduire.
recurrence n répétition f.
recurrent adj répétitif.
red adj rouge:—n rouge m.
redden vt vi rougir.
redeem vt racheter, rembourser.
redemption n rachat m.
redness n rougeur, rousseur f.
redouble vt vi redoubler.
redress vt réparer; redresser.
reduce vt réduire; diminuer.
reduction n réduction f; baisse f.
redundancy n licenciement m.
redundant adj superflu.

reel n bobine f; dévidoir m:—vi chanceler.
re-enter vt rentrer.
re-establish vt rétablir; réhabiliter.
refer vt se référer à:—vi se référer.
referee n arbitre m.
reference n référence f.
refine vt raffiner, affiner.
refinement n raffinement m.
reflect vt réfléchir, refléter:—vi réfléchir.
reflection n réflexion, pensée f.
reform vt réformer:—vi se réformer.
reform n réforme f.
reformer n réformateur m, -trice f.
refrain vi:—~ from s'abstenir de.
refresh vt rafraîchir.
refrigerator n glacière f; réfrigérateur m.
refuge n refuge, asile m.
refugee n réfugié m, -e f.
refund vt rembourser:—n remboursement m.
refusal n refus m.
refuse vt refuser:—n déchets mpl.
regain vt recouvrer.
regal adj royal.
regard vt regarder:—n considération f.
regardless adv quand même.
regenerate vt régénérer.
regeneration n régénération f.
regime n régime m.
region n région f.
register n registre m:—vt enregistrer.
registration n enregistrement m.
regressive adj régressif.
regret n regret m:—vt regretter.
regular adj régulier:—n habitué m, -e f.
regularity n régularité f.
regulate vt régler.
regulation n règlement m.

rehabilitate *vt* réhabiliter.
rehabilitation *n* réhabilitation *f*.
reimburse *vt* rembourser.
reimbursement *n* remboursement *m*.
reinforce *vt* renforcer.
reiterate *vt* réitérer.
reiteration *n* réitération *f*.
reject *vt* rejeter.
rejection *n* refus *m*.
rejoice *vt* réjouir:—*vi* se réjouir.
relapse *vi* retomber:—*n* rechute *f*.
relate *vt* relater:—*vi* se rapporter.
relation *n* rapport *m*; parent *m*.
relationship *n* lien de parenté *m*; relation *f*; rapport *m*.
relative *adj* relatif:—*n* parent *m*, -e *f*.
relax *vt* relâcher:—*vi* se relâcher.
relaxation *n* relâchement *m*; détente *f*.
relay *n* relais *m*:—*vt* retransmettre.
release *vt* libérer:—*n* libération *f*.
relevant *adj* pertinent.
reliable *adj* fiable.
reliance *n* confiance *f*.
relief *n* soulagement *m*; secours *m*.
relieve *vt* soulager, alléger.
religion *n* religion *f*.
religious *adj* religieux.
relinquish *vt* abandonner.
reluctant *adj* peu disposé.
rely *vi* compter sur.
remain *vi* rester, demeurer.
remainder *n* reste, restant *m*.
remark *n* remarque:—*vt* (faire) remarquer.
remarkable *adj* remarquable, notable.
remedy *n* remède *m*:—*vt* remédier à.
remember *vt* se souvenir de.
remind *vt* rappeler.
reminiscence *n* réminiscence *f*.

remit *vt* remettre, pardonner.
remnant *n* reste, restant *m*.
remonstrate *vi* protester.
remote *adj* lointain, éloigné.
remoteness *n* éloignement *m*; isolement *m*.
removable *adj* amovible.
removal *n* suppression *f*.
remove *vt* enlever.
remunerate *vt* rémunérer.
render *vt* rendre, remettre.
renew *vt* renouveler.
renewal *n* renouvellement *m*.
renounce *vt* renoncer à.
renovate *vt* rénover.
renown *n* renommée *f*; célébrité *f*.
rent *n* loyer *m*:—*vt* louer.
renunciation *n* renonciation *f*.
reorganisation *n* réorganisation *f*.
reorganise *vt* réorganiser.
repair *vt* réparer:—*n* réparation *f*.
repatriate *vt* rapatrier.
repay *vt* rembourser.
repayment *n* remboursement *m*.
repeal *vt* abroger:—*n* abrogation.
repeat *vt* répéter.
repel *vt* repousser, rebuter.
repent *vi* se repentir.
repetition *n* répétition *f*.
replace *vt* replacer.
replenish *vt* remplir de nouveau.
replete *adj* rempli.
reply *n* réponse *f*:—*vi* répondre.
report *vt* rapporter:—*n* rapport *m*; compte rendu *m*.
reporter *n* journaliste *mf*.
reprehend *vt* condamner.
reprehensible *adj* répréhensible.
represent *vt* représenter.

representation *n* représentation *f*.

representative *adj* représentatif:—*n* représentant(e) *m(f)*.

repress *vt* réprimer, contenir.

repression *n* répression *f*.

reprieve *n* sursis *m*.

reprimand *vt* réprimander.

reprisal *n* représailles *fpl*.

reproach *n* reproche:—*vt* reprocher.

reproduce *vt* reproduire.

reproduction *n* reproduction *f*.

republic *n* république *f*.

republican *adj n* républicain *m*, -e *f*.

repudiate *vt* renier.

repulse *vt* repousser.

repulsion *n* répulsion *f*.

repulsive *adj* répulsif.

reputation *n* réputation *f*.

request *n* requête *f*:—*vt* demander.

require *vt* demander, nécessiter.

requirement *n* besoin *m*; exigence *f*.

requisite *adj* nécessaire, indispensable.

rescue *vt* sauver, secourir:—*n* secours *m*.

research *vt* faire de la recherche:—*n* recherche *f*.

resemblance *n* ressemblance *f*.

resemble *vt* ressembler à.

resent *vt* être contrarié.

resentment *n* ressentiment *m*.

reservation *n* réservation *f*.

reserve *vt* réserver:—*n* réserve *f*.

reside *vi* résider.

residence *n* résidence *f*.

resident *n* résident *m*, -e *f*.

resign *vt* démissionner de:—*vi* démissionner.

resignation *n* démission *f*.

resist *vt* résister, s'opposer.

resistance *n* résistance *f*.

resolute *adj* résolu.

resolution *n* résolution *f*.

resolve *vt* resoudre:—*vi* (se) résoudre.

resort *vi* recourir:—*n* lieu de vacances *m*.

resource *n* ressource *f*.

respect *n* respect *m*; égard *m*:—*vt* respecter.

respectability *n* respectabilité *f*.

respectable *adj* respectable.

respectful *adj* respectueux.

respecting *prep* en ce qui concerne.

respective *adj* respectif.

respond *vi* répondre.

response *n* réponse.

responsibility *n* responsabilité *f*.

responsible *adj* responsable.

rest *n* repos *m*; reste, restant *m*:—*vi* se reposer.

restitution *n* restitution *f*.

restive *adj* rétif, récalcitrant.

restoration *n* restauration *f*.

restore *vt* restaurer.

restrain *vt* retenir.

restrict *vt* restreindre.

restriction *n* restriction *f*.

restrictive *adj* restrictif.

result *vi* résulter:—*n* résultat *m*.

resume *vt* reprendre; résumer.

resuscitate *vt* réanimer.

retail *vt* détailler:—*n* vente au détail *f*.

retain *vt* retenir, conserver.

retaliate *vi* se venger.

reticence *n* réticence *f*.

retire *vt* retirer:—*vi* se retirer.

retired *adj* retraité.

retirement *n* isolement *m*.

retort *vt* rétorquer:—*n* réplique *f*.

retrace *vt* retracer.

retreat *vi* se retirer.
retribution *n* récompense *f*.
retrieve *vt* récupérer, recouvrer.
return *vt* rendre:—*n* retour *m*.
reunion *n* réunion *f*.
reunite *vt* réunir:—*vi* se réunir.
reveal *vt* révéler.
revelation *n* révélation *f*.
revenge *vt* venger:—*n* vengeance *f*.
revengeful *adj* vindicatif.
revenue *n* revenu *m*; rente *f*.
reverberate *vt* réverbérer:—*vi* résonner.
reverberation *n* réverbération *f*.
reversal *n* renversement *m*.
reverse *vt* renverser:—*vi* faire marche arrière:—*n* inverse *m*.
reversible *adj* réversible.
reversion *n* retour *m*; réversion *f*.
revert *vi* revenir; retourner.
review *vt* revoir:—*n* revue *f*; examen *m*.
revise *vt* réviser.
revision *n* révision *f*.
revival *n* reprise *f*; renouveau *m*.
revive *vt* ranimer.
revoke *vt* révoquer.
revolt *vi* se révolter:—*n* révolte *f*.
revolution *n* révolution *f*.
revolutionary *adj n* révolutionnaire *mf*.
revolve *vt* (re)tourner:—*vi* tourner.
revue *n* revue *f*.
reward *n* récompense *f*:—*vt* récompenser.
rhetorical *adj* rhétorique.
rheumatic *adj* rhumatisant.
rheumatism *n* rhumatisme *m*.
rhyme *n* rime *f*:—*vi* rimer.
rhythm *n* rythme *m*.
rhythmical *adj* rythmique.
rib *n* côte *f*.
ribbon *n* ruban *m*.

rice *n* riz *m*.
rich *adj* riche; somptueux.
richness *n* richesse *f*; abondance *f*.
rid *vt* débarrasser.
riddle *n* crible *m*:—*vt* cribler.
ride *vi* monter (à cheval); aller (en voiture).
ridge *n* arête, crête *f*.
ridicule *n* ridicule *m*:—*vt* ridiculiser.
ridiculous *adj* ~**ly** *adv* ridicule.
rifle *n* fusil *m*.
rig *vt* équiper; truquer:—*n* plate-forme de forage *f*.
right *adj* droit, bien:—~! bien!, bon!; à juste titre:—*n* droit *m*; droite *f*.
righteous *adj* droit, vertueux.
rigid *adj* rigide; sévère.
rigorous *adj* rigoureux.
rigour *n* rigueur *f*; sévérité *f*.
rim *n* bord *m*, monture *f*.
ring *n* anneau, cercle, rond *m*:—*vt* sonner:—*vi* sonner, retentir.
rink *n* (*also* **ice** ~) patinoire *f*.
rinse *vt* rincer.
riot *n* émeute *f*.
riotous *adj* séditieux; dissolu.
rip *vt* déchirer.
ripe *adj* mûr.
ripen *vt vi* mûrir.
ripple *n* ondulation *f*, ride *f*.
rise *vi* se lever; monter:—*n* hausse *f*; augmentation *f*.
rising *n* insurrection *f*.
risk *n* risque:—*vt* risquer.
risky *adj* risqué.
rite *n* rite *m*.
ritual *adj n* rituel *m*.
rival *adj* rival:—*n* rival *m*, -e *f*:—*vt* rivaliser avec.

rivalry n rivalité f.

river n rivière f.

road n route f.

roam vt errer dans:—vi errer.

roar vi rugir:—n rugissement.

roast vt rôtir; griller.

rob vt voler.

robber n voleur m, -euse f.

robbery n vol m.

robust adj robuste.

robustness n robustesse f.

rock n roche f:—vt bercer; balancer.

rocket n fusée f.

rocking chair n fauteuil à bascule m.

rocky adj rocheux.

rodent n rongeur m.

rogue n coquin, polisson m; gredin m.

roll vt rouler:—vi (se) rouler:—n roulement m; rouleau m.

roller n rouleau, cylindre m.

romance n romance f, roman m.

romantic adj romantique.

roof n toit m; voûte f:—vt couvrir.

room n pièce, salle f; espace m.

root n racine f; origine f.

rope n corde f; cordage m.

rose n rose f.

rosemary n (bot) romarin m.

rot vi pourrir:—n pourriture f.

rotate vt faire tourner:—vi tourner.

rotation n rotation f.

rotund adj rond, replet.

rouge n rouge (à joues) m.

rough adj accidenté, rugueux; rude.

roughness n rugosité f; rudesse f.

round adj rond, circulaire:—n cercle m; rond m; tour m; tournée f:—adv autour de; environ:—vt arrondir.

roundness n rondeur f.

rouse vt réveiller; exciter.

rout n déroute f.

route n itinéraire m; route f.

routine adj habituel:—n routine f.

rove vi vagabonder.

row n querelle f.

row n rangée, file f.

royal adj royal; princier.

royalty n royauté f; droits d'auteur mpl.

rub vt frotter; irriter:—n frottement m.

rubber n caoutchouc m.

rubbish n détritus mpl; ordures fpl.

rudder n gouvernail m.

ruddiness n teint vif m, rougeur f.

rude adj impoli, rude.

rudeness n impolitesse f; rudesse f.

ruffle vt ébouriffer, déranger.

rug n tapis m.

rugged adj accidenté, déchiqueté.

ruin n ruine f:—vt ruiner.

ruinous adj ruineux.

rule n règle f; règlement m:—vt gouverner, dominer.

rumble vi gronder, tonner.

ruminate vt ruminer.

rummage vi fouiller.

rumour n rumeur f.

run vt diriger:—vi courir.

rung n barreau, échelon m.

runner n coureur m.

runway n piste de décollage f.

rupture n rupture f:—vt rompre:—vi se rompre.

ruse n ruse f, stratagème m.

rush n ruée f; hâte f:—vi se précipiter.

rust n rouille f:—vi se rouiller.

rustic adj rustique:—n paysan, rustaud m.

rustle *vi* bruire:—*vt* faire bruire; froisser.

rusty *adj* rouillé; roux.

ruthless *adj* cruel, impitoyable.

rye *n* seigle *m*.

S

sabotage *n* sabotage *m*.

sachet *n* sachet *m*.

sack *n* sac *m*

sacrament *n* sacrement *m*.

sacred *adj* saint, sacré.

sacrifice *n* sacrifice *m*:—*vt* sacrifier.

sacrilege *n* sacrilège *m*.

sad *adj* triste, déprimé.

sadden *vt* attrister.

saddle *n* selle *f*; col *m*:—*vt* seller.

sadness *n* tristesse *f*.

safe *adj* sûr, en sécurité:—*n* coffre-fort *m*.

safeguard *n* sauvegarde *f*:—*vt* sauvegarder.

safety *n* sécurité *f*; sûreté *f*.

sage *n* sage *m*:—*adj* sage.

sail *n* voile *f*:—*vt* piloter:—*vi* aller à la voile.

sailing *n* navigation *f*.

sailor *n* marin *m*.

saint *n* saint *m*, -e *f*.

sake *n* bien *m*, égard *m*.

salad *n* salade *f*.

salary *n* salaire *m*.

sale *n* vente *f*; solde *m*.

salesman *n* vendeur *m*.

saliva *n* salive *f*.

salmon *n* saumon *m*.

saloon *n* bar *m*.

salt *n* sel *m*:—*vt* saler.

salt cellar *n* salière *f*.

salubrious *adj* salubre, sain.

salubrity *n* salubrité *f*.

salutary *adj* salutaire.

salute *vt* saluer:—*n* salut *m*.

salvation *n* salut *m*.

same *adj* même, identique.

sameness *n* identité *f*.

sample *n* échantillon *m*:—*vt* goûter.

sanatorium *n* sanatorium *m*.

sanctify *vt* sanctifier.

sanction *n* sanction *f*:—*vt* sanctionner.

sanctuary *n* sanctuaire *m*; asile *m*.

sand *n* sable *m*:—*vt* sabler.

sandal *n* sandale *f*.

sandwich *n* sandwich *m*.

sandy *adj* sablonneux, sableux.

sane *adj* sain.

sanguine *adj* sanguin.

sanity *n* santé mentale, raison *f*.

sapling *n* jeune arbre *m*.

sarcasm *n* sarcasme *m*.

sarcastic *adj* sarcastique.

sardine *n* sardine *f*.

satchel *n* cartable *m*.

satellite *n* satellite *m*.

sate *vt* rassasier, assouvir.

satin *n* satin *m*:—*adj* en *ou* de satin.

satire *n* satire *f*.

satirical *adj* satirique.

satisfaction *n* satisfaction *f*.

satisfactory *adj* satisfaisant.

satisfy *vt* satisfaire.

saturate *vt* saturer.

Saturday *n* samedi *m*.

sauce *n* sauce *f*; assaisonnement *m*.

saucepan *n* casserole *f*.

saucer *n* soucoupe *f*.

saunter *vi* flâner, se balader.

sausage *n* saucisse *f*.

savage *adj* sauvage:—*n* sauvage *mf.*

savagery *n* sauvagerie, barbarie *f.*

save *vt* sauver; économiser:—*adv* sauf, à l'exception de.

saving *prep* sauf, à l'exception de: — *n* sauvetage *m.*

savings bank *n* caisse d'épargne *f.*

savour *n* saveur *f:*—*vt* savourer.

saw *n* scie *f:*—*vt* scier.

say *vt* dire.

saying *n* dicton, proverbe *m.*

scaffolding *n* échafaudage *m.*

scald *vt* échauder:—*n* brûlure *f.*

scale *n* balance *f;* échelle *f:*—*vt* escalader.

scan *vt* scruter; explorer; scander.

scandal *n* scandale *m;* infamie *f.*

scandalise *vt* scandaliser.

scandalous *adj* scandaleux.

scant *adj* rare, insuffisant.

scantiness *n* insuffisance, pauvreté *f.*

scapegoat *n* bouc émissaire *m.*

scar *n* cicatrice *f.*

scarce *adj* rare.

scare *vt* effrayer:—*n* peur; panique *f.*

scarf *n* écharpe *f.*

scarlet *n* écarlate *f:*—*adj* écarlate.

scatter *vt* éparpiller; disperser.

scene *n* scène *f;* lieu *m.*

scenery *n* vue *f;* décor (de théâtre) *m.*

scenic *adj* scénique.

scent *n* parfum *m*, odeur *f:*—*vt* parfumer.

sceptic *n* sceptique *mf.*

sceptic(al) *adj* sceptique.

schedule *n* horaire *m;* programme *m.*

scheme *n* projet, plan *m;* schéma *m:* —*vt* machiner:—*vi* intriguer.

scholar *n* élève *mf;* érudit *m*, -e *f.*

school *n* école *f:*—*vt* instruire.

schoolboy *n* écolier, élève *m.*

schoolgirl *n* écolière, élève *f.*

schoolteacher *n* instituteur/trice *mf;* professeur *m.*

science *n* science *f.*

scientific *adj* scientifique.

scientist *n* scientifique *mf.*

scintillate *vi* scintiller, étinceler.

scissors *npl* ciseaux *mpl.*

scoff *vi* se moquer.

scold *vt* réprimander:—*vi* grogner.

scope *n* portée, envergure.

scorch *vt* brûler:—*vi* se brûler.

score *n* score *m;* marque *f;* entaille *f:* —*vt* marquer.

scorn *vt* mépriser:—*n* mépris *m.*

scornful *adj* dédaigneux.

scoundrel *n* vaurien *m.*

scour *vt* récurer, frotter.

scout *n* (*mil*) éclaireur *m*, -euse *f;* guetteur *m.*

scowl *vi* se renfrogner.

scramble *vi* grimper; se battre, se disputer:—*n* bousculade *f.*

scrap *n* bout *m;* bagarre *f;* ferraille *f.*

scrape *vt vi* racler, gratter:—*vt* érafler.

scratch *vt* griffer, égratigner:—*n* égratignure *f.*

scream *vi* hurler:—*n* hurlement *m.*

screen *n* écran *m;* paravent *m:*—*vt* abriter; sélectionner.

screw *n* vis *f:*—*vt* visser.

screwdriver *n* tournevis *m.*

scribble *vt* gribouiller:—*n* gribouillage *m.*

script *n* scénario *m;* script *m.*

Scripture *n* Ecriture sainte *f.*

scrub *vt* récurer; annuler:—*n* broussailles *fpl.*

scruple *n* scrupule *m*.

scrupulous *adj* scrupuleux.

scuffle *n* rixe *f*:—*vi* se bagarrer.

sculptor *n* sculpteur *m*, -trice *f*.

sculpture *n* sculpture *f*.

scum *n* écume *f*; crasse *f*.

sea *n* mer *f*:—*adj* marin.

seafood *n* fruits de mer *mpl*.

seagull *n* mouette *f*.

seal *n* sceau *m*; phoque *m*:—*vt* sceller.

seamy *adj* sordide.

search *vt* fouiller; inspecter:—*n* fouille *f*; recherche *f*.

seashore *n* bord de mer *m*.

seasickness *n* mal de mer *m*.

season *n* saison *f*.

seasonable *adj* opportun, à propos.

seasoning *n* assaisonnement *m*.

seat *n* siège *m*; place *f*:—*vt* (faire) asseoir.

seaweed *n* algue *f*.

seclude *vt* éloigner, isoler.

seclusion *n* solitude *f*; isolement *m*.

second *adj* deuxième:—*n* second *m*; seconde *f*.

secondary *adj* secondaire.

secrecy *n* secret *m*; discrétion *f*.

secret *adj* *n* secret *m*.

secretary *n* secrétaire *mf*.

secretive *adj* secret, dissimulé.

section *n* section *f*.

sector *n* secteur *m*.

secular *adj* séculaire.

secure *adj* sûr; en sûreté:—*vt* assurer.

security *n* sécurité *f*; sûreté *f*.

sedative *n* sédatif *m*.

sediment *n* sédiment *m*; lie *f*.

sedition *n* sédition *f*.

seduce *vt* séduire.

seduction *n* séduction *f*.

seductive *adj* séduisant.

see *vt* voir, remarquer.

seed *n* graine *f*:—*vi* monter en graine.

seek *vt* chercher; demander.

seem *vi* paraître, sembler.

seemliness *n* bienséance *f*.

seemly *adj* convenable, bienséant.

seesaw *n* bascule *f*:—*vi* osciller.

segment *n* segment *m*.

seize *vt* saisir.

seizure *n* saisie *f*.

seldom *adv* rarement, peu souvent.

select *vt* sélectionner.

selection *n* sélection *f*.

self *n* soi-même:—**the ~** le moi:—*pref* auto-.

self-confident *adj* sûr de soi.

self-defence *n* autodéfense *f*.

self-employed *adj* indépendant.

self-interest *n* intérêt personnel *m*.

selfish *adj* égoïste.

selfishness *n* égoïsme *m*.

self-portrait *n* autoportrait *m*.

self-respect *n* respect de soi *m*.

self-service *adj* libre-service.

self-styled *adj* soi-disant.

self-sufficient *adj* autosuffisant.

self-taught *adj* autodidacte.

sell *vt* vendre:—*vi* se vendre.

seller *n* vendeur *m*, -euse *f*.

semblance *n* semblant *m*.

semicircle *n* demi-cercle *m*.

senate *n* sénat *m*.

senator *n* sénateur *m*, -trice *f*.

send *vt* envoyer.

senile *adj* sénile.

senility *n* sénilité *f*.

senior *n* aîné *m*, -e *f*:—*adj* aîné.

seniority *n* ancienneté *f*.

sensation *n* sensation *f*.

sense *n* sens *m*; sensation *f*.

senseless *adj* insensé.

sensible *adj* sensé; sensible.

sensibly *adj* raisonnablement.

sensitive *adj* sensible.

sensual *adj* sensuel.

sensuality *n* sensualité *f*.

sentence *n* phrase *f*; condamnation *f*.

sentiment *n* sentiment *m*.

sentimental *adj* sentimental.

sentinel *n* sentinelle *f*.

separable *adj* séparable.

separate *vt* séparer:—*vi* se séparer: —*adj* séparé.

separation *n* séparation *f*.

September *n* septembre *m*.

sepulchre *n* sépulcre *m*.

sequel *n* conséquence *f*; suite *f*.

sequence *n* ordre *m*, série *f*.

serenade *n* sérénade *f*:—*vt* jouer une sérénade pour.

serene *adj* serein.

serenity *n* sérénité *f*.

sergeant *n* sergent *m*.

serial *adj* de/en série:—*n* feuilleton *m*.

series *n* série *f*.

serious *adj* sérieux, grave.

sermon *n* sermon *m*.

serpent *n* serpent *m*.

servant *n* domestique *mf*.

serve *vt* servir; desservir:—*vi* servir; être utile.

service *n* service *m*; entretien *m*:—*vt* entretenir.

serviceable *adj* utilisable; pratique.

servile *adj* servile.

servitude *n* servitude *f*.

session *n* séance, session *f*.

set *vt* mettre, poser:—*n* jeu *m*; ensemble *m*:—*adj* fixe, figé.

setting *n* disposition *f*; cadre *m*; monture *f*:—~ **of the sun** coucher du soleil *m*.

settle *vt* poser, installer:—*vi* se poser; s'installer.

settlement *n* règlement *m*; établissement *m*.

seven *adj n* sept *m*.

seventeen *adj n* dix-sept *m*.

seventeenth *adj n* dix-septième *mf*.

seventh *adj n* septième *mf*.

seventieth *adj n* soixante-dixième *mf*.

seventy *adj n* soixante-dix *m*.

several *adj pn* plusieurs.

severe *adj* sévère, rigoureux.

severity *n* sévérité *f*.

sew *vt vi* coudre.

sewer *n* égout *m*.

sex *n* sexe *m*.

sexist *adj n* sexiste *mf*.

sexual *adj* sexuel.

shabby *adj* miteux.

shade *n* ombre *f*; nuance *f*:—*vt* ombrager.

shadow *n* ombre *f*.

shady *adj* ombreux, ombragé.

shaft *n* fût *m*; (*tech*) arbre *m*; rayon *m*.

shake *vt* secouer:—*vi* trembler:—*n* secousse *f*.

shallow *adj* peu profond, superficiel.

sham *vt* feindre:—*n* imposture *f*.

shame *n* honte *f*:—*vt* déshonorer.

shamefaced *adj* honteux, confus.

shameful *adj* honteux; scandaleux.

shampoo *n* shampooing *m*.

shape *vt* former; façonner:—*vi* prendre forme:—*n* forme *f*.

shapely *adj* bien proportionné.

share *n* part, portion *f*:—*vt* partager.

shark *n* requin *m*.

sharp *adj* aigu, acéré.

sharpen *vt* aiguiser, affûter.

sharpness *n* acuité *f*; aigreur *f*.

shatter *vt* fracasser.

shave *vi* se raser.

shaver *n* rasoir électrique *m*.

shaving *n* rasage *m*.

shawl *n* châle *m*.

she *pn* elle.

sheaf *n* gerbe *f*, liasse *f*.

shear *vt* tondre.

shed *n* hangar *m*; cabane *f*.

sheep *n* mouton *m*.

sheer *adj* pur; abrupt:—*adv* abruptement.

sheet *n* drap *m*; plaque *f*.

shelf *n* étagère *f*.

shell *n* coquille *f*; écorce *f*:—*vt* écosser, décortiquer; bombarder.

shelter *n* abri *m*:—*vt* abriter:—*vi* s'abriter.

shepherd *n* berger *m*.

sheriff *n* shérif *m*.

shield *n* bouclier *m*:—*vt* protéger.

shift *vi* changer; se déplacer:—*vt* changer, bouger:—*n* changement *m*.

shine *vi* briller.

shining *adj* resplendissant.

ship *n* bateau *m*; navire *m*:—*vt* embarquer.

shipment *n* cargaison *f*.

shipwreck *n* naufrage *m*.

shirt *n* chemise *f*.

shiver *vi* frissonner.

shock *n* choc *m*; coup *m*:—*vt* bouleverser; choquer.

shoe *n* chaussure *f*.

shoemaker *n* cordonnier *m*.

shoot *vt* tirer:—*vi* pousser:—*n* pousse *f*.

shooting *n* fusillade *f*; tir *m*.

shop *n* magasin *m*; atelier *m*.

shopper *n* acheteur *m*, -euse *f*.

shore *n* rivage, bord *m*.

short *adj* court, bref.

shortcoming *n* insuffisance *f*.

shorten *vt* raccourcir; abréger.

short-sighted *adj* myope.

shortwave *n* ondes courtes *fpl*.

shot *n* coup *m*; décharge *f*.

shotgun *n* fusil de chasse *m*.

shoulder *n* épaule *f*; accotement *m*.

shout *vt vi* crier:—*n* cri *m*.

shove *vt vi* pousser:—*n* poussée *f*.

shovel *n* pelle *f*:—*vt* pelleter.

show *vt* montrer:—*vi* se voir:—*n* exposition *f*.

shower *n* averse *f*; douche *f*.

showy *adj* voyant, ostentatoire.

shred *n* lambeau *m*:—*vt* mettre en lambeaux.

shrewd *adj* astucieux; perspicace.

shriek *vt vi* hurler:—*n* hurlement *m*.

shrill *adj* aigu, strident.

shrimp *n* crevette *f*.

shrink *vi* rétrécir.

shrivel *vi* se ratatiner.

shroud *n* voile *m*; linceul *m*.

shudder *vi* frissonner:—*n* frisson *m*.

shun *vt* fuir, éviter.

shut *vt* fermer; *vi* (se) fermer.

shutter n volet m.
shy adj timide; réservé.
shyness n timidité f.
sick adj malade; écœuré.
sicken vt rendre malade.
sickly adj maladif.
sickness n maladie f.
side n côté m; parti m:—adj latéral.
sideboard n buffet m.
sidelong adj oblique.
siege n (mil) siège m.
sieve n tamis m:—vt tamiser.
sift vt tamiser.
sigh vi soupirer:—n soupir m.
sight n vue f; spectacle m.
sightseeing n tourisme m.
sign n signe m, indication f:—vt signer.
signal n signal m.
signature n signature f.
significance n importance f.
significant adj considérable.
signify vt signifier.
silence n silence m.
silent adj silencieux.
silicon chip n puce de silicium f.
silk n soie f.
silken adj soyeux.
sill n rebord m; seuil m.
silliness n bêtise, niaiserie f.
silly adj bête, stupide.
silver n argent m:—adj en argent.
silvery adj argenté.
similar adj semblable; similaire.
similarity n ressemblance f.
simile n comparaison f.
simmer vi cuire à feux doux, mijoter.
simper vi minauder:—n sourire affecté m.
simple adj simple; naïf.

simplicity n simplicité f.
simplification n simplification f.
simplify vt simplifier.
simulate vt simuler, feindre.
simultaneous adj simultané.
sin n péché m:—vi pécher.
since adv prep depuis:—conj depuis que; puisque.
sincere adj sincère; réel, vrai:—**~ly** adv sincère(ment).
sincerity n sincérité f.
sinew n tendon m; nerf m.
sing vt vi chanter.
singe vt roussir.
singer n chanteur m, -euse f.
single adj seul, unique; célibataire.
singly adv séparément.
singular adj singulier.
singularity n singularité f.
sinister adj sinistre.
sink vi couler:—n évier m.
sinner n pécheur m, pécheresse f.
sinuous adj sinueux.
sir n monsieur m.
sister n sœur f.
sister-in-law n belle-sœur f.
sit vi s'asseoir.
site n emplacement m; site m.
sitting n séance, réunion f.
sitting room n salle de séjour f.
situation n situation f.
six adj n six m.
sixteen adj n seize m.
sixteenth adj n seizième mf.
sixth adj n sixième mf.
sixtieth adj n soixantième mf.
sixty adj n soixante m.
size n taille, grandeur f.
sizeable adj assez grand.

skate n patin m:—vi patiner.
skating rink n patinoire f.
skeleton n squelette m.
sketch n croquis m.
skewer n broche f; brochette f:—vt embrocher.
ski n ski m:—vi skier.
skid n dérapage m:—vi déraper.
skier n skieur m, -euse f.
skiing n ski m.
skill n habileté, adresse f.
skilful adj adroit, habile.
skim vt écrémer; effleurer.
skin n peau f:—vt écorcher.
skinny adj maigre, efflanqué.
skip vi sautiller.
skirmish n escarmouche f.
skirt n jupe f; bordure f:—vt contourner.
skulk vi rôder furtivement.
skull n crâne m.
sky n ciel m.
skylight n lucarne f.
skyscraper n gratte-ciel m invar.
slab n dalle f.
slack adj lâche, négligent.
slack(en) vt relâcher:—vi se relâcher.
slackness n ralentissement m.
slam vt claquer violemment.
slander vt calomnier:—n calomnie f.
slanderous adj calomnieux.
slang n argot m.
slant vi pencher:—n inclinaison f.
slap n gifle f:—vt gifler.
slaughter n carnage, massacre m:—vt abattre.
slave n esclave mf.
slavery n esclavage m.
slay vt tuer.
sleazy adj louche.

sledge n traîneau m.
sleep vi dormir:—n sommeil m.
sleeper n dormeur m, -euse f.
sleepiness n envie de dormir f.
sleepwalking n somnambulisme m.
sleepy adj qui a envie de dormir; endormi.
sleet n neige fondue f.
sleeve n manche f.
slender adj svelte, mince.
slenderness n sveltesse f, minceur f.
slice n tranche f; spatule f:—vt couper.
slide vi glisser:—n glissade f; diapositive f.
slight adj léger, mince:—n affront m.
slightness n fragilité f; insignifiance f.
slim adj mince:—vi maigrir.
slimming n amaigrissement m.
sling n écharpe f:—vt lancer.
slip vi (se) glisser:—vt glisser:—n glissade f; faux pas m.
slipper n pantoufle f.
slippery adj glissant.
slit vt fendre, inciser.
slogan n slogan m.
slope n inclinaison f; pente f:—vt incliner.
sloth n paresse f.
slovenliness n manque de soin m.
slovenly adj négligé, débraillé.
slow adj lent; lourd.
slowness n lenteur, lourdeur f.
sluggish adj paresseux; léthargique.
slum n taudis m.
slump n récession f.
slur vt dénigrer; mal articuler:—n calomnie f.
slush n neige fondante f.

sly *adj* rusé.

slyness *n* ruse, finesse *f*.

smack *n* claque *f*:—*vt* donner une claque à.

small *adj* petit, menu.

smallness *n* petitesse *f*.

smart *adj* élégant; astucieux:—*vi* brûler.

smartness *n* astuce, vivacité, finesse *f*.

smash *vt* casser, briser, se fracasser:—*n* fracas *m*.

smear *vt* enduire; salir.

smell *vt vi* sentir:—*n* odorat *m*; odeur *f*.

smelt *vt* fondre.

smile *vi* sourire:—*n* sourire *m*.

smite *vt* frapper.

smith *n* forgeron *m*.

smoke *n* fumée *f*:—*vt vi* fumer.

smoker *n* fumeur *m*, -euse *f*.

smoky *adj* enfumé; qui fume.

smooth *adj* lisse, uni:—*vt* lisser; adoucir.

smoothness *n* douceur *f*; aspect lisse *m*.

smother *vt* étouffer.

smudge *vt* salir:—*n* tache *f*.

smuggle *vt* passer en contrebande.

smuggler *n* contrebandier *m*, -ière *f*.

snack *n* collation *f*.

snail *n* escargot *m*.

snake *n* serpent *m*.

snap *vt* casser net:—claquer:—*n* claquement *m*.

snare *n* piège *m*; collet *m*.

snatch *vt* saisir.

sneer *vi* ricaner.

sneeze *vi* éternuer.

sniff *vt* renifler.

snivel *n* pleurnicherie *f*.—*vi* pleurnicher.

snob *n* snob *mf*.

snobbish *adj* snob.

snooze *n* petit somme *m*.

snore *vi* ronfler.

snow *n* neige *f*:—*vi* neiger.

snowman *n* bonhomme de neige *m*.

snowplough *n* chasse-neige *m invar*.

snowy *adj* neigeux; enneigé.

snub *vt* repousser, rejeter.

snug *adj* confortable, douillet.

so *adv* si, tellement, aussi; ainsi.

soak *vi* tremper:—*vt* faire tremper.

soap *n* savon *m*:—*vt* savonner.

soar *vi* monter en flèche.

sob *n* sanglot *m*:—*vi* sangloter.

sober *adj* sobre; sérieux.

sobriety *n* sobriété *f*.

sociability *n* sociabilité *f*.

sociable *adj* sociable.

social *adj* social, sociable.

socialist *n* socialiste *mf*.

social worker *n* assistant(e) social(e) *m(f)*.

society *n* société *f*; compagnie *f*.

sociologist *n* sociologue *mf*.

sock *n* chaussette *f*.

socket *n* prise de courant *f*.

sofa *n* sofa *m*.

soft *adj* doux, moelleux.

soften *vt* (r)amollir, adoucir.

softness *n* douceur, mollesse *f*.

software *n* logiciel *m*.

soil *vt* salir:—*n* sol *m*; terre *f*.

solace *vt* consoler:—*n* consolation *f*.

solar *adj* solaire.

solder *vt* souder:—*n* soudure *f*.

soldier *n* soldat *m*.

sole n plante du pied f:—adj seul, unique.

solemn adj solennel.

solemnity n solennité f.

solicit vt solliciter.

solicitor n notaire m.

solicitude n sollicitude f.

solid adj solide, compact:—n solide m.

solidify vt solidifier.

solidity n solidité f.

solitary adj solitaire, retiré.

solitude n solitude f.

solstice n solstice m.

soluble adj soluble.

solution n solution f.

solve vt résoudre.

solvency n solvabilité f.

solvent adj solvable.

some adj du, de la, de l', des; quelques; quelconque; certain(e)s; quelque.

somebody pn quelqu'un.

somehow adv d'une façon ou d'une autre.

something pn quelque chose.

sometimes adv quelquefois, parfois.

somewhat adv quelque peu.

somewhere adv quelque part.

somnolence n somnolence f.

somnolent adj somnolent.

son n fils m.

song n chanson f.

son-in-law n gendre m.

sonorous adj sonore.

soon adv bientôt.

sooner adv plus tôt; plutôt.

soot n suie f.

soothe vt calmer.

sophisticate vt sophistiquer.

sophisticated adj sophistiqué.

soporific adj soporifique.

sordid adj sordide, sale.

sore n plaie f:—adj douloureux, sensible.

sorrow n peine f:—vi se lamenter.

sorrowful adj triste, affligé.

sorry adj désolé; déplorable.

sort n sorte f; genre m:—vt classer; trier.

soul n âme f.

sound adj sain; valide:—n son m; bruit m:—vt sonner (de).

soundness n santé f; solidité f.

soup n soupe f.

sour adj aigre, acide.

source n source f; origine f.

souvenir n souvenir m.

south n sud m.

southern adj du sud, sud, méridional.

southward(s) adv vers le sud.

sovereign adj n souverain m, -e f.

sovereignty n souveraineté f.

sow vt semer.

space n espace m; intervalle m:—vt espacer.

spacious adj spacieux.

spade n bêche f.

span n envergure f:—vt enjamber.

spare vt vi épargner; ménager:—adj de trop; de réserve.

sparing adj limité, modéré.

spark n étincelle f.

sparkle n scintillement m:—vi étinceler.

sparse adj clairsemé.

spasm n spasme m.

spatter vt éclabousser.

speak vt parler; dire.

speaker *n* interlocuteur *m*, -trice *f*; orateur *m*.

spear *n* lance *f*.

special *adj* spécial.

speciality *n* spécialité *f*.

species *n* espèce *f*.

specific *adj* spécifique.

specification *n* spécification *f*.

specify *vt* spécifier.

specimen *n* spécimen *m*.

spectacle *n* spectacle *m*.

spectator *n* spectateur *m*, -trice *f*.

spectre *n* spectre *m*.

speculate *vi* spéculer.

speculation *n* spéculation *f*.

speculative *adj* spéculatif, méditatif.

speech *n* parole *f*; discours *m*.

speed *n* vitesse *f*; rapidité *f*.

speediness *n* promptitude, célérité *f*.

speed limit *n* limitation de vitesse *f*.

speedy *adj* rapide, prompt.

spell *n* charme *m*; période *f*:—*vt* écrire.

spelling *n* orthographe *f*.

spend *vt* dépenser; passer.

sphere *n* sphère *f*.

spherical *adj* sphérique.

spice *n* épice *f*:—*vt* épicer.

spicy *adj* épicé.

spider *n* araignée *f*.

spike *n* clou *m*:—*vt* clouter.

spill *vt* répandre:—*vi* se répandre.

spin *vt* filer:—*vi* tourner:—*n* tournoiement *m*.

spinal *adj* spinal.

spine *n* colonne vertébrale.

spire *n* flèche *f*; aiguille *f*.

spirit *n* esprit *m*; âme *f*; caractère *m*.

spirited *adj* vif, fougueux.

spiritless *adj* sans entrain, abattu.

spiritual *adj* spirituel.

spirituality *n* spiritualité *f*.

spit *n* crachat *m*:—*vt vi* cracher.

spite *n* dépit *m*:—**in ~ of** malgré.

spiteful *adj* rancunier.

splash *vt* éclabousser:—*n* éclaboussure *f*.

splendid *adj* splendide.

splendour *n* splendeur *f*.

splinter *n* éclat *m*:—*vt* (*vi*) (se) fendre en éclats.

split *n* fente *f*:—*vt* fendre.

spoil *vt* abîmer.

spokesman *n* porte-parole *m invar*.

sponge *n* éponge *f*.

sponsor *n* parrain *m*.

sponsorship *n* parrainage *m*.

spontaneity *n* spontanéité *f*.

spontaneous *adj* spontané.

spoon *n* cuiller *f*.

sporadic(al) *adj* sporadique.

sport *n* sport *m*; jeu *m*.

sportsman *n* sportif *m*.

sportswoman *n* sportive *f*.

spot *n* tache *f*; endroit *m*:—*vt* apercevoir.

spotless *adj* impeccable.

spouse *n* époux *m*; épouse *f*.

spout *vi* jaillir:—*vt* faire jaillir:—*n* bec *m*.

sprain *n* entorse *f*.

spray *n* spray *m*; pulvérisation *f*.

spread *vt* étendre:—*vi* s'étendre:—*n* diffusion *f*.

spring *vi* bondir:—*n* printemps *m*; saut *m*.

sprinkle *vt* arroser.

sprout *n* pousse *f*.

spruce *adj* net, impeccable.

spur n éperon m; stimulant m:—vt éperonner; stimuler.

spurn vt repousser avec mépris.

sputter vi bafouiller.

spy n espion m, -onne f:—vt espionner.

squabble vi se quereller:—n querelle f.

squad n équipe f.

squadron n escadron m.

squalid adj misérable, sordide.

squalor n saleté f; misère f.

square adj carré:—n carré m; place f.

squash vt écraser.

squat vi s'accroupir.

squeak vi grincer, crier.

squeal vi couiner.

squeeze vt presser, tordre.

squint vi loucher:—n strabisme.

squirt vt faire gicler:—n giclée f.

stab vt poignarder.

stability n stabilité.

stable n écurie f:—adj stable.

stack n pile f:—vt empiler.

staff n personnel m; bâton m.

stage n étape f; scène f.

stagger vi vaciller.

stagnation n stagnation f.

stagnate vi stagner.

stain vt tacher:—n tache f.

stair n marche f.

stairs n escalier m.

stake n pieu m:—vt marquer.

stale adj rance.

stalk n tige f.

stall n stalle f; étalage m:—vt caler.

stamina n résistance f.

stammer vi bégayer:—n bégaiement m.

stamp vt trépigner; timbrer:—n timbre m; estampille f.

stand vi être debout:—vt supporter: —n position, prise de position f; étalage m.

standard n étendard m; norme f:—adj normal.

standing n importance f; rang m.

standstill n arrêt m.

staple n agrafe f:—adj principal, de base.

star n étoile f.

starch n amidon m.

stare vi:—to ~ at regarder fixement.

starry adj étoilé.

start vi,vt commencer:—n début m.

starter n starter, démarreur m.

startle vt faire sursauter.

starvation n inanition, faim f.

starve vi mourir de faim.

state n état m; condition f:—vt déclarer.

stately adj majestueux, imposant.

statement n déclaration f.

statesman n homme d'Etat m.

static adj statique.

station n station f; (rail) gare f:—vt placer.

stationary adj stationnaire.

stationery n papeterie f.

statistical adj statistique.

statue n statue f.

stature n stature, taille f.

statute n statut m; loi f.

stay n séjour m:—vi rester.

steadfast adj ferme, résolu.

steadiness n fermeté f.

steady adj stable:—vt affermir.

steak n bifteck m; steak m.

steal vt vi voler.

stealthy *adj* furtif.

steam *n* vapeur *f:—vt* cuire à la vapeur.

steam engine *n* locomotive à vapeur *f.*

steel *n* acier *m:—adj* d'acier.

steep *adj* abrupt:—*vt* tremper.

steepness *n* raideur *f.*

steer *vt* diriger.

steering wheel *n* volant *m.*

stem *n* tige *f.*

stenographer *n* sténographe *mf.*

stenography *n* sténographie *f.*

step *n* pas *m*, marche *f:—vi* faire un pas.

stepbrother *n* demi-frère *m.*

stepsister *n* demi-sœur *f.*

stereotype *vt* stéréotyper.

sterile *adj* stérile.

sterility *n* stérilité *f.*

sterling *adj* de bon aloi, veritable.

stern *adj* sévère, rigide.

stew *n* ragoût *m.*

steward *n* intendant *m.*

stewardess *n* hôtesse de l'air *f.*

stick *n* bâton *m:—vt* coller.

sticky *adj* collant, poisseux.

stiff *adj* raide, rigide.

stiffen *vt* raidir:—*vi* se raidir.

stiffness *n* raideur.

stifle *vt* étouffer.

stifling *adj* suffocant.

stigmatise *vt* stigmatiser.

still *vt* calmer:—*adj* calme:—*adv* encore; toujours.

stillness *n* calme *m.*

stimulate *vt* stimuler.

stimulus *n* stimulant *m.*

sting *vt* piquer; piqûre *f.*

stinginess *n* mesquinerie *f.*

stingy *adj* mesquin.

stink *vi* puer:—*n* puanteur *f.*

stipulate *vt* stipuler.

stipulation *n* stipulation *f.*

stir *vt* remuer; agiter.

stitch *vt* coudre:—*n* point *m.*

stock *n* réserve *f*; provision *f:—vt* approvisionner.

stockbroker *n* agent de change *m.*

stock exchange *n* Bourse *f.*

stocking *n* bas *m.*

stoical *adj* stoïque.

stomach *n* estomac *m.*

stone *n* pierre *f:—adj* de pierre:—*vt* empierrer.

stony *adj* pierreux.

stool *n* tabouret *m.*

stoop *vi* se pencher.

stop *vt* arrêter:—*vi* s'arrêter:—*n* arrêt *m.*

stoppage *n* obstruction *f.*

storage *n* emmagasinage *m.*

store *n* provision *f:—vt* emmagasiner.

stork *n* cigogne *f.*

storm *n* tempête *f*, orage *m.*

stormy *adj* orageux.

story *n* histoire *f*; récit *m.*

stout *adj* corpulent, robuste.

stoutness *n* corpulence *f.*

stove *n* cuisinière *f.*

stow *vt* arrimer.

straight *adj* droit; direct:—*adv* droit; directement.

straightaway *adv* immédiatement.

straighten *vt* redresser.

strain *vt* tendre:—*n* tension *f*, effort *m.*

strait *n* détroit *m.*

strand *n* rive *f.*

strange *adj* inconnu; étrange.

strangeness *n* étrangeté *f*.

stranger *n* inconnu(e) *m(f)*, étranger *m*, -ère *f*.

strangle *vt* étrangler.

strap *n* lanière.

stratagem *n* stratagème *m*.

strategic *adj* stratégique *m*.

strategy *n* stratégie *f*.

straw *n* paille *f*.

strawberry *n* fraise *f*.

stray *vi* s'égarer:—*adj* perdu; errant.

streak *n* raie *f*.

stream *n* ruisseau *m*:—*vi* ruisseler.

street *n* rue *f*.

strength *n* force, puissance *f*.

strengthen *vt* fortifier.

stress *n* pression *f*; stress *m*:—*vt* souligner.

stretch *vt* étendre:—*vi* s'étendre:—*n* extension *f*; étendue *f*.

stretcher *n* brancard *m*.

strew *vt* éparpiller.

strict *adj* strict, rigoureux.

strictness *n* sévérité *f*.

stride *n* grand pas *m*.

strife *n* conflit *m*, lutte *f*.

strike *vt* frapper:—*n* coup *m*; grève *f*.

striker *n* gréviste *mf*.

striking *adj* frappant; saisissant.

string *n* ficelle *f*; corde *f*.

stringent *adj* rigoureux.

strip *vi* se déshabiller:—*n* bande *f*; langue *f*.

stripe *n* raie *f*:—*vt* rayer.

strive *vi* s'efforcer.

stroke *n* coup *m*; caresse *f*:—*vt* caresser.

stroll *vi* flâner.

strong *adj* fort, vigoureux.

strongbox *n* coffre-fort *m*.

structure *n* structure *f*; construction *f*.

struggle *vi* lutter:—*n* lutte *f*.

strut *vi* se pavaner.

stubborn *adj* entêté, obstiné.

stubbornness *n* entêtement *m*.

stud *n* clou *m*; crampon *m*.

student *n*, *adj* étudiant *m*, -e *f*.

studio *n* studio, atelier *m*.

studious *adj* studieux.

study *n* étude *f*:—*vt* étudier.

stuff *n* matière *f*; étoffe *f*:—*vt* (rem)bourrer.

stuffing *n* rembourrage *m*.

stumble *vi* trébucher:—*n* trébuchement *m*.

stump *n* souche *f*; moignon *m*.

stun *vt* étourdir.

stunt *n* cascade *f*:—*vt* empêcher de croître.

stupefy *vt* stupéfier.

stupendous *adj* prodigieux.

stupid *adj* stupide.

stupidity *n* stupidité *f*.

stupor *n* stupeur *f*.

sturdiness *n* force, robustesse *f*.

sturdy *adj* robuste; hardi.

stutter *vi* bégayer.

style *n* style *m*:—*vt* appeler; dessiner.

stylish *adj* élégant.

suave *adj* suave.

subdivide *vt* subdiviser.

subdue *vt* assujettir.

subject *adj* soumis; sujet à:—*n* sujet *m*; thème *m*:—*vt* soumettre.

subjection *n* sujétion *f*.

subjugate *vt* subjuguer.

subjugation *n* subjugation *f*.

sublimate *vt* sublimer.

sublime *adj* sublime.

sublimity *n* sublimité *f.*

submarine *adj n* sous-marin *m.*

submerge *vt* submerger.

submersion *n* submersion *f.*

submission *n* soumission *f.*

submissive *adj* soumis.

submit *vt* soumettre:—*vi* se soumettre.

subordinate *adj* subalterne:—*vt* subordonner.

subscribe *vi* souscrire:—*vt* signer.

subscriber *n* souscripteur *m,* -trice *f.*

subscription *n* souscription *f.*

subsequent *adj* ~ly *adv* ultérieur (-ement).

subside *vi* s'affaisser.

subsidence *n* affaissement *m.*

subsidiary *adj* subsidiaire.

subsidise *vt* subventionner.

subsidy *n* subvention *f.*

subsist *vi* subsister; exister.

subsistence *n* subsistance *f.*

substance *n* substance *f;* fond *m.*

substantial *adj* substantiel.

substantiate *vt* justifier.

substitute *vt* substituer.

substitution *n* substitution *f.*

subterranean *adj* souterrain.

subtitle *n* sous-titre *m.*

subtle *adj* subtile.

subtlety *n* subtilité *f.*

subtract *vt* soustraire.

suburb *n* banlieue *f.*

suburban *adj* de banlieue.

subversive *adj* subversif.

subvert *vt* subvertir.

succeed *vi* réussir:—*vt* succéder à, suivre.

success *n* succès *m.*

successful *adj* couronné de succès.

succession *n* succession *f.*

successive *adj* successif.

successor *n* successeur *m.*

succinct *adj* succinct.

succumb *vi* succomber.

such *adj* tel, pareil.

suck *vt vi* sucer.

suckle *vt* allaiter.

sudden *adj* soudain.

suddenness *n* soudaineté *f.*

sue *vt* poursuivre en justice.

suffer *vi* souffrir.

suffering *n* souffrance *f;* douleur *f.*

suffice *vi* suffire, être suffisant.

sufficient *adj* suffisant.

suffocate *vt vi* étouffer.

suffocation *n* suffocation *f.*

sugar *n* sucre *m:*—*vt* sucrer.

sugary *adj* sucré.

suggest *vt* suggérer.

suggestion *n* suggestion *f.*

suicidal *adj* suicidaire.

suicide *n* suicide *m;* suicidé *m,* -e *f.*

suit *n* pétition *f;* costume *m:*—*vt* convenir à.

suitable *adj* approprié.

suitcase *n* valise *f.*

sulky *adj* boudeur, maussade.

sullen *adj* maussade; sombre.

sultry *adj* étouffant; chaud.

sum *n* somme *f;* total *m:*—**to ~ up** *vt* résumer.

summary *adj n* résumé *m.*

summer *n* été *m.*

summit *n* sommet *m;* cime *f.*

summon *vt* convoquer.

summons *n* convocation *f.*

sumptuous *adj* somptueux.

sun *n* soleil *m.*

sunbathe *vi* se faire bronzer.
sunburnt *adj* bronzé.
Sunday *n* dimanche *m*.
sundry *adj* divers, différent.
sunflower *n* tournesol *m*.
sunny *adj* ensoleillé.
sunrise *n* lever du soleil *m*.
sunset *n* coucher du soleil *m*.
sunshade *n* parasol *m*.
sunshine *n* ensoleillement *m*.
sunstroke *n* insolation *f*.
suntan *n* bronzage *m*.
super *adj* (*fam*) sensationnel.
superb *adj* superbe.
supercilious *adj* hautain.
superficial *adj* superficiel.
superfluity *n* superfluité *f*.
superfluous *adj* superflu.
superior *adj n* supérieur *m*, -e *f*.
superiority *n* supériorité *f*.
superlative *adj n* superlatif *m*.
supermarket *n* supermarché *m*.
supernatural *n* surnaturel.
supersede *vt* remplacer.
supersonic *adj* supersonique.
superstition *n* superstition *f*.
superstitious *adj* superstitieux.
supervene *vi* survenir.
supervise *vt* superviser.
supervision *n* surveillance *f*.
supervisor *n* surveillant *m*, -e *f*.
supper *n* dîner *m*.
supplant *vt* supplanter.
supple *adj* souple.
supplement *n* supplément *m*.
supplementary *adj* supplémentaire.
suppleness *n* souplesse *f*.
supplicate *vt* supplier.
supplication *n* supplication *f*.

supplier *n* fournisseur *m*.
supply *vt* fournir:—*n* approvisionnement *m*; provision *f*.
support *vt* soutenir:—*n* appui *m*.
supporter *n* partisan *m*.
suppose *vt vi* supposer.
supposition *n* supposition *f*.
suppress *vt* supprimer.
suppression *n* suppression *f*.
supremacy *n* suprématie *f*.
supreme *adj* suprême.
surcharge *vt* surcharger:—*n* surtaxe *f*.
sure *adj* sûr, certain:—*ly* *adv* sûrement.
sureness *n* certitude, sûreté *f*.
surf *n* (*mar*) ressac *m*.
surface *n* surface *f*:—*vi* remonter à la surface.
surfboard *n* planche (de surf) *f*.
surge *n* vague, montée *f*.
surgeon *n* chirurgien *m*.
surgery *n* chirurgie *m*.
surgical *adj* chirurgical.
surly *adj* revêche, bourru.
surmise *vt* conjecturer:—*n* conjecture *f*.
surmount *vt* surmonter.
surname *n* nom de famille *m*.
surpass *vt* surpasser.
surplus *n* excédent *m*:—*adj* en surplus.
surprise *vt* surprendre:—*n* surprise *f*.
surrender *vi* se rendre:—*n* reddition *f*.
surreptitious *adj* subreptice.
surrogate *n* substitut *m*.
surround *vt* entourer.
survey *vt* examiner:—*n* enquête *f*.
survive *vi* survivre:—*vt* survivre à.
survivor *n* survivant *m*, -e *f*.
susceptibility *n* sensibilité *f*.

susceptible *adj* sensible.

suspect *vt* soupçonner:—*n* suspect *m*, -e *f*.

suspend *vt* suspendre.

suspense *n* incertitude *f*; suspense *m*.

suspicion *n* soupçon *m*.

suspicious *adj* soupçonneux.

sustain *vt* soutenir.

sustenance *n* (moyens de) subsistance *f*.

swagger *vi* plastronner.

swallow *vt* avaler.

swap *vt* échanger:—*n* échange *m*.

swarm *n* essaim *m*:—*vi* fourmiller.

swathe *vt* emmailloter:—*n* bande *f*.

sway *vi* se balancer, osciller:—*n* balancement *m*; emprise.

swear *vt* jurer:—*vi* jurer.

sweat *n* sueur *f*:—*vi* suer.

sweep *vt* balayer.

sweet *adj* doux, agréable; suave:—*n* bonbon *m*.

sweeten *vt* sucrer; adoucir.

sweetener *n* édulcorant *m*.

sweetness *n* goût sucré *m*, douceur *f*.

swell *vi* gonfler:—*n* houle *f*.

swelling *n* gonflement *m*.

swerve *vi* dévier.

swift *adj* rapide.

swiftness *n* rapidité, promptitude *f*.

swim *vi* nager:—*n* baignade *f*.

swimming *n* natation *f*.

swimming pool *n* piscine *f*.

swimsuit *n* maillot de bain *m*.

swindle *vt* escroquer.

swing *vi* se balancer:—*vt* balancer: — *n* balancement *m*.

swirl *n* tourbillon.

switch *n* interrupteur *m*:—*vt* changer de:—**to ~ off** éteindre:—**to ~ on** allumer.

swivel *vt* faire pivoter.

swoon *vi* s'évanouir:—*n* évanouissement *m*.

swoop *vi* fondre sur.

sword *n* épée *f*.

sycophant *n* sycophante *mf*.

syllabic *adj* syllabique.

syllable *n* syllabe *f*.

syllabus *n* programme d'un cours *m*.

symbol *n* symbole *m*.

symbolic(al) *adj* symbolique.

symbolise *vt* symboliser.

symmetrical *adj* symétrique.

symmetry *n* symétrie *f*.

sympathetic *adj* compatissant.

sympathise *vi* compatir.

sympathy *n* compassion *f*.

symphony *n* symphonie *f*.

symptom *n* symptôme *m*.

synagogue *n* synagogue *f*.

syndrome *n* syndrome *m*.

synonym *n* synonyme *m*.

synonymous *adj* synonyme.

synopsis *n* synopsis *f*; résumé *m*.

syntax *n* syntaxe *f*.

synthesis *n* synthèse *f*.

syringe *n* seringue *f*.

system *n* système *m*.

systematic *adj* systématique.

T

table *n* table *f*:—*vt* mettre en forme de tableau.

tablecloth *n* nappe *f*.

tablet *n* tablette *f*; comprimé *m*.

tacit *adj* tacite.

taciturn *adj* taciturne.

tack *n* broquette *f*:—*vt* clouer.

tact *n* tact *m*.

tactics *npl* tactique *f*.

tag *n* ferret *m*:—*vt* ferrer.

tail *n* queue *f*.

tailor *n* tailleur *m*.

tailoring *n* métier de tailleur *m*.

taint *vt* infecter.

tainted *adj* infecté.

take *vt* prendre.

takeoff *n* décollage *m*.

takeover *n* prise de possession *f*.

takings *npl* recette *f*.

talc *n* talc *m*.

talent *n* talent *m*.

talented *adj* talentueux.

talk *vi* parler; causer:—*n* conversation *f*.

talkative *adj* loquace.

tall *adj* grand, élevé.

tally *vi* correspondre.

tame *adj* apprivoisé:—*vt* apprivoiser.

tamper *vi* toucher à.

tan *vt vi* bronzer:—*n* bronzage *m*.

tangible *adj* tangible.

tangle *vt* enchevêtrer.

tank *n* réservoir *m*.

tanker *n* pétrolier *m*.

tantrum *n* accès de colère *m*.

tap *vt* taper doucement:—*n* petite tape *f*; robinet *m*.

tape *n* ruban *m*:—*vt* enregistrer.

tape recorder *n* magnétophone *m*.

target *n* cible *f*.

tariff *n* tarif *m*.

tarnish *vt* ternir.

tart *n* tarte, tartelette *f*.

task *n* tâche *f*.

taste *n* goût *m*; saveur *f*:—*vt* déguster.

tasteful *adj* de bon goût.

tasty *adj* savoureux.

tattoo *n* tatouage *m*:—*vt* tatouer.

taunt *vt* railler:—*n* raillerie *f*.

taut *adj* tendu.

tawdry *adj* tapageur.

tax *n* impôt *m*:—*vt* imposer.

taxable *adj* imposable.

taxation *n* imposition *f*.

taxi *n* taxi *m*.

tax payer *n* contribuable *mf*.

tea *n* thé *m*.

teach *vt* enseigner.

teacher *n* professeur *m*.

teaching *n* enseignement *m*.

team *n* équipe *f*.

teapot *n* théière *f*.

tear *vt* déchirer.

tear *n* larme *f*.

tearful *adj* larmoyant.

tease *vt* taquiner.

teaspoon *n* petite cuiller *f*.

technical *adj* technique.

technician *n* technicien *m*, -ienne *f*.

technique *n* technique *f*.

technological *adj* technologique.

technology *n* technologie *f*.

tedious *adj* ennuyeux.

tedium n ennui, manque d'intérêt m.

teenage adj adolescent:—**r** n ado-lescent(e) m(f).

teethe vi faire ses premières dents.

telegram n télégramme m.

telegraph n télégraphe m.

telepathy n télépathie f.

telephone n téléphone m.

telephone directory n annuaire m.

telephone number n numéro de téléphone m.

telescope n télescope m.

telescopic adj télescopique.

televise vt téléviser.

television n télévision f.

television set n téléviseur m.

tell vt dire; raconter.

temper vt tempérer:—n colère f.

temperament n tempérament m.

temperate adj tempéré.

temperature n température f.

tempest n tempête f.

temple n temple m; tempe f.

temporary adj temporaire.

tempt vt tenter.

temptation n tentation f.

ten adj n dix m.

tenacious adj tenance.

tenacity n ténacité f.

tenant n locataire mf.

tend vt garder.

tendency n tendance f.

tender adj tendre:—n offre f:—vt offrir.

tendon n tendon m.

tennis n tennis m.

tenor n (mus) ténor m; sens m.

tense adj tendu:—n (gr) temps m.

tension n tension f.

tent n tente f.

tentative adj timide, hésitant.

tenth adj n dixième mf.

tenuous adj ténu.

tepid adj tiède.

term n terme m:—vt appeler.

terminal adj terminal:—n aérogare f; terminal m.

terminate vt terminer.

termination n fin, conclusion f.

terrace n terrace f.

terrain n terrain m.

terrestrial adj terrestre.

terrible adj terrible.

terrific adj terrifiant.

terrify vt terrifier.

territorial adj territorial.

territory n territoire m.

terror n terreur f.

terrorise vt terroriser.

terrorist n terroriste mf.

terse adj concis, net.

test n essai m:—vt essayer.

testify vt témoigner.

testimony n témoignage m.

test tube n éprouvette f.

tether vt attacher.

text n texte m.

textual adj textuel.

texture n texture f.

than adv que; de.

thank vt remercier.

thankful adj reconnaissant.

thanks npl remerciement(s) m(pl).

that pn cela, ça, ce; qui, que; celui-là:— conj que.

thatch n chaume m.

thaw n dégel m:—vi dégeler.

the art le, la, l', les.

theatre n théâtre m.

theatrical adj théâtral.

theft n vol m.

their poss adj leur(s).

theirs poss pn le leur; la leur; les leurs.

them pn les; leur.

theme n thème m.

themselves pn pl eux-mêmes mpl, elles-mêmes fpl; se.

then adv alors; ensuite:—conj donc; en ce cas.

theological adj théologique.

theology n théologie f.

theorem n théorème m.

theoretic(al) adj théorique.

theory n théorie f.

therapist n thérapeute mf.

therapy n thérapie f.

there adv y, là.

thereafter adv par la suite; après.

therefore adv donc, par conséquent.

thermal adj thermal.

thermometer n thermomètre m.

these pn pl ceux-ci, celles-ci.

thesis n thèse f.

they pn pl ils, elles.

thick adj épais, gros.

thicken vi (s')épaissir.

thickness n épaisseur f.

thickset adj trapu.

thief n voleur m, -euse f.

thigh n cuisse f.

thin adj mince, fin.

thing n chose f; objet m; truc m.

think vi vt penser:—~ over vt réfléchir à.

thinker n penseur m, -euse f.

thinking n pensée f; réflexion f.

third adj troisième:—n troisième mf; tiers m.

thirst n soif f.

thirsty adj assoiffé.

thirteen adj n treize m.

thirteenth adj n treizième mf.

thirtieth adj n trentième mf.

thirty adj n trente m.

this adj ce, cet, cette, ces:—pn ceci, ce.

thistle n chardon m.

thorn n épine f.

thorough adj consciencieux, approfondi:—~ly adv minutieusement, à fond.

thoroughfare n rue, artère f.

those pn pl ceux-là, celles-la:—adj ces, ces… là.

though conj bien que:—adv pourtant.

thought n pensée, réflexion f.

thoughtful adj pensif.

thoughtless adj étourdi; irréfléchi.

thousand adj n mille m.

thousandth adj n millième mf.

thrash vt battre.

thread n fil m.

threat n menace f.

threaten vt menacer.

three adj n trois m.

threshold n seuil m.

thrifty adj économe.

thrill vt faire frissonner:—n frisson m.

thrive vi prospérer.

throat n gorge f.

throb vi palpiter.

throne n trône m.

throng n foule f.

throttle n accélérateur m:—vt étrangler.

through *prep* à travers; pendant; par:
—*adj* direct.

throughout *prep* partout dans:—*adv*
partout.

throw *vt* jeter:—*n* jet *m*; lancement *m*.

throwaway *adj* à jeter.

thrust *vt* enfoncer:—*n* poussée *f*.

thug *n* voyou *m*.

thumb *n* pouce *m*.

thump *n* coup de poing *m*:—*vt* cogner à.

thunder *n* tonnerre *m*:—*vi* tonner.

thunderclap *n* coup de tonnerre *m*.

thunderstorm *n* orage *m*.

Thursday *n* jeudi *m*.

thus *adv* ainsi.

thwart *vt* contrecarrer.

tic *n* tic *m*.

tick *n* tic-tac *m*; instant *m*.

ticket *n* billet, ticket *m*.

ticket office *n* guichet *m*.

tickle *vt* chatouiller.

tidal wave *n* raz-de-marée *m*.

tide *n* marée *f*.

tidy *adj* rangé, en ordre.

tie *vt* attacher:—*n* attache *f*; lacet *m*.

tier *n* gradin *m*; étage *m*.

tiger *n* tigre *m*.

tight *adj* raide, tendu.

tighten *vt* (re)serrer, tendre.

tile *n* tuile *f*, carreau *m*.

till *n* caisse *f*:—*vt* labourer.

tilt *vt* pencher:—*vi* s'incliner.

timber *n* bois de construction *m*.

time *n* temps *m*; période *f*; heure *f*:—*vt*
fixer; chronométrer.

time lag *n* décalage *m*.

timeless *adj* éternel.

timely *adj* opportun.

time zone *n* fuseau horaire *m*.

timid *adj* timide.

timidity *n* timidité *f*.

tin *n* étain *m*; boîte (de conserve) *f*.

tinge *n* teinte *f*.

tingle *vi* picoter.

tinkle *vi* tinter.

tint *n* teinte *f*:—*vt* teinter.

tinted *adj* teinté; fumé.

tiny *adj* minuscule.

tip *n* pointe *f*, bout *m*; pourboire *m*: —
vt donner un pourboire à.

tirade *n* diatribe *f*.

tire *vt* fatiguer:—*vi* se fatiguer.

tireless *adj* infatigable.

tiresome *adj* ennuyeux, fatigant.

tissue *n* tissu *m*.

titbit *n* friandise *f*.

titillate *vt* titiller.

title *n* titre *m*.

titular *adj* titulaire.

to *prep* à; vers; en.

toast *vt* (faire) griller:—*n* toast *m*.

toaster *n* grille-pain *m invar*.

tobacco *n* tabac *m*.

toboggan *n* toboggan *m*.

today *adv* aujourd'hui.

toe *n* orteil *m*; pointe *f*.

together *adv* ensemble.

toil *vi* travailler dur:—*n* labeur *m*;
peine *f*.

toilet *n* toilette *f*; toilettes *fpl*:—*adj* de
toilette.

toilet paper *n* papier hygiénique *m*.

toiletries *npl* articles de toilette *mpl*.

token *n* signe *m*; marque *f*; jeton *m*.

tolerable *adj* tolérable.

tolerant *adj* tolérant.

tolerate *vt* tolérer.

toll *n* péage *m*:—*vi* sonner.

tomato n tomate f.

tomb n tombeau m; tombe f.

tombstone n pierre tombale f.

tomorrow adv n demain m.

ton n tonne f.

tone n ton m; tonalité f:—vi s'harmoniser.

tongs npl pinces fpl.

tongue n langue f.

tonight adv n ce soir (m).

too adv aussi; trop.

tool n outil m; ustensile m.

tooth n dent f.

toothache n rage de dents f.

toothbrush n brosse à dents f.

toothpaste n dentifrice m.

top n sommet m; haut m; tête f; dessus m:—adj du haut:—vt dépasser.

topic n sujet m.

topical adj d'actualité.

topmost adj le plus haut.

topographic(al) adj topographique.

topography n topographie f.

topple vt renverser:—vi basculer.

torch n torche f.

torment vt tourmenter:—n tourment m.

tornado n tornade f.

torrent n torrent m.

tortuous adj tortueux, sinueux.

torture n torture f:—vt torturer.

toss vt lancer, secouer.

total adj total, global.

totality n totalité f.

totter vi chanceler.

touch vt toucher; contact m; touche f.

touchdown n atterrissage m; but m.

touching adj touchant.

tough adj dur; pénible.

toughen vt durcir.

tour n voyage m; visite f.

tourism n tourisme m.

tourist n touriste mf.

tournament n tournoi m.

tow n remorquage m:—vt remorquer.

toward(s) prep vers.

towel n serviette f.

tower n tour f.

town n ville f.

town hall n mairie f.

towrope n câble de remorquage m.

toy n jouet m.

trace n trace, piste f:—vt tracer.

track n trace f; empreinte f.

tract n étendue; brochure f.

traction n traction f.

trade n commerce m; métier m:—vi commercer.

trademark n marque de fabrique f.

trader n négociant m, -e f.

trade(s) union n syndicat m.

trade unionist n syndicaliste mf.

trading n commerce m:—adj commercial.

tradition n tradition f

traditional adj traditionnel.

traffic n circulation f; négoce m.

traffic jam n embouteillage m.

tragedy n tragédie f.

tragic adj tragique.

trail vt traîner:—n traînée f.

train vt entraîner:—n train m.

trainer n entraîneur m.

training n entraînement m.

trait n trait m.

traitor n traître m.

tramp n clochard m, -e f:—vt piétiner.

trance n transe f; extase f.

tranquil *adj* tranquille.
transact *vt* traiter.
transaction *n* transaction *f*.
transcend *vt* transcender.
transcription *n* transcription *f*.
transfer *vt* transférer:—*n* transfert *m*.
transform *vt* transformer.
transfusion *n* transfusion *f*.
transition *n* transition *f*.
transitional *adj* de transition.
translate *vt* traduire.
translation *n* traduction *f*.
translator *n* traducteur *m*, -trice *f*.
transmission *n* transmision *f*.
transmit *vt* transmettre.
transparency *n* transparence *f*.
transparent *adj* transparent.
transplant *vt* transplanter.
transport *vt* transporter:—*n* transport *m*.
trap *n* piège *m*:—*vt* prendre au piège.
travel *vi* voyager:—*n* voyage *m*.
traveller *n* voyageur *m*, -euse *f*.
traveller's cheque *n* chèque de voyage *m*.
travesty *n* parodie *f*.
tray *n* plateau *m*.
treacherous *adj* traître.
treachery *n* traîtrise *f*.
tread *vi* marcher:—*n* pas *m*.
treason *n* trahison *f*.
treasure *n* trésor *m*.
treasurer *n* trésorier *m*, -ière *f*.
treat *vt* traiter:—*n* cadeau *m*.
treatment *n* traitement *m*.
treaty *n* traité *m*.
treble *adj* triple:—*vt vi* tripler.
tree *n* arbre *m*.
trek *n* randonnée *f*; étape *f*.
tremble *vi* trembler.

tremendous *adj* terrible; formidable.
trend *n* tendance *f*; mode *f*.
trespass *vt* transgresser.
trial *n* procès *m*; essai *m*.
triangle *n* triangle *m*.
tribal *adj* tribal.
tribe *n* tribu *f*.
tribunal *n* tribunal *m*.
tributary *adj n* tributaire *m*.
trick *n* ruse, astuce *f*:—*vt* attraper.
tricky *adj* délicat; difficile.
trifle *n* bagatelle, vétille *f*.
trifling *adj* futile, insignifiant.
trigger *n* détente *f*.
trim *adj* net, soigné:—*vt* arranger.
trip *vi* trébucher:—*n* faux pas *m*; voyage *m*.
triple *adj* triple:—*vt vi* tripler.
trite *adj* banal; usé.
triumph *n* triomphe *m*:—*vi* triompher.
triumphant *adj* triomphant.
trivia *npl* futilités *fpl*.
trivial *adj* insignifiant.
triviality *n* banalité *f*.
troop *n* bande *f*.
tropical *adj* tropical.
trouble *vt* affliger:—*n* problème *m*; ennui *m*.
troublesome *adj* pénible.
trousers *npl* pantalon *m*.
trout *n* truite *f*.
truck *n* camion *m*; wagon *m*.
truck driver *n* routier *m*.
truculent *adj* brutal, agressif.
true *adj* vrai, véritable.
trump *n* atout *m*.
trumpet *n* trompette *f*.
trunk *n* malle *f*.
trust *n* confiance *f*:—*vt* confier à.

trustworthy *adj* digne de confiance.
trusty *adj* fidèle, loyal.
truth *n* vérité *f*.
truthful *adj* véridique.
truthfulness *n* véracité *f*.
try *vt* essayer:—*n* tentative *f*; essai *m*.
tub *n* cuve *f*, bac *m*.
tube *n* tube *m*.
tuck *n* pli *m*:—*vt* mettre.
Tuesday *n* mardi *m*.
tug *vt* remorquer:—*n* remorqueur *m*.
tuition *n* cours, enseignement *m*.
tulip *n* tulipe *f*.
tumble *vi* tomber:—*n* chute *f*.
tumbler *n* verre *m*.
tumultuous *adj* tumultueux.
tune *n* air *m*; accord *m*.
tuneful *adj* mélodieux, harmonieux.
tunnel *n* tunnel *m*.
turbulence *n* turbulence.
turbulent *adj* turbulent.
turf *n* gazon *m*.
turkey *n* dinde *f*.
turmoil *n* agitation *f*; trouble *m*.
turn *vtr* (se) tourner; *vt* monter:—*n* tour *m*; tournure.
turning *n* embranchement *m*.
turnover *n* chiffre d'affaires *m*.
turnstile *n* tourniquet *m*.

turquoise *n* turquoise *f*.
turtle *n* tortue marine *f*.
tusk *n* défense *f*.
tutor *n* professeur particulier *m*.
tweezers *npl* pince à épiler *f*.
twelfth *adj n* douzième *mf*.
twelve *adj n* douze *m*.
twentieth *adj n* vingtième *mf*.
twenty *adj n* vingt *m*.
twice *adv* deux fois.
twilight *n* crépuscule *m*.
twin *n* jumeau *m*, -elle *f*.
twine *vi* s'enrouler.
twinkle *vi* scintiller.
twirl *vi* tournoyer.
twist *vt* tordre, tortiller.
twitch *n* tic *m*.
two *adj n* deux *m*.
twofold *adj* double:—*adv* au double.
tycoon *n* magnat *m*.
type *n* type *m*:—*vi* taper à la machine.
typeface *n* œil de caractère *m*.
typewriter *n* machine à écrire *f*.
typical *adj* typique.
tyrannical *adj* tyrannique.
tyrant *n* tyran *m*.
tyre *n* pneu *m*.

U

ugliness *n* laideur *f*.
ugly *adj* laid.
ulcer *n* ulcère *m*.
ulterior *adj* ultérieur.
ultimate *adj* final:—~**ly** *adv* finalement; à la fin.
ultimatum *n* ultimatum *m*.
umbrella *n* parapluie *m*.

umpire *n* arbitre *m*.
unable *adj* incapable.
unaccomplished *adj* inaccompli.
unaccountable *adj* inexplicable.
unaccustomed *adj* inaccoutumé.
unacknowledged *adj* non reconnu.
unadulterated *adj* pur; sans mélange.

unaltered *adj* inchangé.

unanimity *n* unanimité *f*.

unanimous *adj* unanime.

unanswerable *adj* incontestable.

unapproachable *adj* inaccessible.

unarmed *adj* désarmé.

unattached *adj* indépendant; libre.

unattainable *adj* inaccessible.

unavoidable *adj* inévitable.

unaware *adj* ignorant; inconscient.

unbalanced *adj* déséquilibré.

unbearable *adj* insupportable.

unbelievable *adj* incroyable.

unbiased *adj* impartial.

unbreakable *adj* incassable.

unbroken *adj* intact; ininterrompu.

unbutton *vt* déboutonner.

unceasing *adj* incessant.

uncertain *adj* incertain.

uncertainty *n* incertitude *f*.

unchangeable *adj* immuable.

uncharitable *adj* peu charitable.

uncivil *adj* impoli, grossier.

uncivilised *adj* non civilisé.

uncle *n* oncle *m*.

uncomfortable *adj* inconfortable.

uncommon *adj* rare, extraordinaire.

uncompromising *adj* intransigeant.

unconcerned *adj* indifférent.

unconditional *adj* inconditionnel, absolu.

unconscious *adj* inconscient.

uncork *vt* déboucher.

uncouth *adj* grossier.

uncover *vt* découvrir.

uncultivated *adj* inculte.

undecided *adj* indécis.

undeniable *adj* indéniable.

under *prep* sous; dessous:—*adv* audessous.

underclothing *n* sous-vêtements *mpl*.

undercover *adj* secret, clandestin.

underdeveloped *adj* sousdéveloppé.

underestimate *vt* sous-estimer.

undergo *vt* subir.

undergraduate *n* étudiant(e) en licence *m(f)*.

undergrowth *n* brouissailles *fpl*.

underhand *adj* secret, clandestin.

underline *vt* souligner.

underneath *adv* (en) dessous:—*prep* sous, au-dessous de.

underpaid *adj* sous-payé.

underprivileged *adj* défavorisé.

underside *n* dessous *m*.

understand *vt* comprendre.

understandable *adj* compréhensible.

understanding *n* compréhension:—*adj* compréhensif.

undertake *vt* entreprendre.

undertaking *n* entreprise *f*.

undervalue *vt* sous-estimer.

underwater *adj* sous-marin:—*adv* sous l'eau.

underwear *n* sous-vêtements *mpl*.

underwrite *vt* souscrire à.

undeserved *adj* immérité.

undetermined *adj* indéterminé.

undisciplined *adj* indiscipliné.

undisputed *adj* incontesté.

undivided *adj* indivisé, entier.

undo *vt* défaire; détruire.

undoing *n* ruine *f*.

undoubted *adj* ~**ly** *adv* indubitable(ment).

undress vi se déshabiller.

undue adj excessif.

unduly adv trop, excessivement.

uneasy adj inquiet; gêné.

uneducated adj sans instruction.

unemployed adj au chômage.

unemployment n chômage m.

unending adj interminable.

unequal adj inégal.

unequalled adj inégalé.

uneven adj inégal; impair.

unexpected adj inattendu.

unfailing adj infaillible, certain.

unfair adj injuste.

unfaithful adj infidèle.

unfashionable adj démodé.

unfasten vt détacher, défaire.

unfavourable adj défavorable.

unfeeling adj insensible.

unfinished adj inachevé.

unfit adj inapte; impropre.

unfold vt déplier.

unforeseen adj imprévu.

unforgettable adj inoubliable.

unfortunate adj malheureux.

unfounded adj sans fondement.

unfriendly adj inamical.

ungrateful adj ingrat.

unhappiness n tristesse f.

unhappy adj malheureux.

unhealthy adj malsain.

unheeding adj insouciant.

unhook vt décrocher.

unhurt adj indemne.

uniform adj uniforme.

uniformity adj uniformité f.

unify vt unifier.

unimaginable adj inimaginable.

uninhabitable adj inhabitable.

uninhabited adj inhabité, désert.

uninjured adj indemne.

unintelligible adj inintelligible.

unintentional adj involontaire.

uninterested adj indifférent.

uninterrupted adj ininterrompu.

union n union f; syndicat m.

unique adj unique, exceptionnel.

unison n unisson m.

unit n unité f.

unite vt unir:—vi s'unir.

unity n unité, harmonie f, accord m.

universal adv universel.

universe n univers m.

university n université f.

unjust adj injuste.

unknown adj inconnu.

unlawful adj illégal.

unlawfulness n illégalité f.

unleash vt lâcher.

unless conj à moins que/de, sauf.

unlicensed adj illicite.

unlikely adj improbable.

unlikelihood n improbabilité f.

unlimited adj illimité.

unload vt décharger.

unlucky adj malchanceux.

unmask vt démasquer.

unmerited adj immérité.

unmistakable adj indubitable

unmoved adj insensible, impassible.

unnecessary adj inutile, superflu.

unnoticed adj inaperçu.

unobserved adj inaperçu.

unoccupied adj inoccupé.

unoffending adj inoffensif.

unpack vt défaire.

unparalleled adj incomparable; sans pareil.

unpleasant *adj* désagréable.

unpopular *adj* impopulaire.

unprecedented *adj* sans précédent.

unpredictable *adj* imprévisible.

unprejudiced *adj* impartial.

unprofitable *adj* inutile; peu rentable.

unpublished *adj* inédit.

unqualified *adj* non qualifié; sans réserve.

unquestionable *adj* incontestable, indiscutable.

unreal *adj* irréel.

unreasonable *adv* déraisonnable.

unrelated *adj* sans rapport.

unrelenting *adj* implacable.

unreserved *adj* sans réserve; franc.

unrest *n* agitation *f*; troubles *mpl*.

unripe *adj* vert, pas mûr.

unroll *vt* dérouler.

unsafe *adj* dangereux, peu sûr.

unsatisfactory *adj* peu satisfaisant.

unscrew *vt* dévisser.

unseasonable *adj* hors de saison, inopportun.

unseemly *adj* inconvenant.

unsettle *vt* perturber.

unsociable *adj* insociable.

unspeakable *adj* ineffable.

unstable *adj* instable.

unsteady *adj* instable.

untamed *adj* sauvage.

untapped *adj* non exploité.

untenable *adj* insoutenable.

unthinkable *adj* inconcevable.

untidiness *n* désordre *m*.

untidy *adj* en désordre.

untie *vt* dénouer, défaire.

until *prep* jusqu'à:—*conj* jusqu'à ce que.

untimely *adj* intempestif.

untold *adj* jamais révélé; indicible.

untouched *adj* intact.

untroubled *adj* tranquille, paisible.

untrue *adj* faux.

untrustworthy *adj* indigne de confiance.

unused *adj* neuf, inutilisé.

unusual *adj* inhabituel, exceptionnel:—**~ly** *adv* exceptionnellement.

unveil *vt* dévoiler.

unwelcome *adj* importun.

unwell *adj* indisposé.

unwilling *adj* peu disposé:—**~ly** *adv* de mauvaise grâce.

unwind *vt* dérouler:—*vi* se détendre.

unwise *adj* imprudent.

unwitting *adj* involontaire.

unworkable *adj* impraticable.

unworthy *adj* indigne.

up *adv* en haut, en l'air; levé:—*prep* au haut de; vers.

upbringing *n* éducation *f*.

update *vt* mettre à jour.

upheaval *n* bouleversement *m*.

uphold *vt* soutenir.

upholstery *n* tapisserie *f*.

upkeep *n* entretien *m*.

upon *prep* sur.

upper *adj* supérieur; (plus) élevé.

uppermost *adj* le plus haut, le plus élevé:—**to be ~** prédominer.

upright *adj* droit; honnête.

uprising *n* soulèvement *m*.

uproar *n* tumulte, vacarme *m*.

uproot *vt* déraciner.

upset *vt* renverser; déranger, bouleverser:—*n* désordre *m*; bouleversement *m*:—*adj* vexé; bouleversé.

upshot n résultat m; aboutissement m.

upside-down adv sens dessus dessous.

upstairs adv en haut (d'un escalier).

up-to-date adj à jour.

upturn n amélioration f.

urban adj urbain.

urbane adj courtois.

urchin n oursin m.

urge vt pousser:—n impulsion f.

urgency n urgence f.

urgent adj urgent.

urinate vi uriner.

urn n urne f.

us pn nous.

usage n traitement m; usage m.

use n usage m; emploi m:—vt utiliser.

used adj usagé.

useful adj utile.

usefulness n utilité f.

useless adj inutile.

uselessness n inutilité f.

usher n huissier m; placeur m.

usual adj habituel, courant.

usurp vt usurper.

utensil n ustensile m.

uterus n utérus m.

utility n utilité f.

utmost adj extrême.

utter adj complet; total:—vt prononcer.

utterly adv complètement.

V

vacancy n chambre libre f.

vacant adj vacant.

vacate vt quitter.

vacation n vacances fpl.

vaccinate vt vacciner.

vacuum n vide m.

vague adj vague.

vain adj vain.

valiant adj courageux.

valid adj valide.

valley n vallée f.

valuable adj précieux, de valeur.

value n valeur f:—vt évaluer.

valve n soupape f.

van n camionnette f.

vandalise vt saccager.

vanish vi disparaître.

vanity n vanité f.

vanquish vt vaincre.

vantage point n position avantageuse f.

vapour n vapeur f.

variable adj variable; changeant.

variation n variation f.

variety n variété f.

various adj divers, différent.

vary vt vi varier:—vi changer.

vase n vase m.

vast adj vaste; immense.

vault n voûte f:—vi sauter.

vegetable adj végétal:—n légume m.

vegetarian n végétarien m, -ienne f.

vegetate vi végéter.

vegetation n végétation f.

vehemence n véhémence.

vehement adj véhément.

vehicle n véhicule m.

veil n voile m.

vein n veine f; nervure f.

velocity n vitesse f.

velvet n velours m.

vendor n vendeur m.
venerate vt vénérer.
veneration n vénération f.
vengeance n vengeance f.
venom n venin m.
venomous adj vénéneux.
ventilate vt aérer.
ventilation n ventilation, aération f.
venture n entreprise f:—vi s'aventurer.
verb n (gr) verbe m.
verbal adj verbal, oral.
verification n vérification f.
verify vt vérifier.
versatile adj versatile.
verse n vers m.
version n version f.
versus prep contre.
vertical adj vertical.
vertigo n vertige m.
very adv très, fort, bien.
vessel n récipient m; navire m.
veteran adj n vétéran m.
veterinarian n vétérinaire mf.
veterinary adj vétérinaire.
veto n véto m.
vex vt contrarier.
vexed adj contrarié.
via prep via, par.
viaduct n viaduc m.
vibrate vi vibrer.
vibration n vibration f.
vice n vice m; défaut m.
vicinity n voisinage m.
vicious adj méchant.
victim n victime f.
victor n vainqueur m.
victory n victoire f.
video n vidéo f; vidéocassette f.
viewer n téléspectateur m, -trice f.

vie vi rivaliser.
view n vue f:—vt voir; examiner.
vigil n veille f; vigile f.
vigilance n vigilance f.
vigilant adj vigilant.
vigorous adj vigoureux.
vigour n vigueur f.
vile adj vil.
village n village m.
vindicate vt venger.
vindication n défense f.
vindictive adj vindicatif.
vine n vigne f.
vinegar n vinaigre m.
vineyard n vignoble m.
violate vt violer.
violation n violation f.
violence n violence f.
violent adj violent.
violin n (mus) violon m.
virgin n, adj vierge f.
virile adj viril.
virility n virilité f.
virtual adj vrai, virtuel.
virtue n vertu f.
virtuous adj virtueux.
virulent adj virulent.
visa n visa m.
vis-a-vis prep vis-à-vis.
visibility n visibilité f.
visible adj visible.
vision n vision f; vue f.
visit vt visiter:—n visite f.
visitor n visiteur m, -euse f.
visual adj visuel.
visualise vt s'imaginer.
vital adj vital; essentiel.
vitality n vitalité f.
vitamin n vitamine f.

vivacious *adj* vif.
vivid *adj* vif; vivant.
vocabulary *n* vocabulaire *m*.
vocal *adj* oral.
vocation *n* vocation *f*.
voice *n* voix *f*:—*vt* exprimer.
void *adj* vide:—*n* vide *m*.
volatile *adj* volatile.
volcano *n* volcan *m*.
volition *n* volonté *f*.
voltage *n* voltage *m*.
voluble *adj* volubile.
volume *n* volume *m*.

voluntary *adj* volontaire.
volunteer *n* volontaire *mf*.
voluptuous *adj* voluptueux.
vomit *vt vi* vomir.
voracious *adj* vorace.
vote *n* vote *m*; voix *f*:—*vt* voter.
voter *n* électeur *m*, -trice *f*.
voucher *n* bon *m*.
vow *n* vœu *m*:—*vt* jurer.
voyage *n* traversée *f*.
vulgar *adj* vulgaire; grossier.
vulnerable *adj* vulnérable.

W

wade *vi* patauger.
wafer *n* gaufrette *f*; plaque *f*.
wag *vt vi* remuer.
wage *n* salaire *m*.
wager *n* pari *m*:—*vt* parier.
wages *npl* salaire *m*.
waggon *n* chariot *m*; (*rail*) wagon *m*.
wail *n* gémissement *m*:—*vi* gémir.
waist *n* taille *f*.
wait *vi* attendre:—*n* attente *f*.
waiter *n* garçon *m*; serveur *m*.
waive *vt* renoncer à.
wake *vi* se réveiller:—*vt* réveiller.
walk *vi* marcher:—*vt* parcourir:—*n* promenade *f*.
walker *n* marcheur *m*, -euse *f*.
walking stick *n* canne *f*.
wall *n* mur *m*; paroi *f*.
wallet *n* portefeuille *m*.
wallow *vi* se vautrer.
wallpaper *n* papier peint *m*.
walnut *n* noix *f*; noyer *m*.
wander *vi* errer.
wane *vi* décroître.

want *vt* vouloir:—*vi* manquer:—*n* besoin *m*.
wanton *adj* lascif.
war *n* guerre *f*.
wardrobe *n* garde-robe *f*.
warehouse *n* entrepôt *m*.
wariness *n* circonspection *f*.
warm *adj* chaud; chaleureux:—*vt* réchauffer.
warm-hearted *adj* affectueux.
warmth *n* chaleur *f*.
warn *vt* prévenir.
warning *n* avertissement *m*.
warp *vi* se voiler:—*vt* voiler.
warrant *n* garantie *f*; mandat *m*.
warrior *n* guerrier *m*, -ière *f*.
wary *adj* prudent, circonspect.
wash *vt* laver:—*vi* se laver.
washbowl *n* lavabo *m*.
washing *n* lessive *f*.
washing machine *n* machine à laver *f*.
washing-up *n* vaisselle *f*.
wasp *n* abeille *f*.
wastage *n* gaspillage *m*.

waste vt gaspiller:—n gaspillage m.

wasteful adj gaspilleur.

watch n montre f:—vt regarder.

watchful adj vigilant.

water n eau f:—vt arroser.

water closet n W.C. mpl.

watercolour n aquarelle f.

waterfall n cascade f.

watering-can n arrosoir m.

watermark n filigrane m.

watershed n moment critique m.

watertight adj étanche.

wave n vague:—vi faire signe de la main.

waver vi vaciller, osciller.

wavy adj ondulé.

wax n cire f.

way n chemin m; voie.

wayward adj capricieux.

we pn nous.

weak adj faible.

weaken vt affaiblir.

weakness n faiblesse f.

wealth n richesse f.

wealthy adj riche.

weapon n arme f.

wear vt porter; user:—vi s'user:—n usage m.

weariness n lassitude f.

weary adj las.

weather n temps m:—~ **forecast** n prévisions météorologiques fpl.

weave vt tisser.

web n toile f.

wed vi se marier.

wedding n mariage m; noces fpl.

wedding ring n alliance f.

wedge n cale f:—vt caler.

Wednesday n mercredi m.

weed n mauvaise herbe f:—vt désherber.

week n semaine f.

weekday n jour de semaine m.

weekend n week-end m, fin de semaine f.

weekly adj de la semaine, hebdomadaire.

weep vt vi pleurer.

weigh vt vi peser.

weight n poids m.

weighty adj lourd; important.

welcome adj opportun:—~! bienvenue!:—n accueil m:—vt accueillir.

welfare n bien-être m.

well n puits m:—adj bien, bon:—adv bien.

well-being n bien-être m.

well-bred adj bien élevé.

well-deserved adj bien mérité.

well-known adj connu, célèbre.

well-off adj aisé, dans l'aisance.

west n ouest, Occident m:—adj ouest, de/à l'ouest:—adv vers/à l'ouest.

westerly, western adj (d')ouest.

wet adj humide:—n humidité f:—vt mouiller.

whale n baleine f.

wharf n quai m.

what pn qu'est-ce qui,(qu'est-ce) que, quoi; que, qui; ce qui, ce que; quel(le), que:—adj quel(s), quelle(s):—excl quoi! comment!

whatever pn quoi que; n'importe quoi.

wheat n blé m.

wheel n roue f:—rouler.

wheelbarrow n brouette f.

wheelchair n fauteuil roulant m.

when *adv conj* quand.

whenever *adv* quand; chaque fois que.

where *adv* où:—*conj* où.

whereas *conj* tandis que; attendu que.

whereby *pn* par lequel (laquelle).

wherever *adv* où que.

whereupon *conj* sur quoi.

whether *conj* si.

which *pn* lequel; celui que, celui qui; ce qui, ce que; quoi, ce dont: —*adj* quel(s), quelle(s).

while *n* moment *m*:—*conj* pendant que; alors que; quoique.

whim *n* caprice *m*.

whimsical *adj* capricieux.

whip *n* fouet *m*:—*vt* fouetter.

whirl *vi* tourbillonner.

whirlpool *n* tourbillon *m*.

whirlwind *n* tornade *f*.

whisper *vi* chuchoter:—*n* chuchotement *m*.

whistle *vi* siffler:—*n* sifflement *m*.

white *adj* blanc:—*n* blanc *m*.

whiten *vt vi* blanchir.

whiteness *n* blancheur *f*.

who *pn* qui.

whoever *pn* quiconque, quel(le) que soit.

whole *adj* tout, entier:—*n* tout *m*; ensemble *m*.

wholesale *n* vente en gros *f*.

wholesome *adj* sain, salubre.

wholly *adv* complètement.

whom *pn* qui; que.

why *n* pourquoi *m*:—*conj* pourquoi.

wicked *adj* méchant, mauvais.

wickedness *n* méchanceté.

wide *adj* large, ample.

widen *vt* élargir, agrandir.

widow *n* veuve *f*.

widower *n* veuf *m*.

width *n* largeur *f*.

wield *vt* manier, brandir.

wife *n* femme *f*; épouse *f*.

wild *adj* sauvage, féroce.

wild life *n* faune *f*.

wilful *adj* délibéré.

wilfulness *n* obstination *f*.

will *n* volonté *f*; testament *m*.

willing *adj* prêt, disposé:—*-ly adv* volontiers.

willpower *n* volonté *f*.

wily *adj* astucieux.

win *vt* gagner.

wind *n* vent *m*; souffle *m*.

wind *vt* enrouler:—*vi* serpenter.

windmill *n* moulin à vent *m*.

window *n* fenêtre *f*.

window pane *n* carreau *m*.

windpipe *n* tranchée *f*.

windscreen *n* pare-brise *m invar*.

windy *adj* venteux.

wine *n* vin *m*.

wine cellar *n* cave (à vin) *f*.

wing *n* aile *f*.

wink *n* clin d'œil *m*.

winner *n* gagnant *m*, -e *f*.

winter *n* hiver *m*:—*vi* hiverner.

wintry *adj* d'hiver, hivernal.

wipe *vt* essuyer.

wire *n* fil *m*.

wisdom *n* sagesse, prudence *f*.

wise *adj* sage, avisé.

wish *vt* souhaiter, désirer:—*n* souhait, désir *m*.

wit *n* esprit *m*, intelligence *f*.

witch n sorcière f.

with prep avec; à; de; contre.

withdraw vt retirer:—vi se retirer.

withdrawal n retrait m.

withhold vt retenir.

within prep à l'intérieur de:—adv dedans.

without prep sans.

withstand vt résister à.

witness n témoin m:—vt attester.

wittingly adv sciemment, à dessein.

witty adj spirituel, plein d'esprit.

woe n malheur m; affliction f.

woeful adj triste, malheureux.

wolf n loup m.

woman n femme f.

womanly adj féminin, de femme.

womb n utérus m.

wonder n merveille f:—vi s'émerveiller.

wonderful adj merveilleux.

woo vt faire la cour à.

wood n bois m.

woodcut n gravure sur bois f.

wooden adj de bois, en bois.

woodwork n menuiserie f.

wool n laine f.

woollen adj de laine.

word n mot m; parole f:—vt exprimer

wording n rédaction f.

word processing n traitement de texte m.

work vi travailler:—vt faire fonctionner; façonner:—n travail m; œuvre f; emploi m.

worker n travailleur m, -euse f.

workforce n main-d'œuvre f.

workshop n atelier m.

world n monde m.

worldly adj mondain.

worldwide adj mondial.

worn-out adj épuisé; usé.

worry vt inquiéter; n souci m.

worrying adj inquiétant.

worse adj adv pire.

worship n culte m; adoration f:—vt adorer.

worst adj le pire:—adv le plus mal: —n le pire m.

worth n valeur f; mérite m.

worthily adv dignement.

worthless adj sans valeur.

worthy adj digne; louable.

wound n blessure f:—vt blesser.

wrap vt envelopper.

wreath n couronne, guirlande f.

wreck n naufrage m; ruines fpl:—vt démolir.

wrench vt tordre:—n clé f; torsion violente f.

wrestle vi lutter.

wretched adj misérable.

wrinkle n ride f:—vt rider:—vi se rider.

wrist n poignet m.

wristwatch n montre-bracelet f.

write vt écrire; composer.

writer n écrivain m; auteur m.

writing n écriture f.

wrong n mal m; tort m:—adj mauvais; injuste:—adv mal, inexactement:— vt faire du tort à, léser.

wrongful adj injuste.

wrongly adv injustement.

wry adj ironique.

XYZ

xenophobe *n* xénophobe *mf.*
xenophobic *adj* xénophobique.
X-ray *n* rayon X *m.*
xylophone *n* xylophone *m.*
yacht *n* yacht *m.*
yawn *vi* bâiller:—*n* bâillement *m.*
year *n* année *f.*
yearbook *n* annuaire *m.*
yearly *adj adv* annuel(lement).
yearn *vi* languir.
yeast *n* levure *f.*
yell *vi* hurler:—*n* hurlement *m.*
yellow *adj n* jaune *m.*
yes *adv* oui.
yesterday *adv n* hier *m.*
yet *conj* pourtant:—*adv* encore.
yield *vt* produire:—*vi* se rendre:—*n* production *f.*
yog(h)urt *n* yaourt *m.*

you *pn* vous; tu; te; toi.
young *adj* jeune.
youngster *n* jeune *mf.*
your *poss adj* ton, ta, tes; votre, vos.
yours *poss pn* le tien; le vôtre.
yourself *pn* toi-même; vous-même(s).
youth *n* jeunesse *f*; jeune homme *m.*
zeal *n* zèle *m*; ardeur *f.*
zealous *adj* zélé.
zenith *n* zénith *m.*
zero *n* zéro *m.*
zest *n* enthousiasme *m.*
zigzag *n* zigzag *m.*
zip *n* fermeture éclair *f.*
zodiac *n* zodiaque *m.*
zone *n* zone *f*; secteur *m.*
zoo *n* zoo *m.*
zoologist *n* zoologiste *mf.*
zoology *n* zoologie *f.*